ADVANCES
IN CHILD DEVELOPMENT
AND BEHAVIOR

VOLUME 37

Contributors to This Volume

Ivy Brooker

Virginia Chow

Gail D. Heyman

Maria Legerstee

Beatriz Luna

Diane Poulin-Dubois

Elaine Reese

Kimberly J. Saudino

ADVANCES IN CHILD DEVELOPMENT AND BEHAVIOR

edited by

Patricia Bauer
Department of Psychology
Emory University
Atlanta, GA 30322, USA

Volume 37

AMSTERDAM • BOSTON • HEIDELBERG • LONDON
NEW YORK • OXFORD • PARIS • SAN DIEGO
SAN FRANCISCO • SINGAPORE • SYDNEY • TOKYO
Academic Press is an imprint of Elsevier

ELSEVIER

Academic Press is an imprint of Elsevier
32 Jamestown Road, London NW1 7BY, UK
Radarweg 29, PO Box 211, 1000 AE Amsterdam, The Netherlands
30 Corporate Drive, Suite 400, Burlington, MA 01803, USA
525 B Street, Suite 1900, San Diego, CA 92101-4495, USA

First edition 2009

 Recognizing the importance of preserving what has been written, Elsevier prints
its books on acid-free paper whenever possible.

Library of Congress Cataloging-in-Publication Data
A catalog record for this book is available from the Library of Congress

British Library Cataloguing-in-Publication Data
A catalogue record for this book is available from the British Library

ISBN: 978-0-12-374470-8
ISSN: 0065-2407 (Series)

For information on all Academic Press publications
visit our website at elsevierdirect.com

Printed in the United States of America

09 10 11 12 13   10 9 8 7 6 5 4 3 2 1

Contents

The Role of Dyadic Communication in Social Cognitive Development

MARIA LEGERSTEE

The Developmental Origins of Naïve Psychology in Infancy

DIANE POULIN-DUBOIS, IVY BROOKER, AND VIRGINIA CHOW

Children's Reasoning about Traits

GAIL D. HEYMAN

Contributors

IVY BROOKER
Centre for Research in Human Development, Department of Psychology (PY-170), Concordia University, 7141 Sherbrooke Street West, Montréal, Quebec, H4B 1R6, Canada

VIRGINIA CHOW
Centre for Research in Human Development, Department of Psychology (PY-170), Concordia University, 7141 Sherbrooke Street West, Montréal, Quebec, H4B 1R6, Canada

GAIL D. HEYMAN
Department of Psychology, University of California, San Diego, CA 92093-0109, USA

MARIA LEGERSTEE
Department of Psychology, York University, Toronto, ON M3J 1P3, Canada

BEATRIZ LUNA
Laboratory of Neurocognitive Development, Western Psychiatric Institute and Clinic, University of Pittsburgh Medical Center, Pittsburgh, PA 15213, USA

DIANE POULIN-DUBOIS
Centre for Research in Human Development, Department of Psychology (PY-170), Concordia University, 7141 Sherbrooke Street West, Montréal, Quebec, H4B 1R6, Canada

ELAINE REESE
Psychology Department, University of Otago, Dunedin, NZ 9054, New Zealand

KIMBERLY J. SAUDINO
Psychology Department, Boston University, Boston, MA 02215, USA

THE ROLE OF DYADIC COMMUNICATION IN SOCIAL COGNITIVE DEVELOPMENT

Maria Legerstee

DEPARTMENT OF PSYCHOLOGY, YORK UNIVERSITY, TORONTO,
ON M3J 1P3, CANADA

I. Introduction

Before language takes over as the instrument of interaction one cannot interact humanly with others without some proto-linguistic "theory of mind." (Bruner, 1990, p. 75)

"Communication is dramatically central in the lives of human adults, in diverse spheres of life, of non-human primates, of neurons in engagement with each other in an embodied world, of computer programs and machines

1

Advances in Child Development and Behavior
Patricia Bauer : Editor

designed to 'communicate' and respond in the contexts they are embedded in, and above all, in the lives of very young infants" (Reddy & Legerstee, 2007). In this chapter, I examine communication for its importance in the development of infant social cognition. That is, how through dyadic, face-to-face communication infants reveal that they are people and become more so with development. They are people, because from birth they share simple emotional experiences with conspecifics, and they become people because through communicating with others they construct more complex representations of them that are important for the development of language and theory of mind. I address the questions of when communication can be said to begin and how it develops. While doing so, I highlight the theoretical controversies and debates that promote but also limit the study of dyadic communication in developmental psychology. I begin with a theoretical overview of dyadic communication and examine the relation between infant communication and social cognition. I then touch on the prerequisites to the development of dyadic communication, such as (a) the recognition of conspecifics and their behavior, (b) the ability to differentiate people from things, and (c) the processes that ensure that infants connect to the social world. Subsequently, I describe development during the first year of life when infants are engaged with responsive adults in dyadic face-to-face communication to highlight those aspects of sociality that may reveal the infants' earliest communicative experiences, such as (a) meaningful dyadic communication, (b) mechanisms that promote development, and (c) relations between infants' core abilities and later language and theory of mind.

II. Theoretical Controversies

If infant members of a mind-reading species give us the strong feeling that they are doing some kind of mind reading, they probably are. (Flavell, 1999, p. 32)

Within the context of dyadic interactions, infants communicate with eye contact, facial expression, vocalizations, and gestures while assimilating the rhythm of their interactions to that of their caretakers. Together, the members of the dyad appear to engage in subtle turn-taking and co-constructive dialogues (Fogel, 1993; Stern, 1985). Because language and communication development depend fundamentally on being able to read the intentions of others, there is much controversy over the nature of infant social cognition that underlies the emerging dyadic communicative abilities. Some theorists propose that infants for the first 9 months

(Carpenter, Nagell, & Tomasello, 1998) or 18 months (Barresi & Moore, 1996; Perner, 1991; Piaget, 1954) are not aware of the mental states of others, and consequently during that time are incapable of communication. In contrast, others (Bruner, 1983; Legerstee, 2005; Trevarthen, 1979) argue that infants are born with a natural ability for primary inter-subjectivity, and that development proceeds from simple to more complex communication. In general, intersubjectivity is defined as the process in which mental activity—including motives and emotions—is transferred between minds. It is transmitted by body movements (especially of face, vocal tract, and hands) that are adapted to give visual, auditory, or tactile information about interests and emotions (Trevarthen, 1999).

Advocates of these views differ in their opinion about the continuity of mental state awareness. Their theories have, therefore, been divided into continuous and discontinuous accounts. Because of the relevance of these views for the role of dyadic communication in infants' socio-cognitive development, in what follows, I describe and contrast these two theoretical approaches.

A. CONTINUOUS PERSPECTIVES

Infants (like most other mammals) are social creatures that spend the beginning of their lives in close proximity with their caretakers. Continuous theorists propose that human infants have some special socio-cognitive capacities that make them particularly social and distin-guish them from other mammals. That is, because human infants not only differentiate members of their own species from inanimate objects (Bruner, 1973; Gelman & Spelke, 1981; Legerstee, 1992; Legerstee *et al.*, 1987), capacities which higher primates possess also (Tomasello & Call, 1997), but infants are born with a primitive awareness of the mental world that allows them to relate to others and to share emotions with them, and thus to exhibit their natural ability for intersubjectivity.

What does it mean to engage in intersubjective communication for the infant? Communication is by definition intersubjective (between two or more subjects) (Trevarthen, 1999). If one proposes that infants are born with an innate ability for intersubjectivity, then one argues that newborns relate to their caregivers on a person-to-person basis. According to Hobson (2007, p. 267) intersubjectivity is a uniquely human form of communication that has its roots in infancy, shapes cognitive development, and, more specifically, provides the foundation for symbolic functioning. It is concerned with interpersonal engagement rather than simply transmitting information between people. The uniqueness of interpersonal engagement is the result of the human ability to identify with conspecifics from the beginning of life. This identification not only allows infants to perceive others to be like the self (i.e., "like me") physically (Meltzoff & Brooks, 2001), but more importantly, to perceive people to be "with me" emotionally (Legerstee, 2005; Markova & Legerstee, 2006). Although this socio-cognitive ability becomes more complex with development, it is characterized *from the onset* by the desire to share experiences with others. In fact, continuous theorists propose that there is continuity between early and later social cognitive abilities of language and thought, because infants are born with *domain-specific abilities* that allow them to connect with the social world from the start.

Theorists interested in domain specificity view the mind as a group of specialized domains that process and represent specific kinds of information (Legerstee, 2005; Wellman & Gelman, 1998). With respect to social cognition, the domain contains representations and principles that direct infants to the necessary social input. Consequently, infants are not only sensitive to domain-specific information at birth, but they pick up concrete information through interacting with others and thus construct knowledge about people. These processes allow infants to deal with people's actions in ways that are both precursory and continuous with more mature conceptual understandings of people.

Accordingly, continuous theorists propose that at birth young infants are pre-adapted to the early structure of communication (Bruner, 1983; Stern, 1985; Trevarthen, 1979). They argue that intersubjective sharing can be observed initially during *dyadic* interactions between caregiver and infant (Bruner, 1999; Fogel, 1993; Legerstee, 2005; Stern, 1985; Trevarthen, 1979; Tronick, 1981), and later during *triadic* interactions, which extends the communicative context to a third party or object (Bakeman & Adamson, 1984; Legerstee, Markova, & Fisher, 2007). Because both basic and complex abilities imply mentalist construal, there is a connection between the earliest pre-linguistic communicative behaviors during the first half year of life, and more complex communicative abilities such as triadic communication, intentional gesturing, and mental state language later on (Legerstee, 2008). According to Flavell (1999) such continuity makes sense "... because older human infants are making genuine mental state attributions in a few short months ... it is not unreasonable to suppose that they might be doing some precursory or early version of the same thing now" (p. 33).

In support of continuous theorists, extensive research has revealed that as early as the second month of life infants distinguish between people and objects when perceptual differences are controlled (see Legerstee, 1992, for a review; Legerstee, Corter, & Kienapple, 1990; Legerstee, 1991). However, it appears that no studies have examined whether such conceptual differentiation is available to infants from birth. Consequently, the debate concerning the hypothesis that infants' understanding of people is domain-specific remains active. More research is needed that tests the idea that domain-general mechanisms, such as contingencies and analyses of perceptual features, guides infant' awareness of people (Baird & Saylor, 2006; but see Markova & Legerstee, 2006). Given that infants' limited response repertoire makes it difficult to assess whether they are able to engage in intersubjective sharing from birth, future studies combining behavioral with neurological evidence are needed to shed light on the truly initial state of infant knowledge in the domain of social understanding.

B. DISCONTINUOUS PERSPECTIVES

The majority of cognitive developmental psychologists do not disagree that infant behavior is driven by mental states. If they did, there would be no reason to study the existence of such states. Instead, the debate surrounds the age of onset of an *awareness* of mental states. Some discontinuous theorists view triadic interactions emerging around 9 months as the beginning of meaningful communication in infants (Carpenter *et al.*, 1998). It is argued that at this age infants become aware of their own intentions, and because they are born with an ability to perceive others to be "like me," transfer this understanding to others. In contrast, other theorists (Moore & Corkum, 1994; Perner, 1991; Piaget, 1954) place the onset of an awareness of intentions even later, namely at the end of the sensori-motor period between 18 and 24 months, coinciding with the beginning of symbolic behaviors such as pretence and language. These classical cognitivists (Carpendale & Lewis, 2004; Perner, 1991; Piaget, 1954) and prepared learning theorists (Barresi & Moore, 1996) argue that during the first 2 years of life, infants do not infer the meaning of others' behavior, but rather focus on what they see people do. It is not until the end of the sensori-motor period that infants begin to perceive people's actions as driven by ideas in the mind. Within this view, an understanding of the self as an intentional agent only lays *the foundation* for an awareness that the other is an intentional agent who has internal experiences, such as emotions, beliefs, and desires. These theorists argue that the infants' socio-cognitive development is the result of innate biological processes (e.g., assimilation, accommodation, and interiorization) that prepare the infant to act intentionally around 8–10 months and to perceive others as intentional agents around 18–24 months. For instance, according to the domain-general theory of Piaget (1954), infants are at birth devoid of any cognitive structures and knowledge about the world. Rather, the infant that Piaget described comes equipped with reflexes that only react to incoming stimulation for the first month of life. After much reflexive action on the world (e.g., sucking on the breast or a blanket) and with the help of biological mechanisms of assimilation and accommodation, infants learn to discriminate between various objects in the world (one provides milk and the other comfort, respectively). It is at that moment, around the second month of life, that reflexes turn into action schemas and cognitive structures develop, which direct infants for the first time to act on (rather than being acted upon) the environment. Infants now enter the second stage of the sensori-motor period, namely primary circular reactions, when their actions become discriminatory and voluntary. Although during the subsequent months of the sensori-motor period the cognitive structures allow for more enriched and refined experiences, they never enable the infant a glimpse into the mind of the other. People are experienced behaviorally but never psychologically. It is not until the end of the sensori-motor period that action schemas turn into mental schemas that allow infants to become aware that others have minds (see also Barresi & Moore, 1996; Perner, 1991). Thus, according to Piaget, before the pre-operational period the infant has no representations: she discriminates between people and objects behaviorally (based on perceptual aspects), but never conceptually (based on attributes one cannot see, such as mental states—emotions, feelings, goals, and desires). The infant recognizes her mother because of recognitory assimilation, which is a perceptual process of matching the action schema the child has with the one she sees, but not through matching what she sees with the image she has in her head. The infant does not have the ability to share experiences such as emotions and feelings with others (i.e., intersubjectivity) but responds purely to the stimulation emanating from the adult. It is only during the second year of life that there is a gradual shift from subjective to objective understanding, or from knowing the world perceptually to knowing the world conceptually. The end of the sensori-motor period then marks the beginning of thought. According to Piaget, infants at this stage are becoming social: people are differentiated from objects on their social dimensions (mental states) rather than their physical ones (Barresi & Moore, 1996; Carpenter *et al.*, 1998; Moore & Corkum, 1994; Perner, 1991; Piaget, 1954).

   Although discontinuous theory is well justified in that it provides a well-defined ontogenetic trajectory, it is not without its problems. Most importantly, it is implied that during the first months of life infants have a perceptual, rather than a conceptual understanding of the social world (i.e., understand human communication in terms of physical actions rather than sharing of experiences). Because mental state awareness is not continuous, but develops from an absence to its presence, there is no connection between early and later abilities. A particular problem with the perception/conception distinction is, how one can differentiate between these two cognitive processes (the conceptual or high-functioning cognitive mode and the experiential or low-functioning cognitive mode) and at the same time explain the emergence of both modes of processing from the same origin, as resulting from interactions among innateness (maturation) and experience (learning) (Pascual-Leone & Johnson, 1998).

Thus, although the strength of the discontinuous position is that intentionality is definitely present by one or two years of age, the three weaknesses are that (1) there is no discussion of the mechanisms that bring about developmental changes in behavior (e.g., how does the infant proceed from being a behaviorist to becoming a psychologist), (2) there is no explanation or description on what the origin of mental representation is (it is suddenly there), and (3) there are no theoretical assumptions about how sensitivity to others' psychological states develops (Legerstee, 2001; Zeedyk, 1996).

III. Prerequisites for Human Communication

Let me begin with the ontogeny of the matter. If one adopts a continuous view of mental state awareness, then one can expect to find prerequisites to meaningful communication. That is, to engage in meaningful interpersonal exchanges infants must be able to (a) recognize people as similar to self and (b) differentiate them from non-social stimulation.

A. RECOGNITION OF HUMAN STIMULI

Before we can assume that infants are motivated to interact with social agents in dyadic communication, we need to establish that, rather than having to learn everything about people (cf. Piaget, 1954), infants have some endogenous factors by which they recognize people. What might this be? Research focusing on visual perception has shown that from birth infants are attracted to movement, contour, contrast, certain levels of complexity, and curvature (Banks & Salapatek, 1983; Haith, 1966), especially when they are arranged in a socially relevant face-like pattern rather than in random and abstract ways (Goren, Sarty, & Wu, 1975). In addition, it appears that 1-month-old infants recognize their mothers' faces because they spend more time looking at her face than at strangers' faces

(Barrera & Maurer, 1981; Bushnell, Sai, & Mullin, 1989). Maurer (2007) highlights how important face recognition is for the infants' socio-cognitive development. Apparently, when infant vision is blocked by bilateral congenital cataracts, they fail to develop normal face processing, despite treatment. These visual limitations have an impact on effective dyadic communication in infancy, and beyond.

Auditory perception also appears ready for processing socially relevant information in newborns. The auditory system is stimulated in utero (DeCasper, Lecanuet, Bushnell, Granier-Deferre, & Maugeais, 1994). Newborns recognize the voices of their mothers, to which they were familiarized in the womb, from those of female strangers (DeCasper & Fifer, 1980). At 1 month, infants make fine distinctions among speech sounds (Eimas *et al.*, 1971), discriminate linguistic contrasts not available in their mother tongue (Trehub, 1976), and retain information about syllables (Jusczyk, Kennedy, & Jusczyk, 1995). At 6 months, infants' phonetic perception predicts language development at 24 months of life (Tsao, Liu, & Kuhl, 2004). According to Kuhl (2007) this link between natural speech and language learning depends on children's awareness of the communicative intentions of others.

Another important prerequisite for meaningful dyadic interaction is that infants must separate themselves from surrounding environments. According to Piaget (1954) it is only when infants understand that people and things continue to exist when not perceptually discernable, at the end of the sensori-motor period (18–24 months) that infants truly separate self from the external world and begin to place themselves within a common space with other objects. However, numerous studies have demonstrated that infants are not only aware of their surroundings, but also perceive themselves as independent agents. They have shown that infants are conscious of their own bodies, thereby refuting the notion that infants begin life unable to separate self from others. For instance, newborns become distressed when hearing a recording of another infant but not when they hear a recording of themselves (Dondi, Simion, & Caltran, 1999). Moreover, by 5 months, infants in a preferential looking paradigm visually discriminate the moving images of themselves from those of peers and dolls, and by 8 months differentiate the non-moving, and thus more novel image of self and doll (Legerstee, Anderson, & Schaffer, 1998).

Although infants' ability to recognize faces and voices documents their capacity for storing and recalling information from memory, until recently, they were assumed to lack this ability (Bauer, 2006). However, the ability to reliably recall information improves rapidly between 6 and 20 months. That is, infants not only memorize items or actions, but they remember the order in which the events occur. After seeing a sequence of events, 25% of the 6-month-old infants showed *ordered recall* 24 hours later (Barr, Dowden, & Hayne, 1996), 50% of 9-month-olds showed *ordered recall* 1 month later (Carver & Bauer, 1999, 2001), but by 20 months *all* infants recalled the order of events 1 month later (Bauer, Wemner, Dropik, & Wewerka, 2000). Moreover, emotionally salient events are better remembered by infants. For instance, Bornstein, Arterberry and Mash (2004), in a non-verbal communication paradigm, revealed long-term memory in 20-month-olds who had participated in a social interaction where an adult looked at them but refrained from communicating (a perturbation condition called the still-face procedure) at 5 months. These infants (experience group) fixated the face of the person who had instigated the still-face significantly less than the faces of two other novel persons. Control 20-month-olds (no-experience group) looked longer overall and fixated the target person equally or more than the two novel persons. The still-face response has been said to violate the expectations of infants that in face-to-face communication people will communicate with them (Tronick *et al.*, 1978). That 2-year-olds were able to remember something that happened when they were 5 months of age not only reveals their advanced mental capacity, but also their intersubjective nature and how communication is represented during the first months of life.

In summary, not only do infants' perceptual abilities draw them to the physical properties of people, such as faces, voices, and movements, but they also appear to have early inferential abilities that allow them to make sense of this information. Thus, rather than developing from a perceptual to a conceptual processing of human behavior, infants reveal that they have representations that guide their search for perceptual or concrete information from birth (Legerstee, 2001).

A particularly important question is whether infant responses to persons are different from their responses to objects, and whether this differential responsiveness is based on their different reasoning abilities (Legerstee, 1991, 1992, 1994, 1997, 2001; Legerstee, Barna, & DiAdamo, 2000; Legerstee & Bowman, 1989; Legerstee & Markova, 2008; Legerstee *et al.*, 1987). Indeed, given that the primary function of language is to communicate with one or several persons, distinguishing between people and things seems an important prerequisite.

B. PERSON–OBJECT DIFFERENTIATION

As discussed earlier, several authors (Bruner, 1973; Gelman & Spelke, 1981) put forth the idea that infants are born with specific knowledge about people organized in domains as well as principles about how to interact with them. People and inanimate objects differ in significant ways, and consequently the rules and regulations on how to interact with the physical domain should be different from those we use to interact with the social domain. Although people and objects are similar in physical properties (size, shape), they are different, because only people communicate, and have feelings and intentions. Objects do not have inner states and consequently we would only pay attention to the physical attributes of objects and their functions.

As a result of these differences, adults, but also 2-year-olds interact differently with the two classes: they talk to people, but act on objects. That is, when 2-year-olds want something from their parents they communicate a need to them. If the parent does not respond for some reason, they will continue with great persistence. Children may talk to their toys at times, but will not get upset when they do not receive an answer. Indeed, 2-year-olds take the absence of communication by non-social objects as a matter of fact. If, however, they want their toys to move, they will manipulate them. Young children clearly differentiate between people and things for purposes of communication. They know that the two classes have different functions and require different ways of interacting. One communicates with people and manipulates things.

When is the onset of this differential responsiveness? Some of the traditional observational work addressing this question showed that by 2 months, infants communicate with people and not with things. Faced with a responsive adult, infants produce expressive facial movements, make pre-speech sounds, and participate in conversational turn-taking. Faced with a graspable, non-social object, infants initiate pre-reaching movements defined as hand and arm activity directed toward it (Brazelton, Koslowski, & Main, 1974; Rader & Stern, 1982; Trevarthen, 1979). However, this research has been criticized as not systematic. For instance, the studies failed to control for contingent responding (Watson, 1972), familiarity (Ellsworth, Muir, & Hains, 1993), size, and facial features (Klein & Jennings, 1979) that might have influenced differential responding in infants. However, the many replications of others introducing more stringent controls (for a review see Legerstee, 1992; Legerstee & Markova, 2007) with typically developing infants as well as with infants with Down syndrome, at an age when the infants had approximately the same mental age or level of perceptual-cognitive sophistication as the non-delayed infants (Legerstee & Bowman, 1989; Legerstee, Bowman, & Fels, 1992), all revealed the same pattern of differential responsiveness in infants during the first year of life. In particular, this research showed that during their first month of life infants communicate with people and act on interactive dolls (Legerstee *et al.*, 1990). Between 2 and 3 months, infants imitate mouth openings and tongue protrusions of people but not of inanimate objects that simulate these gestures. Moreover, at that age, infants expect people to share their affective states with them, but they do not have such expectations of inanimate objects (Legerstee & Markova, 2007; Legerstee *et al.*, 1987). Between 5 and 8 months of age, infants begin to recognize their own faces and voices as familiar stimuli and differentiate them from those of peers and inanimate stimuli (Legerstee *et al.*, 1998). By 6 months, infants expect *others* to communicate with persons and to manipulate inanimate objects (Legerstee *et al.*, 2000) and by 10 months, infants complete failed actions of people but imitate failed acts of inanimate agents (Legerstee & Markova, 2008). This early differential responsiveness together with important developmental changes during the first year of life suggests that infants are reacting to communication-related cues in the presence of social stimuli (Legerstee & Markova, 2007; Legerstee *et al.*, 1987).

Although infant's differential responsiveness to people and objects and their relatively advanced social relationships lend credence to the idea that infants have developed a concept of people, an important feature of a concept of a person is that it is distinguished from the self. "One's concept of self is a concept of a person; one's concept of persons cannot be a concept applicable only to a single individual (one-self), for the reason that in this case it would no longer constitute a concept" (Hobson, 1990, p. 165).

The ability to identify with others and to distinguish between self as different from others plays an important role in intersubjective relationships. Human adaptation involves an understanding of others, but also an understanding of the self as different from others. Indeed, the self cannot be viewed in isolation from our view of others, but relies deeply on how we represent people. Thus, the self is perceived in relation to the other (Fogel, 1993). Research shows that from early on infants recognize people as similar to the self, because they imitate mouth openings and tongue protrusions of people, but not inanimate agents simulating these gestures (Legerstee, 1991). In response to an elongated object that moved toward their mouths (simulating a tongue protrusion), infants produced mouth opening as if they perceived a bottle. When an inanimate object simulated mouth opening and closing (a box in the shape of a mouth) infants increased tongue movements as if they wanted to explore the object. Infant imitative responsiveness to people and not to physical objects not only suggests that imitation is a social response, but also supports the contention put forth by Gelman and Spelke (1981, p. 54) that "the infant implicitly 'knows' that he and another person can act in kind."

In summary, from birth infants interact differently with people and objects and have different expectations of them, because they have learned about them through perceiving both the frequency of occurrence of particular actions (i.e., people communicate, objects do not) and the constraints on the particular relations among these occurrences. Although the precise nature of these constraints is unclear (they can range from innate intuitions to precise rules), infants could not have concepts without both components. They need associations to detect new information and theoretical inference to guide the inquiry (Keil *et al.*, 1998).

Although infants' sensitivity to social stimuli is an important aspect of learning about the social world, it is through the dynamics of social interaction that infants get to know people. Dyadic communication plays a central role in the development of the self because people not only react (contingency), but they interact and elaborate on the infants' emotions (Legerstee & Varghese, 2001; Markova & Legerstee, 2006). It is through these intersubjective forms of communication that infants construct a more complex conceptual understanding of their conspecifics, of which the self is a member (Chapman, 1992). As a result, dyadic communication has often been given a major explanatory role in infants' developing understanding of people (Bruner, 1973). Accordingly, one of the main roles of dyadic communication in infant socio-cognitive development is to establish connections with the social world. In what follows, I discuss a study that specifically addressed this proposition.

C. FOUNDATION OF INFANT SOCIAL AWARENESS: CONNECTING WITH THE SOCIAL WORLD

A theoretical question that until recently has received little empirical investigation is how infants become linked with the social world. Or in Hobson's (2007) words, how do infants recognize a special form of occurrence, characterized by sharing, "that only occurs, in relation to some special kind of embodied thing, namely a person, ... and if they do, how are we to characterize the structure and psychological means to such relatedness" (p. 270). As explained earlier, empirical findings reveal that infants know more, and at earlier ages, than had been predicted by classical theory (i.e., Piaget, 1954). These findings have led to a call for a revision of Piaget's theory. As a consequence, new theoretical frameworks have developed that address the question of the foundation of infants' social awareness. Pertinent to the present discussion are the Social Biofeedback or Contingency Detection Model of Gergely and Watson (1999), the Active Intermodal Mapping theory of Meltzoff and Moore (1983), and the Affect Sharing Model by Legerstee (2005). Although all agree that the social partner is important for the development of social cognition, these theories have different opinions about how infants become *connected* to the social world.

The Contingency Detection Model (Gergely & Watson, 1999) focuses on the detection of contingencies and social mirroring as explanatory tools for the infant's developing social understanding. Contingency detection theorists argue that intersubjectivity is a result of infants' perception of social contingencies. Specifically, these authors propose that in the beginning, infants are able to detect only the effect their own actions have in the world, which is important for the development of an awareness of the self (by kicking the sides of the crib I become aware of my body), but it is not until 3 months of age that infants begin to be sensitive to the type of "intermittent" contingent interactions provided by people (Gergely & Watson, 1999). As a result, infants do not orient toward people before the age of 3 months, and thus are not able to establish interpersonal connections with them in the first few months of life.

The Active Intermodal Mapping theory proposes that infants establish intersubjective connections with people by detecting similarities between own and others' actions (Meltzoff & Moore, 1983). How infants do that is the core of this theory. It is proposed that infants are born with multimodal coordination which allows them to operate with multimodal information, thereby recognizing equivalences in information across different sensory modalities. Intermodal coordination enables infants to imitate early communicative facial gestures of people. Imitation is an "attention getter" and through it infants begin to perceive others to be "like me." Thus the infant's ability for multimodal coordination allows them to recognize people as physically similar through imitation. This process lays the foundation for a later developing reciprocal communication system that allows infants to understand and sympathize with others (Meltzoff & Moore, 1983).

The Affect Sharing Model (Legerstee, 2005) provides a framework to explain how infants connect with the social world by relying on innate predispositions and attuned social relationships. Accordingly, infants are born with three important predispositions that allow them to learn about the minds of others: (a) the ability to recognize people as similar to themselves, (b) the awareness of their own and others' emotions, and (c) the recognition of the caregivers' attunement to the infant's emotions and needs. The interplay between these three predispositions results in affectively attuned relationships that are important mechanisms for infants' socio-cognitive development (Legerstee & Varghese, 2001; Markova & Legerstee, 2006). Thus, the Affect Sharing Model postulates that infants' connections with the social world develop through sharing emotional experiences with attuned adults, who reciprocate the infants' communicative behaviors. As a result, infants not only begin to perceive others to be "like me," but more importantly "with me," which is the gateway to the development of an awareness of other minds (Legerstee, 2005).

The assumptions of these three theories have been put to test. In Markova and Legerstee (2006), predictions about the role of contingency, imitation, and affect sharing in the development of social awareness were tested in infants during natural, imitative, and yoked conditions with their mothers at 5 and 13 weeks of age. During the natural condition (Figure 1a) mothers were asked to interact naturally with their infants. During the imitative conditions (see Figure 1b) mothers were instructed to imitate all infants' behaviors, including movements and vocalizations. During the yoked condition (see Figure 1c) mothers listened to an earlier interaction she had engaged in with her infant at 4 and 12 weeks of age, which was now replayed over a portable cassette recorder into earphones only the mother wore. By repeating what they had said a week earlier, mothers produced the same emotions and the same amount of stimulation as during the previous normal interaction. However, mothers' talk was not contingent, nor imitative, because it was not in response to the infants' signals.

We further used the 3-min interactions at 4 and 11 months to assess mothers on their affect attunement. Maternal affect attunement was defined as maintaining infant attention, warm sensitivity, and social responsiveness (see Landry *et al.*, 1998; Legerstee & Varghese, 2001). *Maintaining attention* was defined as a maternal request, or comment that related to or elaborated on the activity the infant is currently visually engaged with, physically engaged with, or both. Maintaining can also be a maternal request, question, or comment that was in direct response to the infant's attempt to attract the mother's attention to an object or activity. *Warm sensitivity* was a composite assessment of the degree of sensitivity that mothers display to infants' affective cues, including promptness and appropriateness of reactions, acceptance of the infants' interest, amount of physical affection, positive affect, and tone of voice. Five-point rating scales were used to make global ratings for three separate behaviors: (1) positive affect, (2) warm concern/acceptance, and (3) social responsiveness. Three ratings were made for each of the behaviors, once every minute of the 3-min natural inter-action and an average was calculated for each category. *Social responsive-ness* was defined as maternal imitative responses to infants' smiles and vocalizations, and as modulations of infants' negative affect. Based on these measures, mothers and infants were divided into high- and low-attuned groups. To determine whether infants enjoyed their mothers' interactions, infant smiles, vocalizations, negative face, and gazes were coded. This allowed for the assessment of "goodness of fit" of the interaction.

The various models have specific predictions about the paradigm in which the infants were observed. The Contingency Detection theory

(a) Natural Interaction

(b) Imitative interaction

(c) Yoked interaction

Fig. 1. (a) Natural, (b) imitative, and (c) yoked interactions with mother (Copyright @ Cambridge University Press).

predicts that both high- and low-attuned groups of infants prefer the imitative interaction at 5 weeks of age, because both are perfectly contingent. Because infant preference switches at 3 months from perfect contingencies to intermittent contingencies, infants in the high-attuned, but not the low-attuned groups would switch their preference to the natural interaction at 13 weeks of age, and react negatively during yoked interactions, due to the lack of sufficient contingency. The Active Intermodal Mapping theory predicts that infants of both high- and low-attuned groups prefer imitative behaviors of their mothers at both ages and react negatively during yoked interactions due to its decreased degree of match. Theories of affect sharing predict that infants in the high-attuned group favor natural interactions with their mothers over the imitative and yoked interactions at both ages because of the high level of affective attunement. In contrast, infants in the low-attuned group should not discriminate between the three conditions at both ages, because less-attuned mothers provide low levels of affective and responsive interactions.

The results supported the predictions put forth by the Affect Sharing Model. At 5 weeks of age infants of high-attuned mothers showed a preference for the natural interaction over imitative and yoked interactions, as indicated by elevated levels of gazes, smiles, and positive vocalizations. However, the infants increased negative vocalizations during the yoked interaction instead. Overall, infants of low-attuned mothers did not react differently to the three conditions (Figure 2a).

Similarly, at 13 weeks infants of high-attuned mothers clearly preferred the natural interaction, over the imitative and yoked interactions and increased their frequency of negative vocalizations during the yoked interaction. Infants of low-attuned mothers gazed significantly more at their mothers' imitative behaviors (probably due to novelty) but did not discriminate between the three conditions with smiles, positive, and negative vocalizations (see Figure 2b).

These findings support the Affect Sharing Model which predicts that infants' connections with the social world develop through sharing emotional experiences with attuned adults who reciprocate the infants' communicative behaviors. Although contingent responding and imitative games may draw infant attention to their social partner, *affective dyadic communication* appears to lay the foundation for infants' appreciation that others are not only similar to the self (like me), but also emotionally in tune with them (with me). Infants' early intersubjective capacities are facilitated by mothers who are attuned to the infants' communicative behaviors. Warm, responsive, and nurturing relationships with caregivers who harmonize their own behaviors with those of their infants enable infants to appreciate that others are similar, responsive, and attuned to

(a)

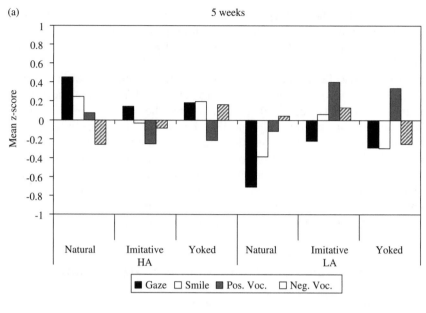

(b)

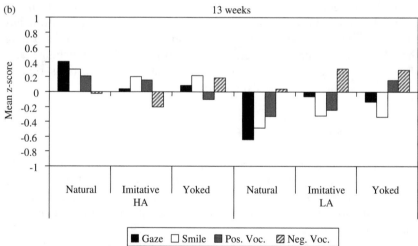

Fig. 2. Results at (a) 5 weeks and (b) 13 weeks (Copyright @ Cambridge University Press).

them. The effectiveness of maternal attunement for infant socio-cognitive development has been confirmed in studies of dysfunctional mother–infant interactions. For instance, depressed mothers spend less time looking at, touching, and talking to their infants, show little positive and negative affect, and often fail to respond contingently to infants' signals. Infants in turn show abnormal activity levels and little positive affect (Field, Healy, Goldstein, Perry, Bendell, & Schanberg, 1988; Legerstee & Varghese, 2001).

In summary, soon after birth, infants are (a) sensitive to social stimuli, (b) recognize conspecifics as similar to self and differentiate them from inanimate objects, and (c) connect with the social world through participating in affective relationships. I now turn to an examination of the development of communication during the first year of life, to provide evidence for those aspects of sociality that allow for the conclusion that (a) infants' earliest communicative experiences are meaningful, (b) affect attunement is the mechanism that promotes their development, and (c) early dyadic competencies provide the foundation for and are continuous with later language and theory of mind abilities.

IV. Dyadic Communication: Is It Meaningful?

If infants connect with others through the sharing of emotions during attuned interactions, then the question arises what infants understand of other's behavior during these early exchanges. Although much work has focused on what goes on during dyadic interactions in terms of describing the dialogue as proto-conversations (mutual gazing, touching, and vocalizing) that serve to share basic emotions, many questions remain about the meaning of these dyadic processes.

A. STILL-FACE: WHY IS CONTACT BROKEN?

We know that as early as 5 weeks, infants expect people to communicate with them when mutual gaze is established (Legerstee *et al.*, 1987) because when people refrain from communicating with them for no apparent reason, infants get upset. In a classic experimental procedure called the still-face paradigm (Tronick, Als, & Adamson, 1979) infants are studied in three conditions: a face-to-face interaction with their mothers; a still-face condition during which mothers maintain eye contact, assume a passive, unresponsive face; and the so-called reunion episode during which mothers and infants engage again in face-to-face interaction (Toda & Fogel, 1993; Weinberg & Tronick, 1996). Infants' reactions to the still-face paradigm are quite consistent. That is, during the normal and reunion conditions they smile and vocalize and alternate gazes. However, during the still-face condition, infants try to engage the adults with smiles and vocalizations, but when repeated attempts fail they become dejected which they express with sad facial expressions and through averting their gazes.

The still-face paradigm has inspired much research to determine which features of the communicative partner are responsible for the still-face response. This research focused on infant sensitivity to various perceptual features, such as the face, voice, or numerous combinations of face, gaze, and voice. Through varying the parameters of the interactions with the help of a closed-circuit television set-up, it was shown that infants were mostly perturbed when their mothers' face was motionless, even though she retained eye-contact and continued to interact vocally (Gusella, Muir, & Tronick, 1988). However, by manipulating the face, voice, or gaze, the social interactive format within which infants' communicative competence is being investigated is distorted (Delgado, Messinger, & Yale, 2002). Reddy and Trevarthen (2004) point out that "emotional acts need emotional perception and one cannot do this easily without emotional engagement" (p. 14), thereby emphasizing the importance of socially interactive structures to gauge the social significance of infants' responses.

To address this methodological problem, Murray and Trevarthen (1985) presented 2- to 3-month-old infants with 3 conditions in which the natural interactions remained intact but the features under investigation were controlled, namely a face-to-face condition, a still-face condition, and a condition during which mothers tried to communicate with their infants, but for some obvious reason (e.g., a third person interrupted the mother) were not able to continue to do so. This time infants displayed more negative affect and withdrawal during the still-face than during the interrupted episode. Infants' lack of negative responsiveness during the interrupted condition suggested that they were aware of the reason why contact was broken. However, it should be noted that in Murray and Trevarthen's (1985) study mothers changed their eye contact during the interrupted condition, because they turned away to look at the person who interrupted them. Given the importance of eye contact as a signal for communication (Legerstee *et al.*, 1987), infants may have interpreted the lack of eye contact as a sign to terminate the communicative interaction.

To examine this hypothesis, Legerstee and Markova (2007) observed infant awareness of the reason why contact is broken in conditions that did not preclude affective stimulation and that controlled for gaze orientation. Infants at 3, 6, and 9 months of age were observed in 2 studies. In Study 1, infants were presented with (a) a natural condition in which mothers were instructed to interact with their infants as they usually would (Figure 3a), (b) a still-face condition during which mothers were asked to maintain visual contact and a friendly face but otherwise to stop communicating

(a) Natural condition with mother

(b) Still-Face Condition (mother)

(c) Masked Condition (mother)

Fig. 3. (a) Natural, (b) still-face, and (c) masked-face conditions with mother (Copyright @ Maria Legerstee).

with their infants (see Figure 3b), and (c) a condition during which mothers wore a mask to conceal their facial expressions, but were instructed to talk to their infants as usual (see Figure 3c). Thus, during the mask condition mothers were unable to communicate with their infants as they usually did, because something interfered with this activity, thereby providing infants with a cue or reason (mask) why there were changes in their communicative repertoire. Only in the still-face condition was there no apparent reason why mothers refrained from communicating.

Although it is theoretically important to determine whether infant responses indicate that they distinguish between the various communicative conditions as a function of the different intentions of their communicative partners despite possible perceptual similarities, there remains a methodological problem. That is, to do so, it is necessary to manipulate certain features that differentiate these intentions. Thus, infants are not only reacting to the changing motives of their mothers (i.e., unwilling or unable to talk), but also to perceptual features (i.e., eye contact, affective stimulation, mask, etc.). To control for confounding stimulus features we included interactions with a non-social object, a large Raggedy Ann doll.

In the natural condition, the doll was moved as soon as the infant fixated the doll's face (Figure 4a) while bells that were fastened to the doll sounded in synchrony. In the still-face condition the doll remained immobile (see Figure 4b), and in the mask condition the doll wore the same mask as the mother (see Figure 4c).

Infants as young as 3 months differentiated between the social and non-social stimuli and also among the three social conditions, and continued to do so until 9 months. They produced a classic still-face response during the still-face condition, but not during the masked condition. Infants also produced significantly more positive affect during the natural conditions than during the masked condition and least during the still-face.

It could be argued that infants' differential responsiveness was due to the modulation of affective stimulation they received from people (i.e., most during face-to-face interactions, less during the masked-face, and least during the still-face). To investigate this suggestion, we continued the inquiry by presenting infants with two still-face conditions: one in which mothers kept eye contact, but presented no affective stimulation, and a modified still-face in which mothers appeared to drink from a bottle, maintained eye contact with their children, but did not speak (Figure 5). Consequently, mothers displayed a classic still-face and a modified still-face.

Because by 9 months there is strong evidence that infants perceive intentions in people's communicative behavior (see Carpenter *et al.*, 1998, for a review), in Study 2 we focused on the theoretically more important ages by studying infants at 3 and 6 months (Delgado *et al.*, 2002; Ellsworth *et al.*, 1993; Gusella *et al.*, 1988; Murray & Trevarthen, 1985). Again, to control for perceptual differences, infants were also presented with matching doll conditions.

The results of Study 2 confirmed our previous findings. Although the bottle condition in Study 2 did not allow mothers to actively engage with their infants (and thus was comparable to the classic still-face), infants did

(a) Natural Condition (Doll)

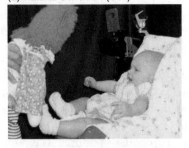

(b) Still Face Condition (Doll)

(c) Masked Condition (Doll)

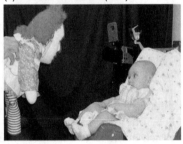

Fig. 4. (a) Natural, (b) still-face, and (c) masked-face conditions with doll (Copyright @ Maria Legerstee).

not get upset. Overall, the results of the two studies revealed that across the ages tested infants responded consistently and appropriately to the various social and non-social conditions. They got upset when mothers refrained from communicating with them for no apparent reason (still-face), but not when mothers were unable to communicate (they wore a mask, or drank a refreshment). Thus in both studies infants discriminated between situations where mothers did not communicate with them because they had a reason from conditions where no reason was provided.

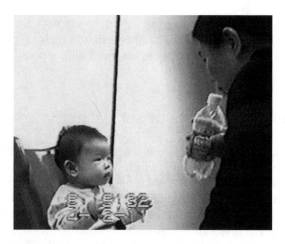

Fig. 5. Bottle condition with mother (Copyright @ Maria Legerstee).

To our knowledge, this was the first study that compared infant responsiveness in the classic still-face with responses to modified still-face conditions where mothers maintained eye contact and affective stimulation either remained high (i.e., mask) or was completely absent (i.e., bottle). The similarity of infant responses in the mask and bottle conditions indicated that infants were not simply responding to variations in stimulation. In addition, the lack of negative responses indicated that emotional distress could not have interfered with infants' abilities to evaluate the reason why contact was broken, confirming the hypotheses put forth by Murray and Trevarthen (1985).

The assumption that infants should discriminate with appropriate reactions among the three social conditions, but react differently to the non-social conditions, was also confirmed, and is consistent with the findings of studies discussed earlier (see Legerstee, 1992; for a review Legerstee *et al.*, 1998; Legerstee *et al.*, 1990; Legerstee *et al.*, 1987). Thus through proper controls, it was ruled out that simple perceptual features of people's communicative acts were the basis for early discrimination among the face-to-face, still-face and modified still-face conditions, and between social and non-social stimuli in young infants. Thus, "we can fool infants into engaging with clever stimuli as if they were humans, of course, just as we can fool adults with holograms, but that does not detract from the fact that there is a categorical distinction between person and personal forms of relatedness from early life" (Hobson, 2007, p. 270). As the above studies indicate, infants expect people and not puppets to relate to them and to share emotions when in face-to-face interactions. As a consequence infants develop preferential relationships or social bonds with their caretakers. One way to examine the meaning infants assign to their relationships with others is to observe their reactions when faced with a possible loss of this relationship.

B. THE IMPORTANCE OF SOCIAL RELATIONSHIPS

One of the earliest forms of losing a relationship is when infants are separated from their parents to which they react with sadness and if prolonged, panic. According to Panksepp (forthcoming): "The correspondence between the brain regions activated during human sadness and those activated during animal separation distress suggests that human feelings may arise from the instinctual emotional action systems of ancient regions of the mammalian brain" (Panksepp, 2003). Thus both the ability to form social bonds and the fear of losing this bond (separation distress) seem wired in the human brain. A more complex social exclusion situation occurs when infants' relationships with caregivers are threatened by a third person.

The fear of losing a loved one to a third party is called jealousy. If this is what infants experience, albeit faintly so, when they are excluded by their mother because she engages with someone else, then this indicates that infants are aware of three relationships. The *primary* relationship, the one the baby has with the mother, called the social bond; the *secondary* relationship, the one between mother and the other (the rival), and the third or *tertiary* relationship, namely the aversive relationship the infants have with the rival (White & Muller, 1989). Thus, whereas separation distress and jealousy may have similar roots, for infants to feel jealous, they need to differentiate among the three people in the social triangle. Even though infants do not need to represent these relationships, they need to perceive and respond to the interpersonal dynamics of this social triad. According to Fogel (1993) infants come to know themselves and other people through ongoing relationships: "Infants are participants in these relationships from the beginning of life and they share with significant others in the creation of meaning" (p. 85). It is through these relationships that infants self-organize and construct new forms of interactions. Thus early in life, infants construct meaningful relationships with those they have frequent social encounters with such as their parents and discriminate between these relationships and other less important ones.

To determine whether young infants experience jealousy, they need to be studied in a social triad. In addition, controls need to be implemented that preclude alternative interpretations. To do that, infant reactions to the exclusion by a loved one in favor of another, the rival, should be contrasted with the exclusion by the loved one in favor of someone the infant does not perceive as a rival. These conditions should be pitted against each other in *one* experimental paradigm. Consequently, we conducted a study with 3- and 6-month-old infants where infants interacted with a female stranger during a natural, still-face, and bottle condition, and two conditions where the female experimenter who communicated with the infant was interrupted by the mother. In one condition, the female experimenter, after being interrupted, began to talk to the mother in a continuous fashion, while explaining the experimental paradigm to her, while the mother looked on. We called this the *monologue* condition. In the other interrupted condition, the experimenter began to engage the mother in an exciting dialogue during which the two adults talked animatedly about the baby. We called this the *dialogue* condition. In both situations, the adults excluded the infant.

At both ages infants reacted with sadness and dejection to the still-face and with quiet interest during the bottle and monologue conditions, replicating earlier findings (Legerstee & Markova, 2007). However, when the experimenter engaged the mother in a dialogue, where they both talked excitedly and had lots of fun, the infants got upset, they kicked their legs, put their feet into their mouth (Figure 6a), vocalized intensely, tried to turn in their seats, and covered their faces with their arms (see Figure 6b).

The combination of the various infant responses was unique and unlike anything observed in the other conditions. Remember that in both the monologue and the dialogue conditions the infants were excluded by the mother, but only in the dialogue condition did mothers show an interest in a third party. The finding that infants reacted negatively to the dialogue, but not the monologue condition, suggests that the infants perceived the third party as someone negative, as a rival. These responses demonstrated "the affective precondition for the emergence of human jealousy, namely the existence of a social bond that is threatened by the perceived intervention of a third party" (Panksepp, forthcoming).

In summary, the various studies reported above show that from early on, infants do not react merely to the changing perceptual features of people (cf. Wellman, 1990), nor do they show inherent tendencies or deep-seated inclinations to communicate with others regardless of whether others intent to communicate with them or not. Rather, during early communicative exchanges infants actively participate in their partners' emotional life, which seems to motivate them to share their own feelings (Hobson, 2007; see also Kugiumutzakis *et al.*, 2006). When maternal responses focus on the meaning of the infants' expressions, thereby tuning in to the child's emotions, infants' communicative signals bring about desired outcomes. Successful dyadic communication depends on reciprocal following and enactment of communicative rules that specify how to interact with a

Maria Legerstee

(a) Dialogue condition - Baby puts foot in mouth

(b) Dialogue Condition - Baby covers face

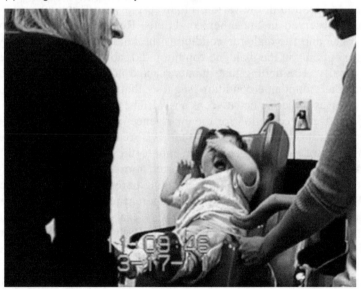

Fig. 6. (a) Baby puts foot in mouth in dialogue condition, and (b) Baby covers face in dialogue condition (Copyright @ Maria Legerstee).

conspecific. If in the mother–infant communicative system this process is engaged in by both partners, then both partners may share not only basic emotions, attention, and expectations, but communicative goals as well. The motivation to engage in communication with another person is a necessary condition for meanings to be exchanged (Tronick *et al.*, 1979), and overlooking the role the child plays in this interaction would leave psychological growth unexplained (Trevarthen, 1979). Although one should not assume that mother–infant communication is intentional by both partners all of the time, when mutuality appears, intentionality, or as Stern (1985) proposes, inter-intentionality, is there.

C. DYADIC COMMUNICATION AND SOCIAL COMPETENCE

Dyadic communication involves exchanges of shareable feelings between infant and caregivers. *From the start*, it is the infants' awareness of the caregiver's attunement (Legerstee, 2005) that gives them a sense of connecting or "being with the other," and allows for the co-creation and regulation of these communicative exchanges which are then progressively integrated into the infant's internal representations to eventually become explicit. However, it is the *caregivers' attunement* to the infants' earliest communicative signals that serves as a crucial catalyst in completing the infant's representations of communication. Thus, the caregivers' attunement and the infant's awareness and acceptance of it drive infant socio-cognitive development, in particular (a) the infant's connection with the social world, (b) self/other differentiation, and (c) the experience that others are "with me."

In a study discussed earlier, Markova and Legerstee (2006) showed that 5- and 13-week-old infants of mothers who ranked high on affect attunement discriminated between the natural, contingently imitative, and random interactions, whereas infants of less affectively attuned mothers failed to discriminate among the various social interactions. This suggests that affective rather than contingent responding connects infants with the social world. Furthermore, Legerstee and Varghese (2001) found that affect attunement influences infants' social expectancy or helplessness at 3 months. According to Seligman (1975) maladaptive attitudes and beliefs in adulthood, such as helplessness, have their roots in early development. If mothers react *affectively* during communicative turn-taking episodes, then infants develop a sense of control or "social expectancy" which is imperative for future social, emotional, and cognitive health. Depriving infants of the ability to learn these affective sequences can result in learned helplessness, as Seligman's research with dogs illustrates. Dogs, who were unable to escape from differentially emitted shocks (i.e., they received continued exposure to an uncontrollable event), were unwilling to escape the shocks, even when it was possible for them to do so. Seligman argued that the dogs had failed to establish a relation between their responses and environmental events, which resulted in learned helplessness and had profound consequences for the entire repertoire of behavior. Learned helplessness produces a cognitive set in which people believe that success and failure are independent of their actions, and they have difficulty learning that their responses or actions are consequential (Seligman, 1975).

Legerstee and Varghese (2001) conducted a study to assess the effects of various levels of maternal affect attunement on social expectancy in 3-month-old infants. In this context, social expectancy was defined as the ability to discriminate between natural and replay interactions with their mothers. During the natural interactions mothers engaged normally with their infants through a double closed-circuit television system. Infants were seated in an infant seat, approximately 50 cm in front of one of the video monitors. In an adjoining room, mothers sat in front of a television monitor tilted at a 90 degree angle, which projected the image of the infant onto an upright, transparent screen behind which a camera was positioned. The mother sat facing the upright screen and was filmed as she looked at her infant on the screen. Her image was then projected to her infant. Because the lens of the camera filming the mother was positioned directly behind the image of the infant's eyes and the mother was looking at the image of her infant's eyes while she interacted, both mother and infant had full eye contact and saw each other's face. These interactions were video recorded and in the subsequent condition replayed to the infants. Because mothers in the natural interaction could respond to their infants' signals during the replay interaction, they looked "natural" to their infants, but because their responses were played back or "yoked" they were not in response to the communicative bids of the infants. Mothers and infants were randomly assigned to receive either the natural or replay interaction first. Maternal attunement was measured during an earlier 3-min face-to-face interaction and was defined as the level of maintaining infant attention, warm sensitivity, and social responsiveness (for a full definition of maternal attunement see earlier discussion of Markova & Legerstee, 2006). A natural split was observed with 58% of mothers ranking high and 42% ranking low on these measures.

The findings were very interesting. Infants of mothers who ranked high on attunement seemed to reflect back this affect: they smiled, vocalized, and gazed at their mothers during the natural interaction. During the replay interaction when mothers displayed the same amount of smiles and vocalizations as in the natural interaction, infants reduced their display of positive affect, suggesting that during the natural episode they were *sharing* affective states with their mothers rather than mimicking them. Infants of highly attuned mothers also ranked high on social expectancy because they discriminated with their responses (smiles, vocalizations, and gazes) between the natural and replay interactions, regardless of the order of presentation.

The responses of the infants of low-attuned mothers revealed a completely different pattern. These infants did *not* differentiate with smiles and vocalizations between the natural and replay interactions. However, this did not mean that these infants were not able to discriminate between the two interactions, because they looked significantly less at their mothers in the replay than in the natural interaction but only when the natural interaction was presented first. When the replay interaction was presented first, they did not recuperate during the subsequent natural interaction (as the infants of highly attuned mothers had), but instead appeared to avoid all further interaction.

Field *et al.* (1988) has developed the "unresponsive mother model" that allows for an interpretation of these results. In this model, infants of mothers who are responsive and sensitive to the infants' communicative bids, develop a sense of control, or efficacy, whereas infants of mothers who are not, experience behavioral disorganization, lack of control, and efficacy. This model predicts that when infants of affectively attuned mothers are presented with a change in responsiveness of their mothers, they do not change their own behavior drastically because these infants have developed stable affective relationships with them, which results in efficacy. In contrast, when infants of mothers who are generally less responsive to the behavior of their infants are confronted with a change in the behavior of their mothers they become helpless (Seligman, 1975). These infants have not consistently experienced affective synchrony and attention of their mothers, and consequently they lack feelings of control or efficacy.

Researchers focusing on the importance of affect sharing often stress the social origin of infants. These authors postulate that infants begin life with an awareness of their own affective states and an ability to share these states with others (Bruner, 1990; Legerstee, 2005; Trevarthen, 1979). Consequently, they engage in mutually affective relationships with sympathetic adults from the beginning (Stern, 1985; Trevarthen, 1979). The hypothesis is that infant core abilities, such as an awareness of emotions, attention and intentions are related to later mental state understanding, such as desires and beliefs (Legerstee, 2005; Wellman & Gelman, 1998). If the earlier and later socio-cognitive abilities are related, then there should be a demonstrable link between the two. Brooks and Meltzoff (2007) revealed that gaze following and pointing at 10–11 months predicted accelerated vocabulary growth longitudinally through two years of age. Vaughn Von Hecke *et al.*

(2007) found that joint attention at 12 months was related to social competence and externalizing behaviors at 30 months, and Wellman *et al.* (2008) revealed that infant social attention at 12 months was related to performance on a false belief task at 4 years of age.

However, these studies did not examine the mechanisms that may promote the link between the earlier and later abilities. Mental state awareness takes place during social interactions where it transforms and is transformed by interpersonal relationships and by language (Hughes & Leekam, 2004). In the next and final section of this chapter, I address what type of parental skills play a role in the relation between the earliest dyadic communicative behaviors and later communication skills. These questions are important because they not only address the socio-cognitive continuity hypothesis, but also the mechanisms that promote this development (Legerstee, 2005; Legerstee & Varghese, 2001; Markova & Legerstee, 2006; Meaney, 2008).

V. Continuity Between Basic and Complex Communicative Abilities and Mechanisms of Change

Traditionally, research focusing on *the mechanisms of change* in communication has been situated within Vygotsky's (1962) framework suggesting that social interactions play an important role in facilitating higher-order mental functioning. Within this context, Vygotsky proposes two fundamental principles of development. First, before infants can subject a function to intentional control, they must already be capable of exercising this function. Second, every ability appears in the infant's development on two planes successively, first on the social plane between infants and parents (intermental), and then on the psychological plane within the child (intramental). Andrew Locke (1980) provides a most interesting example on how these principles work. He describes, how, at one point the child has her arms lifted in the air (is exercising a function) and her mother turns to look at her, smiling she says "You want to be lifted up?" and proceeds to pick up her infant. Through these actions she attributes meaning to the outstretched arms of her child. After various repetitions of the stimulus (gestures) and response (being picked up) between mother and child (intermental), the child begins to produce these actions intentionally (intra-psychologically).

Although it is interesting, Vygotsky's theory provides little information about how infants become connected with the social world. If infant abilities initially exist between parent and child (intermental), before it becomes intramental (within the child), then infants' initial understanding is based solely on experience or social learning rather than the product of endogenous and learning factors (Legerstee, 2001). Thus, Vygotsky perceives the infant initially as a little behaviorist rather than a psychologist.

In the beginning of this chapter, I made the case that the human infant has innate predispositions to recognize and interact with people. To document this, I discussed evidence indicating that infants are attracted to social stimuli and are able to discriminate between social and non-social objects. I further described research revealing that sensitive and attuned human interactions rather than physical parameters such as contingencies connect infants with the social world. I also discussed empirical studies demonstrating that the dyadic interactions infants engage in are meaningful because infants are aware of people's communicative motives and discriminate between them. That is, they recognize whether their caregivers are willing, unwilling or unable to communicate with them.

In all these studies it was shown that infants who had been reared in sensitive and warm relationships were more pro-social because they engaged in more positive interactions with their caregivers and were also more socially competent because they discriminated between the communicative motives of their conspecifics. Smiles, vocalizations, or gestures are social signals that provide information about another person's intentions as well as directions for one's own actions (Montague & Walker-Andrews, 2002). It follows that mothers who provide more information about their own intentions have infants who may begin to act intentionally themselves and to understand intentions in others sooner than infants of mothers who do not provide such information.

The presence of these early socio-cognitive competencies suggests that infants have domain-specific abilities to recognize conspecifics, to share simple mental states, such as basic emotions with them, and to perceive others to be like them physically, but also to be "with them" mentally. However, to assume that what infants reveal during dyadic communication with their caretakers is evidence of the origins of childhood social cognition, these basic understandings need to be continuous with later more complex abilities, such as language and theory of mind. I finish this chapter by providing such evidence. I discuss three studies showing that (a) infant mutual gazing during dyadic interactions at 3 months predicts coordinated attention during triadic communication at 10 months, but only for infants whose mothers are attuned (scaffold infant capacities; Legerstee *et al.*, 2007); (b) infant coordinated attention at 10 months predicts infant declarative pointing at 15 months when infants play with mature communicators (their mothers) but not when playing with same aged peers (Legerstee & Fisher, 2008); and (c) non-verbal gesturing about the mind at 15 months is linked to talking about the mind at 30 months, and that maternal mental state talk at 15 months promotes this link (Legerstee, 2008).

A. FROM DYADIC TO TRIADIC COMMUNICATION

Between 1 and 3 months, infants show a peak in social responsiveness during dyadic communication. However, after approximately 3–4 months of age and as a result of infants' developing motor and cognitive skills permitting more effective interactions and explorations with an expanding environment (Legerstee, 2005; Legerstee et al., 2007; Legerstee et al., 1987) infants begin to coordinate their attention between people and things external to the dyad (Mundy & Newell, 2007). Coordinated attention is the ability to alternate gazes back and forth between a person and an object (social or non-social) during social interactions and signals an interest in this object. This capacity demands that infants monitor other's attention in relation to self, and the other person's attention toward the same object or event, revealing infants' uniquely human representations. The emergence of this skill represents a critical socio-cognitive advance for the developing infant (Werner & Kaplan, 1963). It reflects awareness that meanings can be exchanged between people and it suggests an understanding that social partners can serve an instrumental function. As such, coordinated attention is considered an intention to communicate and to play a central role in the infants' communicative and subsequent linguistic development. Compared to typically developing infants with the same mental age, children with autism have difficulty making eye contact and tend not to monitor the gazes of others during triadic interactions. The lack of these skills in infants with autism has also been linked to their problems with language and theory of mind development (Baron-Cohen, 1991; Charman, et al., 2000).

Bruner (1999) argues that the progression from primary intersubjectivity (dyadic sharing of attention) to secondary intersubjectivity (triadic sharing of attention—person/object/child) is facilitated through "narrative scaffolding" where caretakers treat infants as if "they have things in mind." Bakeman and Adamson (1984) supported this reasoning. The authors found that infants produced significantly more joint attention with mothers and a female stranger than with same-aged peers. This suggests that coordinated attention is scaffolded by more mature social partners.

To investigate this hypothesis, we measured maternal scaffolding directly with the use of the maternal attunement scale (i.e., Markova & Legerstee, 2006; Legerstee & Varghese, 2001) and through observing infant gazes during dyadic interactions at 3 months and to relate these to

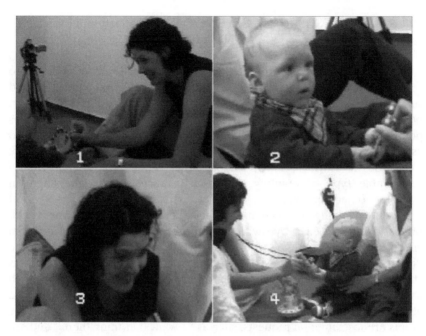

Fig. 7. Five-month-old infant coordinates attention between mother and toy (Copyright @ Maria Legerstee).

the production of coordinated attention at 5, 7, and 10 months (Legerstee *et al.*, 2007). We expected that mothers who ranked high on maternal attunement would have infants who engaged in more mutual gazes at 3 months and that mutual gaze would predict higher levels of coordinated attention later on. At 3 months, the frequencies and durations of infant gaze monitoring of the adult's face was recorded each time the infant looked at the partner's face. At 5, 7, and 10 months, the frequencies and durations of infant coordinated attention were coded (Figure 7). Coordinated attention was defined as the infants' alternation of gazes between an object and a person's face and then back to the same object (see also Bakeman & Adamson, 1984; Carpenter *et al.*, 1998; Legerstee & Fisher, 2008; Legerstee, Van Beek, & Varghese, 2002; Legerstee & Weintraub, 1997).

A regression analysis revealed that gaze monitoring at 3 months significantly predicted coordinated attention at 10 months, but only within the highly attuned group. To our knowledge, this study is the first to show this relation and that maternal attunement is a mechanism that fosters this link.

B. FROM SHARING ATTENTION TO REDIRECTING ATTENTION

As indicated earlier, coordinated attention is considered an intention to communicate, and to play a central role in infants' communicative and subsequent linguistic development (Werner & Kaplan, 1963). However, before infants use speech to communicate, they use gestures such as pointing, showing, giving, and requesting to direct people's attention to aspects of their environment (Bates, Camaioni, & Volterra, 1975; Legerstee & Barillas, 2003; Legerstee *et al.*, 2002). A particularly remarkable type of pointing gesture is a *declarative point*, when an indicated object or event is used as a means of making a non-verbal comment involving the recognition that one can share experiences with others about it (e.g., "Wow, look at that! It's beautiful;" Camaioni *et al.*, 2004; Legerstee & Barillas, 2003). Camaioni (1993) developed the "joint attention" hypothesis, postulating that declarative pointing is structurally and functionally different from other types of pointing such as imperative pointing, because a declarative point, just like coordinated attention, is used to share mental states with others. In contrast, imperative points are instrumental requests, such as "I want that thing there" and are used to direct another's behavior. Baron-Cohen (1986) revealed that declarative pointing is not used nor responded to by children with autism, whereas they do use imperative pointing. If the "joint attention" hypothesis is correct, then there should be a developmental relation between coordinated attention and declarative pointing, but not between coordinated attention and imperative pointing.

It appears that coordinated attention is less impaired in higher functioning infants with Down syndrome compared to infants with autism, but more impaired compared to typically developing infants. Whereas infants with Down syndrome may show a reduction in pre-verbal gestures, infants with autism often show a complete absence of these behaviors (Sigman & Ruskin, 1999). Iverson, Longobardi and Caselli, (2003) attributed the lower production of gestures by infants with Down syndrome and their subsequent delay in two-word utterances to the deficits in early gestural communication. These findings suggest that differences in the development of coordinated attention and pre-linguistic referential gestures during the pre-verbal period in infants with Down syndrome may shed light on language delays in these children later in development.

Surprisingly, although it has been claimed that coordinated attention is "the impelling force behind early indicating forms of communication"

(Bruner, 1990, p. 162), no past research has specifically investigated the relation between coordinated attention and declarative pointing, nor between coordinated attention and other types of indicating such as imperative pointing. Consequently, we examined the "joint attention" hypothesis in a longitudinal sample of typically developing infants and infants with Down syndrome (Legerstee & Fisher, 2008). Infants were assessed at two mean mental ages (10 and 15 months) across four visits (two months apart). Three predictions influenced the research. First, if infants with Down syndrome are delayed in coordinated attention (Beeghly, Weiss-Perry, & Cicchetti, 1990; Landry & Chapieski, 1990; Legerstee & Weintraub, 1997) and declarative pointing (Mundy, Sigman, Kasari, & Yirmiya, 1988), but not imperative pointing (Greenwald & Leonard, 1979), then we expect typically developing infants to produce more coordinated attention and declarative pointing, but a similar amount of imperative pointing compared to infants with Down syndrome. Second, if according to the "joint attention" hypothesis (Camaioni, 1993), coordinated attention is linked to declarative but not imperative pointing, then coordinated attention should predict declarative pointing only. Finally, if coordinated attention is scaffolded by mature communicators (Bakeman & Adamson, 1984; Bruner, 1999), then infants should produce more coordinated attention and also declarative pointing when interacting with mature communicators than with less mature communicators. These predictions were supported. Most interestingly, a regression analysis revealed that coordinated attention at Visit 1 ($M = 10$ months) with mothers predicted declarative pointing at Visit 4 ($M = 15$ months) for typically developing infants. No such findings were found for imperative pointing.

Overall, the results supported Camaioni's (1993) "joint attention" hypothesis that coordinated attention and declarative pointing are triadic relations between two minds and an object, which are thought to be uniquely human representations (Baron-Cohen, 1995; Camaioni, 1993; Camaioni *et al.*, 2004; Legerstee & Barillas, 2003; Sugarman-Bell, 1978; Zinober & Martlew, 1985). The finding that infants produced these coordinated attention bids and declarative points more with mothers and peer's mothers than with same aged peers supports the idea that infants' psychological states benefit from maternal scaffolding as suggested by Bruner (1999). Research that shows that problems with joint attention (coordinated attention and pointing) are linked to problems with later language and theory of mind (Charman *et al.*, 2000) is directly relevant to the issue regarding which foundational skills are related to later cognitive and communicative abilities.

C. FROM NON-VERBAL GESTURES TO TALKING
ABOUT THE MIND

As demonstrated by Legerstee and Fisher (2008) by 15 months, infants begin to use intentional gestures to communicate. Feldman and Green-baum (1997) propose that pre-verbal communication, language and mental state talk form a hierarchical model where pre-linguistic communication, which develops first, involves displaying abstract concepts while remaining within the framework of the here-and-now. Communicative gestures eventually unfold into language as words begin to label objects but also mental states such as emotions, desires and thoughts. Ultimately, the development of mental language, emerging around 30 months, marks the acquisition of a functional theory of mind. However, it will be at least another 12 months before infants begin to talk about the beliefs of others to indicate that they have begun to understand that these beliefs may be different from their own (Bartsch & Wellman, 1995).

Bretherton and Bates (1979) posit that infants' use of pre-verbal gestures "occurs in step with the construction of an internal model of the perceptions, intentions, and feelings of other human beings" (p. 97), suggesting that there is a link between these signals and verbal communication about mental states. Thus, although communicative gestures are restricted to situations in the presence, they are qualitatively similar to linguistic communication, because infants seem to use them in identical ways.

Studies have considered the social factors that might influence the development of mental talk (Tager-Flusberg, 1989; Hughes & Leekam, 2004). Meins and colleagues (Meins, Fernyhough, Wainwright, Gupta, Fradley, & Tucker, 2002) have shown that maternal mental talk at 6 months predicts children's performance on a battery of False Belief tasks at 48 months. However, mothers who talk much about the mind may also rank high on attunement and unless controlled for it is not possible to determine the independent contributions of these maternal skills. It is possible that maternal attunement may promote infant gestures during the primarily non-verbal period at 15 months, but when infants begin to talk at 30 months, maternal mental state language might facilitate child mental language.

In a study reported in Legerstee (2008), the aim was to provide evidence for the continuity between child gestures and later language about mental states, and to investigate whether maternal skills such as her attunement and mental language would promote this link. Children were observed longitudinally at 15 and 30 months during free-play interactions with their mothers. At 15 months, infant intentional communicative gestures such as pointing, showing, giving, and requesting were observed and were accompanied by a look at the partner's face within 2 s before or after the gesture. At 30 months, child mental words such as desire, emotion, cognition/belief, and moral words were measured. To find out which maternal skill helped children make the connection between gestures and mental state words, maternal mental words (desire, emotion, cognition/belief, and moral words), and attunement (maintaining attention, sensitivity, and responsiveness) were also measured during the free-play interactions at both 15 and 30 months. At 15 months, infants were also given the Words and Gestures Scale and at 30 months the Words and Sentence scale of the MacArthur Communicative Development Inventory (MCDI; Fenson, et al., 1994).

First, we examined the relations between maternal skills and child variables at each age. Partial correlations, controlling for child general language at 30 months showed that child gestures at 15 months related to child mental worlds at 30 months. Thus, through these gestures children begin to implicitly conceptualize their ideas about mental states (Bretherton & Bates, 1979).

In a second step we tested the independent contributions of maternal skills at 15 months to child mental language at 30 months. Maternal attunement and her mental talk affected child gestures at 15 months though only maternal mental language but not her emotional attunement, related to children's mental words at 30 months. Moreover, maternal mental talk at 15 months was a unique correlate of child mental words at 30 months independently of maternal affect attunement and child language at 15 months and maternal mental talk at 30 months.

Finally, based on the results of the previous analyses we investigated the moderating or mediating role of maternal skills on the link between gestures and mental language. We found that the initial relation between child gestures and later mental words (when only child language was controlled) became non-significant when accounting for maternal mental language indicating that maternal talk about mental states mediated this relation. Thus mothers reliably mapped infant gestures with mental talk (Figure 8a and b), which must deepen children's understanding of the communicative nature of these gestures and facilitate the process of relating them to mental language later on.

The unique and theoretically important contribution of the Legerstee (2008) study is that communicative gestures produced by pre-verbal children relate to later mental language and that maternal skills scaffold this link. Gestures, such as pointing, giving, showing, and requesting are acts of intentional communication because they are used to direct the attention of people to an object or some other interesting event. These gestures occur within a social context where responsive adults treat infants

(a) Mapping gestures (Point) with words: "You want that?"

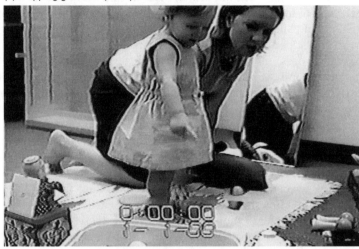

(b) Mapping gestures (sharing) with words: "I think that is a nice dolly"

Fig. 8. (a) Mapping gestures (Point) with words: "You want that?" and (b) mapping gestures (Sharing) with words "I think that is a nice dolly" (Copyright @ Maria Legerstee).

as if they have a mind scaffold the link between these gestures and later mental words as part of a process of learning how and for what purpose words are used (Montgomery, 2002).

To conclude, the three studies just described show that early core abilities are related to later socio-cognitive achievements: (1) gaze monitoring during dyadic communication at 3 months is related to joint attention during triadic communication at 10 months (Legerstee *et al.*, 2007), (2) joint attention at 10 months is related to declarative pointing at 15 months (Legerstee & Fisher, 2008), and (3) non-verbal communicative gestures at 15 months are related to mental state talk at 30 months (Legerstee, 2008). It appears that the ability that underlies this continuity is mental state awareness, and that the mechanisms that promote this awareness are caregivers' interactive skills, such as their affect attunement and talk about the child's mind. These studies highlight the importance of dyadic communication in the development of infant social cognition, and support the idea that during dyadic communication, infants reveal basic core capacities that are the origins of childhood mentalist social cognition.

VI. Conclusions and Future Directions

The first interactions infants engage in are dyadic in nature. During these interactions infants as young as 1 week monitor people's gazes and exchange facial expressions, vocalizations, and movements with them in a reciprocal fashion. Such interactions have been labeled proto-conversations (Bateson, 1979) because they have a turn-taking structure that very much resembles adult-like verbal communication (Legerstee & Varghese, 2001; Markova & Legerstee, 2006).

Adults not only interpret infant behavior as meaningful and communicative, but infants also perceive the adults' acts as meaningful and respond appropriately. Such sharing of experiences is the essence of what Trevarthen (1979) calls *intersubjectivity*, namely the "linking of subjects who are active in transmitting their understanding to each other" (p. 347). As early as 5 weeks of age (Legerstee *et al.*, 1987; Markova & Legerstee, 2006) infants recognize whether they are in tune with the other person. That is, infants have certain *communicative expectations* of their partners, because when people refuse to communicate (pose a still-face) infants get upset (Tronick *et al.*, 1978) and often try to get mothers to respond to them in order to re-establish the dialogue (Legerstee *et al.*, 1990; Legerstee & Markova, 2007; Papousek & Papousek, 1987). However, infants only have such expectations if their mothers are systematically attuned to their signals. If parents are not attuned, or are depressed, infants do not get

upset, revealing that they have not developed expectations of affect
sharing with their mothers (Field *et al.*, 1998; Legerstee & Markova, 2007;
Legerstee & Varghese, 2001). Thus affective sharing is a pivotal
mechanism that links the infant with the social world, promotes
subsequent meaningful communication, and assures that infants become
aware that people are not only "like me" physically, but also "with me"
mentally. An awareness that people are attuned to their emotions, leads
infants to subsequently feel empathy for others (Baldwin, 1902; Hoffman,
1981; Markova & Legerstee, 2006).

With ontogeny, and through careful guiding of parents, infants develop
an increasingly sophisticated understanding of the minds of others. At 3
months of age they distinguish among the different communicative motives
of adults during interpersonal exchanges (Legerstee *et al.*, forthcoming;
Legerstee, 2008; Legerstee & Varghese, 2001). The duration of gaze monitoring at 3 months predicts coordinating attention with others at 10 months
(Legerstee *et al.*, 2007). This relationship, in turn, provides the basis for
using declarative points to direct others' attention to interesting aspects in
the world (Legerstee & Barillas, 2003; Legerstee & Fisher, 2008). Gesturing
about the mind at 15 months is related to talking about the mind at 30
months, when confounding variables are controlled (Legerstee, 2008). The
continuity between early foundational abilities and later socio-cognitive
achievements supports the idea that infants are born with domain-specific
predispositions that contain core areas of thought (Figure 9).

Thus behavioral evidence shows that infants' early communicative
behaviors are not simply reactions to events in the environment or
randomly occurring acts that others respond to, but instead are tools that
infants use to connect with others and to share experiences with them
(Newson, 1979). This finding is in sharp contrast with the idea that infants
do not perceive mental states until the end of the sensori-motor period and
therefore cannot play a determining role in development. Increasingly,
developmental research is beginning to address the ontogeny of socio-
cognitive development and to describe its function and developmental
trajectory through examining the predispositions of the very young infants
and relating them to later complex abilities. As discussed, findings from
dyadic communication have revealed that soon after birth infants are
aware of the intersubjective relations they establish with others and do so
before the onset of more advanced socio-cognitive abilities. The "with me"
experienced during dyadic communication connects infants with the social
world, makes dyadic communication meaningful, and provides the
foundation for continuity between basic foundational skills and later
thought. These data validate the argument that dyadic communication of
infants is continuous with later language abilities and theory of mind and

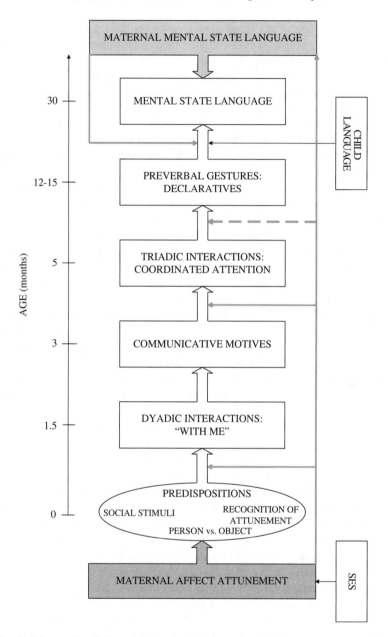

Fig. 9. Schema of multi-factorial interplay between infant dyadic communicative abilities, social cognitive development, and parental behavior (Copyright @ Maria Legerstee).

allows for making predictions about psychopathologies, such as infant failure to strive (helplessness) and autism. For example, deficits in dyadic communication may help to understand the pattern of impairments exhibited by children with autism who have deficits in emotion sharing, coordinated attention and mental state talk (Charman, 2003; Hobson *et al.*, 2006; Mundy & Newell, 2007; Rogers & Pennington, 1991). Even though these developmental processes are becoming better understood, there is a need to continue the study of socio-cognitive development in children in order to provide theoretical frameworks and behavioral data for future research and deepen the potential for intervention.

Until now, the investigation of infant core abilities as revealed during dyadic communication, their relation to later socio-cognitive abilities, and the role the environment plays in this relation has relied on behavioral evidence. As a result of methodological and technological advances, future research will be in a better position to understand the biological underpinnings of this development. A growing interest in developmental social neuroscience is providing insights into how the brain reacts and processes information. Some important issues that might be informed by findings from cognitive neuroscience in infants are to what extent genetic factors might influence such abilities. As revealed in this chapter, infant social cognitive development is complex, involving a multi-factorial interplay between innate core abilities and parental behavior.

As argued earlier, the perception and recognition of social cues as containing socio-emotional meaning is the first step towards social cognition (Legerstee, 2005, 2007). There is evidence from developmental social neuroscience that there are specific areas in the brain collectively called the "social brain" that contain neural systems specialized for the processing of socially relevant information. Specifically, there are groups of neurons in the inferotemporal cortex that respond to human faces, gaze and head direction, and also specific information about faces such as emotions. For instance, when 4-month-olds are presented with facial communication signals, areas are activated in the infant temporal and prefrontal cortex that correspond to the brain regions implicated in these processes in adults (Grossman *et al.*, 2007). In addition, it is known from the still-face paradigm (Legerstee *et al.*, 1987, 1990; Weinberg & Tronick, 1996) that infants soon after birth react to eye gaze of others as an intention to communicate. Studies show that on a neural level, the medial prefrontal cortex becomes activated when gaze is directed at, but not when gaze is averted away from, the self (Kampe, Frith, & Frith, 2003; Schilbach, Wohlschlager, Newen, Shah, Fink, & Vogeley, 2006). Johnson, Grossmann and Farroni (2008) propose that because gamma oscillations measured with EEG are correlated with the BOLD response used in fMRI with adults, eye contact detection in 4-month-old infants may well recruit very similar brain mechanisms as in adults.

Together, these findings suggest that infants have an early specialization of the cortical network involved in the perception of facial communication cues, which prepares infants to engage in communication with conspecifics and to learn from them (Grossmann *et al.*, 2007). In addition, the finding that similar brain activity is evident in infants and adults implies that these early core abilities are continuous with later socio-cognitive abilities. Thus, there appears to be more to the initial blueprint of the brain than classic constructivists propose (e.g., Piaget, 1945; Perner, 1991).

Although there is increasing biological evidence for infants' sensitivity to social stimuli, further research is needed to find neuro-physiological correlates for important behavioral data examined in this chapter, such as person–object differentiation, the role of emotions in social cognition, the relation between non-verbal and verbal communication about the mind, and the role of parents in promoting these abilities. Although there are theoretical models and studies with adults and animals, studies with infants are sparse, largely due to technical constraints. For instance, infants as young as 5 weeks differentiate between people and objects when important physical differences between the stimuli are controlled (see Legerstee, 1992, for a review). Apparently, different neural mechanisms underlie the processing of the two classes of stimuli in adults (see Blakemore, *et al.*, 2003). Evidence for the independence of social and non-social cognition points to neural components that appear to have a high degree of domain specificity in persons with autism (impairments in social cognition, but relatively preserved cognitive skills) and with Williams syndrome (pre-served social skills, but deficits in spatial abilities; Adolphs, 1999). Research with infants may show whether this modularity in adults is the result of genes or the lengthy developmental interactions with the very distinct social and non-social environments (Gelman & Spelke, 1981; Legerstee, 1992).

There is evidence that areas of the brain that are important for emotional processing are also implicated for social cognition in adults (Adolphs, 1999). To comprehend another person's mental state, it is important to be able to feel what they feel and to represent what they represent or feel. Decety and Sommerville (2003) suggest that the right hemisphere, which is predominant early in life, is implicated in the ability for shared representations and thus may be responsible for the infant's feeling of empathy, namely that others are "with me" (Legerstee, 2005). Investigating the neural systems implicated in mother-infant interactions may support the behavioral data that maternal attunement to infant emotions is one of the mechanisms that promotes empathy and the subsequent developmental components of a theory of mind, such as sharing attention (Legerstee *et al.*, 2007; Legerstee & Barillas, 2003), gesturing and talking about the mind (Legerstee, 2008).

Social or moral emotions such as jealousy, shame, guilt, and embarrassment only have meaning within a social context and may have their foundation in the infants' feel of being with the other (Trevarthen & Aitken, 2001). However, there are intense debates whether the social emotion of jealousy, might present itself in infants (see Hart & Legerstee, forthcoming). Although there is behavioral evidence for the existence of the affective precondition for the emergence of human jealousy in 3- to 6-month-old infants (Legerstee *et al.*, forthcoming), apart from very informative and stimulating theoretical models (see Panksepp, forthcoming), there are no studies that have examined what is happening in the human infant brain. Given that jealousy is not a single emotion, but is more appropriately labelled "a state" that one experiences and that depending the context, may conjure up emotions such as sadness (loss), anger (betrayal), fear/anxiety (loneliness), and so forth, jealousy does not have accompanying coherent infra structures in the brain and thus mapping jealousy onto a specific region is not possible (Panksepp, forthcoming). Future research may reveal whether infants feel the pain of social loss that adults speak of, when being excluded. Functional magnetic resonance imaging has shown that when adult participants were excluded from a virtual tossing video-game (the other players stopped throwing the ball to them) while blood flow was monitored by MRI, they experienced emotional distress as measured by substantial blood flow in the anterior cingulate cortex, an area associated with physical pain (Eisenberger, Lieberman, & Williams, 2003; see also Panksepp, 2003).

In this chapter, I have provided behavioral evidence to support the view that social cognition is both domain specific and the product of learning by examining the various child and parental factors as critical aspects in the developmental process. Drawing on core abilities, the neural architecture in which there is interaction between components that are innately specified and others whose operation emerges through experience, elucidate the importance of early social interactions and their emotional quality (i.e., affect attunement). For instance, coordinated attention is foundational to developing language and sharing emotions. Consequently, an important developmental milestone occurs when infants change between 3 and 5 months from sharing attention with others in dyadic situations (face-to-face) to sharing attention with others over objects in triadic situations. Legerstee *et al.* (2007) showed that this development was facilitated through maternal attunement. However, research addressing the brain structures and mechanism that support such change has not been conducted.

A deep controversy remains also about the onset of an awareness of intentions in others. Behne *et al.* (2005) addressed this topic by comparing the responses of 6-, 9-, 12-, and 18-month-old infants towards an adult who was either unwilling (teasing) or unable (dropped) to give the infant a toy. The authors measured how often infants looked away from the adult and reached for the object, and showed that 6-month-old infants did not differentiate between varying intentions of the adult. However, if an awareness of intentions exists in very young infants, one might expect this understanding to be expressed in a different manner than in older infants. It would make sense to use measures such as gaze aversions and other emotional responses that are known to be indices of discrimination by infants when people refrain from engaging in shared contexts (e.g., Hsu & Fogel, 2003; Markova & Legerstee, 2006; Murray & Trevarthen, 1985). Consequently, Marsh *et al.* (2009) set out to replicate and expand the research by Behne *et al.* (2005). Interestingly, the results showed that infants in both age groups systematically discriminated between the unwilling and unable conditions if a different constellation of behavioral measures was used such as positive and negative affect. To shed light on these contrasting findings, behavioral and neural correlates of an awareness of intentions in others are needed at 6 and 9 months. If no different correlates exist at these ages then a continuous rather than discontinuous development of intention understanding is supported.

There are data on continuity between coordinated attention and later socio-cognitive skills such as language. Mundy and colleagues (Mundy, Card, & Fox, 2000) found that initiating coordinated attention skills in infants aged 14 and 18 months were associated with EEG coherence of left frontal and left and right central activity. In a subsequent study (Mundy, Fox & Card, 2003) measures of joint attention and EEG coherence at 14 months were related to language development at 24 months. Thus some form of coordinated attention skills (including pointing) that emerge early in infancy are associated with socio-cognitive processes that emerge later in development. These converging findings are certainly interesting and further support the behavioral data I reported here.

In summary, the study of the biological mechanisms that subserve social interactions, is based on the idea that identifying the biological, cognitive, and social levels of analysis contributes to more comprehensive explanations of human socio-cognitive development. Consequently, future research should focus on collaborations between traditional socio-cognitive developmental theory and developmental social neuroscience in order to provide a more detailed account of the relative contributions that innate and environmental components make to social cognition, with the goal of advancing an understanding of child development and behavior.

Acknowledgements

The studies reported in this chapter were supported by grants from the Social Sciences and Humanities Research Council (Canada) to Maria Legerstee. Gratitude is expressed to the infants and parents who participated in the studies and to the research team of the Centre for Infancy studies at York University for help in the many phases of the research reported here. Thanks to Gabriela Markova, Vanessa Skrainka, and Giulia Zucal for providing interesting comments regarding an earlier draft of this chapter and to Gabriela Markova for preparing the Schema.

REFERENCES

Adolphs, R. (1999). Social cognition and the human brain. *Trends in Cognitive Sciences, 3*, 469–479.

Baird, J. A., & Saylor, M. S. (2006). Knowing others in the First Year of Life: Essay review of Infants' sense of People – Precursors to a Theory of Mind by Maria Legerstee. *Human Development, 49*, 363–368.

Bakeman, R., & Adamson, L. (1984). Coordinating attention to people and objects in mother–infant and peer–infant interaction. *Child Development, 55*, 1278–1289.

Baldwin, J. (1902). *Social and ethical interpretations in mental development.* New York: MacMillan.

Banks, M. S., & Salapatek, P. (1983). Infant visual perception. In M. M. Haith, & J. J. Campos (Vol. Eds.), *Infancy and developmental psychobiology* (Vol. II). In P. H. Mussen (Gen. Ed.), *Handbook of Child Psychology* (4th ed.). New York: Wiley.

Baron-Cohen, S. (1986). Perceptual role-taking and proto-declarative pointing in autism. *British Journal of Developmental Psychology, 7*, 113–127.

Baron-Cohen, S. (1991). Precursors to a theory of mind: Understanding attention in others. In A. Whiten (Ed.), *Natural theories of mind: Evolution, development and simulation of everyday mindreading.* Cambridge, MA: Basil Blackwell.

Baron-Cohen, S. (1995). *Mindblindness: An essay on autism and theory of mind.* Cambridge, MA: MIT Press.

Barr, R., Dowden, A., & Hayne, H. (1996). Developmental change in deferred imitation by 6-to 24-month-old infants. *Infant Behavior and Development, 19*, 159–170.

Barrera, M. E., & Maurer, D. (1981). Recognition of mother's photographed face by the three-month-old infant. *Child Development, 52*, 714–716.

Barresi, J., & Moore, C. (1996). Intentional relations and social understanding. *Behavioral and Brain Sciences, 19*, 107–154.

Bartsch, K., & Wellman, H. M. (1995). *Children talk about the mind.* Oxford: Oxford University Press.

Bates, E., Camaioni, L., & Volterra, V. (1975). The acquisition of performatives prior to speech. *Merrill-Palmer Quarterly, 21*, 205–226.

Bateson, M. C. (1979). The epigenesist of conversational interaction: A personal account of research development. In M. Bullowa (Ed.), *Before speech: The beginning of human communication* (pp. 63–77). Cambridge: Cambridge University Press.

Bauer, P. (2006). Constructing a past in Infancy: A neuro-developmental account. *Trends in Cognitive Sciences, 10,* 175–181.

Bauer, P. J., Wemner, J. A., Dropik, P. L., & Wewerka, S. S. (2000). Parameters of remembering and forgetting in the transition from infancy to early childhood. *Monograph for the Society for Research in Child Development, 65,* 4.

Beeghly, M., Weiss-Perry, B., & Cicchetti, D. (1990). Beyond sensorimotor functioning: Early communicative and play development of children with Down syndrome. In M. Beeghly & D. Cicchetti (Eds.), *Children with Down syndrome: A developmental perspective* (pp. 329–368). New York: Cambridge University Press.

Behne, T., Carpenter, M., Call, J., & Tomasello, M. (2005). Unwilling versus unable: Infants' understanding of intentional action. *Developmental Psychology, 41,* 328–337.

Blakemore, S.-J., Boyer, P., Pachot-Clouard, M., Meltzoff, A., Segebarth, C., & Decetey, J. (2003). The detection of contingency and animacy from simple animations in the human brain. *Cerebral Cortex, 13,* 837–844.

Bornstein, M. H., Arterberry, M. E., & Mash, C. (2004). Long-term memory for an emotional interpersonal interaction occurring at 5 months of age. *Infancy, 6,* 407–416.

Brazelton, T. B., Koslowski, B., & Main, M. (1974). The origins of reciprocity: The early mother-infant interaction. In M. Lewis & L. S. Rosenblum (Eds.), *The effects of the infant on its caregiver* (pp. 49–76). New York: Wiley.

Bretherton, I., & Bates, E. (1979). The emergence of intentional communication. In I. Uzgiris (Ed.), *Social interaction and communication during infancy* (pp. 81–100). San Fransisco: Jossey Bass Brooks.

Brooks, R., & Meltzoff, A. N. (2007). Infant gaze following and pointing predict accelerated vocabulary growth through two years of age: A longitudinal, growth curve modeling study. *Journal of Child Language, 34,* 1–14.

Bruner, J. S. (1973). Organization of early skilled action. *Child Development, 44,* 11.

Bruner, J. S. (1983). *Child's talk: Learning to use language.* New York: Norton.

Bruner, J. S. (1990). *Acts of meaning.* Cambridge, MA: Harvard University Press.

Bruner, J. S. (1999). The intentionality of referring. In P. Zelazo & J. W. Astington (Eds.), *Developing theories of intention: Social understanding and self-control* (pp. 329–339). Mahwah, NJ: Erlbaum.

Bushnell, I. W. R., Sai, F., & Mullin, J. T. (1989). Neonatal recognition of the mother's face. *British Journal of Developmental Psychology, 7,* 3–15.

Camaioni, L. (1993). The development of intentional communication: A re-analysis. In J. Nadel & L. Camaioni (Eds.), *New perspectives in early communicative development* (pp. 82–96). London: Routledge.

Camaioni, L., Perucchini, P., Bellagamba, F., & Colonnesi, C. (2004). The role of declarative pointing in developing a theory of mind. *Infancy, 5,* 291–308.

Carpendale, J., & Lewis, M. (2004). Constructing an understanding of mind: The development of children's social understanding within social interaction. *Behavioral and Brain Sciences, 27,* 79–151.

Carpenter, M., Nagell, K., & Tomasello, M. (1998). Social cognition, joint attention, and communicative competence from 9 to 15 months of age. *Monographs of the Society for Research in Child Development, 63*(4), Serial No. 255.

Carver, L. J., & Bauer, P. J. (1999). When the event is more than the sum of its parts: Nine-month-olds' long-term ordered recall. *Memory, 7,* 147–174.

Carver, L. J., & Bauer, P. J. (2001). The dawning of a past: The emergence of long-term explicit memory in infancy. *Journal of Experimental Psychology (General), 130,* 726–745.

Chapman, M. (1992). Equilibration and the dialectic of organization. In H. Beiling & P. Putfall (Eds.), *Piaget's theory: Prospects and possibilities* (pp. 39–59). Hillsdale, NJ: Erlbaum.

Charman, T. (2003). Why is joint attention a pivotal skill in autism? *Philosophical Transactions of the Royal Society B: Biological Transactions, 358*, 315–324.

Charman, T., Baron-Cohen, S., Swettenham, J., Baird, G., Cox, A., & Drew, A. (2000). Testing joint attention, imitation, and play as infancy precursors to language and theory of mind. *Cognitive Development, 15*, 481–498.

DeCasper, A. J., & Fifer, W. P. (1980). Of human bonding: Newborns prefer their mother's voice. *Science, 208*, 1174–1176.

DeCasper, A. J., Lecanuet, J. P., Bushnell, M. C., Granier-Deferre, C., & Maugeais, R. (1994). Fetal reactions to recurrent maternal speech sounds. *Infant Behavior and Development, 9*, 133–150.

Decety, J., & Sommerville, J. A. (2003). Shared representations between self and others: A social cognitive neuroscience view. *Trends in Cognitive Science, 7/12*, 527–533.

Delgado, C. E. F., Messinger, D. S., & Yale, M. E. (2002). Infant responses to direction of parental gaze: A comparison of two still-face conditions. *Infant Behavior and Development, 25*, 311–318.

Dondi, M., Simion, F., & Caltran, G. (1999). Can newborns discriminate between their own cry and the cry of another newborn infant? *Developmental Psychology, 35*, 418–426.

Eimas, P. D., Siqueland, E. R., Juscyk, P., & Vigorito, J. (1971). Speech perception in infants. *Science, 171*, 303–306.

Eisenberger, N. I., Lieberman, M. D., & Williams, K. (2003). Does rejection hurt? An fMRI study of social exclusion. *Science, 302*, 290–292.

Ellsworth, C. P., Muir, D., & Hains, S. (1993). Social competence and person–object differentiation: An analysis of the still-face effect. *Developmental Psychology, 39*, 63–73.

Feldman, R., & Greenbaum, C. W. (1997). Affect regulation and synchrony in mother–infant play as precursors to the development of symbolic competence. *Infant Mental Health Journal, 18*, 4–23.

Fenson, L., Dale, P., Reznick, J., Bates, E., Thal, D., & Pethick, S. (1994). Variability in early communicative development. *Monographs of the Society for Research in Child Development, 59*(5), Serial No. 242.

Field, T., Healy, B., Goldstein, S., Perry, S., Bendell, D., Schanberg, S., *et al.* (1988). Infants of depressed mothers show "depressed" behaviors even with non-depressed adults. *Child Development, 59*, 1569–1579.

Flavell, J. H. (1999). Cognitive development: Children's knowledge about the mind. *Annual Review of Psychology, 50*, 21–45.

Fogel, A. (1993). *Developing through relationships: Origins of communication, self and culture.* Chicago, IL: University of Chicago Press.

Gelman, R., & Spelke, E. (1981). The development of thoughts about animate and inanimate objects: Implications for research on social cognition. In J. H. Flavell & L. Ross (Eds.), *Social cognition development: Frontiers and possible futures.* New York: Cambridge University Press.

Gergely, G., & Watson, J. S. (1999). Early socio-emotional development: Contingency perception and the social biofeedback model. In P. Rochat (Ed.), *Early social cognition, understanding others in the first months of life* (pp. 101–136). Mahwah, NJ: Erlbaum.

Goren, C. C., Sarty, M., & Wu, P. Y. K. (1975). Visual following and pattern discrimination of face-like stimuli by newborn infants. *Pediatrics, 56*, 544–549.

Greenwald, C. A., & Leonard, L. B. (1979). Communicative and sensorimotor development of Down's syndrome children. *American Journal of Mental Deficiency, 84*, 296–303.

Grossmann, T., Johnson, M. H., Farroni, T., & Csibra, G. (2007). Social perception in the infant brain: Gamma oscillatory activity in response to eye gaze. *Social Cognitive & Affective Neuroscience, 2,* 284–291.

Gusella, J., Muir, D., & Tronick, E. (1988). The effect of manipulating maternal behavior during an interaction on three- and six-month-olds' affect and attention. *Child Development, 59,* 111–1124.

Haith, M. M. (1966). The response of the human newborn to visual movement. *Journal of Experimental Psychology (Child Psychology), 3,* 243–253.

Hart, S., & Legerstee, M. (Eds.) (forthcoming). *Handbook of jealousy: Theories, principles and multidisciplinary approaches.* Oxford, UK: Wiley-Blackwell.

Hobson, R. P. (1990). On the origins of self and the case of autism. *Development and Psychopathology, 2,* 163–181.

Hobson, R. P. (2007). Communicative depth: Soundings from developmental psychopathology. In: M. Legerstee & V. Reddy (Eds), *What does it mean to communicate for infants? Infant Behavior and Development, 30*(Special Issue), 262–277.

Hobson, P. R., Chidambi, G., Lee, A., & Meyer, J. (2006). Foundations for self- awareness: An exploration through autism. *Monographs of the Society for Research in Child Development, 71,* Serial No. 284.

Hoffman, M. (1981). Perspectives on the difference between understanding people and understanding things: The role of affect. In H. Flavell & L. Ross (Eds.), *Social cognitive development: Frontiers and possible futures* (pp. 67–81). New York: Cambridge University Press.

Hughes, C., & Leekam, S. (2004). What are the links between theory of mind and social relations? Review, reflections and new directions for studies of typical and atypical development. *Social Development, 13,* 590–619.

Hsu, H. C., & Fogel, A. (2003). Stability and transitions in mother–infant face-to-face communication during the first 6 months: A micro-historical approach. *Developmental Psychology, 39,* 1061–1082.

Iverson, J. M., Longobardi, E., & Caselli, M. C. (2003). The relationship between gestures and words in children with Down syndrome and typically-developing children in the early stages of communicative development. *International Journal of Language and Communication Disorders, 38,* 179–197.

Johnson, M. H., Grossmann, T., & Farroni, T. (2008). The social cognitive neuroscience of infancy: Illuminating early development of social brain functions. *Advances in child development and behavior, 36,* 331–372.

Jusczyk, P. W., Kennedy, L. J., & Jusczyk, A. (1995). Young infants' retention of information about syllables. *Infant Behavior and Development, 18,* 24–41.

Kampe, K., Frith, C. D., & Frith, U. (2003). "Hey John": Signals conveying communicative intention toward self activate brain regions associated with "mentalizing," regardless of modality. *Journal of Neuroscience, 12,* 5258–5263.

Keil, C. K., Smith, W. C., Simons, D. J., & Levin, D. T. (1998). Two dogmas of conceptual empiricism: Implications for hybdrid models of the structure of knowledge. *Cognition, 65,* 103–135.

Klein, R. P., & Jennings, K. D. (1979). Responses to social and inanimate stimuli in early infancy. *Journal of Genetic Psychology, 135,* 3–9.

Kugiumutzakis, G., Kokkinaki, T., Markodimitraki, M., & Vitalaki, E. (2006). Emotions in early mimesis. In J. Nadel & D. Muir (Eds.), *Emotional development: Recent research advances.* Oxford: Oxford University Press.

Kuhl, P. K. (2007). Is speech learning 'gated' by the social brain? *Developmental Science, 10,* 110–120.

Landry, S. H., & Chapieski, M. L. (1990). Joint attention of six-month-old Down syndrome and preterm infants: 1 Attention to toys and mother. *American Journal on Mental Retardation, 94*, 488–498.

Landry, S. H., Smith, K. E., Millar-Loncar, C. L., & Swank, P. R. (1998). The relation of change in maternal interactive styles to the developing social competence in full-term and pre-term children. *Child Development, 69*, 105–123.

Legerstee, M. (1991). Changes in the quality of infant sounds as a function of social and nonsocial stimulation. *First Language, 11*, 327–343.

Legerstee, M. (1992). A review of the animate/inanimate distinction in infancy: Implications for models of social and cognitive knowing. *Early Development and Parenting, 1*, 59–67.

Legerstee, M. (1994). The role of familiarity and sound in the development of person and object permanence. *British Journal of Developmental Psychology, 12*, 455–468.

Legerstee, M. (1997). Contingency effects of people and objects on subsequent cognitive functioning in three-month-old infants. *Social Development, 3*, 307–321.

Legerstee, M. (2001). Six-month-old infants rely on explanatory inference when relating communication to people and manipulatory actions to inanimate objects: Reply to Gergely. *Developmental Psychology, 5*, 583–586.

Legerstee, M. (2005). *Infants' sense of people: Precursors to a theory of mind.* Cambridge: Cambridge University Press.

Legerstee, M. (2008). Mental state awareness in infancy and childhood: The role of relationships. In K. H. Brisch & T. Hellbruggge (Eds.), *The infant, attachment, neurobiology and genes* (pp. 266–288). Stuttgart, Germany: Klett-Cotta.

Legerstee, M., & Barillas, Y. (2003). Sharing and pointing to objects at 12 months: Is the intentional stance implied? *Cognitive Development, 18*, 91–110.

Legerstee, M., Barna, J., & DiAdamo, C. (2000). Precursors to the development of intention: Understanding people and their actions at 6 months. *Developmental Psychology, 36*, 627–634.

Legerstee, M., & Bowman, T. (1989). The development responses to people and a toy in infants with Down syndrome. *Infant Behavior and Development, 12*, 462–473.

Legerstee, M., Bowman, T., & Fels, S. (1992). People and objects affect the quality of vocalizations in infants with Down syndrome. *Early Development and Parenting, 1*, 149–156.

Legerstee, M., Corter, C., & Kienapple, K. (1990). Hand, arm and facial actions of young infants to a social and nonsocial stimulus. *Child Development, 61*, 774–784.

Legerstee, M., Ellenbogen, B., Nienhuis, T., & Marsh, H. (forthcoming). Social bonds, goals and thirdness: Preconditions for the emergence of human jealousy. In S. Hart, & M. Legerstee (Eds.), *Handbook of jealousy: Theories, principles and multidisciplinary approaches.* Oxford, UK: Wiley-Blackwell.

Legerstee, M., & Fisher, T. (2008). Coordinated attention, imperative and declarative pointing in infants with and without down syndrome: Sharing experiences with adults and peers. *First Language, 28*, 281–311.

Legerstee, M., & Markova, G. (2007). Intentions make a difference: Infant responses to still-face and modified still-face conditions. *Infant Behavior and Development, 30*, 232–250.

Legerstee, M., & Markova, G. (2008). Variations in 10-month-old infant imitation of people and things. *Infant Behavior and Development, 31*, 81–91.

Legerstee, M., & Varghese, J. M. (2001). The role of maternal affect mirroring on social expectancies in 3-month-old infants. *Child Development, 5*, 1301–1313.

Legerstee, M., Pomerleau, A., Malcuit, G., & Feider, H. (1987). The development of infants' responses to people and a doll: Implications for research in communication. *Infant Behavior and Development, 10*, 81–95.

Legerstee, M., Anderson, D., & Schaffer, M. (1998). Five- and eight-month-old infants recognize their faces and voices as familiar and social stimuli. *Child Development*, *69*, 37–50.

Legerstee, M., Van Beek, Y., & Varghese, J. (2002). Effects of maintaining and redirecting infant attention on the production of referential communication in infants with and without Down syndrome. *Journal of Child Language*, *29*, 23–48.

Legerstee, M., Markova, G., & Fisher, T. (2007). The role of maternal affect attunement in dyadic and triadic communication. *Infant Behavior and Development*, *2*, 296–306.

Legerstee, M., & Weintraub, J. (1997). The integration of person and object attention in infants with and without Down syndrome. *Infant Behavior and Development*, *20*, 71–83.

Locke, A. (1980). *The guided reinvention of language*. London: Academic Press.

Markova, G., & Legerstee, M. (2006). Contingency, imitation, and affect sharing: Foundations of infants' social awareness. *Developmental Psychology*, *42*, 132–141.

Marsh, H., Stavropoulos, J. Nienhuis, T., & Legerstee, M. (2009). *Six and Nine Month-olds discriminate between unwilling and unable social partners*. Poster presented at the Biennial Meeting of the Society for Research in Child Development (SRCD), Denver, Colorado.

Maurer, D. (2007). The development of face processing: Visual limitations and their social implications, October 10. Advanced Research Seminar Talk. York University.

Meaney, M. (2008). Maternal programming of endocrine function and behaviour through epigenetic effects on gene expression, January 10. Advanced Research Seminar Talk. York University.

Meins, E., Fernyhough, C., Wainwright, R., Gupta, M. D., Fradley, E., & Tuckey, M. (2002). Maternal mind-mindedness and attachment security as predictors of theory of mind understanding. *Child Development*, *73*, 1715–1726.

Meltzoff, A. N., & Moore, M. K. (1983). The origins of imitation in infancy: Paradigm, phenomena, and theories. In L. P. Lipsitt & C. Rovee-Collier (Eds.), *Advances in infancy research*. Norwood, NJ: Ablex.

Meltzoff, A. N., & Brooks, R. (2001). "Like me" as a building block for understanding other minds: Bodily acts, attention, and intention. In B. F. Malle & L. J. Bertram (Eds.), *Intentions and intentionality: Foundations of social cognition* (pp. 171–195). Cambridge, MA: MIT Press.

Montague, D. P. F., & Walker-Andrews, A. S. (2002). Mothers, fathers, and infants: The role of familiarity and parental involvement in infants' perception of emotion expressions. *Child Development*, *73*, 1339–1352.

Montgomery, D. (2002). Mental verbs and semantic development. *Journal of Cognition and Development*, *3*(4), 357–384.

Moore, C., & Corkum, V. (1994). Social understanding at the end of the first year of life. *Developmental Review*, *14*, 349–372.

Mundy, P., & Newell, L. (2007). Joint attention, social cognition and the interior/posterior attention systems. *Current Directions in Psychological Science*, *16*, 269–274.

Mundy, P., Card, J., & Fox, N. (2000). Fourteen month cortical activity and different infant joint attention skills. *Developmental Psychobiology*, *36*, 325–338.

Mundy, P., Fox, N., & Card, J. (2003). EEG coherence, joint attention and language development in the second year. *Developmental Science*, *6*, 48–54.

Mundy, P., Sigman, M., Kasari, C., & Yirmiya, N. (1988). Nonverbal communication skills in Down syndrome children. *Child Development*, *59*, 235–249.

Murray, L., & Trevarthen, C. (1985). Emotional regulations of interactions between two-month-olds and their mothers. In T. M. Field & N. A. Fox (Eds.), *Social perception in infants* (pp. 177–197). Norwood, NJ: Ablex.

Newson, J. (1979). The growth of shared understanding between infant and caregiver. In M. Bullowa (Ed.), *Before speech: The beginning of human communication* (pp. 207–222). Cambridge: Cambridge University Press.

Panksepp, J. (2003). Feeling the pain of social loss. *Science, 302*, 237–238.

Panksepp, J. (forthcoming). The evolutionary sources of jealousy: Cross-species approaches to fundamental issues. In S. Hart, & M. Legerstee (Eds.), *Handbook of Jealousy: Theories, principles and multidisciplinary approaches.* Oxford, UK: Wiley-Blackwell.

Papousek, H., & Papousek, M. (1987). Intuitive parenting: A dialectic counterpart to the infant's integrative competence. In J. D. Osofsky (Ed.), *Handbook of infant development* (2nd ed., pp. 669–720). New York: Wiley.

Pascual-Leone, J., & Johnson, J. (1998). A dialectical constructivist view of representation: The role of mental attention, executives, and symbols. In I. E. Sigel (Ed.), *The development of representational thought: Theoretical perspectives* (pp. 169–200). Mahwah, NJ: Erlbaum.

Perner, J. (1991). *Understanding the representational mind.* Cambridge, MA: MIT Press.

Piaget, J. (1954). *The origins of intelligence in children.* New York: Norton.

Rader, N., & Stern, J. D. (1982). Visually elicited reaching in neonates. *Child Development, 53*, 1004–1007.

Reddy, V., & Legerstee, M. (2007). What does it mean to communicate? *What does it mean to communicate for infants.* Special issue: *Infant Behavior and Development, 30*, 177–297.

Rogers, S. J., & Pennington, B. F. (1991). A theoretical approach to the deficits in infantile autism. *Development and Psychopathology, 3*, 137–162.

Schilbach, L., Wohlschlager, A. M., Newen, A., Shah, N. J., Fink, G. R., & Vogeley, K. (2006). Being with virtual others: neural correlates of social interaction. *Neuropsychologica, 44*, 718–730.

Seligman, M. E. P. (1975). *Helplessness: On depression, development and death.* San Francisco, CA: Freeman.

Sigman, M., & Ruskin, E. (1999). Continuity and change in the social competence of children with autism, Down syndrome, and developmental delays. *Monographs of the Society for Research in Child Development, 63*(1, Serial No. 256).

Stern, D. N. (1985). *The interpersonal world of the infant.* New York: Basic Books.

Sugarman-Bell, S. (1978). Some organizational aspects of pre-verbal communication. In I. Markova (Ed.), *The social context of language* (pp. 49–66). New York: Wiley.

Tager-Flusberg, H. (1989). *An analysis of discourse ability and internal state lexicons in a longitudinal study of autistic children.* Paper presented at Biennial Meeting of Society for Research in Child Development, Kansas City.

Toda, S., & Fogel, A. (1993). Infant response to still-face situation at 3 and 6 months. *Developmental Psychology, 29*, 532–538.

Tomasello, M., & Call, J. (1997). *Primate cognition.* London: Oxford University Press.

Trehub, S. (1976). The discrimination of foreign speech contrasts by infants and adults. *Child Development, 47*, 466–472.

Trevarthen, C. (1979). Communication and cooperation in early infancy: A description of primary intersubjectivity. In M. Bullowa (Ed.), *Before speech: The beginning of human communication* (pp. 321–347). London: Cambridge University Press.

Trevarthen, C. (1999). Intersubjectivity. In R. Wilson & F. Keil (Eds.), *The MIT Encyclopedia of Cognitive Sciences* (pp. 415–419). Cambridge, MA: MIT Press.

Trevarthen, C., & Aitken, K. J. (2001). Infant intersubjectivity: Research, theory, and clinical applications. *Journal of Child Psychology and Psychiatry, 42*, 3–48.

Tronick, E. Z. (1981). Infant communication intent: The infant's reference to social interaction. In R. E. Stark (Ed.), *Language behavior in infancy and early childhood* (pp. 5–16). New York: Elsevier.

Tronick, E. Z., Als, H., Adamson, L., Wise, S., & Brazelton, T. B. (1978). The infant's response to entrapment between contradictory messages in face-to-face interaction. *Journal of the American Academy of Child Psychiatry, 17,* 1–13.

Tronick, E. Z., Als, H., & Adamson, L. (1979). The communicative structure of early face-to-face interactions. In M. Bullowa (Ed.), *Before speech: The beginnings of interpersonal communication* (pp. 349–372). Cambridge, UK: Cambridge University Press.

Tsao, F.-M., Liu, H. M., & Kuhl, P. K. (2004). Speech perception in infancy predicts language development in the second year of life: A longitudinal study. *Child Development, 75,* 1067–1084.

Vaughan Van Hecke, A., Mundy, P. C., Acra, C. F., Block, J., Delgado, C. E. F., Parlade, M. V., Meyer, J. A., *et al.* (2007). Infant joint attention, temperament, and social competence in preschool children. *Child Development, 78,* 53–69.

Vygotsky, L. S. (1962). *Thought and language.* . Cambridge: MIT Press (edited and translated by Eugenia Haufmann & Gertrude Vakar).

Watson, J. S. (1972). Smiling, cooing, and 'the game'. *Merrill-Palmer Quarterly, 18,* 323–339.

Weinberg, M. K., & Tronick, E. Z. (1996). Infant affective reactions to the resumption of maternal interaction after the still-face. *Child Development, 67,* 905–914.

Wellman, H. (1990). *The child's theory of mind.* Cambridge, MA: MIT Press.

Wellman, H. M., & Gelman, S. A. (1998). Knowledge acquisition in foundational domains. In D. Kuhn & R. Siegler (Eds.), *Cognition, perception and language: Vol. 2. Handbook of child psychology* (5th ed.,pp 523–573). New York: Wiley.

Wellman, H. M., Lopez-Duran, S., Labounty, J., & Hamilton, B. (2008). Infant attention of intentional action predicts preschool theory of mind. *Developmental Psychology, 4,* 618–623.

Werner, H., & Kaplan, B. (1963). *Symbol formation: An organismic developmental Approach to language and the expression of thought.* New York: Wiley.

White, G. L., & Muller, P. E. (1989). *Jealousy: Theory, research and clinical strategies.* New York: Guilford Press.

Zeedyk, S. M. (1996). Developmental accounts of intentionality: Toward integration. *Developmental Review, 16,* 416–461.

Zinober, B., & Martlew, M. (1985). Developmental changes in four types of gestures in relation to acts and vocalizations from 10 to 21 months. *British Journal of Developmental Psychology, 3,* 293–306.

THE DEVELOPMENTAL ORIGINS OF NAÏVE PSYCHOLOGY IN INFANCY

Diane Poulin-Dubois, Ivy Brooker, and Virginia Chow

CENTRE FOR RESEARCH IN HUMAN DEVELOPMENT,
DEPARTMENT OF PSYCHOLOGY (PY-170), CONCORDIA UNIVERSITY,
7141 SHERBROOKE STREET WEST, MONTRÉAL, QUEBEC, H4B 1R6, CANADA

I. Introduction

Folk or naïve psychology assumes that observed behavior can be explained by mental states. This sophisticated system of knowledge about the mental world, also known as theory of mind, takes many years to fully develop. Research on the development of children's knowledge about the mind has a long history, with three main waves of research (see Flavell, 2004 for an excellent history of the area). The first wave was derived from Piaget's theory, which proposed that children are cognitively egocentric. The notion that children do not take into account the conceptual,

55

perceptual, and affective perspectives of others generated a flurry of studies on the development of perspective-taking abilities (Flavell, 1992; Shantz, 1983). The second wave of research on children's concept of the mind started in the early 1970s and focused on metacognitive development (Flavell, Miller, & Miller, 1993). Metacognition is broadly defined as both the knowledge of and the regulation of cognitive abilities (Flavell, 1979). The last and current wave of research started in the early 1980s and has been one of the largest and liveliest topics of research in the area of cognitive development for the past 25 years (Astington, 1993; Flavell & Miller, 1998). Commonly referred to as theory of mind research, it investigates children's knowledge about basic mental states such as desires, percepts, beliefs, knowledge, thoughts, emotions, and intentions. Researchers attempt to determine when and how children recognize the existence of these various mental states as well as what they know about *how* these mental states are causally linked to perceptual and behavioral outputs, and to other mental states.

The research on naïve psychology has taken many directions since the early 1980s. The study of one mental state belief, namely, false belief, has dominated the research in this area. In a series of influential studies, Wimmer and Perner (1983) reported a developmental shift in children's understanding that others or themselves could hold a belief that is false. Using the unexpected transfer task, it was shown that it is only between 3 and 5 years of age that children understand that someone will have a false belief about the location of an object if they do not witness its transfer of location. This milestone in naïve psychology development, which consists of the understanding of mental representations or that people think and act in accordance with the way they represent the world mentally rather than the way the world actually is, also has been confirmed with other false-belief tasks, such as appearance, reality, and unexpected content task (see Wellman, Cross, & Watson, 2001 for a meta-analysis of false-belief research).

Although the study of false belief has dominated the field for many years, researchers have charted the development of many additional mental states. The literature on naïve psychology development is too vast to review, and we only briefly mention the major accomplishments about the understanding of each mental state (see Flavell, 1999 for review). For visual perception, children are first able to infer that one may see something that they do not and vice versa (Level 1, perspective taking) but only later they are able to demonstrate the understanding that the same object can be perceived differently by two people if viewed from different positions (Level 2). Attention is another mental state that develops with children gradually understanding that people's attention is limited, selective, and graded (Moll & Tomasello, 2006). Key points in the development also have been found for the mental states of desires and emotions. Desires are linked to emotions by 3 years of age and differentiated from intentions by the age of 4 years. Regarding emotions, research has demonstrated that even pre-schoolers understand that emotions are subjective states that are different from the actions and expressions that they cause (Feinfield *et al.*, 1999). Only later they grasp the complex nature of emotional states, including the fact that facial expressions do not always match emotional states, emotional experiences may vary as a function of current and past experiences, and that many emotional states can be experienced simultaneously (Flavell & Miller, 1998).

Children's knowledge about mental representations continues to develop after the understanding of false belief at 5 years of age. A few years after false-belief acquisition, second-order beliefs (e.g., she knows that I know that) as well as the insight that the mind is an interpretive device, that is, two people can differently interpret the same object or event develop (Carpendale & Chandler, 1996). Regarding children's grasp of knowledge, although even preschoolers understand that seeing leads to knowing, there is much improvement after the acquisition of this basic concept. Among these more advanced concepts is understanding *how* knowledge is acquired and the perceptual conditions required to produce knowledge (Taylor, Esbensen, & Bennett, 1994). For example, it is not until the age of 6 years that children realize that people must have visual access to an object to know its color or that partial visibility might not allow certain knowledge about the identity of an object (Taylor, 1988; Yaniv & Shatz, 1988). Finally, children only gradually understand the process of thinking. Even if preschoolers already understand thinking as an internal activity that represents real or imaginary things, it takes many years for children to grasp specific aspects of thinking (i.e., conscious vs. unconscious; Flavell, 1999). In sum, research on naïve psychology has demonstrated that even young preschoolers possess some basic knowledge about the mind, and by the elementary school years, children have constructed a sophisticated understanding of how mental states predict and explain behaviors.

In addition to charting the development of all mental states, research on theory of mind has taken many new directions since its emergence in the 1980s (Flavell, 1999, 2000). Now there exists a large body of research that has focused on intercultural and interspecies differences in theory of mind skills (e.g., Tomasello, Call, & Hare, 2003; Yazdi *et al.*, 2006). Further-more, work has progressed on the antecedents and consequents of mentalistic understanding. Many developmental psychologists believe that children's difficulties in theory of mind tasks, such as those testing the false-belief concept, are caused by the limitations of other, more general cognitive abilities such as language and executive functioning (Carlson, Moses, & Hix, 1998; Gerstadt, Hong, & Diamond, 1994; Russel, 1996; Zelazo, Frye, & Rapus, 1996). Moreover, it has been demonstrated that children's theory of mind development has a significant impact on social behavior. Preschool children who have more advanced theory of mind skills have more successful peer relations than less advanced peers (Dunn, 1996; Hughes & Dunn, 1997; Watson *et al.*, 1999). Interestingly, there is also evidence for negative consequents of advanced mind-reading skills with antisocial behavior (e.g., bullies; Sutton, Smith, & Swettenham, 1999). It appears that some children who bully not only understand the emotions their actions cause but also act on the basis of that understanding.

One of the exciting new directions taken by research on naïve psychology is the investigation of the developmental origins of theory of mind in infancy. In one of the first review papers on the topic, Flavell (1999, 2000) identified this as a promising line of research. At that time of the review, there were only a handful of studies directly testing precursors of theory of mind in infants. Other relevant data focused on infants' abilities to analyze and discriminate human stimuli, such as gaze following, imitation of motor movements, and discrimination of facial and vocal expressions (Butterworth & Jarrett, 1991; Cooper & Aslin, 1989; Meltzoff & Moore, 1994). In this chapter, we review the most recent findings from studies that have sought the developmental origins of the understanding of the basic mental states just discussed. Researchers have designed several ingenious tasks, many of them based on the violation of expectancy method, to uncover what many of them believe to be an implicit naïve psychology that develops during the first two years of life. We begin by outlining the theories that have been offered as explanations for the development of children's naïve psychology.

II. Theories

There are several theoretical models that have been proposed to explain the development of naïve or commonsense psychology. There are a number of in-depth treatments of these theoretical views available in the literature (Astington & Gopnik, 1991a; Jarrold *et al.*, 1994; Wellman, 2002). Some of these models have clear implications about the roots of naïve psychology during the infancy period. One type of theory is the theory-theory view (Gopnik & Meltzoff, 1997; Gopnik & Wellman, 1994; Perner, 1991; Wellman & Gelman, 1998). Theory theorists claim that children's psychological understanding is "theory-like" in that unobservable constructs are used to explain, predict, and understand human behavior and experience.

They postulate that domain-specific entities (e.g., beliefs and desires) are causally linked to one another and to behavioral inputs. For example, what we perceive may influence what we think and believe. In turn, our thoughts and beliefs could foster other mental and physiological changes, which can influence our desires and goal-directed activity. According to this constructivist approach, naïve psychology gradually develops in a series of steps toward a full-fledged theory of mind. Around age 2, children possess a desire psychology that is mentalistic but nonrepresentational, that is, they understand that real and represented objects are different entities but cannot grasp that the represented objects vary across individuals. By age 3, children have started to talk about beliefs and understand them as mental representations but still do not link them causally to behaviors, which is the reason why this step is called a desire–belief psychology. For example, they do not recognize that people's emotional reactions to situations are determined by their beliefs. Finally, by age 4, an adult belief–desire psychology is acquired, and like adults, these children have mental representations of their beliefs and desires, and they are able to link them to behavior. The realization of a full-fledged theory of mind is driven by the accumulation of data and information through experience.

In contrast, the modularity model of naïve psychology contends that the development of naïve psychology consists in the maturation of domain-specific and modular mechanisms (Baron-Cohen, 1995; Leslie, 1994a; Leslie & Roth, 1993). In one such model, there are four early maturing modular mechanisms dedicated to mental state computations that mature by the end of the second year (Leslie, 1994a).

A third major theoretical framework that attempts to account for the development of naïve psychology contends that reasoning about the mind proceeds not through abstract constructs but through our own first-hand experiences (Harris, 1991, 1992; Meltzoff, 2007). In one version of this approach, the attribution of mental experiences to others requires a simple process of simulation. In other words, to think about others' state of mind, children imagine themselves in other people's shoes whereby they project themselves into the other person's situation and imagine what they would feel in such situations (Harris, 1991, 1992; Lillard, 2002). In another instantiation of that approach, the recognition of self–other equivalences provides the foundation, not the outcome, of social cognition (Meltzoff, 2007). Infants can represent human movement patterns they see and ones they perform using the same mental code. Early facial imitation is one of the best indicators that infants can map actions of other people onto actions of their own body, as infants have never seen their own faces. This simulation theory of mind-reading is compatible with cognitive neuroscience work concerning mirror neurons. Mirror neurons are visuomotor neurons that respond both when an individual performs a particular action and when that individual observes the same action performed by another individual (Gallese & Goldman, 1998; Oberman & Ramachandran, 2007).

Each of these theoretical viewpoints has generated much of the research that we review in this chapter. In addition, domain-general changes in certain information-processing capacities are very likely to contribute to the rapid development of precursors to a mature naïve psychology. What makes this field one of the most exciting areas of cognitive development is the debate over the depth of infants' sophisticated understanding of human action that has been documented. A full-fledged naïve psychology entails the ability to make lawful inferences about the behavior of other agents on the basis of abstract representations of the causal relation between unobservable mental states and observable states of affairs. Human infants (and nonhuman animals) probably do not understand others in terms of a fully adult-like belief–desire psychology. However, infants and very young children do not seem to only read and react to overt behavior. As this review shows, there is mounting evidence that infants have developed precursors to a full-fledged naïve psychology. We now review empirical evidence for the emerging understanding of mental constructs such as perception, desire, belief, attention, intention, and knowledge, all part of a mature naïve psychology.

III. Visual Perception

Since vision is a primary source of information about others' mental experience, the ability to correctly represent what others can and cannot see is a precondition for the successful attribution of knowledge or beliefs (Sodian, Thoermer, & Metz, 2007). As such, a child's ability to nonego-centrically represent what others see, or Level-1 visual perspective taking (Flavell, 1977), is considered a critical component in social interactions (Argyle & Cook, 1976; Kleinke, 1986; Langton, Watt, & Bruce, 2000) and represents an important precursor to theory of mind later (e.g., Corkum & Moore, 1998). Until recently, the bulk of this research has focused on preschoolers. It has demonstrated that 2-year-olds reach sophisticated levels of understanding others' visual perception (e.g., Flavell, 1992, 1999, 2000; Lempers, Flavell, & Flavell, 1977).

A. UNDERSTANDING WHAT OTHERS SEE

Research has come a long way in terms of charting infants' under-standing of what other people see (e.g., Chow, Poulin-Dubois, & Lewis,

2008; Brooks & Meltzoff, 2002, 2005; Moll & Tomasello, 2004; Sodian *et al.*, 2007). Using a number of different paradigms, infants' understanding of other people's visual perception has been examined through their gaze following skills (i.e., looking at where someone else is looking: Brooks & Meltzoff, 2002, 2005; Caron *et al.*, 2002; Chow *et al.*, 2008; Dunphy-Lelii & Wellman, 2004; Moll & Tomasello, 2004; Sodian *et al.*, 2007). Brooks and Meltzoff (2002) found that 12-month-olds followed an experimenter's gaze direction and head turn more often when the experimenter's eyes were open than when they were closed. Using the same procedure, Brooks and Meltzoff (2005; cited in Meltzoff & Brooks, 2007) replicated this finding in infants as young as 10 months. However, when infants' gaze following was compared when the experimenter's eyes were open, blindfolded, or closed, only 14- and 18-month-olds, but not 12-month-olds, followed gaze more when the eyes were open. In contrast, once all the infants experienced the sight-blocking properties of a blindfold, they behaved similarly (D'Entremont & Morgan, 2006). On the basis of these findings, it has been concluded that infants near the end of their first year understand the link between the person's eyes and his or her directed attention toward an object in the surrounding environment, representing a mentalistic or "rich" interpretation of referential understanding.

B. INTERPRETATION OF GAZE FOLLOWING BEHAVIORS

Despite these promising findings, there is debate concerning how to interpret infants' gaze following actions and his or her attributions about the looker. According to Povinelli and Eddy (1996), knowledge about visual perception could be processed at three different levels of comprehension. At the most parsimonious level, infants can respond to another person's eyes without attributing the mental act of seeing or attending-to-objects to people (Langton *et al.*, 2000; Moore & Corkum, 1994; Moore, 1999; Povinelli, 2001). A person's head-turn could simply be a learned response that draws an infant's attention to a particular location or space because it has become a predictive cue that there is something interesting to look at. However, at a second level of comprehension, visual perception could be understood as an attentional process that connects individuals to the external world (Flavell, 1988), thus linking the perceiver with the perceived (Povinelli & Eddy, 1996). Finally, at the third level of comprehension, there is mentalistic understanding. That is, infants have the ability to represent a "relationship between the eyes and an object, and represent the relationship as being representational in some way" (Doherty, 2006, p. 179). Furthermore, they understand that visual perception in themselves and others can lead to knowledge and belief formation (Gopnik & Graf, 1988; Wimmer, Hogrefe, & Perner, 1988), unless the reliability of the person's gaze following is violated in some way (Poulin-Dubois & Chow, in press). Given the different levels of explanations available for explaining visual perception understanding, we now turn our attention to studies that seek to answer whether infants do indeed reach this third level of comprehension and show a mentalistic understanding of visual perception.

C. MENTALISTIC UNDERSTANDING OF VISUAL PERCEPTION

Compelling evidence for infants' mentalistic understanding of seeing comes from the "Barrier" paradigm, in which the experimenter's line of sight is obstructed by a barrier. In this task, the infant sits opposite the experimenter who looks toward a target on the left or right side of a wall. Butler, Caron, and Brooks (2000) found that both 14- and 18-month-olds looked to the target more often when the experimenter's line of sight was clear than when it was blocked by an opaque screen. However, when a screen with a large window was used,18-month-olds, but not 14-month-olds, followed the experimenter's gaze, suggesting that only 18-month-old infants showed an understanding that the window enabled a clear line of sight. Subsequent studies found competence in this task among 15-month-olds (Caron *et al.*, 2002) and 14-month-olds (Dunphy-Lelii & Wellman, 2004) when the contrast between the opaque barrier and the barrier with a window was made more salient. Taken together, these findings provide support for infants' rich interpretation and attribution of visual reference to others, developing shortly after one year of life.

Using a variation of the Barrier paradigm, Moll and Tomasello (2004) created a more natural situation in which the infants' line of sight to the target was blocked by a barrier but the experimenter's was not. In this way, the setup simulates everyday situations in which the adult has visual access to a target but the child does not. They found that both 12- and 18-month-old infants not only followed the adult's gaze but also moved a short distance to gain a proper viewing of the target at which the experimenter was looking at. The authors argued that these results support Level-1 perspective taking. That is, the child understands that a person sees an object if her or his eyes are directed toward the object and that another person can see something that the child cannot see. These results are also supported by research by Csibra and Volein (2008) in which 8- and 12-month-old infants followed the gaze of the experimenter to one of two locations behind a barrier and were surprised and therefore looked longer when they were confronted with an empty location. These results suggest that young infants expect to find a referent object whenever they follow another person's gaze.

To clarify the debate surrounding the interpretation of infants' gaze following, Chow *et al.* (2008) directly tested Level-1 visual perspective taking in 14-month-olds, by examining whether their gaze following differs depending on the credibility of the person's looking behavior. Past research with preschoolers showed that they can adapt their object-labeling (Clément, Koenig, & Harris, 2004; Koenig, Clément, & Harris, 2004) and word-learning based on the reliability or *trustworthiness* of their informant (Sabbagh & Baldwin, 2001). To test the idea that infants can take into account what each looker sees, Chow *et al.* (2008) first trained 14-month-olds using a variation of Repacholi's (1998) search task. Specifically, infants participated in an object search task in which they witnessed an experimenter show excitement while looking inside a box that either contained a toy (reliable looker condition) or was empty (unreliable looker condition). Following this training phase, a variation of Moll and Tomasello's paradigm (2004) was used to compare infants' gaze following to a target in front (control condition) and behind a barrier (experimental condition). The authors reasoned that if infants were simply following a learned response to a person's head turn, then infants should follow both experimenters' gaze (reliable and unreliable) equally to target objects in both conditions. However, if infants understood the subjective nature of gaze, then infants in the reliable looker condition should be more likely to follow the experimenter's gaze behind the barrier than infants in the unreliable looker condition. In fact, infants were influenced by their previous experience with the looker and adapted their gaze following accordingly across tasks. Even when a more stringent control was used whereby an unfamiliar experimenter was introduced in the barrier task following training with an unreliable looker, infants did not transfer their knowledge of the unreliable looker to the novel experimenter and treated her as though she was reliable by following her gaze equally often to the target in front and behind the barriers (see Figure 1). Taken together, these findings demonstrate for the first time that young infants are sensitive to an individual's record of gaze reliability.

Sodian *et al.* (2007) investigated 12- and 14-month-olds' expectation about another person's goal-directed action based on whether that person could see the old goal-object in the test event when she was reaching for a new goal. Fourteen-month-olds, but not 12-month-olds, looked longer when the experimenter reached for and grasped a new object when the old goal-object was visible than when it was invisible to the person

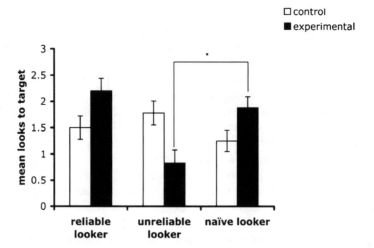

Fig. 1. Mean scores (out of 4) for looking at targets in the control and experimental conditions in the reliable, unreliable, and naïve looker conditions. Error bars show standard errors of the means.

(hidden behind an opaque barrier) but visible to the infant. On the basis of these findings, the authors concluded that 14-month-olds are able to reason or "rationalize" the person's reach for a new object when the old object was out of sight and thus looked longer when these assumptions were violated. Similarly, when the experimenter's visual access to the target was manipulated during the test event using the same paradigm, Luo and Johnson (2009) found that even 6-month-olds recognize that an agent's goal-directed actions are influenced by her perceptions. Overall, these results suggest that infants recognize that a person's goal-directed actions are constrained by their visual access to information (see also Johnson, Ok, & Luo, 2007).

Finally, another line of evidence that supports the precocious understanding that infants have of others' visual perspectives comes from studies using event-related potentials (ERPs). Using ERPs to measure the neural systems involved in information processing, Hoehl *et al.* (2008) investigated how 4-month-olds process the direction of an adult's eye gaze when they are presented with static photographs of adult faces with eye gaze either directed or averted from an object. Hoehl *et al.* (2008) focused on the positive slow wave processing which has been shown in previous studies to be significantly greater for unfamiliar compared to familiar stimuli, suggesting that infants form a stronger memory representation for cued objects (e.g., Nelson *et al.*, 2000; de Haan & Nelson, 1997).

Interestingly, they found that 4-month-olds differentially process the direction of an adult's eye gaze, as evidenced by an enhanced positive slow wave at frontal sites during observation of stimuli depicting gaze-cued objects. In addition, Senju, Johnson, and Csibra (2006) recorded the ERPs of adults and 9-month-old infants while they watched video clips containing gaze shifts either toward or away from the location of a preceding object. They found that both age groups exhibited increased ERP amplitudes over the occipito-temporal area for object-incongruent gaze shifts than for object-congruent gaze shifts, which suggests that 9-month-olds encode referential information of gaze in a way that is similar to adults.

Although it is important to note that understanding visual perception (gaze judgments) continues to develop beyond infancy (Leekam *et al.*, 1997; Doherty, Anderson, & Howieson, 2004), the studies reviewed in this section contribute to the growing body of evidence of infants' developing understanding of what other people see. In addition to their understanding of the requirements of sight, infants appear to be able to track the reliability of the looker, and *rationalize* a person's goal-directed actions on the basis of their visual perception. Furthermore, young infants' understanding of another person's goal-directed actions on the basis of that person's visual access is supported by ERP findings that show that infants and adults process gaze-object relations in similar ways.

IV. Attention

Attention is the cognitive process of selectively focusing on certain information while ignoring other information. It plays a critical role in social development as it is a precondition for learning about the external world, whether it involves acquiring new behaviors or communicating with others. It has many implications for infants' developing theory of mind, including knowledge and understanding of others as intentional agents who possess certain beliefs and desires (Wellman *et al.*, 2008). Indeed, an awareness and understanding of the role of attention in social contexts can lead to the development of social cognition.

The attentional focus of a person can be revealed through certain cues that inform others of their intended referent. Infants are particularly sensitive to cues such as eye-contact, raised eyebrows, being spoken to by name, and contingent turn-taking (Gergely, Egyed, & Király, 2007). For children to determine someone's focus of attention, they must have the prerequisite skills of being sensitive to another's eye and hand movements that are directed toward some external action or object (Cleveland & Striano, 2007). This sensitivity, which emerges at about 3-months of age, is limited to their own visual field until approximately 6 months of age (D'Entremont, Hains, & Muir, 1997). However, as this ability becomes more robust (at 12 months), infants can follow gaze direction to a target located behind a barrier. This suggests that they have some curiosity and understanding of what others see and that they can track and attend to a person's gaze direction that is outside their own field of vision (Moll & Tomasello, 2004).

Once an infant has attended to the intended referent of another person, certain neural processes are required to understand this relationship (Hoehl *et al.*, 2008). Specifically, objects in the external environment previously cued by an observer's gaze become familiar to an infant, requiring differential neural processing than those gazes that are nonobject directed. On the basis of neuro-imaging data, it appears that infants as young as 4 months process socially relevant cues more deeply and therefore establish some expectancy of others' focus of attention to external objects (Hoehl *et al.*, 2008).

For infants to focus on and share the same attentional context with another, they must be able to differentiate between triadic (shared attention among infant, experimenter, and object) and nontriadic interactions (both the infant and experimenter attend to the object but not to each other). Striano and Stahl (2005) found that infants smiled and gazed more during triadic interactions in which an experimenter demonstrated positive affect, while alternating eye gaze with the infant and another object, as opposed to during nontriadic interactions, when the experimenter avoided eye-contact with the infant once attention to the object had been initiated. Importantly, infants were not influenced by others' affect alone, as this condition (without the sharing of attention with an outside referent) did not elicit gaze or smiling. This and other research (Tricia *et al.*, 2007) suggests that infants make the distinction between triadic and nontriadic interactions at the age of 3 months.

Following the development of awareness of different social and attentional contexts, Cleveland and Striano (2007) found that 9-month-old infants can achieve a sophisticated level of object processing. In their study, infants looked longer at novel toys following a familiarization phase that involved the experimenter alternating attention between the infant and a different toy than when the experimenter looked at the toy alone. This suggests that infants are better able to process novel information regarding their external environment when facilitated in a socially cued, joint-attentional context.

In this joint-attentional context the question then becomes, do infants understand if the person is attending to one object in particular? In other words, do infants understand referential intentions? Tomasello and Haberl (2003) showed that by the end of their first year, infants understand that adults get excited and pay attention to new objects as opposed to old ones and thus are able to correctly identify a new toy for the experimenter even though it is not new for them (i.e., the experimenter leaves the room when this new toy is presented to the infant). Additionally, infants at 14–18 months appear to understand that being excited about seeing an old object does not make sense, so when confronted with this situation, infants search for a second object to which they believe the experimenter may be attending (Moll *et al.*, 2006). Taken together, it appears that infants understand and are aware that others are intentional and attentional agents who have voluntary control of their perceptions, thus lending support for the "rich" interpretation of social cognition (Slaughter & McConnell, 2003; Tomasello & Haberl, 2003).

It seems that infants are able to differentially process what others know and have experienced based on the attentional context in which it occurs (Moll & Tomasello, 2007). In contrast to the understanding that occurs in the joint-attention context, both 14- and 18-month-old infants failed to understand whether an experimenter had previously experienced an object solely based on watching the experimenter visually attending to it (Moll, Carpenter, & Tomasello, 2007; Moll & Tomasello, 2007). The need for joint engagement appears to decline at about 15 months of age, and by 18 months the infants in this study were able to distinguish the experimenter's past experience with individual engagement (the experimenter manipulating and verbalizing only with the object; Moll & Tomasello, 2007). Therefore, by the first year of age, infants have sophisticated social-cognitive abilities that initially develop in joint-attentional, triadic contexts.

One way that infants communicate within these contexts is through their pointing behavior. It seems that infants point not only to direct adult's attention (usually positive) to the self but also in a declarative manner to direct others to an external referent in their environment. Liszkowski *et al.* (2004) found that when adults showed affect only toward the infant, as opposed to attending to the infant and the referent to which they were pointing at, infants exhibited dissatisfaction and tried to "message repair" by continually pointing at the intended referent. This dissatisfaction appears to result from the failure to share attention and communicate about the referent with another. If they were pointing merely to draw positive attention to themselves (and not establish a joint-attentional context; a "lean" interpretation of infants' social cognition) than infants should have been pleased with the attention, they were garnering from the experimenter and not try to "message repair" with their pointing behavior.

Infants' desire to communicate with others and learn about their external environment also extends to them attending to another's social cues. When confronted with an ambiguous situation, infants look to another, more knowledgeable person to guide their own behavior, otherwise known as social referencing (Goswami, 2006; Mumme, 1993; Racine & Carpendale, 2007; Slaughter & McConnell, 2003). Particularly within the mother–infant dyad, infants will look to their caregiver and persist in referencing in order to establish a joint-attentional context in which they can seek information regarding their external environment (Stenberg, 2003). When their caregiver does not facilitate a joint-attentional context, infants will reference another external source of information (i.e., a bystander other than the mother) in order to fulfill their desire for information. This suggests that toward the end of the first year of life, infants have a desire for knowledge and a developing understanding that others have internal states such as their capacity for knowledge.

Finally, at around the same time, infants have been found to have intentions to influence another person's mind, by wanting to share with another some object of attention that has to be imagined (Tomasello, Carpenter, & Liszkowski, 2007). In a context in which 12-month-old infants were attending to an object that later "disappeared" from view, the infants pointed toward the location where the object was before, especially if this object was previously not seen by the other person (Liszkowski, Carpenter, & Tomasello, 2007a). Along with findings that infants point more often under conditions in which shared interest, visual accessibility, and joint-attention occur (Liszkowski *et al.*, 2004, 2008; Liszkowski, Carpenter, & Tomasello, 2007b), these findings suggest that by the first year of life, infants are able to communicate intent and have social motives. They also seem to understand the necessary conditions where it can be facilitated, ideally in a joint-attentional context.

To sum, soon after their first birthday, infants appear to understand others' attentional and knowledge states. They also are able to communicate about things that have occurred in the past, as evidenced by their reference to objects that are absent or to events that have already happened. Their use of declarative pointing at this age also highlights their understanding of mental states, specifically what others *know*. There is a clear developmental progression for this understanding of others' experience. This suggests that a good avenue for future research would be to conduct longitudinal studies to examine how infants develop these skills, and whether they are essential precursors for later understanding of more complex knowledge states such as false beliefs (Moll & Tomasello, 2006; Striano & Stahl, 2005).

V. Desires

Adults make inferences about other people's mental states when trying to explain and predict another person's actions. For example, we reason that a person may reach for an apple because he or she is hungry (*a belief*) and therefore desires to eat it. Thus, the mental state of desire does not occur alone but within a constellation of other mental states that informs human action. According to Wellman and Woolley (1990), the understanding of another person's mental state requires the conception of a tripartite relation between beliefs, desire, and action. That is, desires represent a motivational force that is framed by beliefs and that leads to the formation of an intention; an intended action prior to its performance (Astington, 1991). Research has demonstrated that 3-year-olds can explain and predict other people's behaviors given their desires (Wellman & Woolley, 1990) and explain actions with recourse to another agent's desires (Bartsch & Wellman, 1995). Research has extended this investigation to infancy, examining whether infants have a similar and more implicit understanding of desires which may serve as a foundation for a more sophisticated understanding of other people's mental states (see Baron-Cohen, 1995; Bretherton, 1991; Hobson, 1994; Poulin-Dubois & Shultz, 1988; Wellman, 1993, for overviews). By implicit understanding, we refer to knowledge that is nonsymbolic and preconscious but is nevertheless evident in behavior. Language development allows this knowledge to become stored in an explicit, conscious, and accessible format. Such suggestion has been made in other areas of development (Alibali & Goldin-Meadow, 1993; Karmiloff-Smith, 1992; Mandler, 2004). After all, infants often encounter social situations in which their desires may conflict or be incompatible with those of others. Consider an infant wanting to have a toy from a store that the parent refuses to buy. This emotionally charged interaction may serve to highlight the subjective nature of desires and motivate infants to communicate their own wants and needs to others so as to fulfill their desires.

The spontaneous speech that infants produce to communicate their needs and fulfill their desires is also used as evidence that infants can reason about other people's desires. In particular, Wellman and Bartsch (1994) found that infants as early as 18 months begin to use desire terms, such as *want*, to explicitly refer to internal states. Furthermore, by their second birthday they can contrast the desires of different people by reasoning that Jane wants X and Bills wants Y. However, it is not until 30 months that infants demonstrate an appreciation, through use of desire words, that two individuals can have opposing desires for the same object and thereby able to distinguish that Jane wants X but Bill does not want X.

Further evidence for infants' understanding of desires comes from a nonverbal task that examined whether infants understand that others have preferences that are different from their own. Specifically, Repacholi and Gopnik (1997) presented infants with two familiar food items. After tasting each food, the experimenter produced an affective response that was either positive or negative to indicate her preferences. When she requested that the child give her some food, only the 18-month-olds, but not the 14-month-olds, understood that others may have preferences that may diverge from their own. For example, they understood that the other person wanted a broccoli but not a cracker, whereas they preferred a cracker. These results suggest that by 18-months of age, infants use their knowledge of the experimenter's earlier emotional reactions to infer the object of the experimenter's desires thus providing support for a mentalistic interpretation for infants' behavior.

Similarly, infants' understanding of the role of desires underlying human actions and emotional reactions was examined using a preferential looking paradigm. Videotaped scenarios were used featuring an actor expressing a desire for an object by pointing to one of two objects and indicating, "I want that one" (Poulin-Dubois, 1999; Tilden, Poulin-Dubois, & Desroches, 1997). Then, in the test phase, the actor either reached for the desired object or another object. Using their looking time at each object as a measure, results revealed that infants as young as 18 months of age expect people's actions to be congruent with their desires when a combination of visual, gestural, and verbal cues are used. In fact, they seemed surprised when a person reached for an object that was different from the one she wanted in the recent past. However, when gaze direction was controlled for in a follow-up experiment (actor also looked at and extended her arm toward the nondesired object and indicated, "Look at that one."), results revealed that both gaze direction and gestures toward an object are more important indicators of desires for 18- and 24-month-olds than verbal expression.

Although infants show some early competence in desire reasoning, a lean interpretation posits that children under the age of 4 do not truly understand desires as a subjective state, but only as a sophisticated notion of objective desirability (Perner, Zauner, & Sprung, 2005). That is, infants may reason that eating the broccoli is objectively good for the other person but bad for themselves because it is not something they desire. However, infants may not be able to conceptualize a scenario in which two different people hold incompatible desires regarding the same referent. For example, infants may not construe a scenario in which it is subjectively good for them to eat the cracker from person A's perspective, but subjectively bad from person B's perspective. As such, a true subjectivist account could not be demonstrated in Repacholi and Gopnik's study (1997) given that infants did not have to make any inferences regarding the person's psychological state in an incompatible desire scenario. This problem was addressed by Poulin-Dubois and McKoy (1999) when they manipulated the experimenter's expression of desire. In particular, they showed that infants as young as 18 months will give a person the food item that this person desires (e.g., broccoli), even when this desire mismatches their own (crackers; see also Repacholi & Gopnik, 1997). In contrast, these same infants did not attribute the mismatching desire to an experimenter when she only requested some food, without expressing a desire beforehand. The infants also took longer to give food to the experimenter who did not express a desire before requesting it, compared to a condition in which both desire expression and request came from the same person (see Figure 2).

Empirical support for the assumption that children under the age of 4 years do not understand truly subjective desires comes from several studies. First, in a study where 3-year-olds played a jigsaw puzzle game against a puppet character, Moore *et al.* (1995) found that when the children were asked about the puppet's desire when it conflicted with their own, they performed poorly on this task, falsely ascribing to the puppet the same desire they held themselves. In addition, their performance on the standard false-belief task was poor. However, when a replication study was conducted with a control condition in which there was no incompatibility between the desires of the puppet and the child, children in this control condition performed better than children in the original condition (Daxeder & Feichtinger, 2003, cited in Perner *et al.*, 2005). A similar pattern of results was found by Lichtermann (1991), who presented infants

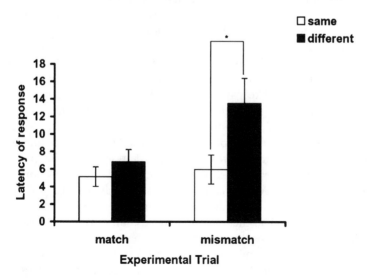

Fig. 2. Latency of response as a function of experimental trial and agent type.

with a scenario involving two characters who had either compatible or incompatible desires. When asked about the character's desire-dependent emotions (whether each was happy after a desired or undesired event), children in both conditions correctly inferred the emotion. However, like the subjects in Moore *et al.*'s study (1995), infants performed better in the compatible condition than in the incompatible condition, thus providing support that children under the age of 4 years do not understand other people's desires as truly subjective. As well, their performance in the incompatible condition was highly correlated with their performance on the false-belief task, lending support to the proposal that children at this age do not possess a representational state of mind.

It is important to point out some limitations in the above-mentioned studies. According to Moore *et al.* (1995), poor performance could be due to a conceptual problem in assigning subjective attitudes. That is, the child has to be able to override his or her own desire for one option in order to answer in terms of the other person's incompatible desire. In addition, in Lichtermann's (1991) study, the child was never made aware that the second character did not desire to go to the place the first character wished to go. Therefore, an alternative explanation for their findings may be that the child reported the second character as sharing similar emotions with the first because she was happy to follow the other character, despite wanting to go in the opposite direction initially.

Given these limitations, the assumption that children under the age of 4 years do not understand the subjectivist notion of desire has been challenged. In particular, Rakoczy, Warneken, and Tomasello (2007) replicated Lichtermann's (1991) methodology using a modified version of the scenario, which involved some quarreling between the protagonists, resulting in one person's desire being fulfilled, but not the other person. In this way, the interaction represents an ecologically valid scenario wherein subjective desires are likely to be incompatible. Children then were asked to infer the character's emotions based on the fulfillment of his or her desire or lack thereof. Using this refined methodology, even 3-year-olds inferred correctly the desire of the two characters in the compatible and incompatible conditions. Interestingly, they demonstrated this proficiency even though the majority failed the standard false-belief task. In contrast to earlier findings by Moore *et al.* (1995) and Lichtermann (1991), these results suggest that young children understand incompatible desires as well as compatible ones. The fact that 3-year-olds can reason with desires but not false beliefs is consistent with the view that a representational theory of mind emerges at around 4 years of age (Perner, 1991). In addition, the results imply that belief reasoning is not a necessary pre-requisite to develop desire reasoning.

Considerable research has documented that children are able to reason about desires earlier than beliefs (Hadwin & Perner, 1991; Wellman & Banerjee, 1991; Wellman & Bartsch, 1988; Yuill, 1984). However, just as Repacholi and Gopnik (1997) and Poulin-Dubois and McKoy (1999) used a nonverbal experimental paradigm to tap into infants' earlier understanding of the subjectivity of desires, it is likely that a nonverbal false-belief task may yield similar results with beliefs, resulting in a symmetry in infants' developmental understanding of other people's desires and beliefs. In fact, a number of studies (Onishi & Baillargeon, 2005; Southgate, Senju, & Csibra, 2007; Surian, Caldi, & Sperber, 2007) have shown that infants as young as 13 months show some understanding of another person's belief as subjective. Therefore, future studies will have to examine how and when infants come to reliably make the connections between several mental states such as desires and beliefs (e.g., Churchland, 1984; Davidson, 1980; Wellman, Phillips, & Rodriguez, 2000).

To summarize, it appears that by 18 months of age infants have some understanding of desires and that they can use emotional cues to make inferences regarding another person's internal psychological state. Also, they appear to understand the role that desires play in human actions. Although this mentalistic interpretation has received some criticism due to the common assumption that children under the age of 4 years do not hold a truly subjective notion of desire, this assumption has been challenged. Research with refined methodologies shows promise that this competency develops earlier. Additionally, even though poor performance on theory of mind tasks is correlated with performance on the false-belief task, it appears that succeeding on the false-belief task is not a necessary prerequisite to understanding the subjectivity of desires.

Although infants seem to show sensitivity to other people's desires, more research is essential to determine whether infants reason about other people's desires in various contexts, not simply with familiar objects such as food. Also, future studies need to clarify the mechanisms by which an infant progresses from an early understanding of desires to a more mature conceptualization of desire in childhood. Finally, with the advent of using nonverbal tasks to examine infants' understanding of other people's desires, it will be interesting to explore how desire understanding is related to other mental states such as intentions and beliefs.

VI. Emotion

It has been argued that infants are born with an innate sense of communicating emotion, as they spontaneously display an extensive range of emotion through varying facial displays, as well as understand those made by others, cross-culturally (Meins, 2003). Emotion, however, is more complex than a simple reflexive process of registering the behavior of the caregiver. It involves the development of an understanding of the meaning of other people's emotional expressions and inferring the referent of their emotional expression. Thus, *how* an infant begins to perceive his or her external environment in addition to the significance of the events that occur within it shapes how they begin to express their emotions. Infants' understanding of others' emotions sheds light into their psychological growth, for it uncovers how infants begin to understand the working of others' minds and how this influences their well-being and later social competency (Thompson & Lagattuta, 2006).

Infants are sensitive to others' expression of emotions, and by about 7 months, they discriminate the facial and vocal emotional expressions of others. At this age, infants can differentiate positive from negative facial expressions (Nelson, 1987), as well as among emotions of the same valence (i.e., happy vs. surprised and anger vs. fearfulness; Kobiella *et al.*, 2008; Soken & Pick, 1999). They also associate vocal and facial affect, as evidenced by their preferential looking behavior at facial expressions that are congruent with the vocal affect being expressed. Specifically, Walker (1982) found that when presented with two filmed facial expressions while hearing an accompanying vocal expression, infants at 7 months preferred to look at the facial expression that matched the vocal expression. These results have been replicated using electrophysiological data (De Groote, Roeyers, & Striano, 2007). Even more impressively, infants have been found to express positive affect in response to "happy" vocalizations and negative affect in response to "angry" vocalizations, even if the vocalizations were not in their mother tongue (Fernald, 1993). Thus, at an early age (7 months), infants appear successful at recognizing and discriminating between various emotional expressions in terms of their differential visual and oral responses.

The capacity to discriminate between different emotions and seek out these affective cues to guide their behavior is known as social referencing and has been found in infants by their first year of life (Meins, 2003; Moses *et al.*, 2001). One of the first studies to demonstrate social referencing was conducted by Sorce *et al.* (1985) who implemented a visual cliff paradigm that was designed to have infants either approach the illusion of a cliff or a relatively flat surface. Only when the situation was ambiguous (i.e., approaching the cliff) did infants' reference and use their mother's facial expression to either approach (when joy or interest was emoted) or avoid (when fear or anger was emoted).

Infants also appear to interpret novel information using vocal affect alone. Mumme, Fernald, and Herrera, (1996) and Mumme and Fernald (2003) found that 12-month-old infants inhibited their playing behavior and displayed increased negative affect after simply hearing fearful vocalizations being directed toward a target toy. Interestingly, none of the above social referencing situations reported a change in infants' behavior and affect following positive feedback. This supports the suggestion that positive information signals infants to maintain their current behavior, whereas negative information signals infants to change their behavior (Cacioppo & Gardner, 1999; Harris, 2006). In these social referencing situations, one may question whether infants are merely reacting to another's emotional expression by modifying their own affect to mirror that of the person observed, or whether they are actually attending to the referent that the person is expressing emotion over. If they are simply reacting to another's emotional expression, they are unaware and/or misunderstand the actual intended referent of the other person.

Indeed, genuine referential understanding was found in infants at 12 months. At this age, infants are sensitive to the referential cues of another by discerning between two salient objects in their environment and modifying their behavior specifically toward the target object of an emoter's reaction (Mumme & Fernald, 2003). In addition, when their own focus of attention was discrepant from the emoter's focus, they changed their focus to that of the emoter's, suggesting some sensitivity to the internal states of others (Moses *et al.*, 2001). The infants appeared to reference more in response to negative than positive outbursts, suggesting that the unfamiliarity of negative outbursts (given they are accustomed to positive feedback) may have influenced results. Another argument is that of temporal contiguity, wherein infants can only link an emotional reaction observed by others to the stimulus to which they themselves are currently attending. However, this "lean" interpretation seems inadequate because when the target to which infants are oriented is different than the emoter's, infants change their focus to the correct referent. This suggests that by their first year, infants are capable of modifying their response to novel stimuli according to another's affective message.

Toward the end of their second year, infants also use others' indirect affective messages to regulate their own object-directed behavior. Specifically, infants who watched another individual demonstrate an action for an experimenter were less likely to imitate following an action that elicited an angry response from the experimenter than one that elicited a happy or neutral response (Repacholi & Meltzoff, 2007; Repacholi, Meltzoff, & Olsen, 2008). However, these results were contingent on visual availability. That is, the differences in imitation emerged only when the experimenter was turned toward the infant or was actually in the room (Repacholi & Meltzoff, 2007). In a follow-up study, the experimenter was in the room and visual availability was more conservatively defined as when the experimenter's eyes were open and/or when she was not visually distracted (i.e., reading a magazine; Repacholi *et al.*, 2008). With this more conservative procedure, infants were more likely to imitate when the experimenter was attending to the referent. In both these studies, a "lean" interpretation of mood contagion is unlikely, as infants did not adopt the mood of the experimenter but rather understood that the affect was directed toward the target object, not them. Instead, these results support the "rich" interpretation that infants understand the link between visual experiences and affective behavior, such that their emotional expression is contingent on their attentional state.

Sometime around 18 months, secondary intersubjectivity occurs wherein the sharing of knowledge and/or emotions extends beyond the mother–infant dyad to some outside referent (Thompson & Lagattuta, 2006; Trevarthen, 1988) and is dependent on certain cues such as visual availability and gaze direction. Infants as young as 14 months followed an experimenter's gaze to a container and based on her emotional expression, inferred that the hidden object within the container was their target referent (Repacholi, 1998). They preferred to explore the contents of the container when the emotional expression was a pleasant one and not one of disgust. This research demonstrates that infants have some referential understanding of others as they interpret the others' gaze and physical action. Similarly, research has demonstrated that infants use an experimenter's gaze direction and emotional expression to predict their object-directed action, looking longer at inconsistent events (where gaze and emotional expression do not match physical action). In particular, it has been found that 12-month-olds look longer when an experimenter grasps an object that was not the previous target of her positive emotional attention and 7-month-olds look longer when an experimenter's teasing behavior is met with a neutral facial expression (Phillips, Wellman, & Spelke, 2002; Striano & Vaish, 2006, respectively). This shows that infants understand that one's visual/facial-emotional behavior should be in line with their physical action, an understanding that is a precursor to intentional understanding.

Perhaps the curiosity and interest in attending to others' looking behavior and inferring their mental states occurs when infants become increasingly self-aware. The rouge-test (in which a spot of rouge is placed on an infant's face and then the infant is oriented in front of a mirror) has shown that infants at 18-month-olds successfully touch their nose to their own self-image, demonstrating their developing self-concept and recognition (Meins, 2003). It is also around this time that infants develop self-conscious emotions such as pride, shame, guilt, and embarrassment (Lagattuta & Thompson, 2007). The ability to properly take another's perspective and understand their mental states also appears to coincide with the development of empathy (Eisenberg, Murphy, & Shepard, 1997; Flavell, Green, & Flavell, 1989).

From a very early age, infants demonstrate empathy by expressing reactive emotions, similar to emotional contagion. By observing another's emotional expression, infants can either imitate another's distressed facial expression (Zahn-Waxler & Radke-Yarrow, 1990) or display reactive crying (Simner, 1971). Later on, by around 12–18 months, infants have been found to comfort another in distress, through such prosocial behavior as kisses or pats (Zahn-Waxler, Robinson, & Emde, 1992). It also has been shown that infants' empathy becomes more sophisticated when they can make a distinction between themselves and others (i.e., have a developed self-concept), as well as have the ability to express empathy in different ways (e.g., through facial expressions, and vocalizations; Roth-Hanania, 2002). As infants' understanding of others' internal states develops, so too does their empathy.

Infants' emotional understanding appears to start with simple reflexive processes, whereby they mimic the emotional responses of their caregiver, often appearing as displays of empathy. Following this, infants recognize and discriminate various forms of emotional expressions in terms of their differential visual and oral responses. This allows them to use these emotional cues either directly or indirectly to predict others' actions toward a specific referent and guide their own object-directed action. Thus, infants are able to use emotional cues to respond flexibly and adapt to their social environment, as well as understand the referential intentions of others. Future research can use these emotion-imitation paradigms to examine how and when young children interpret emotion signals at a greater level of abstraction such as understanding social norms and rules (Repacholi *et al.*, 2008; Repacholi & Meltzoff, 2007).

VII. Knowledge

Research on belief understanding has primarily focused on toddler's ability to attribute knowledge to others. The term "knowledge" or what a person "knows" is described broadly as something a person is "acquainted with" after having been familiarized with it from the immediate past. Importantly, this type of knowledge is acquired through "direct experience-based contact between the "knower" and an object, person, or place"

(Moll *et al.*, 2007, p. 827) and is conceptualized as an epistemic state whereby the child metarepresents beliefs (Astington, 1991). A well-established consensus posits that children under the age of 3–4 years do not have a mature understanding of what other people know because they have been shown to repeatedly fail the standard false-belief task (Wellman *et al.*, 2001; Wimmer & Perner, 1983). This finding has been consistent across various task manipulations (Wellman *et al.*, 2001). On the contrary, passing the false-belief task suggests that children have a conceptual understanding of another person's mental state (Gomez, 2004) and can reason that beliefs or knowledge play a role in motivating others' actions (Bartsch & Wellman, 1989). This interpretation of succeeding on a false-belief task has come under heavy criticism. Many have argued that success does not rely only on understanding other people's mental states but also requires domain-general abilities such as executive functioning skills that include planning, working memory, and inhibitory control (Carlson *et al.*, 1998; Gerstadt *et al.*, 1994; Hood, 1995; Russel, 1996; Zelazo *et al.*, 1996). In particular, the standard false-belief task requires that the child inhibit her or his knowledge about the toy's actual hidden location in order to select the correct response, while keeping in working memory the two different and conflicting representations (her own and that of the protagonist). Therefore, the goals of recent studies involve finding paradigms that tap into early forms of belief understanding that do not require complex cognitive skills.

A growing number of studies have revealed that toddlers and preschoolers show an implicit understanding of what other people know. Several studies using nonverbal tasks (e.g., looking time studies) have revealed that infants demonstrate early sensitivity to what others know. A landmark study conducted by Onishi and Baillargeon (2005) revealed that 15-month-olds expected an agent's search behavior to be guided by her true or false belief about a toy's hidden location. Specifically, using a nonverbal false-belief task, Onishi and Baillargeon familiarized 15-month-old infants to an event that involved an agent hiding a toy in one of two boxes. Next, they observed as the adult either witnessed or did not witness the change in the toy's location. Interestingly, infants who saw the adult witness the change of location were surprised and therefore looked longer when she searched for the toy in the incorrect location as compared to the correct location. The opposite pattern was true when infants observed search in the correct location by the adult, who did not witness the change of location. These results suggest that infants expected the adult to search for the object in the location based on her knowledge of where she had seen it previously, regardless of the toy's true location. Consistent with these findings, Southgate *et al.* (2007) found that 25-month-old infants gazed in anticipation toward a location where the agent was expected to search if he or she held a false belief, suggesting that infants can suspend their belief about the toy's true hidden location and correctly predict the behavior of the agent in terms of his or her false belief. Likewise, a looking time study demonstrated that infants as young as 13 months can predict an agent's future actions toward an object by taking into account the agent's previous exposure to relevant information about the object's location (Surian *et al.*, 2007). Although these findings have been interpreted as infants demonstrating an early sensitivity to what others know, there is some debate about this interpretation. One alternate interpretation of the findings is that infants may have simply learned or are innately predisposed to assume that people look for objects where they last saw them and not because that is where the object actually is. As such, infants may follow the rule without any awareness of the mind acting as a mediator (see Ruffman & Perner, 2005, for a review).

One possible way to address this debate between a precocious mentalistic understanding and a rule-based behavior is by examining the effect of an agent's reliability on infants' attribution of beliefs. Previous research with preschoolers has shown that they appraise the reliability of their informants (Harris, 2007). For example, when presented with two informants, one who provides consistently accurate names for familiar objects and one who provides consistently inaccurate names, 4-year-olds prefer the names offered by the reliable informant (Clément *et al.*, 2004; Koenig *et al.*, 2004). Other research has shown that 3-year-olds learn new words from confident rather than uncertain speakers (Sabbagh & Baldwin, 2001). Also, research has demonstrated that 14-month-old infants are sensitive to the reliability of what a person has previously seen when determining whether to follow the adult's gaze to a target located behind a barrier (Chow *et al.*, 2008).

Poulin-Dubois and Chow (in press) tested whether the reliability of the looker influences 16-month-olds' attribution of knowledge. First, infants were trained using a variant of Repacholi's (1998) search task using the procedure in Chow *et al.* (2008) to develop trust or mistrust toward what the adult has seen. Infants first observed an adult display positive affect (e.g., vocalization, smile) while looking inside a container that contained an attractive object (reliable looker) or was empty (unreliable looker). Although infants from both groups continued to look inside the container, those mislead by the unreliable looker became gradually less motivated to verify the content of the container, as evidenced by their increased latency to open the lid. Following the training phase, infants then watched the same experimenter act as the agent in a nonverbal true-belief task, similar to the one used by Onishi and Baillargeon (2005).

Consistent with Onishi and Baillargeon (2005), infants in the reliable looker group looked longer during the trials where the adult searched in

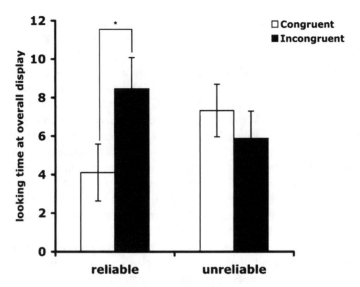

Fig. 3. Mean looking time (max = 30 seconds) at display in congruent and incongruent test conditions for reliable and unreliable looker groups. Error bars show standard error of the means.

the wrong place when the same person had been a reliable looker in the previous search task (control condition). In contrast, infants who had experienced an unreliable looker had no expectations about the success of her search behavior and looked equally long at the correct and incorrect search (see Figure 3). The authors proposed that infants in the unreliable looker condition encoded and recalled the inaccuracy of the looker's gaze during the search task and inferred that her gaze was also unreliable in the new context, thus suspending any attribution of where the adult should be searching for the hidden object. Had infants simply developed (or possess innately) the behavioral rule that people tend to look for objects where they last saw them, then infants in both looker groups would have looked longer at the test event when the actor searched for the target object in the wrong location. Therefore, it seems unlikely that infants' performance on the nonverbal false-belief task can be attributed to their adherence to behavioral rules.

Given that infants appear to demonstrate some implicit understanding of what other people know, some researchers have begun to question the content of that knowledge. That is, what do infants know about what other people have and have not experienced in the past? Tomasello and Haberl (2003) found that when 12- and 18-month-old infants know which of three objects a person has not experienced, they understand what object they are getting excited about now. Likewise, Poulin-Dubois *et al.* (2007) examined infants' understanding that seeing leads to knowing by testing infants' expectation about a person's search for a hidden object based on what the person has witnessed in the immediate past. Using the violation of expectancy paradigm, infants were exposed to videotaped events in which a person either did (true belief) or did not (false belief) witness the location where an object was placed. Their results revealed a developmental progression in infants' understanding of seeing, as evidenced by their increased looking times. Eighteen-month-olds were surprised and looked longer when the person who witnessed the placement of the object searched in the incorrect location as compared to the correct location, and they also looked longer when the person who did *not* witness the placement of the object searched in the correct location. The 18-month-olds' behavior suggests that they understand what others can and cannot see at a particular moment and know that what others have seen influences their subsequent behavior. Taken together, studies indicate that by their first birthday, infants know what others do and do not know from past perceptual experience and follow a developmental progression in their ability to use body orientation and eye gaze cues to make inferences about what a person knows based on what he has seen previously.

Given that infants demonstrate some understanding of what others know, an important question concerns the conditions under which infants' understanding of others' experiences are facilitated. Moll and Tomasello (2007) approached this question by manipulating how 14- and 18-month-olds observe an adult experiencing objects. Using a variation of the Tomasello and Haberl (2003) paradigm, infants were exposed to three different experimental conditions. In the joint-engagement condition, infants played with an adult with two toys. In the individual engagement condition, the adult and the infant did not experience the first two toys together. Finally, in the onlooking condition, the adult simply looked at the known toys from some distance as the infant and assistant played with them together. Following each condition, the experimenter left the room while the infant and assistant played with the third object and then returned and excitedly asked the infant to give her an object. There was a developmental progression such that 14-month-olds knew which objects the adult would be familiar with only in the joint attentional condition in which the infants were engaged personally. In contrast, 18-month-olds knew this in the individual engagement condition as well as the joint engagement condition.

These results were further clarified in a follow-up study (Moll *et al.*, 2007), which showed that it is not sufficient for 14-month-olds to witness from a third person perspective the adult sharing the familiar objects with another person but rather they need to be directly involved in sharing the adult's experience. As Moll and colleagues (2007) have pointed out, infants' performance on this task requires that they have a general understanding that people tend to get excited about things that are new and not old. Furthermore, they are required to identify which of the three objects was new for the adult even if all three objects are old for them. However, because people can express excitement for things other than novelty, it is important to disambiguate whether infants are giving the toy that is novel for the adult or because they are excited about an object that they have previously shared with some other person. This issue was addressed in another study (Moll *et al.*, 2008) in which infants shared all three objects with the adult. In the "Share Condition," the infant and adult had special experiences with one target object whereby they encountered the object several times in unusual places and shared excitement about this. Then, they also shared in a more normal fashion the other two objects for the same length of time. Thus, to successfully choose the target object, infants had to know which of the three objects the adult was excited about, as well as which object they had experienced together in a special way. In fact, infants may have noticed the special quality of the shared experience, because they correctly interpreted the adult's excitement at test as referring back to their shared experience with the target object and therefore offered the toy with which they shared the special experience.

Overall, the extant literature contributes to the growing body of evidence suggesting that over the second year of life, infants gradually develop an implicit understanding of what other people know and what others have experienced in the recent past. It appears that infants' knowledge of other people's experiences changes with age, with joint attentional engagement playing a particularly crucial role in the months immediately after their first birthday and later becoming less important.

Interesting challenges lie ahead for future belief understanding research. Given that studies have demonstrated early competence on nonverbal tasks, it would be of interest to explore why this ability is revealed at an earlier age using nonverbal paradigms, whereas active response measures elicit correct responses only at a later age. Although, infants in these studies appear to have an understanding of the subjective nature of beliefs, whether infants understand that beliefs mediate behavior remains to be investigated. Also, future belief research may incorporate longitudinal designs to explore the continuity of infants' belief understanding by linking their performance on an implicit false-belief task in infancy and their performance on an explicit false-belief task in childhood. Finally, studies using a switch actor design could strengthen the argument that infants understand the subjective nature of beliefs when they differentially attribute beliefs to a person on the basis of whether the person was previously credible or not.

VIII. Intentions

Intention is a mental state that is nonrepresentational but abstract and is one of the earliest developmental forms of theory of mind (Olineck & Poulin-Dubois, 2007b). It can be thought of as purposeful action that follows the rationale for why some action was made. A developmental progression taking place during the preschool period has been reported wherein a more sophisticated understanding of others' intentions that includes their beliefs occurs (Astington & Gopnik, 1991b; Gopnik, 1993). At about 3 or 4 years of age, children appear capable of making inferences about others' intentions (Flavell, 1999). By the end of their second year, infants' intentional understanding is evidenced through their use of internal state words (e.g., want), visual attention to cues such as gaze, facial expressions, and hand gestures (e.g., pointing), as well as their imitation of others' behavior. It appears that infants are at the beginning stages of wanting to share psychological states with other people, whether it is providing information, learning new information, or collectively sharing information, in the form of shared intentions and attention (Tomasello & Carpenter, 2007).

Intentional understanding often comes in the form of attributing goals to others and has been demonstrated in infants using visual attention paradigms. Poulin-Dubois (1999) demonstrated that 18- to 30-month-olds are sensitive to incongruent versus congruent behavior based on watching another's video-recorded gaze and pointing cues. Specifically, infants looked longer at an experimenter who grasped an object not looked at (incongruent behavior) than when she grasped an object that she had looked at and paid attention to (congruent behavior). Infants' sensitivity to incongruent behavior has been found in infants as young as 6 months. Woodward (1998) habituated infants to a situation in which an experimenter's hand reached to grab one of two toys. Subsequently, the experimenter either grasped for the same toy via a different path or for a new toy via the original path. Infants as young as 6 months were sensitive to the new goal more than the new movement, looking longer when a new toy was grasped than when a new movement was chosen. This suggests that infants attributed an expectancy of the experimenter to prefer one toy over the other and thus were surprised and looked longer when the experimenter searched for a new toy.

Extending the findings of Woodward (1998), 12-month-old infants watched the same familiarization demonstration, but with one of the toys initially placed behind either an opaque or transparent screen, such that the experimenter's visual access to one of the toys was either obstructed or not (Luo & Baillargeon, 2007). Infants looked longer in the test phase only when the experimenter searched for a new toy to which they previously had visual access (i.e., was formerly behind a transparent screen in the familiarization phase, not an opaque screen). Subsequent research replicated and extended the findings in infants as young as 6 months, by teasing apart whether infants are more sensitive to visual or physical access (i.e., having the toy hidden behind the experimenter where it could be physically reached but not seen; Luo & Johnson, 2009). In this study, infants only demonstrated a violation of expectation when the experimenter reached for a new toy when both toys were previously in front of her during familiarization as opposed to when one was hidden behind her (no visual access). Taken together, these studies suggest that infants are aware of others' perceptions, even when they differ from their own, and know that in order for one to have a goal to reach an object, one must have appropriate *visual* access. Importantly, it appears infants make these goal attributions for human agents alone, and not when witnessing the same movements made by inanimate agents (e.g., mechanical claw; Woodward, 2005). This suggests that infants have developed expectations about human action and see actions as object directed, specifically when one has the necessary visual perception to make such goals.

The use of another's attentional cues to infer another's goals and infer an actor–object link has been found to have a developmental progression (Phillips *et al.*, 2002; Sodian & Thoermer, 2004; Woodward, 2003, 2005). To illustrate, Phillips et al. (2002) habituated infants to a scene in which an experimenter looked at a target object and then picked it up. During the test phase, they looked and picked up the other toy (consistent) or they looked at the first target toy but picked up the other toy (inconsistent). Only 12-month-olds inferred an actor–object link based on gaze alone. Younger infants appear to need more stimulus cues, such as grasping and/or reaching, to make the relation between overt behavior and mental state more salient (Woodward, 2003). Importantly, if head and eye-turns are embedded within a sequence of fixations on the target object (i.e., multiple looks to the object), infants as young as 9 months infer goal-directedness (Johnson *et al.*, 2007).

Around the same age, infants display what seems to be a more advanced understanding of intention, deciphering between nonintentional and intentional goals based on one's external actions. Behne *et al.* (2005) showed that around 9 months, infants reacted differently to an experimenter who was either "unwilling" or "unable" to give them a toy than to an experimenter who "accidentally" dropped the toy they were passing.

Specifically, infants seemed impatient, reaching longer and looking away from an experimenter who first appeared willing to pass a toy, but then pulled it back in a teasing manner. In contrast, they were more patient when the experimenter was trying to pass them a toy, but dropped it. The infants' differential responding was contingent on their perception of an actor's underlying intentions. This is a clear indication that they are sensitive to and aware of others' goals.

This ability to infer goals from another's overt behavior, also known as *intention-in-action*, has been demonstrated in infants' action-parsing skills. This is evidenced in how an infant responds to action sequences in which actors complete or attempt to complete their intentions. Ten-month-old infants watched an everyday action sequence, wherein a woman reached and grasped a towel on the kitchen floor, placing it on a towel rack. When the woman's actions were interrupted before the intention was fulfilled, infants increased their looking time suggesting a sensitivity to goal-directed actions. This was in opposition to their disinterest and reduced looking time when the interruption occurred at the end of the completed intention (Baird & Baldwin, 2001; Baldwin *et al.*, 2001). These findings have been replicated with infants as young as 8 months, whose looking time and neural activity were found to increase following an incomplete versus completed action (Reid *et al.*, 2007). Using a more stringent test that required intermodal matching (vocal and auditory), infants at 9 months were found to segment intentional action sequences. Specifically, while watching two simultaneous action displays that involved continuous motion on novel objects, infants looked longer at displays where a tone coincided with intentional–action boundaries, as opposed to those in which the tone interrupted intentional sequences (Saylor *et al.*, 2007). This skill of parsing intentional sequences of action is thought to be a prerequisite to the development of genuine intentional understanding.

In addition to intention-in-action, imitation research has shown that by 24 months, children have an understanding of others' intentions *without* actually seeing their behavior. This understanding is contingent on their awareness of others' "prior intentions," such that the other person's goals are communicated to them before the displayed behavior. In one study, a group of children watched an experimenter successfully open a box several different ways, whereas the control group did not. During the test phase, when both groups watched the experimenter pull out a pin and open the box, the children who saw the experimenters prior behavior with the box were more likely to imitate the action (Carpenter, Call, & Tomasello, 2002). Importantly, understanding others' intention without seeing their overt behavior means that by 2 years of age, children have a more mentalistic interpretation of others' intentions, as they had to infer the intentions of others' without direct evidence of their goal-directed behavior.

Also using an imitation paradigm, Carpenter, Akhtar, and Tomasello (1998) showed that 14- to 18-months-olds were more likely to imitate instances of intentional actions (followed by the experimenter saying "there") versus accidental actions (followed by the experimenter saying "oops"). In order to differentiate between the two actions, infants had to both infer the action as intentional and imitate only the intended actions and not the overall, overt behavior. A developmental progression for this ability has been demonstrated, with 18-month-olds being more advanced than 14-month-olds (Olineck & Poulin-Dubois, 2005). This shows that infants represent the behavior of people in a psychological framework involving goals and intended acts rather than purely physical movements, thus demonstrating infants' understanding of intention-in-action (Meltzoff, 1995).

With improved performance in action processing and production, infants are better able to understand others' goal-directed actions, given the perspective gained from their own experience with these actions (Sommerville & Woodward, 2005). For instance, infants as young as 3 months who were given tools (e.g., a sticky mitt) that allowed them to mimic more sophisticated motor skills (e.g., reaching for a toy) were able to understand and therefore looked longer at the same goal-directed behavior of others than those who were not given tools (Sommerville & Woodward, in press). With greater development of motor skills, infants' imitation of others' actions can be used to determine their growing intentional understanding. One of the first studies to do so was Meltzoff (1995), who showed 18-month-olds an actor trying, but failing, to perform various different actions on a selection of objects. Interestingly, infants who watched the actor *trying* to perform the action performed as many target acts as those who actually saw the target action completed. They were also 6 times more likely to imitate when the actor was human as opposed to an inanimate object (a rod). This developmental change in intentional understanding appears to occur between 12 and 18 months (Bellagamba & Tomasello, 1999; Bellagamba, Camaioni, & Colonnesi, 2006; Johnson, Booth, & O'Hearn, 2001). Taken together, the above-mentioned studies show that by 18 months, infants may indeed have intention-reading skills and perhaps an innate sense for attributing goals to people. It also suggests early-precursors for theory of mind abilities.

In the above-mentioned examples, intentional understanding in the form of the person–object link was examined. However, research (e.g., Carpenter, Tomasello, & Striano, 2005) has demonstrated that infants also understand intentions others have toward the self, as well as being able to join in and share these intentions. Specifically, infants imitate an action that an experimenter did to themselves on their own bodies (dyadic role-reversal imitation), as well as learn the rules of a game demonstrated to them and model the expected goal of the game (triadic, person–object role-reversal imitation). Infants at 12 and 18 months participate in dyadic, bodily role-reversal imitation, as well as triadic, person–object role-reversal imitation. This shows that infants imitate after interpreting another's action, such that if the intention of the person giving a demonstration is for the infant to subsequently reverse roles, infants are able to understand this and act appropriately. The authors also found a positive correlation between 18-month-old infants' dyadic role-reversal imitation and comprehension and production of pronouns. This relation between intention understanding and language skills also was found in a longitudinal study in which 14- and 18-month-olds' ability to produce only intentional actions as opposed to accidental actions predicted their significantly larger internal state vocabulary at 32 months (Olineck & Poulin-Dubois, 2005). It also overlaps with other research that shows that by the second year, infants have begun using mental state terms (e.g., want, wish), which has been shown to later predict theory of mind (Bartsch & Wellman, 1995; Olineck & Poulin-Dubois, 2007a; see Table I for the latter study's results).

It appears that infants demonstrate a developmental continuum of understanding of intention. By around 10 months, infants appear capable of parsing action sequences, thereby understanding intention-in-action, and by 14 months, infants distinguish between intentional and accidental

Table I

Intercorrelations between Children's Performance on Infant Imitation Task, Internal State Language, and Their Performance on Preschool Theory of Mind Tasks

	HNP	MP	FB	ToM Scale ($n = 16$)
Infant task: intentional action first	.50**	−.18	.05	−.02
Infant task: difference score	.19	−.01	−.10	−.07
MCDI score (14–18 months)	.02	−.16	.45*	.42
Internal state language at 32 months ($n = 26$)	−.14	.06	.43*	.55*
Target-hitting game: HNP score (HNP)		−.26	−.16	−.19
Target-hitting game: MP score (MP)			−.04	.00
False belief task (FB).				.65*

Note: **$p < .01$; *$p < .05$.

actions, based on their imitative behavior. This shows that infants are aware of others' mental states, even those that may be different from their own. One of the goals of research is to examine whether there is continuity between infants' intention capabilities as measured by these differing tasks at various developmental stages. One of the first studies to address this question was Olineck and Poulin-Dubois (2007b). In this study, 10-month-old infants performed two visual attention tasks: a goal detection task (based on Woodward, 2003) and an action-parsing task (based on Baldwin *et al.*, 2001). The same infants returned to the lab at 14-months to perform a demonstration of intention task (based on Meltzoff, 1995) and action imitation task (Carpenter *et al.*, 1998; Olineck & Poulin-Dubois, 2005, 2007a). The results revealed that the ability to parse ongoing behavior at intentional boundaries at 10 months predicted the ability to re-enact the incomplete action of an actor's "failed intention." In addition, the ability to goal detect at 10 months predicted the ability to discriminate between intentional and accidental actions at 14 months. However, the concurrent measures (i.e., visual-attention tasks at 10 months and imitation tasks at 14 months) were not correlated. It was suggested that the lack of a link between the different measures reflects the nature of the different mechanisms involved: the former reflecting a low-level sensitivity to temporal and physical regularities and the latter reflecting deeper intentional understanding wherein the infant had to link the actor's body orientation and gaze to a specific referent (Olineck & Poulin-Dubois, 2007b). However, causal relations could not be inferred. More longitudinal, within-subject designs promise an important future direction to investigate whether these tasks are measuring the same construct and can help determine the exact precursors for later theory of mind development.

IX. Naïve Psychology: The Quest for Causal Precursors

Many theoretical accounts of naïve psychology development posit that there is a developmental relation between social-cognitive skills in infancy and later theory of mind. The most convincing evidence that supports this hypothesis is a demonstration that some form of folk psychology is present in very young infants. Many of the early socio-cognitive abilities that we have reviewed in this chapter may be precursors for such knowledge. Such fundamental social skills include imitation and joint attention (Csibra & Gergely, 2005; Moll & Tomasello, 2007; Wellman *et al.*, 2008). Regardless of the exact nature of infants' competence, support for the precursor hypothesis can only be generated by longitudinal studies that examine continuity in naïve psychology from infancy to childhood. Until recently, there was little direct empirical evidence for the continuity hypothesis. There has been a growing interest in this topic, and this section proposes an overview of the findings on this important issue.

In one of the first studies on continuity, Youngblade and Dunn (1995) demonstrated longitudinal associations between infants' pretend play with peers at 33 months of age and performance on false-belief tasks at 40 months. Charman *et al.* (2000), conducted another longitudinal study on the potential link among play, joint attention, imitation skills and later theory of mind abilities such as perspective taking and desire. At 20 months, joint attention behaviors, but not imitation skills, predicted theory of mind performance at 44 months. These two studies provided preliminary evidence that fundamental social skills predict later folk psychology abilities.

Other studies on precursors of theory of mind skills have focused on a long-term continuity in social cognition. Wellman *et al.* (2004) conducted the first test of the continuity between infants' social task performance at 14 months and later theory of mind ability. Specifically, infants who showed a greater decrease in attention during a habituation task on human intentional action, performed better on a battery of theory of mind tasks administered at 4 years of age (Wellman & Liu, 2004). However, no such link was found between infants' performance and later verbal ability as measured by the Peabody Picture Vocabulary Test (PPVT) or on the false-belief task. These findings subsequently were replicated with a larger sample ($N = 45$), although the correlation was only significant between decrement of attention at 11 months in the habituation task measuring goal attribution and desire and false-belief task abilities at age 4 years (Wellman *et al.*, 2008). Similar results were reported in a study that extended this line of research initiated by Wellman to an age when goal attribution first emerges (Aschersleben, Hofer, & Jovanic, 2008). A task measuring action interpretation, based on a reaching response, was administered to 6-month-old infants who were retested with the Theory of Mind scale and standardized measure of receptive and productive language at 4 years of age. Consistent with other findings, the results revealed a correlation between infants' decrement of attention to goal-directed action at 6 months and their ability to solve false-belief tasks at the age of 4 years. This was not related to their verbal skills. Overall, these three studies provided some support for the continuity hypothesis, indicating that infants' attention to intentional action displays during their initial exposure to them predicts the development of false beliefs in preschool years.

Although the continuity data validate the looking time paradigm as capturing a form of understanding that is continuous with later, more mature theory of mind skills, it lacks a comparison that is critical to exploring the developmental continuity in the social domain. The crucial comparison is the relation between early nonsocial cognitive abilities and later childhood naïve psychology. Yamaguchi *et al.* (in press) compared 12-month-olds' performance in social and nonsocial tasks with theory of mind competence at 4 years of age. The social task consisted of a habituation procedure that examined infants' understanding of goal-directed actions with computer-animated geometric figures that helped or pushed down another figure that attempted to climb a hill (Kuhlmeier, Wynn, & Bloom, 2003). The test movies showed the target figure approached the helping or hindering figure. The nonsocial task was a duration discrimination study. As expected, a specific link was found between theory of mind skills in preschool and infants' social cognitive skills, with a significant correlation observed only between the social task and theory of mind skills. On the basis of their data, the authors concluded that there are individual differences that are developmentally stable over many years. Furthermore, they cautioned that the processes involved in their social task might not simply be precursors for later theory of mind abilities but part of a larger domain of abilities (e.g., parsing goal units, and detection of animacy cues) that sustain later meta-representational abilities such as false belief.

Other potential precursors of theory of mind skills have been explored using tasks other than those that measure infant attention to goal-directed actions. Olineck and Poulin-Dubois (2005) investigated the link between infants' differentiation of intentional and accidental actions at 14 or 18 months of age with the production of internal state language at 30 months of age. Infants were administered an imitation task in which they had to reproduce a sequence of two actions on small devices (e.g., twisting a handle): one action was accompanied by facial and vocal cues that suggested intentionality (e.g., smile, gaze at device), whereas the other action seemed to be performed accidentally (e.g., looking away). A relation was found between the ability to identify the intentional action in the imitation task and later mental lexicon. The proportion of trials in which infants chose to perform the intentional action alone predicted the size of the internal state vocabulary, even when age was controlled. These data provided the first line of evidence showing that infants' processing of behavioral cues that signal intentional actions is linked to subsequent talk about the mind, which itself is predictive of later theory of mind abilities (Wellman *et al.*, 2000). In a follow-up study, Olineck and Poulin-Dubois (2007a) retested the same sample of infants at the age of 4 years on a task measuring the concept of intention in addition to the theory of mind scale. Children's verbal skills were also assessed with the PPVT in order to rule out language as a potential mediator of any observed link between the social-cognitive abilities in infancy and childhood. Preschoolers' concept of intention was assessed with a game that consisted of winning prizes hidden in a series of colored cans that could be knocked down with a remote control device. The game was controlled by the experimenter, with half of the trials a hit and the other half a miss (a 50% chance of winning a prize). The dependant variable was the infants' ability to correctly recall their intentions in the trials where the intention was inconsistent with the outcome (e.g., hit, no prize). This ability to correctly recall or monitor their intended actions at 4 years of age was predicted by the percentage of times that infants imitated the intentional action in the imitation task at 14–18 months, but no such link was observed with performance on the false-belief task or on the battery of theory of mind tasks. Interestingly, internal state language at 32 months predicted the scores on both the false-belief task and the theory of mind scale.

Finally, another study also focused on infants' understanding of intentional actions and later theory of mind skills (Colonnesi *et al.*, 2008). Infants were tested at 12 and 15 months on their understanding of intentions with the behavior re-enactment task (Meltzoff, 1995) as well as on their comprehension and production of pointing gestures. Later, at 39 months, different measures of folk psychology were administered, including visual perspective taking, intention, and belief understanding. Infants' ability to identify the intended goal of the experimenter in failed attempts predicted later intention and perception understanding, even when age and language skills were partialed out.

To conclude, the combined findings of the recent longitudinal studies on folk psychology suggest that there is continuity in these abilities from infancy to childhood. There are a number of limitations to most of the research conducted so far, including small sample sizes and a lack of nonsocial tasks as control measures. There are also a number of incon-sistencies across the data sets, most notably the absence of links between performance in infancy and composite scores of theory of mind skills. In order to clarify these issues, future research should increase their sample sizes and include a battery of tasks measuring a wide range of theory of mind constructs in infancy that match the theory of mind scale which is widely used in older children. Notwithstanding these limitations, the current data suggest continuity in social cognitive development that provides support for the hypothesis that the sophisticated social cognitive abilities have their roots in infancy.

X. Summary and Conclusions

Research interest in children's understanding of the mind goes back as far as Piaget's claim that children are cognitively egocentric (Flavell, 2000).

Many years later, research on the understanding of the mind was revived in a paper that sought evidence for a theory of mind, not for children but for chimpanzees (Premack & Woodruff, 1978). The researchers claimed that chimpanzees' ability to predict what a human actor will do to achieve certain goals implies that the animal attributes mental states to the actor. This seminal paper generated a flurry of studies on theory of mind in nonhuman primates. A review of this research based on several different experimental paradigms concluded that chimpanzees understand others in terms of a perception-goal psychology (i.e., they can perceive what the other's goal is but not understand the mental states associated with the goal), as opposed to a full-fledged, human-like belief-desire psychology (Call & Tomasello, 2008).

Around the same time, research on children's understanding of the mind was revived in a landmark paper by Wimmer and Perner (1983) and by other developmentalists (Bretherton, McNew, & Beegly-Smith, 1981). In line with the research on nonhuman primates, part of the progress that has been made in recent years is a recognition that theory of mind knowledge is acquired in an extended series of developmental milestones and that this development is based on a rich set of socio-cognitive abilities that develop in infancy (Wellman, 2002). The evidence outlined in the sections of this chapter suggests that infants possess a nascent understanding of mental states that older children use in explaining and predicting human behavior.

Researchers have learned a great deal about the developmental origins of naïve psychology in infancy. Nevertheless, the depth of infants' understanding of human behavior is still a controversial issue. For example, a popular paradigm in naïve psychology is violation of expectancy. In false-belief tasks, infants look longer at a scene in which a protagonist searches for an object in a location she does not know than at a scene in which the protagonist searches for an object in a location where she has previously seen the object disappear. The fact that no active behavioral response is required makes many researchers doubt that an infants' looking pattern reflects a deep level of understanding. Looking pattern may simply reflect the infants' detection that something in the scene is novel (e.g., protagonist looks at a location different than the one infants last saw her look at). Indeed this interpretation may account for the conflicting results in recent studies (e.g., Poulin-Dubois *et al.*, 2007; Onishi & Baillargeon, 2005; Surian *et al.*, 2007). Poulin-Dubois *et al.* (2007) recently reported that the ability to distinguish between knowledge and ignorance (true belief) is absent at 14 months of age and still fragile at 18 months in a violation-of-expectancy task depicting videotaped human actors. In contrast, false-belief attribution to a computer animated caterpillar has been reported in 13-month-old infants (Surian *et al.*, 2007).

Given that infants have had more experience with humans looking at objects than with a caterpillar's looking behavior, the current evidence for an implicit understanding of advanced mental states such as false belief should be interpreted with caution.

As is the case for nonhuman primate research, infants' mind-reading success might be accounted for by a simple behavior-reading explanation. According to some researchers, primates' (and infants') successful performance in theory of mind tasks can be explained by a sophisticated form of behavior reading. Under this view, infants perform well in such tasks because they are adept at calculating the statistical likelihood that some aspects of people's observable features (e.g., gaze) will be linked to future actions (e.g., search at a location). Distinguishing between a mentalistic and rule-based account is very difficult (Povinelli & Vonk, 2004). One way to address this debate would be to design training studies that provide infants with first-person experience of mental states and to use more active behavioral measures. In terms of training, there is some evidence that infants' performance on goal and visual perception attribution tasks is improved if they received training of relevant skills (e.g., wearing a blindfold, reaching with a "sticky mitten": Meltzoff & Brooks, 2007; Sommerville & Woodward, 2004). Furthermore, longitudinal research using more active measures revealed links between goal detection as measured with the violation of expectancy paradigm at 10 months of age and the ability to infer intended goals in an imitation task at 14 months (Olineck & Poulin-Dubois, 2007b).

Developmental changes in the scope of infants' concept of intentional agent also will require more attention from researchers. According to some, infants' attributions of intentional behavior are activated whenever infants recognize an object as a psychological agent, based on an evolutionary designed system which is sensitive to certain cues such as self-propulsion, contingent reactivity or equifinal variation of the action (Baron-Cohen, 1995; Gergely & Csibra, 2003; Johnson, 2000; Leslie, 1994b). Other researchers reject this cue-based perspective and propose that infants' understanding of intentional actions is restricted only to human actions (Meltzoff, 1995; Meltzoff & Brooks, 2001; Woodward, Sommerville, & Guajardo, 2001). Although there is some evidence that infants construe nonhuman agents as intentional beings, to date much of this research has been limited to goal detection and gaze following abilities (Johnson *et al.*, 2001; Johnson, Slaughter, & Carey, 1998; Luo & Baillargeon, 2005). However, research on more advanced forms of psychological processes, such as referential intentions, suggests that the concept of intentional agent has narrowed by 18 months of age (O'Connell *et al.*, in press). Finally, children with autism often are described as deficient in theory of mind. One may hope that nonverbal theory of mind tasks that reliably predict later theory mind skills will be adapted for use with this population and eventually used for the early detection of autism.

In sum, the numerous studies reported here show that by the end of the second year of life, infants have developed ways to predict human actions. The review also makes clear that we do not yet fully understand how deep infants' insight into the mind really is. Nonetheless, there appears to be some consensus that infants, like chimpanzees, understand the goals, intentions, perception, and knowledge of others. This provides the foundations for the full-fledged adult-like naïve psychology that develops gradually in early childhood.

REFERENCES

Alibali, M. W., & Goldin-Meadow, S. (1993). Gesture-speech mismatch and mechanisms of learning: What the hands reveal about a child's state of mind. *Cognitive Psychology, 25,* 468–523.

Argyle, M., & Cook, M. (1976). *Gaze and mutual gaze.* Cambridge, UK: Cambridge University Press.

Aschersleben, G., Hofer, T., & Jovanic, B. (2008). The link between infant attention to goal-directed action and later theory of mind abilities. *Developmental Science, 11,* 862–868.

Astington, J. W. (1991). Intention in the child's theory of mind. In D. Frye & C. Moore (Eds.), *Children's theories of mind: Mental states and social understanding* (pp. 157–172). Hillsdale, NJ: Lawrence Erlbaum Associates.

Astington, J. W. (1993). *The child's discovery of the mind.* Cambridge, MA: Harvard University Press.

Astington, J. W., & Gopnik, A. (1991a). Theoretical explanations of children's understanding of the mind. *British Journal of Developmental Psychology, 9,* 7–31.

Astington, J. W., & Gopnik, A. (1991b). Understanding desire and intention. In A. Whiten (Ed.), *Natural theories of mind: Evolution, development and simulation of everyday mindreading* (pp. 39–50). Oxford: Basil Blackwell.

Baird, J. A., & Baldwin, D. A. (2001). Making sense of human behaviour: Action parsing and intentional reference. In B. F. Bertram, M. J. Louis, & D. A. Baldwin (Eds.), *Intentions and intentionality: Foundations of social cognition* (pp. 193–206). Cambridge, MA: MIT Press.

Baldwin, D. A., Baird, J. A., Saylor, M. M., & Clark, M. A. (2001). Infants parse dynamic action. *Child Development, 72,* 708–717.

Baron-Cohen, S. (1995). *Mindblindness: An essay on autism and theory of mind.* Cambridge, MA: MIT Press.

Bartsch, K., & Wellman, H. (1989). Young children's attribution of action to beliefs and desires. *Child Development, 60,* 946–964.

Bartsch, K., & Wellman, H. M. (1995). *Children talk about the mind.* New York, NY: Oxford University Press.

Behne, T., Carpenter, M., Call, J., & Tomasello, M. (2005). Unwilling versus unable: Infants' understanding of intentional action. *Developmental Psychology, 41,* 328–337.

Bellagamba, F., & Tomasello, M. (1999). Re-enacting intended acts: Comparing 12- and 18-month olds. *Infant Behavior & Development, 22*, 277–282.

Bellagamba, F., Camaioni, L., & Colonnesi, C. (2006). Change in children's understanding of others' intentional actions. *Developmental Science, 9*, 182–188.

Bretherton, I. (1991). Intentional communication and the development of mind. In D. Frye & C. Moore (Eds.), *Children's theories of mind, mental states and social understanding* (pp. 49–76). Hillsdale, NJ: Lawrence Erlbaum Associates.

Bretherton, I., McNew, S., & Beeghly-Smith, M. (1981). Early person knowledge as expressed in gestural and verbal communication. When do infants acquire a "theory of mind"? In M. Lamb & L. Sherrod (Eds.), *Social Cognition in Infancy* (pp. 333–373). Hillsdale, NJ: Erlbaum.

Brooks, R., & Meltzoff, A. N. (2002). The importance of eyes: How infants interpret adult looking behavior. *Developmental Psychology, 38*, 958–966.

Brooks, R., & Meltzoff, A. N. (2005). The development of gaze following and its relation to language. *Developmental Science, 8*, 535–543.

Butler, S. C., Caron, A. J., & Brooks, R. (2000). Infant understanding of the referential nature of looking. *Journal of cognition and Development, 1*, 359–377.

Butterworth, G., & Jarrett, N. (1991). What minds have in common is space: Spatial mechanisms serving joint visual attention in infancy. *British Journal of Developmental Psychology, 9*, 55–72.

Cacioppo, J. T., & Gardner, W. L. (1999). Emotions. *Annual Review of Psychology, 50*, 191–214.

Call, J., & Tomasello, M. (2008). Does the chimpanzee have a theory of mind? 30 years later. *Trends in Cognitive Sciences, 12*, 187–192.

Carlson, S. M., Moses, L. J., & Hix, H. R. (1998). The role of inhibitory processes in young children's difficulties with deception and false belief. *Child Development, 69*, 672–691.

Caron, A. J., Kiel, E. J., Dayton, M., & Butler, S. C. (2002). Comprehension of the referential intent of looking and pointing between 12 and 15 months. *Journal of Cognition and Development, 3*, 445–464.

Carpendale, J. I., & Chandler, M. J. (1996). On the distinction between false belief understanding and subscribing to an interpretive theory of mind. *Child Development, 67*, 1686–1706.

Carpenter, M., Akhtar, N., & Tomasello, M. (1998). Fourteen- through 18-month-old infants differentially imitate intentional and accidental actions. *Infant Behavior & Development, 21*, 315–330.

Carpenter, M., Call, J., & Tomasello, M. (2002). Understanding 'prior intentions' enables two-year-olds to imitatively learn a complex task. *Child Development, 73*, 1431–1441.

Carpenter, M., Tomasello, M., & Striano, T. (2005). Role reversal imitation and language in typically developing infants and children with autism. *Infancy, 8*, 253–278.

Charman, T., Baron-Cohen, S., Swettenham, J., Baird, G., Cox, A., & Drew, A. (2000). Testing joint attention, imitation, and play as infancy precursors to language and theory of mind. *Cognitive Development, 15*, 481–498.

Chow, V., Poulin-Dubois, D., & Lewis, J. (2008). To see or not to see: Infants prefer to follow the gaze of a reliable looker. *Developmental Science, 11*, 761, 770.

Churchland, P. M. (1984). *Matter and consciousness*. Cambridge, MA: Bradford/MIT Press.

Clément, F., Koenig, M., & Harris, P. (2004). The ontogenesis of trust. *Mind and Language, 19*, 360–379.

Cleveland, A., & Striano, T. (2007). The effects of joint attention on object processing in 4- and 9-month-old infants. *Infant Behavior & Development, 30*, 499–504.

Colonnesi, C., Rieffe, C., Koops, W., & Perucchini, P. (2008). Precursors of a theory of mind: A longitudinal study. *British Journal of Developmental Psychology, 26*, 233–247.

Cooper, R. P., & Aslin, R. N. (1989). The language environment of the young infant: Implications for early perceptual development. *Canadian Journal of Psychology, 43*, 247–265.

Corkum, V., & Moore, C. (1998). Origins of joint visual attention in infants. *Developmental Psychology, 34*, 28–38.

Csibra, G., & Gergely, G. (2005). Social learning and social cognition: The case for pedagogy. In M. H. Johnson & Y. Munakata (Eds.), *Processes of change in brain and cognitive development. Attention and performance, XXI*. Oxford: Oxford University Press.

Csibra, G., & Volein, A. (2008). Infants can infer the presence of hidden objects from referential gaze information. *British Journal of Developmental Psychology, 26*, 1–11.

Davidson, D. (1980). *Essays on actions and events*. Oxford, UK: Clarendon Press.

Daxeder, U., & Feichtinger, V. (2003). *Verstehen von unterschiedlichen subjektiven Wünschen-ein Problem in Konfliktsituationen*. Unpublished manuscript.

D'Entremont, B., Hains, S. M. J., & Muir, D. W. (1997). A demonstration of gaze following in 3- to 6-month-olds. *Infant Behavior & Development, 20*, 569–572.

D'Entremont, B., & Morgan, R. (2006). Experience with visual barriers and its effects on subsequent gaze-following in 12- to 13-month-olds. *British Journal of Developmental Psychology, 24*, 465–475.

De Groote, I., Roeyers, H., & Striano, T. (2007). Gaze following as a function of affective expression in 3-, 6- and 9-month-old infants. *Infant Behaviour & Development, 30*, 492–498.

de Haan, M., & Nelson, C. (1997). Recognition of the mother's face by six-month-old infants: A neurobehavioral study. *Child Development, 68*, 187–210.

Doherty, M. J. (2006). The development of mentalistic gaze understanding. *Infant and Child Development, 15*, 179–186.

Doherty, M. J., Anderson, J. R., & Howieson, L. (2004). *The rapid development of explicit gaze judgment ability at 3 years*. Unpublished manuscript.

Dunn, J. (1996). Children's relationships: Bridging the divide between social and cognitive development. *Journal of Child Psychology and Psychiatry, 37*, 507–518.

Dunphy-Lelii, S., & Wellman, H. M. (2004). Infants' understanding of occlusion of others' line-of-sight: Implications for an emerging theory of mind. *European Journal of Developmental Psychology, 1*, 49–66.

Eisenberg, N., Murphy, B. C., & Shepard, S. (1997). The development of empathic accuracy. In W. Ickes (Ed.), *Empathic accuracy*. New York: Guilford Press.

Feinfield, K. A., Lee, P. P., Flavell, E. R., Green, F. L., & Flavell, J. H. (1999). Young children's understanding of intention. *Cognitive Development, 14*, 463–486.

Fernald, A. (1993). Approval and disapproval: Infant responsiveness to vocal affect in familiar and unfamiliar languages. *Child Development, 64*, 657–674.

Flavell, J. H. (1977). *Cognitive development*. Oxford, UK: Prentice Hall.

Flavell, J. H. (1979). Metacognition and cognitive monitoring: A new area of cognitive-developmental inquiry. *American Psychologist, 34*, 906–911.

Flavell, J. H. (1988). The development of children's knowledge about the mind: From cognitive connections to mental representations. In J. W. Astington, P. L. Harris, & D. R. Olson (Eds.), *Developing theories of mind* (pp. 244–267). New York, NY: Cambridge University Press.

Flavell, J. H. (1992). Cognitive development: Past, present, and future. *Developmental Psychology, 28*, 998–1005.

Flavell, J. H. (1999). Cognitive development: Children's knowledge about the mind. *Annual Review of Psychology, 50*, 21–45.

Flavell, J. H. (2000). Development of children's knowledge about the world. *International Journal of Behavioral Development, 24,* 15–23.

Flavell, J. H. (2004). Theory-of-mind development: Retrospect and prospect. *Merrill-Palmer Quarterly, 50,* 274–290.

Flavell, J. H., & Miller, P. H. (1998). Social cognition. In W. Damon (Ed.), *Handbook of child psychology: Cognition, perception, and language* (Vol. 2, pp. 851–898). Hoboken, NJ: Wiley.

Flavell, J. H., Green, F. L., & Flavell, E. R. (1989). Young children's ability to differentiate appearance-reality and level 2 perspectives in tactile modality. *Child Development, 60,* 201–213.

Flavell, J. H., Miller, P. H., & Miller, S. A. (1993). *Cognitive development* (3rd ed.). Englewood Cliffs, NJ: Prentice-Hall, Inc.

Gallese, V., & Goldman, A. (1998). Mirror neurons and the simulation theory of mind-reading. *Trends in Cognitive Sciences, 12,* 493–501.

Gergely, G., & Csibra, G. (2003). Teleological reasoning in infancy: The naive theory of rational action. *Trends in Cognitive Sciences, 7,* 287–292.

Gergely, G., Egyed, K., & Király, I. (2007). On pedagogy. *Developmental Science, 10,* 139–146.

Gerstadt, C. L., Hong, Y. J., & Diamond, A. (1994). The relationship between cognition and action: Performance of children 3½-7 years old on a Stroop-like day-night test. *Cognition, 53,* 129–153.

Gomez, J. C. (2004). *Apes, monkeys, children, and the growth of mind.* Cambridge, MA: Harvard University Press.

Gopnik, A. (1993). How we know our minds: The illusion of first-person knowledge of intentionality. *Behavioural and Brain Sciences, 16,* 1–15.

Gopnik, A., & Graf, P. (1988). Young children's ability to identify and remember the sources of their beliefs. *Child Development, 59,* 1366–1371.

Gopnik, A., & Meltzoff, A. N. (1997). *Words, thoughts, and theories.* Cambridge, MA: Bradford, MIT Press.

Gopnik, A., & Wellman, H. (1994). The "theory theory". In L. Hirschfield & S. Gelman (Eds.), *Domain specificity in culture and cognition.* New York, NY: Cambridge University Press.

Goswami, U. (2006). The foundations of psychological understanding. *Developmental Science, 9,* 545–550.

Hadwin, J., & Perner, J. (1991). Pleased and surprised: Children's cognitive theory of emotion. *British Journal of Developmental Psychology, 9,* 215–234.

Harris, P. L. (1991). The work of the imagination. In A. Whiten (Ed.), *Natural theories of mind* (pp. 283–304). Oxford, UK: Basil Blackwell.

Harris, P. L. (1992). From simulation to folk psychology: The case for development. *Mind & Language, 7,* 120–144.

Harris, P. L. (2006). Social cognitions. In D. Kuhn, R. S. Siegler, W. Damon, & R. M. Lerner (Eds.), *Handbook of child psychology: Cognition, perception, and language* (6th ed., Vol. 2, pp. 811–858). Hoboken, NJ: Wiley.

Harris, P. L. (2007). Commentary. *Monographs of the Society for Research in Child Development, 72,* 113–120.

Hobson, P. (1994). Perceiving attitudes, conceiving minds. In C. Lewis & P. Mitchell (Eds.), *Children's early understanding of mind: Origins and development* (pp. 71–94). Hillsdale, NJ: Erlbaum.

Hoehl, S., Reid, V., Mooney, J., & Striano, T. (2008). What are you looking at? Infants neural processing of an adult's object-directed eye gaze. *Developmental Science, 11,* 10–16.

Hood, B. M. (1995). Gravity rules for 2- to 4-year olds? *Cognitive Development, 10,* 577–598.

Hughes, C., & Dunn, J. (1997). "Pretend you didn't know": Preschoolers' talk about mental states in pretend play. *Cognitive Development, 12*, 477–497.

Jarrold, C., Carruthers, P., Smith, P. K., & Boucher, J. (1994). Pretend play: Is it metarepresentational? *Mind & Language, 9*, 445–468.

Johnson, S. C. (2000). The recognition of mentalistic agents in infancy. *Trends in Cognitive Science, 4*, 22–28.

Johnson, S. C., Slaughter, V., & Carey, S. (1998). Whose gaze will infants follow? Features that elicit gaze-following in 12-month-olds. *Developmental Science, 1*, 233–238.

Johnson, S. C., Booth, A., & O'Hearn, K. (2001). Inferring the goals of a non-human agent. *Cognitive Development, 16*, 637–656.

Johnson, S. C., Ok, S., & Luo, Y. (2007). The attribution of attention: 9-month-olds' interpretation of gaze as goal-directed action. *Developmental Science, 10*, 530–537.

Karmiloff-Smith, A. (1992). *Beyond modularity: A developmental perspective on cognitive science*. Cambridge, MA: The MIT Press.

Kleinke, C. L. (1986). Gaze and eye contact: A research review. *Psychological Bulletin, 100*, 78–100.

Kobiella, A., Grossmann, T., Reid, V. M., & Striano, T. (2008). The discrimination of angry and fearful facial expressions in 7-month-old infants: An event-related potential study. *Cognition and Emotion, 22*, 134–146.

Koenig, M., Clément, F., & Harris, P. L. (2004). Trust in testimony: Children's use of true and false statements. *Psychological Science, 15*, 694–698.

Kuhlmeier, V., Wynn, K., & Bloom, P. (2003). Attribution of dispositional states by 12-month-olds. *Psychological Science, 14*, 402–408.

Lagattuta, K. H., & Thompson, R. A. (2007). The development of self-conscious emotions: Cognitive processes and social influences. In J. L. Tracy, R. W. Robins, & J. P. Tangney (Eds.), *The self-conscious emotions: Theory and research* (pp. 91–113). New York, NY: Guilford Press.

Langton, S. R. H., Watt, R. J., & Bruce, V. (2000). Do the eyes have it? Cues to the direction of social attention. *Trends in Cognitive Sciences, 4*, 50–59.

Leekam, S., Baron-Cohen, S., Perrett, D., Milders, M., & Brown, S. (1997). Eye direction detection: A dissociation between geometric and joint attention skills in autism. *British Journal of Developmental Psychology, 15*, 77–95.

Lempers, J. D., Flavell, E. R., & Flavell, J. H. (1977). The development in very young children of tacit knowledge concerning visual perception. *Genetic Psychology Monographs, 95*, 3–53.

Leslie, A. M. (1994a). ToMM, ToBy, and agency: Core architecture and domain specificity. In L. A. Hirschfeld & S. A. Gelman (Eds.), *Mapping the mind: Domain specificity in cognition and culture* (pp. 119–148). Cambridge, UK: Cambridge University Press.

Leslie, A. M. (1994b). Pretending and believing: Issues in the theory of ToMM. *Cognition, 50*, 211–238.

Leslie, A. M., & Roth, D. (1993). What autism teaches us about metarepresentation. In S. Baron-Cohen, H. Tager-Flusberg, & D. Cohen (Eds.), *Understanding other minds: Perspectives from autism* (pp. 83–111). Oxford: Oxford University Press.

Lichtermann, L. (1991). *Young children's understanding of desires*. Unpublished manuscript.

Lillard, A. (2002). Pretend play and cognitive development. In U. Goswami (Ed.), *Blackwell handbook of childhood cognitive development* (pp. 189–205). Malden, MA: Blackwell Publishing.

Liszkowski, U., Carpenter, M., Henning, A., Striano, T., & Tomasello, M. (2004). Twelve-month-olds point to share attention and interest. *Developmental Science, 7*, 297–307.

Liszkowski, U., Carpenter, M., & Tomasello, M. (2007a). Pointing out new news, old news, and absent referents at 12 months of age. *Developmental Science, 10*, F1–F7.

Liszkowski, U., Carpenter, M., & Tomasello, M. (2007b). Reference and attitude in infant pointing. *Journal of Child Language, 34*, 1–20.

Liszkowski, U., Albrecht, K., Carpenter, M., & Tomasello, M. (2008). Infants' visual and auditory communication when a partner is or is not visually attending. *Infant Behavior & Development, 31*, 157–167.

Luo, Y., & Baillargeon, R. (2005). Can a self-propelled box have a goal? Psychological reasoning in 5-month-old infants. *Psychological Science, 16*, 601–608.

Luo, Y., & Baillargeon, R. (2007). Do 12.5-month-old infants consider what objects others can see when interpreting their actions? *Cognition, 105*, 489–512.

Luo, Y., & Johnson, S. C. (2009). Recognizing the role of perception in action at 6 months. *Developmental Science, 12*, 142–149.

Mandler, J. M. (2004). *The foundations of mind: Origins of conceptual thought.* New York, NY: Oxford University Press.

Meins, E. (2003). Emotional development and early attachment relationships. In A. Slater & G. Bremner (Eds.), *An introduction to developmental psychology* (pp. 141–164). Malden, MA: Blackwell Publishing.

Meltzoff, A. N. (1995). Understanding the intentions of others: Re-enactment of intended acts by 18-month-old children. *Developmental Psychology, 31*, 838–850.

Meltzoff, A. N. (2007). 'Like me': A foundation for social cognition. *Developmental Science, 10*, 126–134.

Meltzoff, A. N., & Brooks, R. (2001). "Like me" as a building block for understanding other minds: Bodily acts, attention, and intention. In B. F. Malle, L. J. Moses, & D. A. Baldwin (Eds.), *Intentions and intentionality: Foundations of social cognition* (pp. 171–191). Cambridge, MA: MIT Press.

Meltzoff, A. N., & Brooks, R. (2007). Eyes wide shut: The importance of eyes in infant gaze-following and understanding other minds. In R. Flom, K. Lee, & D. Muir (Eds.), *Gaze-following: Its development and significance* (pp. 217–241). Mahwah, NJ: Lawrence Erlbaum Associates Publishers.

Meltzoff, A. N., & Moore, M. K. (1994). Imitation, memory, and the representation of persons. *Infant Behavior & Development, 17*, 83–99.

Moll, H., & Tomasello, M. (2004). 12- and 18-month-old infants follow gaze to spaces behind barriers. *Developmental Science, 7*, 1–9.

Moll, H., & Tomasello, M. (2006). Level I perspective-taking at 24 months of age. *British Journal of Developmental Psychology, 24*, 603–613.

Moll, H., & Tomasello, M. (2007). How 14- and 18-month-olds know what others have experienced. *Developmental Psychology, 43*, 309–317.

Moll, H., Koring, C., Carpenter, M., & Tomasello, M. (2006). Infants determine others' focus of attention by pragmatics and exclusion. *Journal of Cognition and Development, 7*, 411–430.

Moll, H., Carpenter, M., & Tomasello, M. (2007). Fourteen-month-olds know what others' experience only in joint engagement. *Developmental Science, 10*, 826–835.

Moll, H., Richter, N., Carpenter, M., & Tomasello, M. (2008). Fourteen-month-olds know what "we" have shared in a special way. *Infancy, 13*, 90–101.

Moore, C. (1999). Gaze-following and the control of attention. In P. Rochat (Ed.), *Early social cognition: Understanding others in the first months of life* (pp. 241–256). Mahwah, NJ: Lawrence Erlbaum Associates.

Moore, C., & Corkum, V. (1994). Social understanding at the end of the first year of life. *Developmental Review, 14*, 349–372.

Moore, C., Jarrold, C., Russell, J., Lumb, A., Sapp, F., & MacCallum, F. (1995). Conflicting desires and the child's theory of mind. *Cognitive Development, 10*, 467–482.

Moses, L. J., Baldwin, D. A., Rosicky, J. G., & Tidball, G. (2001). Evidence for referential understanding in the emotions domain at twelve and eighteen months. *Child Development, 72*, 718–735.

Mumme, D. L. (1993). *Rethinking social referencing: The influence of facial and vocal affect on infant behavior.* US: ProQuest Information & Learning.

Mumme, D. L., & Fernald, A. (2003). The infant as onlooker: Learning from emotional reactions observed in television scenario. *Child Development, 74*, 221–237.

Mumme, D. L., Fernald, A., & Herrera, C. (1996). Infant's responses to facial and vocal emotional signals in a social referencing paradigm. *Child Development, 67*, 3219–3237.

Nelson, C. A. (1987). The recognition of facial expressions in the first two years of life: Mechanisms of development. *Child Development, 58*, 889–909.

Nelson, C. A., Wewerka, S., Thomas, K. M., Tribby-Walbridge, S., deRegnier, R., & Georgieff, M. (2000). Neurocognitive sequelae of infants of diabetic mothers. *Behavioral Neuroscience, 114*, 950–956.

Oberman, L. M., & Ramachandran, V. S. (2007). The simulating social mind: The role of the mirror neuron system and simulation in the social and communicative deficits of autism spectrum disorders. *Psychological Bulletin, 133*, 310–327.

O'Connell, L., Poulin-Dubois, D., Demke, T., & Guay, A. (in press). Do infants use gaze direction to infer the referential intent of a nonhuman speaker? *Infancy.*

Olineck, K. M., & Poulin-Dubois, D. (2005). Infants' ability to distinguish between intentional and accidental actions and its relation to internal state language. *Infancy, 8*, 91–100.

Olineck, K. M., & Poulin-Dubois, D. (2007a). Imitation of intentional actions and internal state language in infancy predict preschool theory of mind skills. *European Journal of Developmental Psychology, 4*, 14–30.

Olineck, K. M., & Poulin-Dubois, D. (2007b, March). Infants' detection of goal-directed action at 10 months predicts their imitation of intentional actions at 14 months. Poster presented at the 2007 Biennial Meeting of the Society for Research in Child Development, Boston, MA.

Onishi, K. H., & Baillargeon, R. (2005). Do 15-month-old infants understand false beliefs? *Science, 308*, 255–258.

Perner, J. (1991). *Understanding the representational mind.* Cambridge, MA: MIT Press.

Perner, J., Zauner, P., & Sprung, M. (2005). What does "that" have to do with point of view? Conflicting desires and "want" in German. In J. W. Astington & J. Baird (Eds.), *Why language matters for theory of mind* (pp. 220–244). New York, NY: Oxford University Press.

Phillips, A. T., Wellman, H. M., & Spelke, E. S. (2002). Infants' ability to connect gaze and emotional expression to intentional action. *Cognition, 85*, 53–78.

Poulin-Dubois, D. (1999). Infants' distinction between animate and inanimate objects: The origins of naïve psychology. In P. Rochat (Ed.), *Early social cognition: Understanding others in the first months of life* (pp. 257–280). Mahwah, NJ: Lawrence Erlbaum Associates.

Poulin-Dubois, D., & Chow, V. (in press). The effects of a looker's past reliability on infant's reasoning about beliefs. *Developmental Psychology.*

Poulin-Dubois, D., & McKoy, K. (1999, April). Understanding of the subjectivity of desires in 18-month-olds. Poster presented at the Biennial Meeting of the Society for Research in Child Development, Albuquerque, NM.

Poulin-Dubois, D., & Shultz, T. R. (1988). The development of the understanding of human behavior: From agency to intentionality. In J. Astington, P. Harris, & D. Olson (Eds.), *Developing theories of mind* (pp. 109–125). New York: Cambridge University Press.

Poulin-Dubois, D., Sodian, B., Metz, U., Tilden, J., & Schoeppner, B. (2007). Out of sight is not out of mind: Developmental changes in infants' understanding of visual perception during the second year. *Journal of Cognition and Development, 8,* 401–425.

Povinelli, D. J. (2001). On the possibilities of detecting intentions prior to understanding them. In B. F. Malle, L. J. Moses, & D. A. Baldwin (Eds.), *Intentions and intentionality: Foundations of social cognition* (pp. 225–248). Cambridge, MA: MIT Press.

Povinelli, D. J., & Eddy, T. J. (1996). What young chimpanzees know about seeing. Monographs of the Society for Research in Child Development (Vol. 61, No. 2, Serial No. 247).

Povinelli, D. J., & Vonk, J. (2004). We don't need a microscope to explore the chimpanzee's mind. *Mind & Language, 19,* 1–28.

Premack, D., & Woodruff, G. (1978). Problem-solving in the chimpanzee: Test for comprehension. *Science, 202,* 532–535.

Racine, T. P., & Carpendale, J. I. M. (2007). The role of shared practice in joint attention. *British Journal of Developmental Psychology, 25,* 3–25.

Rakoczy, H., Warneken, F., & Tomasello, M. (2007). 'This way!', 'No! That way!'—3 year olds know that two people can have mutually incompatible desires. *Cognitive Development, 22,* 47–68.

Reid, V. M., Csibra, G., Belsky, J., & Johnson, M. H. (2007). Neural correlates of the perception of goal-directed action in infants. *Acta Psychologica, 124,* 129–138.

Repacholi, B. M. (1998). Infants' use of attentional cues to identify the referent of another person's emotional expression. *Developmental Psychology, 34,* 1017–1025.

Repacholi, B. M., & Gopnik, A. (1997). Early reasoning about desires: Evidence from 14- and 18-month-olds. *Developmental Psychology, 33,* 12–21.

Repacholi, B. M., & Meltzoff, A. N. (2007). Emotional eavesdropping: Infants selectively respond to indirect emotional signals. *Child Development, 78,* 503–521.

Repacholi, B. M., Meltzoff, A. N., & Olsen, B. (2008). Infants' understanding of the link between visual perception and emotion: "If she can't see me doing it, she won't get angry". *Developmental Psychology, 44,* 561–574.

Roth-Hanania, R. (2002). The role of self-concept development in the development of empathic concern during infancy. *Dissertation Abstracts International: Section B: The Sciences and Engineering, 62,* 1–188.

Ruffman, T., & Perner, J. (2005). Do infants really understand false belief? *Trends in Cognitive Sciences, 9,* 462–463.

Russel, J. (1996). *Agency.* Cambridge: Lawrence Erlbaum Associates/Taylor & Francis Ltd.

Sabbagh, M. A., & Baldwin, D. (2001). Learning words from knowledgeable versus ignorant speakers: Links between preschoolers' theory of mind and semantic development. *Child Development, 72,* 1054–1070.

Saylor, M. M., Baldwin, D. A., Baird, J. A., & LaBounty, J. (2007). Infants' on-line segmentation of dynamic human action. *Journal of Cognition and Development, 8,* 113–128.

Senju, A., Johnson, M. H., & Csibra, G. (2006). The developmental and neural basis of referential gaze perception. *Social Neuroscience, 1,* 220–234.

Shantz, C. U. (1983). Social cognition. In J. H. Flavell & E. Markman (Eds.), *Handbook of child psychology: Cognitive development* (pp. 495–555). New York: Wiley.

Simner, M. L. (1971). Newborn's response to the cry of another infant. *Developmental Psychology, 5,* 136–150.

Slaughter, V., & McConnell, D. (2003). Emergence of joint attention: Relationships between gaze following, social referencing, imitation, and naming in infancy. *Journal of Genetic Psychology, 164,* 54–71.

Sodian, B., & Thoermer, C. (2004). Infants' understanding of looking, pointing, and reaching as cues to goal-directed action. *Journal of Cognition and Development, 5*, 289–316.

Sodian, B., Thoermer, C., & Metz, U. (2007). Now I see it but you don't: 14-month-olds can represent another person's visual perspective. *Developmental Science, 10*, 199–204.

Soken, N. H., & Pick, A. D. (1999). Infants' perception of dynamic affective expressions: Do infants distinguish specific expressions? *Child Development, 70*, 1275–1282.

Sommerville, J. A., & Woodward, A. L. (2004). Action experience alters 3-month-old infants' perception of others' actions. *Cognition, 96*, B1–B11.

Sommerville, J. A., & Woodward, A. L. (2005). Pulling out the intentional structure of action: The relation between action processing and action production in infancy. *Cognition, 95*, 1–30.

Sommerville, J. A., & Woodward, A. L. (in press). The link between action production and action processing in infancy. In F. Grammont, D. Legrand, & P. Livet (Eds.), *Naturalizing intention in action.*

Sorce, J. F., Emde, R. N., Campos, J. J., & Klinnert, M. D. (1985). Maternal emotional signaling: Its effect on the visual cliff behavior of 1-year-olds. *Developmental Psychology, 21*, 195–200.

Southgate, V., Senju, A., & Csibra, G. (2007). Action anticipation through attribution of false belief by 2-year-olds. *Psychological Science, 18*, 587–592.

Stenberg, G. (2003). Effects of maternal inattentiveness on infant social referencing. *Infant and Child Development, 12*, 399–419.

Striano, T., & Stahl, D. (2005). Sensitivity to triadic attention in early infancy. *Developmental Science, 8*, 333–343.

Striano, T., & Vaish, A. (2006). Seven-to-9-month-old infants use facial expressions to interpret others' action. *British Journal of Developmental Psychology, 24*, 750–760.

Surian, L., Caldi, S., & Sperber, D. (2007). Attribution of beliefs by 13-month-old infants. *Psychological Science, 18*, 580–586.

Sutton, J., Smith, P. K., & Swettenham, J. (1999). Bullying and theory of mind: A critique of the social skills deficit view of anti social behaviour. *Social Development, 8*, 117–127.

Taylor, M. (1988). The development of children's understanding of the seeing-knowing distinction. In J. Astington, P. Harris, & D. Olson (Eds.), *Developing theories of mind* (pp. 93–108). London: Cambridge University Press.

Taylor, M., Esbensen, B. M., & Bennett, R. T. (1994). Children's understanding of knowledge acquisition: The tendency for children to report that they have always known what they have just learned. *Child Development, 65*, 1581–1604.

Thompson, R. A., & Lagattuta, K. H. (2006). Feeling and understanding: Early emotional development. In K. McCartney & D. Phillips (Eds.), *Blackwell handbook of early childhood development* (pp. 317–337). Malden, MA: Blackwell Publishing.

Tilden, J., Poulin-Dubois, D., & Desroches, J. (1997). *Young children's understanding of the role of desires in human actions and emotional reactions.* Unpublished raw data, Centre for Research in Human Development, Concordia University.

Tomasello, M., & Carpenter, M. (2007). Shared intentionality. *Developmental Science, 10*, 121–125.

Tomasello, M., & Haberl, K. (2003). Understanding attention: 12- and 18-month-olds know what's new for other persons. *Developmental Psychology, 39*, 906–912.

Tomasello, M., Call, J., & Hare, B. (2003). Chimpanzees understand psychological states – the question is which ones and to what extent. *Trends in Cognitive Sciences, 7*, 153–156.

Tomasello, M., Carpenter, M., & Liszkowski, U. (2007). A new look at infant pointing. *Child Development, 78*, 705–722.

Trevarthen, C. (1988). Universal co-operative motives: How infants begin to know the language and culture of their parents. In G. Jahoda & I. M. Lewis (Eds.), *Acquiring culture: Cross cultural studies in child development* (pp. 37–90). New York, NY: Croom Helm.

Tricia, S., Stahl, D., Cleveland, A., & Hoehl, S. (2007). Sensitivity to triadic attention between 6 weeks and 3 months of age. *Infant Behavior & Development, 30,* 529–534.

Walker, A. S. (1982). Intermodal perception of expressive behaviours by human infants. *Journal of Experimental Child Psychology, 33,* 514–535.

Watson, A. C., Nixon, C. L., Wilson, A., & Capage, L. (1999). Social interaction skills and theory of mind in young children. *Developmental Psychology, 35,* 386–391.

Wellman, H. M. (1993). Early understanding of mind: The normal case. In S. Baron-Cohen, H. Tager-Flusberg, & D. J. Cohen (Eds.), *Understanding other minds: Perspectives from autism* (pp. 10–39). Oxford, UK: Oxford University Press.

Wellman, H. M. (2002). Understanding the psychological world: Developing a theory of mind. In U. Goswami (Ed.), *Handbook of childhood cognitive development* (pp. 167–187). Oxford, UK: Blackwell.

Wellman, H. M., & Banerjee, M. (1991). Mind and emotion: Children's understanding of the emotional consequences of beliefs and desires. *British Journal of Developmental Psychology, 9,* 119–124.

Wellman, H. M., & Bartsch, K. (1988). Young children's reasoning about beliefs. *Cognition, 30,* 239–277.

Wellman, H. M., & Bartsch, K. (1994). Before belief: Children's early psychological theory. In C. Lewis & P. Mitchell (Eds.), *Children's early understanding of mind: Origins and development* (pp. 331–354). Hillsdale, NJ: Erlbaum.

Wellman, H. M., & Gelman, S. A. (1998). Knowledge acquisition in foundational domains. In W. Damon (Series Ed.), D. Kuhn, & R. S. Siegler (Vol. Eds.), *Handbook of child development: Vol. 2. Cognition, perception, and language* (5th ed., pp. 523–573). New York, NY: Wiley.

Wellman, H. M., & Liu, D. (2004). Scaling of theory of mind tasks. *Child Development, 75,* 523–541.

Wellman, H. M., & Woolley, J. D. (1990). From simple desires to ordinary beliefs: The early development of everyday psychology. *Cognition, 35,* 245–275.

Wellman, H. M., Phillips, A. T., & Rodriguez, T. (2000). Young children's understanding of perception, desire, and emotion. *Child Development, 71,* 895–912.

Wellman, H. M., Cross, D., & Watson, J. (2001). Meta-analysis of theory-of-mind development: The truth about false belief. *Child Development, 72,* 655–684.

Wellman, H. M., Phillips, A. T., Dunphy-Lelii, S., & LaLonde, N. (2004). Infant social attention predicts preschool social cognition. *Developmental Science, 7,* 283–288.

Wellman, H. M., Lopez-Duran, S., LaBounty, J., & Hamilton, B. (2008). Infant attention to intentional action predicts preschool theory of mind. *Developmental Psychology, 44,* 618–623.

Wimmer, H., & Perner, J. (1983). Beliefs about beliefs: Representation and constraining function of wrong beliefs in young children's understanding of deception. *Cognition, 13,* 103–128.

Wimmer, H., Hogrefe, G. J., & Perner, J. (1988). Children's understanding of informational access as source of knowledge. *Child Development, 57,* 567–582.

Woodward, A. L. (1998). Infants selectively encode the goal object of an actor's reach. *Cognition, 69,* 1–34.

Woodward, A. L. (2003). Infants' developing understanding of the link between looker and object. *Developmental Science, 6,* 297–311.

Woodward, A. L. (2005). The infant origins of intentional understanding. *Advances in Child Development and Behaviour, 33*, 229–262.

Woodward, A. L., Sommerville, J. A., & Guajardo, J. J. (2001). How infants make sense of intentional action. In B. Malle, L. Moses, & D. Baldwin (Eds.), *Intentions and intentionality: Foundations of Social Cognition* (pp. 149–169). Cambridge, MA: MIT Press.

Yamaguchi, M., Kuhlmeier, V. A., Karen, W., & vanMarle, K. (in press). Continuity in social cognition from infancy to childhood. *Developmental Science.*

Yaniv, I., & Shatz, M. (1988). Children's understanding of perceptibility. In J. Astington, P. Harris, & D. Olson (Eds.), *Developing theories of mind* (pp. 93–108). London: Cambridge University Press.

Yazdi, A. A., German, T. P., Defeyter, M. A., & Siegal, M. (2006). Competence and performance in belief-desire reasoning across two cultures: The truth, the whole truth and nothing but the truth about false belief? *Cognition, 100*, 343–368.

Youngblade, L. M., & Dunn, J. (1995). Individual differences in young children's pretend play with mother and sibling: Links to relationships and understanding of other people's feelings and beliefs. *Child Development, 66*, 1472–1492.

Yuill, N. (1984). Young children's coordination of motive and outcome in judgements of satisfaction and morality. *British Journal of Developmental Psychology, 2*, 73–81.

Zahn-Waxler, C., & Radke-Yarrow, M. (1990). The origins of empathic concern. *Motivation and Emotion, 14*, 107–130.

Zahn-Waxler, C., Robinson, J. L., & Emde, R. N. (1992). The development of empathy in twins. *Developmental Psychology, 28*, 1038–1047.

Zelazo, P. D., Frye, D., & Rapus, T. (1996). An age-related dissociation between knowing rules and using them. *Cognitive Development, 11*, 37–63.

CHILDREN'S REASONING ABOUT TRAITS

Gail D. Heyman

DEPARTMENT OF PSYCHOLOGY, UNIVERSITY OF CALIFORNIA, SAN DIEGO,
CA 92093-0109, USA

I. Children's Reasoning about Traits

Success in navigating the complexities of the human social world requires an ability to look beyond the information that is observable in any given situation. One way adults do this is by drawing inferences about the psychological traits of others and using these inferences to make predictions about future behavior. For example, an adult might use information about whether an individual is honest or smart to determine

Advances in Child Development and Behavior
Patricia Bauer : Editor

whether he or she would make a good president, business partner, or spouse. Children also encounter situations in which trait information is relevant, such as when they are trying to decide who might have good advice about a personal problem, or who would make a good partner for a school project. However, the extent to which children are able to make use of information in an adult-like way has been the subject of considerable debate. I address this question and the role of trait information in children's social cognition more broadly. I argue that despite a widespread assumption that children lack any meaningful notion of traits before middle childhood, they can make use of trait information to make a wide variety of inferences as early as age 5. In the first section, I review research on children's understanding of traits. In the second section, I examine children's tendencies to view traits within an essentialist framework, in which traits are seen as fundamental and stable aspects of what individuals are like. The third section considers influences on children's trait thinking, including factors that promote trait attributions and that promote psychological essentialism when reasoning about traits.

II. Children's Understanding of Traits

When considering children's trait understanding, it is important to define what is meant by the term "trait" because it has been used in a number of different ways in the psychological literature. Some researchers define it narrowly, for example, to refer only to specific characteristics that have met particular statistical criteria, such as those constituting what are often called "the big five" (*openness, conscientiousness, extraversion, agreeableness,* and *neuroticism*; see Pytlik Zillig, Hemenover, & Dienstbier, 2002). Others use the term more broadly, for example, to refer to physical traits such as having poor eyesight, in addition to psychological traits (Lockhart, Chang, & Story, 2002). For purposes of this chapter, the term "trait" is used relatively broadly, but is limited to characteristics that are predominantly psychological in nature because the primary theoretical questions of interest concern children's use of trait concepts to characterize mental life and behavior. It is also important to note that the research covered here addresses children's understanding of traits; a discussion of the nature of traits themselves is beyond the scope of this chapter.

A. STANDARD APPROACH

In the 1970s, researchers typically assumed that children do not conceptualize people with reference to traits until after age of 7 years, and younger children were thought to focus primarily on observable characteristics and behaviors. This view was supported by studies that used a free-description methodology, in which individuals across a range of ages were asked to describe themselves or others (Livesley & Bromley, 1973; Peevers & Secord, 1973). Children aged 7 years and younger tend to focus on "peripheral statements" that concern matters such as appearance, possessions, and activities. Around 8 years of age, children shift to using more "central statements" that concern matters such as traits and motives. These results are consistent with Piaget's preoperational stage of development (Piaget & Inhelder, 1969), in which children between the ages of 2 and 7 are described as being distracted by the surface features of reasoning tasks. Some researchers have suggested that children's notions of invariance in the social world may be a by-product of their understanding of invariance more generally (Flavell, 1977; Livesley & Bromley, 1973; Rotenberg, 1982). For example, Flavell (1977) offered the following explanation.

> Children gradually come to think of themselves and others as stable human beings who conserve, over time and circumstances, their personhoods, personalities, social and sexual roles and identities, and many other attributes. Day to day changes in one's own or another's mood and behavior come to be construed as variations on an enduring theme, rather than a succession of unrelated melodies. (p. 12)

An alternative explanation is that children see broad themes emerging from the variability of observable human actions but lack the verbal ability to articulate their understanding in response to open-ended questions. To investigate this possibility, methodologies were developed as a means to examine children's trait understanding in a manner that minimizes verbal demands. One such approach is the behavioral prediction methodology, in which participants hear about a character who engages in one or more trait-relevant behaviors and predict whether the character will engage in trait-consistent behaviors in other contexts. Some studies that have used this paradigm indicate that children younger than 7 years do not expect individuals to behave in a trait-consistent manner (Kalish, 2002; Rholes & Ruble, 1984; Rotenberg, 1982; see Rholes, Newman & Ruble, 1990). Rholes and Ruble (1984) showed participants a series of vignettes in which a character performs a trait-relevant behavior and asked them to identify which of three other behaviors the character had also performed. For example, in one vignette a character was described as sharing his lunch, which represents *generosity*, and children selected among possible behaviors that were either trait-consistent (helping to rake leaves), trait-inconsistent (refusing to help rake leaves), or unrelated to the trait. Older children (9- to 10-year-olds) tended to select trait-consistent behaviors, but younger children (5- to 6-year-olds) did not. However, other studies using similar methodologies have suggested that children younger than 7 do indeed expect trait-consistent behavior from others (Dozier, 1991; Heller & Berndt, 1981). Heller and Berndt (1981) found that kindergartners made different predictions for a child who shared his lunch on two occasions than for a child who refused to share his lunch on two occasions. Previous sharing was associated with greater expectations of future sharing in the form of sharing food and helping in the form of collecting money for UNICEF and helping a sibling.

The reason for these apparently conflicting findings has been the subject of considerable debate (Ruble & Dweck, 1995; Yuill, 1992). Several of the studies on this topic have shown diverging patterns of results despite having similar methodologies, which suggests that relatively subtle methodological factors can determine whether children's responses will indicate an expectation of trait-consistent behavior. An alternative possibility is that young children are indeed unable to make trait inferences, but certain methodologies allow them respond in ways that resemble the responses of individuals who do hold a meaningful understanding of trait categories. For example, a child might reason that a character who shares a cookie is likely to share a banana based on a global evaluative judgment of the character, in the absence of any specific trait inferences (Alvarez, Ruble, & Bolger, 2001; see also Rholes & Ruble, 1984; Ruble & Dweck, 1995).

B. ADAPTATIONS OF THE BEHAVIORAL PREDICTION METHODOLOGY

1. Concepts and Properties

Heyman and Gelman (1999) pointed out that concepts from the categorization literature can be applied to the study of children's trait reasoning, such that traits are treated as categories and behaviors are treated as properties. Within the categorization literature, information about properties supports inferences about categories, and information about categories supports inferences about properties. For example, one could use the knowledge that an animal is a bird (category information) to infer that the animal is likely to have the properties *has feathers* and *flies* (property information). One could also draw an inference in the opposite direction by using knowledge that an animal has the properties *has feathers* and *flies* to infer that it is a bird. From this perspective, the standard behavioral prediction methodology in which children are asked to make generalizations about future behavior based on their knowledge of past behavior involves property-to-property inferences.

Liu, Gelman, and Wellman (2007) argued that this methodology requires children to draw two component inferences: they must first infer the trait based on past behavior, and then they must predict future behavior based on the trait. Liu *et al.* asked children to make these component inferential processes in addition to asking them to make the kind of property-to-property inferences that characterize the standard behavioral prediction methodology. For example, in addition to examining whether children will infer the future behavior *not sharing* from past instances of *not sharing* (property to property), they were asked to infer the trait *selfish* from past instances of *not sharing* (property to category) and to infer the future behavior *not sharing* from the trait *selfish* (category to property). They found that 4- and 5-year olds tended to perform poorly on the standard (property to property) version of the task, but did well with each of the component inferences. This finding suggests that the participants had difficulty in combining information from the two component processes, which is consistent with the possibility that children's understanding in this domain is not sufficiently robust for them to integrate these two types of information spontaneously. Liu *et al.* also asked participants to evaluate how much they liked each story character and used participants' evaluations as a covariate in the statistical analysis. Even after controlling for their judgments about how much they liked each story character, young children still made sensible judgments of the story characters' traits. The finding that children's responses could not be explained solely in terms of global evaluative processes suggests that their trait reasoning is not simply an expression of the extent to which they like the individuals about whom they are reasoning.

2. Generalization across Traits

Other researchers have extended the basic behavioral consistency paradigm by examining how children generalize across traits. For example, if a boy behaves in an antisocial way, do children assume that he has other negative characteristics as well, such as low academic ability? The evidence suggests that children do not hold trait conceptions that are wholly undifferentiated (Cain, Heyman, & Walker, 1997a; Stipek & Daniels, 1990). Cain *et al.* (1997a, 1997b) found that among 4-year-olds, instances of antisocial behavior held stronger implications for a character's future antisocial behavior than for his or her future academic or athletic performance. However, there was evidence of generalizing across traits of the same valence, is that participants predicted poorer academic and athletic outcomes for a character who behaved in an antisocial way versus a character who behaved in a prosocial way (see also Yussen & Kane, 1985 for related findings). Studies using memory recall measures have also found that young children tend to have difficulty in differentiating between traits of the same valence. Heyman, Gee, and Giles (2003) found that preschoolers were better able to recall a character's traits when the traits were consistent in valence (e.g., *nice* and *smart*) rather than conflicting in valence (e.g., *mean* and *smart*).

There is also evidence that the tendency to generalize across traits of the same valence is greater among younger children. Stipek and Tannatt (1984) asked 4- to 8-year-olds to judge their own academic abilities and those of their classmates and to explain their reasoning. A content analysis revealed that the younger children were more likely to make reference to sociability than the older children. This may be the result of a tendency for young children to focus on the extent to which individuals are prosocial, to the exclusion of other traits. For example, Feldman and Ruble (1988) asked children to select partners for a game that would give them a chance to earn prizes and found that 9- to 11-year-olds chose partners with relevant skills (e.g., an athletically coordinated partner for a kickball competition), whereas 5- to 6-year-olds tended to select the partner they found the most likeable. This finding is consistent with the possibility that children use traits in a relatively global way early in development and in a more differentiated way later (see Livesley & Bromley, 1973). However, even young children have some understanding that individuals can hold traits of conflicting valence. Heyman *et al.* (2003) found that more than 90% of preschool-age participants agreed that it is possible for an individual to hold a positive trait on one dimension and a negative trait on another (e.g., to be both *smart* and *mean*). Of course, it may be that children conceptualize traits as distinct, but also understand that information about one trait can have implications for other traits as well. This possibility is suggested by an explanation provided by one participant in a study by Heyman and Dweck (1998). In that study, children were asked whether it is possible to infer that someone who does mean things is lacking in academic ability (Heyman & Dweck, 1998). One second grader responded yes and explained, "They fight a lot. They are probably fighting when they are supposed to be working." This response suggests that children might think that one can infer one trait based on another trait for reasons other than an inability to differentiate between traits.

3. Mental States and Processes

A third approach to understand the nature of trait conceptions has been to investigate them in relation to the understanding of other aspects of mental states and processes (Heyman & Gelman, 1998, 1999; Yuill, 1992).

From this perspective, mental states and processes can serve as potential mediators between traits and behaviors. Heyman and Gelman (1998, 1999) defined this ability to reason about traits in relation to mental states and processes as a psychologically meaningful understanding of traits. Children with a psychologically meaningful understanding of traits have an appreciation of the notion that specific behaviors can point to different trait implications. For example, an individual who says things that hurt other people's feelings may be antisocial, uninhibited, or both. The same behavioral information can even point to conflicting trait inferences: a person who takes candy from a baby is antisocial if the goal is to make the baby cry, but prosocial if the goal is to prevent the baby from choking. Such an understanding also involves knowing that trait-relevant information can hold a wide range of implications for understanding psychological experience. For instance, knowing that an individual is shy might tell you not only about how she or he is likely to act at a large social event but also about the emotions the individual might experience. A child with a psychologically meaningful understanding is able to view mental states and processes as potential mediators between traits and behaviors (Heyman & Gelman, 1998, 1999).

The possibility of an early emerging capacity to conceptualize traits in a psychologically meaningful way is consistent with evidence that psychological reasoning is central to how young children reason about people. Lillard and Flavell (1990) found that 3-year-olds showed a preference for mentalistic rather than behavioral descriptions of human actions. It is also consistent with an extensive body of evidence that children acquire a rich understanding of mental states early in life. By age 5, most children understand that beliefs are representational, as reflected by their performance on false-belief tasks (Wellman, Cross, & Watson, 2001), and most 3-year-olds have some understanding of connections between past events and present emotions and between thinking and feeling (Lagattuta & Wellman, 2001). Some appreciation of mental life emerges even before children reach their second birthday. For example, by 18 months of age, children have some capacity to understand that different individuals can have different desires (Repacholi & Gopnik, 1997) and are capable of imitating based on the perceived intentions of others (Meltzoff, 1995). These findings suggest that by the time children reach elementary school age, they have acquired a large body of knowledge about psychological experience that could potentially inform their understanding of traits.

It is possible that understanding mental states is necessary for a psychologically meaningful trait understanding, but not sufficient. A child might reason about someone's psychological experience in a specific context without drawing inferences about their psychological experiences in other contexts. For example, a child may be able to infer that someone wants to help in a particular situation without having any kind of assumption that there may be individual differences in how strongly people generally desire to help others. It may also be that children have theories of mind in which mental states are viewed as closely tied to situations and that are not linked to notions of stable properties of individuals (see Kalish, 2002).

One approach to examining whether young children are capable of conceptualizing traits in a psychologically meaningful way is to examine whether they use information about mental states to make trait inferences. In one study taking this approach, Heyman and Gelman (1998) presented participants (kindergartners, second graders, fifth graders, and adults) with scenarios in which protagonists perform actions that cause targets to respond in a favorable or an unfavorable way. In these scenarios, the motives of protagonists were systematically manipulated: protagonists acted with prosocial intent, antisocial intent, or an incidental intent that involved a goal that had nothing to do with how the target might respond. For example, in one story the protagonist finishes a puzzle that the target had been working on and the target is either pleased or upset upon discovering the completed puzzle. In the prosocial motive version of the story, the protagonist assumed that the target was tired of working on it and would be happy to see it finished. In the antisocial version, the protagonist assumed that the target had wanted to finish the puzzle and that finishing it would make the target angry. In the incidental version, participants were told the protagonist did it because he liked doing puzzles. We reasoned that if participants were making appropriate trait inferences merely based on the general positive or negative valence of the event, their responses should correspond to the outcome information at least as much as to the motive information since the outcome information was emphasized to a greater extent (unlike the motive information it was repeated and also presented visually). However, if children have a psychological understanding of traits, motive information should be more important in determining their responses. Our findings were consistent with the latter possibility: participants in all age groups were sensitive to the motive information when making trait-relevant inferences and used motive information to a greater extent than information about the outcome. For instance, they tended to infer that protagonists who acted with prosocial or with incidental motives were nicer and were more willing to share pennies and help a child who was hurt on the playground than would protagonists who acted with antisocial motives, but largely ignored the outcome of the protagonists' actions in making these predictions.

This general approach also has been applied to look specifically at conceptions of ability. Older children and adults typically assume that smart people are capable of doing many cognitive tasks with less effort than individuals who are not as smart. We examined whether young children also held such an assumption by asking preschool participants about two children who completed identical puzzles (Heyman *et al.*, 2003). Participants were told that one individual found the puzzle easy to do and that the other found it hard to do and then were asked to make judgments about the relative ability of the two individuals. Participants showed a systematic tendency to assume that individuals who perceived the task to be easier are smarter. This research provides further evidence that young children are capable of using information about an individual's psychological experience to make trait inferences.

Other research has examined children's conceptions of traits in a psychologically meaningful way by asking whether trait information is used to make inferences about mental states. Gnepp and Chilamkurti (1988) addressed this issue by testing whether children use trait information to predict an individual's emotional response to a particular situation. They presented kindergartners, second graders, fourth graders, and college students with a story that included one of three behavioral manifestations of a trait or no trait information (a control condition). Participants were then asked to rate the actor's emotional response in a new context. For example, for the trait *helpful*, the characteristic behaviors were "helps old people walk down the stairs," "shows new kids around the school," and "sets the table for his mom whenever he can." Participants were asked whether the character would feel happy or sad when his mother asked him to clean his room. Gnepp and Chilamkurti found that even kindergartners showed some evidence of using the trait information in their emotion predictions (see also Yuill & Pearson, 1998, for further evidence of early sophistication in the use of trait information to make emotion predictions).

Heyman and Gelman (1999) also examined how children use trait information to make inferences about mental states, using a procedure adapted from Heyman and Gelman (1998). Four-year-olds heard a description of a character who is either shy or not shy and goes to a location and finds that either no people or many people are present. For instance, in one set of scenarios, participants are told that a character is shy and that he went to a swimming pool and found that there were many people there. Even these young participants used the trait information to make mental state inferences such as using information that an individual is shy to infer that they were less likely to have wanted there to be a lot of people to be at the location in question. Similar results were also seen for the traits *nice* and *mean*. For example, a character who was described as nice who was shown doing something that caused a target to become upset was judged as less likely to have foreseen the negative reaction than was a protagonist who was described as mean.

The findings on children's reasoning about traits in relation to mental states suggests that by as early as 4 years of age, children begin to understand traits as having the potential to do more than simply describe overt behavior. However, it is important to note that this capacity does not mean that they consistently reason about traits in relation to mental life. Much of the research that demonstrates early capacities to conceptualize traits in these ways demonstrates an age-related increase in the tendency to engage in such reasoning (e.g., Gnepp & Chilamkurti, 1988; Yuill & Pearson, 1998). It may even be inappropriate for children to view some traits in relation to mental states, given that traits better characterize consistencies in behavior than consistencies in psychological states (Fletcher, 1984). Yuill (1997a) points out that one can reasonably attribute a trait of generosity to someone even if they rarely succeed in displaying generous behavior, as long as they have intentions to act generously, but that one cannot reasonably attribute a trait of punctuality to an individual who strives to be early but is never on time. Nevertheless, the evidence that young children can reason about traits in a psychologically meaningful way indicates that they are not limited to form simple associations between behaviors and instead are capable of developing more complex representations. It is likely that these representations serve as building blocks as children refine their notions of what individual people are generally like.

C. SUMMARY

Researchers had previously assumed that children do not reason about others in terms of traits before they reach 7 years of age, but recent findings suggest otherwise. Children have some ability to differentiate between traits of the same valence and can reason about traits in relation to the mental life of others. However, the reasoning of young children in this domain is far from complete. Even after children have acquired many of the precursors to a psychologically meaningful understanding of traits, they sometimes fail to apply it.

III. Psychological Essentialism and Trait Reasoning

Once children have the capacity to understand traits, do they see them as fundamental and stable or as superficial and transient? Researchers have addressed these questions from the perspective of psychological essentialism, which is a tendency to believe that entities have natures or underlying essences that have causal properties that make them what they are. From this perspective, essences are viewed as generating or constraining potentially observable properties and observable properties are used to diagnose underlying essences (Medin, 1989). When concepts are viewed in essentialist ways, they tend to be seen as rooted in nature and relatively difficult to change (Gelman, 2003). For example, an individual who holds essentialist beliefs about musical ability would tend to endorse the notion that some individuals are born with an innate potential to develop special skills in music and that knowing their level of music skill at one time point is likely to be highly informative about their long-term potential to acquire skills in music.

A. BIOLOGICAL ESSENTIALISM

The framework of psychological essentialism has been most extensively studied in the biological domain. Researchers addressing this question have used a wide range of methodologies and have provided strong evidence of essentialist reasoning among children as young as preschool age. One issue that has been examined within this general framework is the extent to which category labels promote nonobvious inferences. To the extent that such labels promote such inferences, it suggests that entities with shared category labels may also share essences. In one study, Gelman and Markman (1986) used a triad task to address this question with 3- and 4-year-olds. On each trial, children were presented with three drawings of creatures, such as a flamingo, a blackbird, and a bat. Two of the creatures looked similar to each other (the blackbird and the bat). Children were told about the category membership of two of the creatures (e.g., that the blackbird and the flamingo are both birds). They were then told a property of one creature (such as that the flamingo feeds its young mashed-up food), and a different property of another creature (such as that the bat feeds its young milk). Children were then asked which property the third creature possesses (i.e., whether the blackbird feeds its young mashed-up food or milk). Children tended to report the property possessed by the creature that looked different but shared category membership (i.e., to report that the blackbird feeds its young mashed-up food). This result shows that even at a very early age, children use category labels in the biological domain in making inferences about unseen properties. Further research by Gelman and Wellman (1991) provides evidence that preschool children also make assumptions about the innate potential of animals and plants. For example, by age 4 children predicted that a baby kangaroo that is raised with goats would grow up to have a pouch and be good at hopping.

B. PSYCHOLOGICAL ESSENTIALISM

Researchers have argued that children sometimes apply essentialist reasoning to the social world. Most work on this topic has examined such reasoning with reference to social categories. For example, children often emphasize the importance of nature over nurture when reasoning about gender (Taylor, 1996) and race (Hirschfeld, 1995). Hirschfeld (1996) argued that an important reason is people's "innate human-kind creating potential." (See Atran, 1990, and Sperber, 1996 for further discussion of why children might essentialize social categories.)

To what extent do children of different ages apply essentialist reasoning to traits? Prior research suggests that the answer to this question is likely to have important psychological and social implications (see Dweck, 1999). This work suggests that essentialist beliefs are associated with a tendency to view academic difficulties in terms of whether one has what it takes to succeed, rather than as problems to be solved (Heyman & Dweck, 1998). Much of the work in this area has concerned whether children conceive of traits as *malleable* or *stable*. These are distinct properties, although they are often confused. Malleability concerns whether individuals have the capacity to change, whereas stability has to do with the likelihood that change will happen. Individuals are said to conceive of traits as malleable to the extent that they believe people are capable of changing their traits over time. For example, the belief that intelligence is malleable is often assessed by asking participants to rate their level of agreement with statements such as "You can learn new things but you can't really change how smart you are." People who tend to reject such statements are often described as holding entity or fixed beliefs about ability. In contrast, people who tend to endorse such statements are often described as holding incremental or malleable ability conceptions. Individuals are said to conceive of traits as stable to the extent that they believe people are likely to maintain the same traits over time. Such beliefs are often assessed by asking participants whether a particular pattern of trait-relevant behavior that characterizes an individual at one point in time will still characterize the individual in the future. For instance, the following question was used by Giles and Heyman (2003) to look at stability beliefs related to antisocial behavior.

> Imagine you see a girl who takes another kid's lunch, steps on the sandwich, and then spills the drink. Do you think she will stop acting this way when she gets older?

People who tend to expect the behaviors to continue are classified as conceiving of traits as stable. The tendency to view traits as low in malleability, or to view them as high in stability, each serve as in index of essentialism. However, individuals who hold essentialist views based on one of these measures do not necessarily hold essentialist views based on the other. For example, someone might reason that an individual exhibits the trait of laziness by choice (a high malleability, anti-essentialist belief), but predict that the individual will remain lazy over time because he or she is in an environment that rewards laziness and will most likely remain in that environment (a high stability, essentialist belief; see the next section for further discussion of relations among essentialist measures, and see also Pomerantz & Saxon, 2001, for evidence of distinctions between these types of measures).

Research on the extent to which children conceive of traits as malleable suggests a link to maladaptive motivational consequences (see Dweck, 1999). Cain and Dweck (1995) found that fifth graders who conceived of traits as malleable were more likely than their peers to exhibit the characteristics of motivational helplessness in the face of obstacles, including decreased persistence and more negative expectations about their future performance. Blackwell, Trzesniewski, and Dweck (2007) found that children who held incremental views of ability were better able to cope with the challenges posed by the transition to middle school. One explanation for these findings is that beliefs about intelligence are associated with different concerns and goals (Dweck & Leggett, 1988; Leggett, 1985). For individuals who hold entity views of intelligence, poor performance is seen as a threat to intellectual adequacy. In contrast, for individuals who hold incremental beliefs about intelligence, poor performance simply indicates that skills need to be improved (Leggett, 1985; Wood & Bandura, 1989), because limited skill in the present is not seen as precluding significant improvement in the future.

There is evidence suggesting that essentialist beliefs are associated with maladaptive motivational responses even among early elementary school children. Heyman and Dweck (1998) found that 7- and 8-year-olds who endorsed a belief in the long-term stability of sociomoral traits (by agreeing that a child who exhibits negative behavior will continue to do so over a long period of time) tended to equate academic difficulty with inability and to de-emphasize the importance of task-relevant processes such as effort and strategy generation. Heyman, Dweck, and Cain (1992) found that 5- and 6-year-olds who agreed that traits are stable were more likely to show low persistence and to make negative self-inferences in the face of difficulty.

Essentialist beliefs carry implications for peer relations as well. Erdley *et al.* (1997) examined late elementary school children's beliefs about the malleability of personality in relation to how they respond to social rejection. In this paradigm, participants tried out for a pen pal club in which children were asked to write a letter to a child representative of the club and told that the letter would be sent by radio transmission. After being told that their letter had been transmitted, all participants received a mild rejection in which they were told that the representative was not sure yet whether or not to invite them to join the club. (After the rejection, participants were then invited to write a second letter and invited to join the club.) An entity view of personality was associated with a tendency to focus on social evaluation, which led to behaviors and attributions characteristic of motivational helplessness in the face of peer rejection. For example, participants with an entity view of personality were more likely to endorse social strategies directed toward avoiding social rejection, such as only inviting children to a birthday party who "are sure to say yes," and were more likely to attribute their rejection to difficulties making friends. Other research suggests that children with an entity view of personality are more likely to make rigid and global evaluative judgments of people who commit transgressions (Chiu, Hong, & Dweck, 1997; Erdley & Dweck, 1993) and are more likely to engage in stereotyping (Levy & Dweck, 1999).

C. DEVELOPMENT AND ESSENTIALIST BELIEFS

1. Appearances versus Traits

One way that researchers have examined the development of essentialist beliefs about traits has been to examine the extent to which young children tend to make inductive inferences based on information about traits, as opposed to information about appearance. Evidence that children use trait information to a greater extent than appearance information to guide their inference would provide evidence for essentialist reasoning.

Hoffner and Cantor (1985) addressed this question in a study in which children aged 3 to 10 saw one of four possible videotapes in which the appearance of a female character was varied factorially with the trait-relevant behavior she exhibited. The characters were designed to appear as either ugly with a pointed chin and crooked nose and resembling the common stereotype of a witch or with a round face and resembling the common stereotype of a kindly grandmother. The characters were shown engaging in either kind behavior in which they picked up a cat gently and fed it or cruel behavior in which they threatened to starve a cat and threw it down the stairs. Participants of all ages of were more likely to rate the character who engaged in kind behavior as nice, but there was an age-related change in relative emphasis on behavior versus appearance: for 3- to 5-year-olds the character's appearance accounted for greater variability than her behavior, and the reverse pattern was found among older children.

Heyman and Gelman (2000b) hypothesized that preschool children might use trait information to a greater extent than appearance information if the trait information was presented in the form of a trait label, and if the appearance information was presented in a way that avoided strong value-laden associations. This study used an adapted version of the triad task developed by Gelman and Markman (1986) that was described previously, in which trait labels such as "shy" and "outgoing" were pitted against appearance information. Participants learned novel properties associated with each of two children, and were asked which of the properties best characterizes a third target child. On each trial, the target child looked similar to one child but shared the same trait label with another child (see Figure 1). For example, participants might be told that one child is shy and likes to play "tibbits" and that another child is outgoing and likes to play "jimjam." Participants were then asked whether a third child who looks like the child labeled as "shy" but is labeled as "outgoing" likes to play tibbits or jimjam. Results indicated a systematic tendency to draw inferences based on the trait information rather than the appearance information. Taken together, the results of Heyman and Gelman (2000b) and Hoffner and Cantor (1985) suggest that preschool children do not always give appearance information greater weight than trait information, but may do so when presented with appearance information that is highly stereotypical.

2. Malleable or Stable?

Another way researchers have examined the development of essentialist beliefs about traits has been to ask whether different traits are perceived to be malleable or stable. As discussed in the preceding section, malleability and stability are of particular interest because of their implications for how children respond to academic and social difficulties. One general conclusion of this research has been that children often give more weight to evidence of positive traits than to evidence of negative traits. For example, Heyman and Giles (2004) found that 7- to 9-year-olds were more likely to expect that a child who is smarter than most of her peers will hold the same status in two years than to have the corresponding expectation for a child who is less smart. Participants were also more likely to endorse the possibility than a character could work to gain favorable traits (e.g., becoming nicer or smarter) than unfavorable ones (e.g., becoming meaner or less smart). This difference is unlikely to have resulted from the

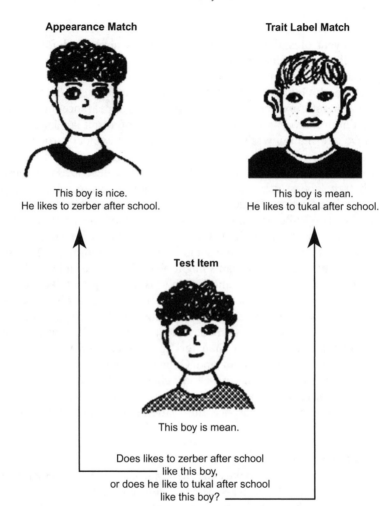

Appearance Match

This boy is nice.
He likes to zerber after school.

Trait Label Match

This boy is mean.
He likes to tukal after school.

Test Item

This boy is mean.

Does likes to zerber after school
like this boy,
or does he like to tukal after school
like this boy?

Fig. 1. Example procedure from Heyman and Gelman (2000b, Study 1). In each triad that was presented, participants saw one test item, one appearance match item, and one trait label item. In this example, participants were asked whether the mean boy in the test trial likes to zerber after school like the nice boy with a similar appearance or likes to tukal after school like the mean boy with a dissimilar appearance.

assumption that individuals would not really want to have negative traits since participants were given explicit justifications for these changes. For example, in one scenario they heard about a boy who is smart and wanted to become less smart so that he could have more fun and stop worrying about problems.

This tendency toward optimism when reasoning about traits tends to be stronger among younger children (Droege & Stipek, 1993; Lockhart *et al.*, 2002; Newman, 1991). In a study of trait inferences among 5- to 6-year-olds and 7- to 10-year-olds, Lockhart *et al.* (2002) found the younger children were more likely to believe that negative traits can become positive and that extremely positive traits will persist over time. Boseovski and Lee (2008) found that preschool children only rarely attributed antisocial traits to story characters, even ones who engaged in antisocial behaviors repeatedly.

Droege and Stipek (1993) found optimism about traits among early elementary school children who were asked to reason about the academic abilities of their classmates. Participants were asked whether the classmates they had rated as relatively low in academic competence could, with effort, improve their abilities. Sixth graders endorsed the possibility of moderate change by reporting that the children could attain a level of competence comparable to that of a peer who they had rated as only slightly more capable. In contrast, kindergartners tended to express great optimism about possible change, reporting that the children could acquire a level of competence comparable to that of a peer who they had rated as highly capable.

Related research suggests that young children often maintain positive assessments of their abilities even in the face of contradictory evidence (Stipek & Mac Iver, 1989; Ruble, Eisenberg, & Higgins, 1994). Children may benefit from cognitive limitations that make it easier for them to disregard information that they find unpleasant, but as their cognitive capacities become more sophisticated, they may face increasing pressure to acknowledge it (Schuster, Ruble, & Weinert, 1998). Stipek and Daniels (1988) suggested that the age at which children begin to acknowledge their own limitations comes earlier when their social environment makes their limitations more salient. They compared kindergarteners who attended classes in which normative evaluation was emphasized (*high salience* classrooms) with kindergarteners who attended classes in which normative evaluation was de-emphasized (*low salience* classrooms). For example, in high salience classrooms, but not low salience classrooms, teachers graded papers using checks, stars, happy, and sad faces and displayed papers that had mostly correct answers on bulletin boards. Stipek and Daniels (1988) found that kindergarteners in high salience classrooms perceived their competence to be lower than kindergarteners attending low salience classrooms.

There is evidence that the extent to which children conceive of traits as stable or malleable sometimes differ as a function of the trait in question. Giles and Heyman (2004a) investigated preschool children's reasoning about aggression and withdrawal and found that children expected aggression to be more resistant to change and more stable over time. Giles (2003) noted that young children's tendency to reason in an essentialist manner about aggression may lead them to "pigeonhole transgressors into evaluative categories, and to support punitive means of dealing with aggression," as adults often do.

Even young children expect that some individuals will be better than others in helping people to change their traits. Giles and Heyman (2004a) asked preschoolers which of four possible agents would be effective in helping a child change his or her aggressive or withdrawn behavior: a friend, a doctor, a parent, or a teacher. Participants were significantly more likely to expect that a friend would be effective, as compared to a doctor, parent, or teacher. Giles and Heyman (2004a) followed up on this finding by examining what preschoolers thought of the effectiveness of different kinds of intervention efforts by friends. Participants expected prosocial strategies such as showing how to make friends to be more effective than simply telling a child to stop engaging in undesirable behavior. There is evidence that over time, children become more skeptical about the extent to which characteristics can be modified by effort or behavioral change alone and begin to incorporate other factors into their models of how traits can change (Maas, Marecek, & Travers, 1978; Yuill, 1997b). For instance, in a study of beliefs about potential mechanisms of trait change among children aged 4 to 11, Yuill (1997b) found that younger children tended to believe that people can change their traits simply by changing their behavior, whereas older children were more likely to emphasize the importance of cognitive control.

3. Innateness or Nature versus Nurture

There has been some research on the extent to which children believe traits to be innate. Heyman and Gelman (2000a) posed a nature–nurture conflict in the form of a switched-at-birth task (see Hirschfeld, 1995) to participants ranging in age from kindergarten to fifth grade. Participants were told that due to an accidental switch at a hospital that went undetected, two babies grew up with the wrong set of parents. Each baby's birth parents were described as having a trait that contrasted with the trait of the parents who raised him or her. For example, participants were asked about a baby born to "smart" parents, who was raised by "not smart" parents, and about a baby born to "not smart" parents, who was raised by "smart" parents. In each case, participants were asked whether the baby would grow up to share the trait of the birth parents (nature response) or the upbringing parents (nurture response) and to explain why. Physical characteristics such as ear shape were included to allow comparisons with children's reasoning about psychological traits. Children of all ages were more likely to provide nature responses to physical characteristics. This tendency increased with age and almost all fourth and fifth graders responded in this way. In contrast, for psychological traits there were strong individual differences in all age groups.

Within each age group, children's explanations tended to be consistent with their predictions about which set of parents the story characters would resemble. For example, nurture responses tended to be justified in terms of environmental influences, but not nature responses. Specific mechanisms for environmental influences were described by children in all age groups, as in the following examples, which were in response to a question about a child born to "not smart" parents who grew up with "smart" parents.

She learns how to be smart. The more you read, the smarter you get. (kindergarten)

The parents would read all the time and they would see what the parents are doing and would read along. (second grade)

It grew up with people who encourage learning. (fifth grade)

More of the age-related change was seen in children's justifications for their nature responses, with only children in the oldest age group describing mechanisms through which children might come to have the traits of their birth parents, as in the following examples.

He wasn't born to smart parents. (kindergarten)

The family would try but the baby would always stay not very smart. (second grade)

It will have trouble. It's in its genes. (fifth grade)

It will have their blood and stuff. (fourth grade)

Another developmental change that was some of the oldest children offered complex justifications of their responses that are not captured by a simple distinction between nature and nurture. Some fourth and fifth graders suggested that environmental influences would work against natural tendencies. In some cases, children viewed the environmental influence as winning out in the end. One participant expressed this view in response to a scenario in which a child is born to active parents but grows up with inactive parents, with the argument that "The child would want to be active but would be forced into not being more active and would get used to it." Others saw the natural tendencies corresponding to the traits of the birth parents as winning out in the end. This view was expressed by one participant in response to the scenario in which a child was born to smart parents but grew up with parents who were not smart: "The baby will not be smart at first, but in school it will get smart. The baby learns well because of the original parents. The new parents will be proud of the child for doing better than they expected."

Some fourth and fifth graders made a distinction between overt behavior and underlying traits. For example, one participant responded to a scenario in which a baby was born to shy parents but raised by outgoing parents by explaining, "The original parents are shy so the kid will be shy too. The child looks outgoing. The parents will teach him to converse with people and look like he is having fun, but he will not be. Something like a feeling depends on the original parents, not like activity."

Another age-related change was that the older children showed different patterns of reasoning for different traits, but the younger children did not. The clearest distinction was seen between intellectual ability and prosocial tendencies. Participants expected a greater influence from the biological parents in determining intellectual ability. One possible explanation is that because being smart is sometimes referred to in terms of "having brains." Brains are associated with biology, and children may have thought more about biological influences. As is consistent with this possibility, children sometimes referred to the brain in their justifications of their responses to questions concerning the trait "smart," as in the following example of a response provided by a fifth grader: "You can change the way you act but you can't change the brain. If the baby was born to not so smart people, it couldn't learn things as well because it has a low IQ." It may also be that environmental influences are seen as especially important for prosocial traits since parents are often observed explicitly telling children to be nice to others.

D. SUMMARY

In summary, children sometimes apply essentialist reasoning to traits. When they do so, it appears to have important implications for how they reason about themselves and others. For example, individuals with essentialist beliefs are especially likely to respond to their academic and social difficulties by questioning whether they have what it takes to succeed rather than by focusing on what needs to be done to overcome the difficulties and on building their skills. They are also more likely to be more rigid in their judgments of others, for example, by readily engaging in stereotyping. By early elementary school, children show some tendencies to essentialize traits, although they do so less than with physical characteristics and are often quite optimistic about the possibility of positive trait change. As children get older, they begin to think about the interplay between different influences in trait development and increasingly make distinctions in the extent to which they essentialize different traits.

IV. Influences on Trait Thinking

The preceding sections have shown that by early elementary school, children hold meaningful trait conceptions and sometimes reason about traits in essentialist ways. In this section, I review research that has addressed what is known about factors that affect the way children make trait inferences.

A. CONTEXTS FOR TRAIT EXPLANATIONS

One set of questions concerns the contexts for which children consider trait explanations to be appropriate. The work of Kelley (1973) provides the theoretical foundation for much of the research examining this question. Kelley (1973) proposed that when adults are deciding whether to attribute the behaviors they observe to underlying traits versus other factors, they perform something resembling a statistical analysis (see also Boseovski & Lee, 2006; Schuster *et al.*, 1998). According to Kelley's model, the process of making a trait attribution involves three components. The first component, *consensus*, concerns whether others in the same situation as the actor would behave in the same way. When individuals make a *low consensus inference*, it means they expect that others would act similarly. The second component, *distinctiveness*, concerns whether the actors' behavior tends to generalize across contexts. When individuals make a *low distinctiveness inference*, it means that such generalization is expected. The third component, *consistency*, concerns whether the individual will behave in the same manner in similar situations over time. When individuals make a *high consistency inference*, it means that such consistency is expected. Inferences of low consensus, low distinctiveness, and high consistency are associated with making trait attributions. Schuster *et al.* (1998) found that by second grade, children make appropriate inferences when they are given information about all three factors. Other research has focused on how children reason about specific subsets of the factors. Boseovski and Lee (2008) found that preschool children ignore consensus information when reasoning about prosocial versus antisocial behavior. Boseovski and Lee

(2006) found that the use of consistency information precedes the use of distinctiveness information, perhaps because appropriate reasoning about distinctiveness involves covariation reasoning (see also Ferguson *et al.*, 1984).

Other research has investigated whether social category information influences trait attributions in situations that are open to interpretation. In one such study, Heyman (2001) examined how 7- to 9-year-olds use gender information to make inferences. Participants were shown photographs of male and female children and a behavior that was consistent with at least one positive interpretation and one negative interpretation. When the unfamiliar child was male, participants were more likely to remember the behavior in unfavorable ways and to select more negative attributions for it. For example, they were more likely to attribute antisocial motives to a boy who asked lots of questions than to a girl who did so. This pattern of response was seen even among male participants, who reported a greater expectation of liking male than female peers. Giles and Heyman (2004b) extended these findings by demonstrating that even preschool children make more negative trait attributions when a glass of milk is knocked over by a boy than a girl. In addition, preschool children made more negative trait attributions when the action was done by an 8-year-old rather than a 3-year-old, and by a person rather than a dog. This finding suggests that social categories can influence how children make use of behavioral information to make trait inferences and that preschool children's reasoning in this domain goes beyond simply identifying overt behavioral tendencies that they applied to all individuals.

B. COLLECTING TRAIT-RELEVANT INFORMATION

In most studies addressing children's trait reasoning, researchers present the known information and examine how children use it to make inferences. However, in real life children face the additional step of determining how to seek out and evaluate trait-relevant information. Just as researchers must decide upon a data-collection strategy, children often need to decide upon a strategy for collecting trait-relevant information. For example, is it best to learn about people's traits by asking them, by observing what they do, or by asking a third party? Furthermore, children are sometimes faced with conflicting trait-relevant information, such as when an individual is observed lying on repeated occasions but professes to be honest.

When a trait carries evaluative implications, there is a motive for people to lie about it. Heyman and Legare (2005) investigated this topic by asking children of ages 6–7 and 10–11 years whether they consider self-report to be a good source of information about particular evaluative traits such as honesty or intelligence, as well as comparison traits such as a tendency to be outgoing. (An additional set of children confirmed the distinction between evaluative and comparison traits by reporting they would be happy if others thought they held a positive evaluative trait, unhappy if others thought they held a negative evaluative trait, and did not care much about how others judged them regarding the comparison traits.) The goal was to determine whether children would be skeptical about the value of self-report as a means to gain information about evaluative traits.

For each characteristic, participants were given a simple definition and asked a *self-report endorsement* question. For example, children were told "smart people are good at learning new things" and asked "is asking someone if they are smart a good way to find out how smart they are?" If children understand that the presence of potential motives to lie suggests skepticism is warranted, they should be more wary of self-report concerning evaluative traits than comparison traits. An age-related difference was seen, with only the older children showing more skepticism about self-report for the evaluative versus the comparison traits. Children's explanations of their responses to the self-report endorsement measure also indicated that the older children were aware of the possibility of distortion, as in the following examples.

> People don't want to tell you they're not good at something.

> You can't always trust people by what they say because sometimes people make up what they talk about.

> Maybe they don't want to admit they aren't honest.

> They might boast and make it seem like others aren't smart.

In contrast, the younger children were much more likely to express a belief that the character would or should tell the truth.

> I don't think they would lie about how they feel.

> If you ask them to tell the truth then they better tell the truth, otherwise it would be a lie.

> Because telling the truth is the right thing.

> Because if they tell you you'll know they're telling the truth.

Heyman and Legare (2005) also asked children of ages 6–7 and 10–11 to select among different sources of information as a means to learn about the evaluative traits and comparison characteristics of others. Choices included self-report, behavioral observation, teacher report, and peer report as a way to learn about an individual. As is consistent with the findings using self-report endorsement measure, the younger children were more likely to identify self-report as the best way to learn about evaluative characteristics, but there was no age-related difference concerning the comparison characteristics. These findings suggest that between the ages of 7 and 10, children become increasingly skeptical of self-report as a means to learn about the traits of others when there appear to be clear motives to present oneself in a favorable way.

A puzzling aspect of this age-related shift is why it appears so late, given the evidence that young children are capable of understanding that others sometimes lie. For example, during the preschool years, children begin to make distinctions between appearance and reality (Flavell, Green, & Flavell, 1989; Sapp, Lee & Muir, 2000) and to understand that verbal statements do not always reflect a speaker's true beliefs (Lee & Cameron, 2000). If 6- and 7-year-olds understand that people sometimes lie, why would they fail to question the statements of individuals who have obvious motives to do so? One possibility is that social experiences help children move from the understanding that distortion is possible to being able to identify the contexts in which lying is likely to occur. Heyman, Fu, and Lee (2007) took a first step toward investigating this possibility by investigating the reasoning of children from the U.S. and China. Children who grow up in these two countries are exposed to substantially different cultural values about the types of information about the self that are socially appropriate to express. For example, there is a stronger tendency to emphasize positive information about the self in North America as compared to East Asia (Lee *et al.*, 1997; Lee *et al.*, 2001). There also appears to be a greater emphasis on impression management in China, which appears to relate to traditional Confucian Chinese values that discourage self-disclosure (see Gao, Ting-Toomey, & Gudykunst, 1996).

Participants of ages 6–7 and 10–11 were tested using a set of self-endorsement measures from Heyman and Legare (2005) that was adapted for use in both countries. As in that study, children were asked about both evaluative and comparison traits. In response to the evaluative traits (e.g., honest) the older children within each country expressed more skepticism than the younger children, and children in China expressed more skepticism overall (see Figure 2). However, there were no corresponding effects of age or country in response to the comparison characteristics (e.g., outgoing). These results suggest that social experience can substantially effect how children evaluate sources of information about traits.

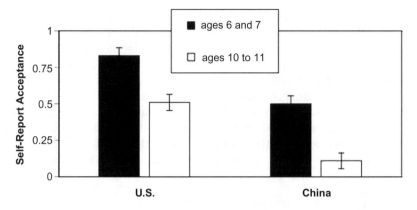

Fig. 2. Proportion of responses in which participants accepted self-report as a good way to learn about highly value-laden evaluative characteristics such as honest (data from Heyman et al., 2007, Study 1), by age group and country. Lower values indicate an appreciation that self report may be unreliable in the presence of self-presentational motives.

C. FACTORS THAT PROMOTE ESSENTIALIST REASONING

Another focus of research in this area has been to examine factors that are likely to promote essentialist reasoning about traits. Context sensitivity in children's trait thinking could be expected if children lack firm beliefs or hold conflicting sets of beliefs and use whatever cues are available in the environment to guide their responses. For example, a child might hold both essentialist and anti-essentialist conceptions of intellectual ability, but apply only one of them within a particular situation. This would parallel a pattern seen by Harris and Giménez (2005) concerning children's reasoning about death. They found that children can simultaneously hold both a biological view of death in which it implies the cessation of mental and bodily functions and a spiritual view of death in which aspects of these functions can continue after death and that contextual cues help determine which view applies within a given context. For instance, they found that 7- to 11-year-olds were more likely to predict that an elderly person who dies would continue to have functioning eyes and ears within the context of a narrative in which a priest informs the family of the death, as compared to a narrative in which a doctor informs the family of the death. Similarly, in response to the context involving a priest, children were more likely to endorse the notion that the deceased person would be able to think and to feel emotions.

A basic question about factors that promote essentialist reasoning is whether learning about one property associated with an essentialist trait conception holds implications for other properties. For example, does knowing that a trait is present at birth imply it will be more resistant to change or that it might be detectable through biological assessments such as blood tests? Gelman, Heyman, and Legare (2007, Study 4) described characters to first and third graders using novel trait labels such as "banana hater" and "easy laugher." Children then heard a novel fact about the character that was either consistent with an essentialist interpretation, such as that the character was born with the trait, or not consistent, or inconsistent with an essentialist interpretation, such as that the character was not born with the trait. Children were then asked to make inferences about other properties. For example:

> Rachel thinks bananas taste yucky. She is a banana-hater. She was born that way; she was born a banana-hater. Do you think Rachel could change whether or not she's a banana-hater, if she wants to?

Only the third graders considered information about one aspect of essentialism to be informative about other aspects. For example, after learning that a trait was present at birth, they were more likely to assume that it would not change and that scientists would one day be able to identify who has the trait by examining their blood under a microscope. This result suggests that during the early elementary school years, children come to expect coherence among different aspects of essentialist trait conceptions and that this coherence of beliefs allows them to make generalizations when reasoning about traits.

Other research suggests there are some less direct ways of encouraging essentialist reasoning. One example was seen in the Heyman and Gelman (2000a) research that was described previously, in which elementary school children reasoned about the importance of nature versus nurture on the switched-at birth task. For some of the participants, the first scenario concerned a psychological trait, and for others it concerned a physical characteristic such as ear shape. Among early elementary-school-aged participants, those who reasoned about a physical characteristic first were more likely to reason in an essentialist way, as evidenced by their stronger tendency to predict that the baby would grow up to share the traits of his or her birth parents, than those who were asked about a psychological trait first. For example, 63% of the second graders who heard a story about a physical characteristic first responded in a way that was consistent with a nature interpretation compared with 27% of the second graders who heard a story about psychological traits. However, this order effect was not seen in the responses of older children. One possible explanation for the age difference is that children are the most susceptible to this type of priming effect before they have spent time thinking about of trait origins.

Other research has focused on linguistic factors associated with essentialist reasoning about traits. One approach is based on the fact that certain languages differ in the way characteristics of people are described. For example, Spanish speakers can describe people using the verb *ser* or *estar*, but there is no lexicalized equivalent for speakers of English. Each word is translated into English as *to be*, with *ser* used to refer to permanent properties and *estar* used to refer to temporary properties (see Sera, Bales, & del Castillo Pintado, 1997). Heyman and Diesendruck (2002) randomly assigned 6- to 10-year-old bilingual speakers of Spanish and English to one of three conditions. Two of the groups heard descriptions of characters in Spanish, one using *ser* form, and the other using the *estar* form, and the third group heard the same descriptions in English using the form *to be*. For example, participants in the English condition heard about a female character who "is shy," which was translated to "es penosa" and "está penosa" for the two Spanish conditions. All children made inferences about whether the characters would be likely to engage in trait-consistent ways at other times and in other contexts. Children treated *ser* and *to be* as more likely to convey the stability of psychological characteristics than *estar*. The fact that children made distinctions between the two Spanish forms suggests that it may serve as a cue for Spanish-speaking children when learning about the nature of traits.

There also have been studies of the role of linguistic form within a single language. Gelman and Heyman (1999) examined the effect of nominalized novel phrases on children's inferences about people. Children of ages 5 and 7 years heard descriptions of characters such as "Rose eats a lot of carrots." In a between-subjects design, each description was followed by either a noun label, such as "she is a carrot-eater," or a verbal predicate, such as "she eats carrots whenever she can." All participants then were asked the same series of questions about the character's behavior, which related to past behavior ("did Rose eat a lot of carrots when she was 4 years old?"), future behavior ("will Rose eat a lot of carrots when she is grown up?"), behavior with no family support ("would Rose eat a lot of carrots if she grew up in a family where no one liked carrots?"), and behavior opposed by the character's family ("would Rose stop eating a lot of carrots if her family tried to stop her from eating carrots?"). Children predicted that the characteristics that had been referred to with a noun label would be significantly more stable over time and across contexts than those that had been referred to with a verbal predicate. This finding suggests that when adults use noun labels to describe children's behavior, it may encourage children to reason about traits in essentialist ways. For example, a parent who calls her child a "picky eater" may be unintentionally implying that the child's eating habits are unlikely to change.

These results are consistent with Waxman's (1999) suggestion that common names carry implications of deeper commonalities.

Other work on the relation between labeling and essentialism has focused on children's reasoning about academic ability. Heyman (2008) presented children of ages 8–12 with two scenarios, one that describes a character who performs successfully in math and another that describes a character who performs successfully in spelling. Half of the participants were assigned to a label condition, in which a teacher informs the class that whoever gets the highest score in the class will earn the title of "math whiz" or "spelling master" and applies the label to the child who performed most successfully. The math scenario for the label condition read as follows.

> There is a class just like yours. In this class, the teacher said that whoever does the best in the class on the math test will be called a "math whiz." Joseph did the best in the class, so he was called a "math whiz."

The other half of the participants were assigned to a no label condition, which was the same except that the performance information was simply repeated.

> There is a class just like yours. In the class the teacher said, "Let's see who does the best in the class on the math test." Joseph did the best in the class. He did better than anyone else in the class on the math test.

The participants in the label condition were more likely to infer that the character was born with special ability and would continue to do well without subsequent practice. This result suggests that the use of ability labels encourages children to view ability as a gift some individuals are born with, rather than a set of skills that can be developed over time. This way of thinking raises the question of who else does or does not have such a gift and shifts attention away from the processes that are involved in developing skills. Mueller and Dweck (1998) made a similar critique of labeling children as "talented" or "gifted," by arguing that it leads some children to "become overly concerned with justifying that label and less concerned with meeting challenges that enhance their skills" and to "react more poorly to setbacks because they worry that mistakes, confusions, or failures mean that they do not deserve to be labeled as gifted" (p. 50). Mueller and Dweck (1998) found that children in late elementary school who received global ability praise for their successes were more vulnerable to motivational difficulty in the face of obstacles than were those who were praised for their effort.

Heyman and Compton (2006) showed that merely asking children questions can prime different ways of conceptualizing ability. For example, in Study 3 of that paper 5- and 6-year-olds were told about a character who finished a puzzle task more slowly than his or her peers, and were then asked a priming question. For half of the children, the priming question involved whether the character found the task to be hard or easy, and for the other half it involved whether the character worked hard on the task. The children who had been asked the priming question about perceived difficulty were more likely to later agree that ability is a stable quality, for example, by endorsing the statement that "there are some people who could never be really good at puzzles." This result suggests that asking children to consider the role of effort encourages them to conceive of ability in terms of an expandable set of skills, whereas asking children to consider perceived difficulty encourages them to focus on individual differences in ability and to see a lack of ability as placing a limit on the effectiveness of effort (see also Heyman *et al.*, 2003). As a result, it may be possible for adults to teach children about the nature of ability even as they are unaware of doing so.

The composition of children's families may affect the extent to which they hold essentialist trait conceptions. Himelstein, Graham, and Weiner (1991) found that parents who have more than one child were more likely to emphasize the importance of genes in determining their child's level of success than were parents who have only one child. They argued that parents with one child tend to interpret their child's outcomes with reference to parenting practices, whereas parents with multiple children often observe strong differences among their children cannot be easily explained with reference to parenting practices, so they look for other explanations. Parents may communicate these beliefs to their children in direct or indirect ways. It is also likely that these types of effects extend beyond traits that are related to ability. Meerum Terwogt, Hoeksma, and Koops (1993) found that parents with adopted children tend to have relatively strong beliefs about the importance of biological inheritance in determining psychological traits.

For many children, salient examples of individuals they know may give rise to broader theories about people and traits. When children are asked to reason about traits, it is not uncommon for them to mention a specific individual they know as they explain their responses. For example, one participant who responded to the switched at birth task (Heyman & Gelman, 2000a) predicted that a baby who was born to outgoing parents and grew up with shy parents would grow up to be outgoing, and explained, "My friend's mother is an orphan. Her birth mom was outgoing, but the mom she was brought up by liked to stay at home. [So] she [the friend's mother] would just go off and do stuff." It may be that as children reason about their own traits or those of others, they often draw upon specific examples that are highly familiar but are also unrepresentative.

D. SOME CAVEATS

One reason for the interest in essentialist reasoning about people is the idea that limiting it could help children to solve problems more effectively. For example, if children learn to think about their academic and social difficulties in less essentialist ways they are more likely focus on what they can do to solve problems and build skills, which is likely to have long-term benefits (see Dweck, 1999). However, the effects of anti-essentialist messages may not always be positive. For instance, Heyman and Legare (2007, October) found that late elementary school children were less likely to blame a child for difficulty in paying attention if the child was labeled as "hyperactive." This reduction in blame could translate into fewer negative peer interactions. Essentialist reasoning about to one's difficulties is likely to lead a reduction in self-blame when little effort is exerted. For example, a woman who is known to the author was once told by a music teacher that she is "tone deaf" and could never learn to play the piano. As a result, she says she does not feel bad that she has never made a serious effort to develop her musical skills, because such an effort would be futile (see Himelstein *et al.*, 1991, for similar arguments concerning parent's responsibility for their children's difficulties).

Another consideration is that the relation between behavior and essentialist reasoning about traits is unlikely to be unidirectional. Although essentialist beliefs clearly drive behavior, behavior and outcomes of behavior may also influence essentialist beliefs. For example, children may generate essentialist explanations to make sense of particular experiences, as in the following conversation between an 8-year-old and a 7-year-old that was overheard by the author.

> Child 1: You're lucky. You make friends so easily. I have a hard time making friends. I guess it's because we have different genes.
>
> Child 2: That doesn't come from genes! I'll teach you. If you're shy, you just go up to someone and say. "Hello what's your name? Do you want to come over today? Do you want to play at recess?"
>
> Child 1: But that's hard for me. You're more comfortable than I am. I'm not good at doing that. I'm afraid people will think I'm weird.

Children may be especially likely to reach essentialist conclusions about their ability when they have repeatedly tried and failed to develop a skill, especially when peers are seen mastering the skill quickly. Consequently, effective interventions must teach children how to think about traits and also how to interpret trait-relevant behavior and outcomes. For example, teaching children in late elementary about the difficulties others have faced before achieving success tends to limit children's essentialist reasoning and promote optimism about the prospect of overcoming their own difficulties (Heyman, 2008; see Wilson & Linville, 1985, for a related intervention with college students). It also may be useful to draw children's attention to improvements they have made, such as having them compare writing samples from the beginning and end of the school and teaching them to be skeptical of peers who claim to have reached success with minimal effort (see Juvonen & Murdock, 1995).

E. SUMMARY

Trait reasoning is influenced by various factors associated with the target, including what social category she or he belongs to. For example, when the evidence is ambiguous, children are more likely to infer negative sociomoral traits when they are reasoning about boys than when they are reasoning about girls.

Children's beliefs about the appropriate ways to learn about the traits of others vary as a function of their age and culture. For example, early elementary school children are much more likely than older children to consider self-report to be a useful way to learn about highly evaluative traits of others, and skepticism about the value of self report in this context is substantially lower among elementary schools in the U.S. than their age-matched counterparts in China.

Subtle differences in the way individuals are described can influence the extent to which individuals engage in essentialist reasoning. For example, describing traits in terms of verbal labels can carry implications beyond describing what an individual is like at a particular time in a particular context and may sometimes implicitly convey that it in some way characterizes what the individual is essentially like (Gelman, 2003).

Finally, children's trait reasoning may be influenced by experiences of attempting to change their own traits or those of others. It is likely that failed attempts to change traits would lead to more essentialist trait reasoning and that learning about individuals who have changed traits over time would lead to less essentialist trait reasoning.

V. Future Directions

Future research on children's reasoning about traits will need to address a number of important questions. One question concerns how children first come to understand traits. It is possible that components of this understanding first emerge as children begin to consider how they, or the people close to them, tend to differ from others. The work of Eder (1990) suggests that children are beginning to consider these questions by the age of 3 years. She showed children pairs of puppets that demonstrated either a high or a low level of a particular trait. For example, for the trait *angry,* one puppet said, "When I get angry I feel like hitting someone," and another said, "When I get angry I feel like being quiet." For the trait *control* one puppet said, "When I color I try to stay inside the lines," and another said, "When I color I don't try to stay inside the lines." After each pair of puppets was presented, children were asked, "how about you?" Even among the 3-year-olds, responses tended to be internally consistent and ratings were moderately stable over a one-month period. Perhaps as children reflect upon these types of individual differences, they begin to form more theory-like trait conceptions that they can use as a basis for predicting and explaining behavior across a wide range of contexts.

In examining how children's trait conceptions emerge and develop over time, it will be important to determine whether their reasoning tends to reflect domain-specific versus domain-general reasoning processes. This question is important to address given the broader debates about the extent to which cognition can be appropriately characterized as differing in important ways across content areas (Wellman & Gelman, 1998). It will also be important to determine the source of similarities and differences. For example, similarities could reflect generalizations from one domain to another or domain-general reasoning processes applied across domains, and differences could reflect diverging learning processes or social experiences.

Another topic for future research is the role of motives and emotional states. For example, might ambivalence about changing one's negative traits lead people to reason essentialist ways as a means to evade responsibility? Is positive mood associated with a tendency to focus on evidence that casts one's traits is a positive light?

Finally, more research is needed on the role of the social environment. It may be that when adults draw comparison between people, it encourages children to focus on individual differences. For example, a father who tells his daughter that she is always too loud and asks why she can't be more like her brother may not only be teaching the child about her own traits and standing in the family but also be prompting her to think about individual differences among people. The telling of stories may also contribute to this process, as many stories for children focus on clear contrasts between good and bad characters, which may promote a valence-based classification and serve as a precursor to trait understanding. Stories also often emphasize specific traits. For example, the *Curious George* series may help children to understand what it means to be curious and trigger discussions with caregivers that expand upon this understanding.

A deeper understanding of the role of the social environment will need to include possible cross-cultural differences. As noted previously, one such difference is that children in China are much more skeptical about the utility of self report for learning about value-laden traits, which suggests that children in different cultures learn different rules about how to acquire information about the traits others. There also are likely to be cross-cultural differences in the way children interpret and make generalizations about information that holds possible trait implications. For example, Miller (1984) found evidence that people in India were more likely to favor situational explanations rather than trait explanations for behavior, as compared to people in the U.S. (see also Choi, Nisbett & Norenzayan, 1999, concerning a greater belief in the importance of the situations among East Asians than Westerners). There may be cross-cultural differences in the way children view the mapping between traits and behavior. Heyman, Fu, and Lee (2008) found that late elementary school children in the U.S. expected a child who revealed his or her own academic success to poorly performing classmates would be seen as trying to showing off, whereas their Chinese counterparts expected such disclosure would be seen as an implicit offer of help. A better understanding of these types of cross-cultural differences should provide clues to the way children's reasoning about people is affected by their social experiences and offer insight into the variability in children's reasoning about the social world.

VI. Conclusion

Even before children reach school age, they have developed trait conceptions that extend beyond mere descriptions or evaluations of observable behavior. These trait conceptions help to guide children as they make inferences about the mental states of others and reason about their social world. There is evidence that trait conceptions undergo some important changes during the elementary school years. For example, children learn to coordinate different trait inferences and to make trait inferences across a broader range of contexts.

In some cases, children interpret information about traits as though it indicates what individuals are like in general across time and contexts, which is a form of psychological essentialism. This way of conceptualizing traits is associated with an increased risk of maladaptive responses to academic and social challenges, and a tendency to interpret negative social and academic outcomes as diagnostic of underlying traits. Across the elementary school years, children develop more coherent essentialist belief systems that correspond to aspects of their emerging understanding of the biological domain.

Children's essentialist reasoning, as well as other aspects of their trait reasoning, is influenced by their immediate social context. For instance, the application of verbal labels to people often promotes essentialist reasoning. It is likely that these social contextual influences extend to the broader context in which children are developing, including their school and home environments.

Acknowledgments

This article was supported by NICHD Grant HD38529. I thank Brian Compton and David Liu for helpful comments. Address requests for further information to Gail D. Heyman, Department of Psychology, University of California, San Diego, 9500 Gilman Dr., La Jolla CA 92093-0109. E-mail: gheyman@ucsd.edu.

REFERENCES

Alvarez, J. M., Ruble, D. N., & Bolger, N. (2001). Trait understanding or evaluative reasoning? An analysis of children's behavioral predictions. *Child Development, 72*, 1409–1425.

Atran, S. (1990). *The cognitive foundations of natural history*. New York: Cambridge University Press.

Blackwell, L., Trzesniewski, K., & Dweck, C. S. (2007). Implicit theories of intelligence predict achievement across an adolescent transition: A longitudinal study and an intervention. *Child Development, 78*, 246–263.

Boseovski, J. J., & Lee, K. (2006). Children's use of frequency information for trait categorization and behavioral prediction. *Developmental Psychology, 42*, 500–513.

Boseovski, J. J., & Lee, K. (2008). Seeing the world through rose-colored glasses? Neglect of consensus information in young children's personality judgments. *Social Development, 17*, 399–416.

Cain, K. M., & Dweck, C. S. (1995). The relation between motivational patterns and achievement cognitions through the elementary school years. *Merrill-Palmer Quarterly, 41*, 25–52.

Cain, K. M., Heyman, G. D., & Walker, M. E. (1997a). Preschoolers' ability to make dispositional predictions within and across domains. *Social Development, 6*, 53–75.

Chiu, C., Hong, Y., & Dweck, C. S. (1997b). Lay dispositionism and implicit theories of personality. *Journal of Personality and Social Psychology, 73*, 19–30.

Choi, I., Nisbett, R. E., & Norenzayan, A. (1999). Causal attribution across cultures: Variation and universality. *Psychological Bulletin, 125*, 47–63.

Dozier, M. (1991). Functional measurement assessment of young children's ability to predict future behavior. *Child Development, 62,* 1091–1099.

Droege, K. L., & Stipek, D. J. (1993). Children's use of dispositions to predict classmates' behavior. *Developmental Psychology, 29,* 646–654.

Dweck, C. S. (1999). *Self-theories: Their role in motivation, personality, and development.* Philadelphia, PA: Psychology Press/Taylor & Francis.

Dweck, C. S., & Leggett, E. L. (1988). A social-cognitive approach to motivation and personality. *Psychological Review, 95,* 256–273.

Eder, R. A. (1990). Uncovering young children's psychological selves: Individual and developmental differences. *Child Development, 61,* 849–863.

Erdley, C. A., & Dweck, C. S. (1993). Children's implicit personality theories as predictors of their social judgments. *Child Development, 64,* 863–878.

Erdley, C. A., Cain, K. M., Loomis, C. C., Dumas-Hines, F., & Dweck, C. S. (1997). Relations among children's social goals, implicit personality theories, and responses to social failure. *Developmental Psychology, 33,* 263–272.

Feldman, N. S., & Ruble, D. N. (1988). The effect of personal relevance on psychological inference: A developmental analysis. *Child Development, 59,* 1339–1352.

Ferguson, T. J., Olthof, T., Luiten, A., & Rule, B. G. (1984). Children's use of observed behavioral frequency versus behavioral covariation in ascribing dispositions to others. *Child Development, 55,* 2094–2105.

Flavell, J. H. (1977). *Cognitive development.* Englewood Cliffs, NJ: Prentice-Hall.

Flavell, J. H., Green, F. L., & Flavell, E. R. (1989). Young children's ability to differentiate appearance-reality and Level 2 perspectives in the tactile modality. *Child Development, 60,* 201–213.

Fletcher, G. (1984). Psychology and common sense. *American Psychologist, 39*(3), 203–213.

Gao, G., Ting-Toomey, S., & Gudykunst, W. B. (1996). Chinese communication processes. In M. Bond (Ed.), *The handbook of Chinese psychology* (pp. 280–293). Hong Kong: Oxford University Press.

Gelman, S. A. (2003). *The essential child: Origins of essentialism in everyday thought.* New York: Oxford University Press.

Gelman, S. A., & Heyman, G. D. (1999). Carrot-eaters and creature-believers: The effects of lexicalization on children's inferences about social categories. *Psychological Science, 10,* 489–493.

Gelman, S. A., & Markman, E. M. (1986). Categories and induction in young children. *Cognition, 23,* 183–209.

Gelman, S. A., & Wellman, H. M. (1991). Insides and essences: Early understandings of the non-obvious. *Cognition, 38,* 213–244.

Gelman, S. A., Heyman, G. D., & Legare, C. H. (2007). Developmental changes in the coherence of essentialist beliefs about psychological characteristics. *Child Development, 78,* 757–774.

Giles, J. W. (2003). Children's essentialist beliefs about aggression. *Developmental Review, 23,* 413–443.

Giles, J. W., & Heyman, G. D. (2003). Preschoolers' beliefs about the stability of antisocial behavior: Implications for navigating social challenges. *Social Development, 12,* 182–197.

Giles, J. W., & Heyman, G. D. (2004a). Conceptions of aggression and withdrawal in early childhood. *Infant and Child Development, 13,* 407–421.

Giles, J. W., & Heyman, G. D. (2004b). When to cry over spilled milk: Young children's use of category information to guide inferences about ambiguous behavior. *Journal of Cognition and Development, 5,* 359–382.

Gnepp, J., & Chilamkurti, C. (1988). Children's use of personality attributions to predict other people's emotional and behavioral reactions. *Child Development, 59,* 743–754.

Harris, P. L., & Giménez, M. (2005). Children's acceptance of conflicting testimony: the case of death. *Journal of Cognition and Culture, 5,* 143–164.

Heller, K. A., & Berndt, T. J. (1981). Developmental changes in the formation and organization of personality attributions. *Child Development, 52,* 683–691.

Heyman, G. D. (2001). Children's interpretation of ambiguous behavior: Evidence for a "boys are bad" bias. *Social Development, 10,* 230–247.

Heyman, G. D. (2008). Talking about success: Implications for achievement motivation. *Journal of Applied Developmental Psychology, 5,* 361–370.

Heyman, G. D., & Compton, B. J. (2006). Context sensitivity in children's reasoning about ability across the elementary school years. *Developmental Science, 9,* 616–627.

Heyman, G. D., & Diesendruck, G. (2002). The Spanish ser/estar distinction in bilingual children's reasoning about human psychological characteristics. *Developmental Psychology, 38,* 407–417.

Heyman, G. D., & Dweck, C. S. (1998). Children's thinking about traits: Implications for judgments of the self and others. *Child Development, 69,* 392–403.

Heyman, G. D., & Gelman, S. A. (1998). Young children use motive information to make trait inferences. *Developmental Psychology, 34,* 310–321.

Heyman, G. D., & Gelman, S. A. (1999). The use of trait labels in making psychological inferences. *Child Development, 70,* 604–619.

Heyman, G. D., & Gelman, S. A. (2000a). Beliefs about the origins of human psychological traits. *Developmental Psychology, 36,* 663–678.

Heyman, G. D., & Gelman, S. A. (2000b). Preschool children's use of trait labels to make inductive inferences about people. *Journal of Experimental Child Psychology, 77,* 1–19.

Heyman, G. D., & Giles, J. W. (2004). Valence effects in reasoning about evaluative traits. *Merrill-Palmer Quarterly, 50,* 86–109.

Heyman, G. D., & Legare, C. H. (2005). Children's evaluation of sources of information about traits. *Developmental Psychology, 41,* 636–647.

Heyman, G.D., & Legare, C.H. (2007, October). *Noun labels and social categories.* Paper presented as part of a symposium on "Cognitive developmental perspectives on social categorization and the implications for intergroup bias" at the biennial meeting of the Cognitive Development Society in Santa Fe, New Mexico.

Heyman, G. D., Dweck, C. S., & Cain, K. M. (1992). Young children's vulnerability to self-blame and helplessness: Relationship to beliefs about goodness. *Child Development, 63,* 401–415.

Heyman, G. D., Gee, C. L., & Giles, J. W. (2003). Preschool children's reasoning about ability. *Child Development, 74,* 516–534.

Heyman, G. D., Fu, G., & Lee, K. (2007). Evaluating claims people make about themselves: The development of skepticism. *Child Development, 78,* 367–375.

Heyman, G. D., Fu, G., & Lee, K. (2008). Reasoning about the disclosure of success and failure to friends among children in the U.S. and China. *Developmental Psychology, 44,* 908–918.

Himelstein, S., Graham, S., & Weiner, B. (1991). An attributional analysis of maternal beliefs about the importance of child-rearing practices. *Child Development, 62,* 301–310.

Hirschfeld, L. A. (1995). Do children have a theory of race? *Cognition, 54,* 209–252.

Hirschfeld, L. A. (1996). *Race in the making: Cognition, culture, and the child's construction of human kinds.* Cambridge, MA: MIT Press.

Hoffner, C., & Cantor, J. (1985). Developmental differences in responses to a television character's appearance and behavior. *Developmental Psychology, 21,* 1065–1074.

Juvonen, J., & Murdock, T. B. (1995). Grade-level differences in the social value of effort: Implications for self-presentation tactics of early adolescents. *Child Development, 66,* 1694–1705.

Kalish, C. W. (2002). Essentialist to some degree: The structure of natural kind categories. *Memory & Cognition, 30,* 340–352.

Kelley, H. H. (1973). The processes of causal attribution. *American Psychologist, 28,* 107–128.

Lagattuta, K. H., & Wellman, H. M. (2001). Thinking about the past: Early knowledge about links between prior experience, thinking, and emotion. *Child Development, 72,* 82–102.

Lee, K., & Cameron, C. A. (2000). Extracting truth information from lies: The emergence of representation-expression distinction in preschool children. *Merrill-Palmer Quarterly, 40,* 1–20.

Lee, K., Cameron, C. A., Xu, F., Fu, G., & Board, J. (1997). Chinese and Canadian children's evaluations of lying and truth-telling. *Child Development, 68,* 924–934.

Lee, K., Xu, F., Fu, G., Cameron, C. A., & Chen, S. (2001). Taiwan and Mainland Chinese and Canadian children's categorization and evaluation of lie- and truth-telling: A modesty effect. *British Journal of Developmental Psychology, 19,* 525–542.

Leggett, E.L. (1985, March). *Children's entity and incremental theories of intelligence: Relationships to achievement behavior.* Paper presented at the annual meeting of the Eastern Psychological Association, Boston.

Levy, SR., & Dweck, C. S. (1999). The impact of children's static versus dynamic conceptions of people on stereotype formation. *Child Development, 70,* 1163–1180.

Lillard, A. S., & Flavell, J. H. (1990). Young children's preference for mental state versus behavioral descriptions of human action. *Child Development, 61,* 731–741.

Liu, D., Gelman, S. A., & Wellman, H. M. (2007). Components of young children's trait understanding: Behavior-to-trait inferences and trait-to-behavior predictions. *Child Development, 78,* 1543–1558.

Livesley, W. J., & Bromley, B. D. (1973). *Person perception in childhood and adolescence.* New York: Basic.

Lockhart, K. L., Chang, B., & Story, T. (2002). Young children's beliefs about the stability of traits: Protective optimism? *Child Development, 73,* 1408–1430.

Maas, E., Marecek, J., & Travers, J. R. (1978). Children's conceptions of disordered behavior. *Child Development, 49,* 146–154.

Medin, D. L. (1989). Concepts and conceptual structure. *American Psychologist, 44,* 1469–1481.

Meerum Terwogt, M., Hoeksma, J. B., & Koops, W. (1993). Common beliefs about the heredity of human characteristics. *British Journal of Experimental Psychology, 84,* 499–503.

Meltzoff, A. N. (1995). Understanding the intentions of others: Re-enactment of intended acts by 18-month-old children. *Developmental Psychology, 31,* 838–850.

Miller, J. G. (1984). Culture and the development of everyday social explanation. *Journal of Personality & Social Psychology, 46,* 961–978.

Mueller, C. M., & Dweck, C. S. (1998). Praise for intelligence can undermine children's motivation and performance. *Journal of Personality and Social Psychology, 75,* 33–52.

Newman, L. S. (1991). Why are traits inferred spontaneously? A developmental approach. *Social Cognition, 9,* 221–253.

Peevers, B. H., & Secord, P. F. (1973). Developmental changes in attribution of descriptive concepts to persons. *Journal of Personality and Social Psychology, 27,* 120–128.

Piaget, J., & Inhelder, B. (1969). *The Psychology of the child.* New York: Basic.

Pomerantz, E. M., & Saxon, J. L. (2001). Children's conceptions of ability as stable and self-evaluative processes: A longitudinal examination. *Child Development, 72,* 152–173.

Pytlik Zillig, L. M., Hemenover, S. H., & Dienstbier, R. A. (2002). What do we assess when we assess a Big 5 trait? A content analysis of the affective, behavioral and cognitive processes represented in the Big 5 personality inventories. *Personality & Social Psychology Bulletin*, *28*, 847–858.

Repacholi, B. M., & Gopnik, A. M. (1997). Early reasoning about desires: Evidence from 14- and 18-month-olds. *Developmental Psychology*, *33*, 12–21.

Rholes, W. S., & Ruble, D. N. (1984). Children's understanding of dispositional characteristics of others. *Child Development*, *55*, 550–560.

Rholes, W. S., Newman, L. S., & Ruble, D. N. (1990). Understanding self and other: Developmental and motivational aspects of perceiving others in terms of invariant dispositions. In E. T. Higgins & R. Sorrentino (Eds.), *Handbook of motivation and cognition: Foundations of social behavior* (Vol. II, pp. 369–407). New York: Guilford Press.

Rotenberg, K. J. (1982). Development of character constancy of self and other. *Child Development*, *53*, 505–515.

Ruble, D. N., & Dweck, C. S. (1995). Self-conceptions, person conceptions and their development. In N. Eisenberg (Ed.), *Review of personality and social psychology: Social development* (Vol. 15, pp. 109–139). Thousand Oaks, CA: Sage.

Ruble, D. N., Eisenberg, R. N., & Higgins, E. (1994). Developmental changes in achievement evaluation: Motivational implications of self-other differences. *Child Development*, *65*, 1095–1110.

Sapp, F., Lee, K., & Muir, D. (2000). Three-year-olds' difficulty with the appearance-reality distinction: Is it real or apparent? *Developmental Psychology*, *36*, 547–560.

Schuster, B., Ruble, D., & Weinert, F. (1998). Causal inferences and the positivity bias in children: The role of the covariation principle. *Child Development*, *69*, 1577–1596.

Sera, M. D., Bales, D. W., & del Castillo Pintado, J. (1997). Ser helps Spanish speakers identify "real" properties. *Child Development*, *68*, 820–831.

Sperber, D. (1996). *Explaining culture: A naturalistic approach*. Cambridge, MA: Blackwell Publishers.

Stipek, D. J., & Daniels, D. H. (1988). Declining perceptions of competence: A consequence of changes in the child or in the educational environment? *Journal of Educational Psychology*, *80*, 352–356.

Stipek, D. J., & Daniels, D. H. (1990). Children's use of dispositional attributions in predicting the performance and behavior of classmates. *Journal of Applied Developmental Psychology*, *11*, 13–28.

Stipek, D. J., & Mac Iver, D. J. (1989). Developmental change in children's assessment of intellectual competence. *Child Development*, *60*, 521–538.

Stipek, D. J., & Tannatt, L. M. (1984). Children's judgments of their own and their peers' academic competence. *Journal of Educational Psychology*, *76*, 75–84.

Taylor, M. G. (1996). The development of children's beliefs about social and biological aspects of gender differences. *Child Development*, *67*, 1555–1571.

Waxman, S. R. (1999). The dubbing ceremony revisited: Object naming and categorization in infancy and early childhood. In D. L. Medin & S. Atran (Eds.), *Folkbiology* (pp. 233–284). Cambridge, MA: MIT Press.

Wellman, H.M., & Gelman, S.A. (1998). Knowledge acquisition in foundational domains. In W. Damon (Ed.), and D. Kuhn & R.S. Siegler (Vol. Eds.), *Handbook of child psychology: Volume 2, Cognition, perception, and language*. (pp. 523–573). New York: Wiley.

Wellman, H. M., Cross, D., & Watson, J. (2001). Meta-analysis of theory-of-mind development: The truth about false belief. *Child Development*, *72*, 655–684.

Wilson, T. D., & Linville, P. W. (1985). Improving the performance of college freshmen with attributional techniques. *Journal of Personality and Social Psychology*, *49*, 287–293.

Wood, R., & Bandura, A. (1989). Impact of conceptions of ability on self-regulatory mechanisms and complex decision making. *Journal of Personality and Social Psychology, 56*, 407–415.

Yuill, N. (1992). Children's conception of personality traits. *Human Development, 35*, 265–279.

Yuill, N. (1997a). Children's understanding of traits. In S. Hala (Ed.), *The development of social cognition* (pp. 273–295). East Sussex, UK: Psychology Press.

Yuill, N. (1997b). English children as personality theorists: Accounts of the modifiability, development, and origin of traits. *Genetic, social, and general psychology monographs, 123*, 5–26.

Yuill, N., & Pearson, A. (1998). The development of bases for trait attribution: Children's understanding of traits as causal mechanisms based on desire. *Developmental Psychology, 34*, 574–586.

Yussen, S. R., & Kane, P. T. (1985). Children's conception of intelligence. In S. R. Yussen (Ed.), *The growth of reflection in children* (pp. 207–241). Orlando, FL: Academic Press.

THE DEVELOPMENT OF AUTOBIOGRAPHICAL MEMORY: ORIGINS AND CONSEQUENCES

Elaine Reese

PSYCHOLOGY DEPARTMENT, UNIVERSITY OF OTAGO, DUNEDIN, NZ 9054,
NEW ZEALAND

I. The Development of Autobiographical Memory: Origins and Consequences

Our memories lend a sense of continuity to our present self. Like a trail marking our steps through life, our memories stretch backward in time to childhood. The memories are closer together and more visible at some points along the trail, sparser and fainter at others, and they never lead back to the very beginning of our journey. Nevertheless, the existence of these memories makes us feel like essentially the same person through time (James, 1890/1950).

145

Advances in Child Development and Behavior
Patricia Bauer : Editor

How do autobiographical memories develop from early childhood to adulthood? What forces shape their existence, their vividness, and their durability? Why are memories from some life periods less frequent than are memories from other life periods? Finally, of what use is autobiographical memory? Do autobiographical memories make us smarter, happier, and more successful?

In this chapter, I first offer an overview of the milestones in autobiographical memory development from infancy to adolescence. Then I present contemporary theories of autobiographical memory and evaluate the evidence for those theories. Finally, I consider the value of autobiographical memory in children's and adolescents' everyday lives. I argue that autobiographical memory evolves gradually from the nonverbal memories of infants to the life stories of adolescents. Autobiographical memory arises from a complex interaction among children's cognitive, linguistic, and socioemotional skills and the way that adults talk with them about the past. I conclude that autobiographical memory appears to have positive spinoffs for social and emotional development in childhood and adolescence, but additional research needs to be conducted to confirm these benefits.

II. The Growth of Autobiographical Memory from Infancy to Adolescence

A. MEMORY IN INFANCY

1. Nonverbal Memory

Even infants display evidence of long-term memory (see Table I for memory milestones). In deferred imitation paradigms, an experimenter demonstrates to the infant target actions with novel objects, and then after a delay allows the infant to manipulate the objects. Infants as young as 6 months demonstrate long-term memory: infants in experimental conditions produce significantly more target actions after a 24-hour delay than do infants in control conditions, who saw the objects one day earlier but not the target actions (Barr, Dowden, & Hayne, 1996; Collie & Hayne, 1999). At 6 months, however, infants' long-term memory is extremely specific and forgetting is rapid. Even when 6-month-olds demonstrate immediate memory for an action, they do not always retain that memory over 24 hours (Herbert, Gross, & Hayne, 2006). Six-month-olds must view twice the number of demonstrations of the target action as 12-month-olds to

Table I

Milestones in the Development of Autobiographical Memory

Memory accomplishment	Age at earliest occurrence	Evidence
Long-term (24-hour) nonverbal event recall	6 months	Barr *et al.* (1996) Collie and Hayne (1999)
Ordered long-term nonverbal event recall	9–10 months	Carver and Bauer (1999, 2001)
Verbal reference to a past event or absent object	15–17 months	Reese (1999) Sachs (1983)
Initiates past event talk with others	18 months for a verbal reference ("Hand. Door")	Reese (1999)
	27 months for a true conversation ("Do you remember ...?")	Hudson (1991)
Verbal reference to a preverbal event	22 months	Morris and Baker-Ward (2007) Peterson and Rideout (1998)
Provides an understandable account of a past event to naïve listener	3 to 3 1/2 years	Fivush, Haden, and Adam (1995) Peterson & McCabe (1983)
Provides a full narrative account of a past event	6 years	Peterson and McCabe (1983)
Responds appropriately to prompt for life story	8–9 years	Bohn and Berntsen (2008) Habermas and de Silveira (2008)
Integrates life story and autobiographical narratives with respect to time and place	12 years	Habermas and de Silveira (2008)
Projects life story into future	14 years	Bohn and Berntsen (2008)
Life story is coherent and thematic	16–20 years	Habermas and de Silveira (2008)

retain the memory (Barr *et al.*, 1996), and at best, 6-month-olds only tolerate a 24-hour delay (Barr, Vieira, & Rovee-Collier, 2001). By 9 months, infants can retain the memory of a novel event for as long as 4 weeks, and some infants can even reproduce the correct sequence of actions from a two-step event (Carver & Bauer, 1999). By 10–16 months, most infants are capable of ordered recall and can retain memories of novel actions for several months (Barr & Hayne, 2000; Bauer *et al.*, 2000; Carver & Bauer, 2001; Klein & Meltzoff, 1999; Meltzoff, 1995). It is important to note that a similar pattern of results emerges when other nonverbal memory tasks are used (see Hayne, 2004 for a review).

These maximum retention intervals in deferred imitation paradigms are plastic at each age, depending on the events to be remembered, and upon the presence of "reminders" of the original event. A reminder can consist of a part of the original event (e.g., an object) that is displayed to the infant at different points before the test. Reminders dramatically extend memories during the first two years of life (e.g., Barr, Rovee-Collier, & Campanella, 2005; Bauer *et al.*, 2001; Carver & Bauer, 1999; Sheffield & Hudson, 2006). The memory test itself acts as a full reminder of the event. At 6 months, infants who had the opportunity to retrieve an event 4 times after exposure (at 1, 10, 30, and 60 days after the event) still demonstrated memory of the target action 2½ months after exposure (Barr *et al.*, 2005). These retrieval opportunities, if timed near the end of the normal retention period, strengthen the memory exponentially. For instance, normally a 6-month-old infant would only retain a novel event for 24 hours, but if allowed to retrieve the event, their memory then extends to 10 days past the original exposure.

These early memory feats are impressive, yet are these memories autobiographical? Tulving (1985, 2002) proposed that for a memory to count as episodic, and all autobiographical memories are episodic, the memory must contain information about the "what," "where," and "when" of the event. Remembering must also be accompanied by a sense of recollection, or of being transported back in time to the original event. Certainly infants hold information about the "what" in their memories or they would not be able to produce actions from the target events. Their memories may also contain information about the "where" in the sense that the memories are closely tied to their original context. If any aspect of the context is changed (e.g., encoding is at home and test is at laboratory), younger infants' memory is disrupted. By the second year of life, toddlers' memories are more robust and remain even when the test takes place in a different location to the encoding phase (Hayne, Boniface, & Barr, 2000). But it is not until children begin to talk that we can ask them more directly about where and when the event took place. The ability to verbalize a memory may also imply some level of conscious awareness (Bauer, 2008; Reese, 1999, 2002a).

A final critical element of an autobiographical memory is a sense of embodiment that the experience happened to someone, and specifically to *me*. Howe and Courage (1993) argued that autobiographical memories are impossible before the advent of a sense of self, as measured in the mirror test of visual recognition. In the standard mirror test (Lewis & Brooks-Gunn, 1979), a researcher discreetly marks a child's nose with rouge, waits several minutes to ensure that the child does not feel the mark, and then places the child in front of a mirror. Children are considered to pass the mirror test if they engage in mark-directed behavior (i.e., touching their nose). Using this criterion, nearly all children pass the mirror test between 18 and 24 months of age (Lewis & Brooks-Gunn, 1979; Priel & de Schonen, 1986; but see Keller *et al.*, 2005). Mirror recognition is followed a few months later by children's use of personal pronouns (Courage, Edison, & Howe, 2004). Indeed, toddlers who pass the mirror test earlier show more advanced nonverbal memory skills in deferred imitation (Prudhomme, 2005) and in a hide-and-seek memory task (Howe, Courage, & Edison, 2003). These studies do not necessarily show that children with better visual self-recognition skills are specifically remembering more self-relevant or autobiographical information, however. Children with advanced self-recognition skills may simply be more mature neurocognitively, and as a consequence are advanced on a number of cognitive tasks (see Povinelli, 2001).

In the 20th century, knowledge of the neurological underpinnings of memory development was limited. Lesion research with primates isolated a later-developing memory system based on medial-temporal structures (see Alvarado & Bachevalier, 2000, for a review). These later developing structures supported declarative or explicit memory for events and facts (Squire, 1992). Most researchers agree that deferred imitation is an instance of declarative memory. Imitation paradigms have also been used to draw inferences about the development of underlying neurological structures. Because adults with temporal lobe amnesia cannot imitate after a delay (McDonough *et al.*, 1995), the inference is that deferred imitation depends upon intact medial-temporal structures. Because infants can perform deferred imitation from 6 months (e.g., Barr *et al.*, 1996), the analogous inference is that medial-temporal structures must be developed enough by 6 months to support fledgling long-term declarative memory (Hayne, 2004).

In the 21st century, an exciting new source of evidence for the neurology of memory development in infancy became possible with the use of noninvasive functional-imaging techniques (event-related potentials or ERP; e.g., Bauer *et al.*, 2003a; see Bauer, 2007a, 2007b, 2008 for reviews). This technique identifies patterns of electrical activity in the brain in response to a specific stimulus, but is unable to locate precisely the neural sources of stimulation (Bauer *et al.*, 2006). Event-related potentials are recorded during recognition tests as infants view old and new event sequences either immediately after exposure (accessing encoding) or two days to one week later. Memories themselves go through a developmental process that begins at encoding. Over the next few days or even weeks, the memory is consolidated as it integrates with existing knowledge structures, and then is stored in a more stable form awaiting retrieval (Howe, 2000). Of course, as the Barr *et al.* (2005) study illustrates, the act of retrieval itself can activate a new cycle of consolidation and storage.

In ERP studies using deferred imitation, the ERP responses of infants who later demonstrate long-term recall for an event are compared to the ERP responses of infants who did not demonstrate long-term recall. Although an early ERP study with 9-month-olds implicated consolidation, storage, and retrieval differences as the main contributors to long-term memory development in infancy (e.g., Bauer *et al.*, 2003a), a later study with a broader age range (9–10 months) also pointed to encoding as a major contributor to age-related increases in the durability of memories (Bauer *et al.*, 2006). Bauer (2008) concluded that developments in encoding and consolidation, as opposed to storage and retrieval, are the primary reasons for increased recall with age in the infancy period. Older infants encode events faster and more deeply than do younger infants. Moreover, older infants retain events better over 48 hours than do younger infants. Because consolidation of a memory is proposed to take at least several days, a significant portion of the age-related differences in long-term retrieval is thus due to encoding and consolidation (cf. Richmond & Nelson, 2007).

The proposal that advances in encoding and consolidation are primarily responsible for memory development in infancy is controversial. Other theories maintain that age-related differences in long-term memory are primarily due to developments in storage and retrieval (e.g., Hayne, 2004; Liston & Kagan, 2002), and the weight of the evidence still favors the retrieval hypothesis. These "forgetting" theories are based mainly on behavioral data and animal models, however, not on brain-imaging techniques. Bauer (2008) proposed that over the course of infancy and early childhood, a gradual shift may occur such that storage and retrieval differences then account for more variance in the durability of memories than do encoding and consolidation. Future research employing brain-imaging techniques with older children is needed to test this theory, given the continued development past infancy of the dentate gyrus and prefrontal cortex (Goldman-Rakic, 1987), both of which are implicated in storage and retrieval processes (Bauer, 2008; Richmond & Nelson, 2007).

Will brain-imaging research, however, offer insight into the seemingly intractable problem of whether infants and toddlers experience a sense of recollection during remembering?

2. Verbal Memory

Another critical accomplishment in the growth of autobiographical memory in the second year of life is the beginning of children's verbal references to the past (see Table I; cf. Reese, 2002a, for a review). I propose that when, unprompted, children refer verbally to the past, they are mentally re-experiencing a previous event. Most children begin to talk about the past at around 1½ years (Fenson *et al.*, 1993; Hudson, 1991; Nelson & Ross, 1980; Reese, 1999; Sachs, 1983). At first, these verbal memories comprise one or two words referring to recently completed actions or to absent objects. Soon after, children refer to events experienced several days or even weeks in the past. Sometimes these verbal memories are in response to parents' questions, but children also initiate these verbal references to the past with increasing frequency in the second and third year of life. At first, these memory initiations are primitive. For instance, in Reese (1999), an 18-month-old child attempted to tell his uncle about pinching his hand in a door several days earlier by pointing to his hand and saying "Hand" and then pointing to the door and saying "Door."

Memory talk also features in young children's self-directed speech. One toddler's presleep monologues about events from the day offer some insights. Nelson (1989) recorded Emily's night-time talk to herself in her crib several times a week from age 21 to 36 months. Emily referred to specific memories more often in her night-time monologues than in her daytime dialogues with others. Nelson argued that Emily showed evidence of episodic memory at age 2 through her use of temporal terms that correctly distinguished past from future events (*yesterday, tomorrow morning, and then, after*). By age 2 to 2½ years, children independently initiate conversations about past events with adults using the conventional opener "Do you remember ...?" (Hudson, 1991).

A vital question for the study of autobiographical memory development is whether infants' nonverbal memories can ultimately be translated into language and expressed verbally. If so, the nonverbal memories of infancy could evolve in a continuous fashion into the autobiographical memories of early childhood. Research on this question has produced evidence for both sides. For example, in an experimental study, preschool children described their memories of a "magic shrinking machine" using only words that had been in their productive vocabularies at the time of encoding at ages 2–3 years (Simcock & Hayne, 2002). Research with children who experienced a trauma that necessitated a visit to the emergency room largely concurs that preverbal memories do not cross the language barrier. Only children who were over 20 months at the time of the trauma, and who produced a verbal memory soon after the event, were able to produce a complete verbal memory of the trauma in the long term (Peterson & Rideout, 1998). In a similar vein, when children aged 13–20 months participated in deferred imitation tests, and then at age 3 years were questioned about those events, children younger than 20 months at the time of the event did not produce any verbal recall (Bauer *et al.*, 2004). Unlike the younger children, those who were 20 months at encoding were later able to verbally access their memories even with a change in context (from lab to home) from encoding to test. Taken together, this evidence suggests that only children who are older and already able to express their memories through language at encoding are able to maintain these memories verbally in the long term.

Several important pieces of evidence, however, do not fit this pattern. In the Peterson and Rideout (1998) study, 7 of the 12 children who were below 19 months at the time of the trauma later produced at least some verbal recall of the event. This exception to the general pattern suggests that it may be possible for preverbal experiences to be translated later into language, but due to the naturalistic conditions of this study, it is also possible that the children were repeating information that they had gained through subsequent conversations. In a more controlled experimental study, Cheatham and Bauer (2005) analyzed the verbal recall at 3 years of children who had participated in imitation studies at either 16 or 20 months of age, and who had participated in 2 retrieval tests in the interim. The best predictor of children's ability to produce verbal recall at 3 years was their verbal recall at one of the later tests, not their language or age at the time of encoding, implying that memories could later be expressed using language acquired after the experience. Note that in this study, children's task-specific vocabulary at encoding or retrieval was not assessed, so it is possible, although unlikely, that at encoding these children already possessed the words they later used to describe the events.

In the most fine-grained analysis of this question to date, Morris and Baker-Ward (2007) tracked toddlers' comprehension and production of specific color words before and after a novel bubble machine event. Between the event and the memory test, researchers attempted to teach children the new color words from the event. Of the 31 toddlers who did not comprehend or produce the color words at exposure, but who acquired one or more of the color words after the event, a small but significant percentage (29%) were able to use those new words in their later verbal memories of the bubble machine two months later. Thus, memories can cross the verbal divide, but only under highly supportive conditions (cf. Bauer & Wewerka, 1995). Note that the children were taught the new color words close in time to the experience. Perhaps the ability to translate a preverbal experience into language depends upon acquiring the words to describe the experience fairly close in time to encoding. If the nonverbal memory trace is still vivid when the new words are learned, the nonverbal memory may integrate more readily with language during consolidation, akin to a time-window effect for maintaining nonverbal memories (see Barr *et al.*, 2005). Even once verbal recall of preverbal memories is possible, however, preschool children express only a fraction of their memories through language (Simcock & Hayne, 2003). Much more is left unsaid than said at this age.

3. Summary of Infant Memory

Infants are capable of long-term memory from 6 months of age, but their ability to encode, consolidate, store, and retrieve memories at this young age is limited. Brain-imaging research pinpoints changes in the encoding and consolidation of memories as undergoing especially rapid development at around 9–10 months of age. Memory capacity then appears to develop relatively continuously through the second year of life. Verbal memory begins to develop in the second year of life but lags behind children's general language development. Two-year-olds' verbal memories contain references to the self as well as to the "what," "where," and "when" of the event. By the end of the second year of life, toddlers are capable of translating at least some of their preverbal memories into language. It is an open question as to whether these early memories are already, or can later become, autobiographical.

B. AUTOBIOGRAPHICAL MEMORY IN THE PRESCHOOL YEARS

By 3 to 3½ of age, verbal memory has developed steadily such that children can now tell an understandable story about an event they experienced up to 1 year in the past to an adult who was not present at the event (see Table I; Fivush *et al.*, 1995; Peterson & McCabe, 1983). Existing studies of children's nonverbal memory during this period also demonstrate continued advances in children's encoding and retrieval of events (e.g., Fivush, Kuebli, & Clubb, 1992; Morgan & Hayne, 2007; Simcock &

Table II

A Child's (C) Typical Past Event Narrative with a Researcher (R) at 40 Months

R:	Cos do you know what else your Mum said you did?
R:	She said that you went in an earthquake house
C:	And a girl went in th- a table
R:	A table, yeah?
C:	Yeah, and she didn't shakes and she didn't go in the kitchen wh- when everything was shaking in there
R:	Ooh
C:	She crept hideded outside
R:	Yeah?
C:	Yeah
R:	Ohh. And what else happened when you went to see the earthquake house?
C:	And, there was a robot
R:	A robot?
C:	The robot did that
R:	Oh the r-, mmm?
C:	And then it was finished
R:	And it was finished?
C:	Yeah
R:	Oh right
C:	Then someone else went in

Hayne, 2003). Given preschoolers' facility with verbal recall, though, the most popular method of assessing children's memory at these ages is through language.

Preschoolers' verbal recall, however, is by no means fully developed. At best, preschool children can tell a listener some of the "what," a bit of the "where" and "when," and perhaps even why the event was interesting or relevant. Preschoolers still provide only limited information about time and place in their autobiographical narratives, and they have difficulty narrating the order in which events occurred (Reese *et al.*, 2009). Table II contains an example of a typical 3-year-old's autobiographical narrative. Although the child in this example tells a relatively understandable account of the past event to the naïve listener, she still needs prompts to produce her account, and her recall is somewhat disjointed.

Cultural differences in children's autobiographical narratives in their native language begin to emerge in the preschool period (see Reese *et al.*, 2009, for a review). Compared to European American children, Chinese children tell shorter stories of the past and offer fewer memories of specific events, instead preferring to talk about general past occurrences (e.g., *My mom told me stories every night*; Wang, 2004, p. 6). In contrast, African-American children's autobiographical narratives are already in classic form with a beginning, middle, high point, and resolution by age 6–7 years (Champion, Seymour, & Camarata, 1995), whereas Native American and Japanese children's event narratives are still not in classic form by age 9 (Minami, 1996; Pesco & Crago, 1996). Hispanic American children's event narratives in English tend to be shorter and less detailed than European American children's event narratives, regardless of whether English is their first or second language (Leyva *et al.*, 2008; McCabe & Bliss, 2003). These differences appear to reflect children's acquisition of the conventional narrative forms within the culture (see Minami, 1996). Cultural differences in autobiographical narratives are especially intriguing given the finding that adults in Asian cultures have later memories from early childhood compared to adults from European cultures (e.g., Mullen, 1994), indicating that narrative form is an important factor in the durability of memories.

Another intriguing parallel with the adult memory literature is the emergence of a female advantage in autobiographical narratives during the preschool period, in line with the growing evidence in adult studies that women have an episodic memory advantage over men (e.g., Bauer, Stennes, & Haight, 2003b; Pillemer *et al.*, 2003). In some but certainly not all studies with preschoolers, girls produce longer and richer autobiographical narratives than do boys (e.g., Reese & Fivush, 1993), and these differences are not completely accounted for by a linguistic advantage for girls. For instance, in a longitudinal study with New Zealand children, girls had a linguistic advantage over boys in the early preschool period, but were not yet displaying advanced autobiographical memory skills. By the end of the preschool period at age 5 ½, girls no longer had a linguistic advantage over boys, but girls recalled both recent and distant past events more vividly and accurately than did boys (Cleveland & Reese, 2008; Figure 1). These gender differences in autobiographical memory may arise from different reminiscing environments for girls and boys (see Reese & Fivush, 1993). I address this argument with additional evidence in later sections.

Are these cultural, gender, and age differences in narrative an aspect of autobiographical memory development, or simply of language development? Along with others, I argue that narrative molds memories at all phases of the memory-making process, from encoding to consolidation and storage to expression (Bauer, 2007b; Fivush, Haden, & Reese, 1996; Nelson, 1996; Ornstein, Haden, & Elischberger, 2006; Reese *et al.*, 2009). At the time of the actual encoding of an event and during the consolidation phase, the narrative templates to which the child has access shape his or her understanding of the event taking place. Memories in narrative form are more likely to survive than memories in nonnarrative

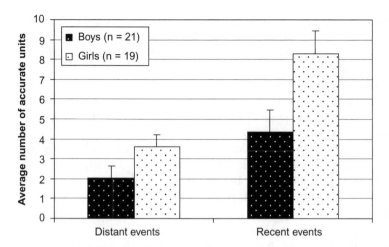

Fig. 1. Average number of accurate units of information boys and girls recalled at age 5 ½ for distant and recent events (from Cleveland & Reese, 2008, Figure 5).

form (Mandler & Johnson, 1977). Later, at retrieval, narrative is often the form in which the memory is expressed (Peterson & McCabe, 1983; e.g., "Guess what? One time I got stung by a bee ..."). Narrative also provides a vehicle for telling others why an event was interesting or important in our lives. In our everyday lives, we use memory not to showcase our prodigious and accurate knowledge of the past, but to entertain others and to divulge experiences that have shaped who we are (Thorne, 2000).

Acknowledging that autobiographical memory is not just about the medium but also about the message, what aspects of events are memorable for preschoolers? Nelson (1989) reported that 2-year-old Emily talked about aspects of her life that are mundane by adult standards, such as going to get diapers, not the birth of her baby brother. Young preschoolers' relative emphasis on the mundane is echoed in larger studies. In one study, mothers kept diary records of their 2-year-old children's spontaneous verbal references to the past (Reese, 1999). For the most part, the events that children brought up on their own were mundane by adults' standards. For instance, one child talked about his memory of throwing a pair of dice up in the air, not about going to a wildlife park, which he experienced at around the same time. Fivush and Hamond (1990) noted that at age 2½, children talked about mundane aspects of novel events, such as the following account of a camping trip: "And then we waked up and eat dinner. First we eat dinner, then go to bed, and then wake up and eat breakfast" (p. 231). By the older preschool years, this

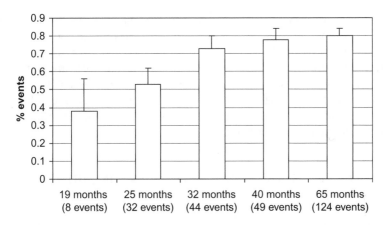

Fig. 2. Percentage of events for which 5½-year-olds recalled any accurate information as a function of time of original conversation (from Cleveland & Reese, 2008, Figure 3).

emphasis on the mundane has waned. At age 4 years, the same children in Fivush and Hamond's study talked instead about new and distinctive aspects of the same events.

Given the mundane focus and primitive narrative forms of young preschoolers' memories, how many of these verbal memories will survive? Childhood amnesia is the phenomenon by which adults cannot remember, on average, any experiences before age 3 or 4 (Dudycha & Dudycha, 1933). Has this phenomenon already begun by the end of early childhood? Cleveland and Reese (2008) tracked the retention and demise of children's verbal memories longitudinally from 1 ½ to 5 ½ years of age. Children verbally recalled at least one unit of accurate information from more than 75% of the events they were questioned about that occurred after age 2, but fewer than half of the memories of events from before age 2 were retained verbally with any accuracy to the end of preschool (Figure 2). The events tracked were all discussed with some frequency within the family, however, so it is not possible to know whether children directly recalled the original experiences or were repeating information gained from subsequent conversations. A large body of research shows that during preschool, children are especially prone to changing their memories in response to misinformation provided by an adult (see Bruck & Ceci, 1999, for a review). The children in the Cleveland and Reese study participated in everyday conversations about the past in which adults did not (at least knowingly) mislead them. Under these supportive conditions, at least some events from very early childhood are still verbally accessible by the end of preschool.

Summary of preschoolers' autobiographical memory. In the preschool years, children can produce an understandable account of a past event to others, but their autobiographical narratives grow closer to the classic narrative form of the culture throughout this period. Girls are starting to show an advantage over boys in their autobiographical memory, although this advantage is not evident across every sample. By age 5, children can verbally recall at least some events from early childhood, but primarily for events that occurred after age 2.

C. AUTOBIOGRAPHICAL MEMORY IN MIDDLE CHILDHOOD

Children's autobiographical memories continue to develop in the school years, although research is sparser on development during this period (see Table I). The preferred methodology for studying autobiographical memory in middle childhood is verbal recall. Continued development is especially evident in children's provision of the *where, when*, and *why* of events into adolescence (Reese *et al.*, 2009). For instance, children now spontaneously provide some information about the time and place of events, although provision of specific information about time and place does not occur until adolescence (Reese *et al.*, 2009). At the beginning of middle childhood, only about half of children's event propositions are chronologically ordered. By adolescence, more than 75% of their event propositions are chronologically ordered. Surprisingly, children's provision of "what" information about recent past events does not increase significantly during middle childhood (van Abbema & Bauer, 2005), although children at this age provide more core features, details, and internal states than they did in early childhood for the same events (see Fivush *et al.*, 2004). Over middle childhood and early adolescence, an increasingly higher proportion of children's autobiographical narratives fit Tulving's (1985, 2002) criteria for a strictly episodic memory, with specific information provided about time, place, and event details (Piolino *et al.*, 2007). Children also need less prompting to recall a specific past event over this period (Piolino *et al.*, 2007).

Surprisingly, the accuracy of children's memory for the time of an event bears little or no relation to the volume of accurate memory they provide about the event (Friedman & Lyon, 2005). Children, like adults (Friedman, 2004), can produce a great deal of accurate information about an event without being able to date the event with precision. Although Tulving (1985, 2002) proposed that knowledge of the "when" of an event is a prerequisite for episodic memory, a less stringent criterion may be in order. Friedman argued that even adults do not directly remember the date and time of most past events; instead, they reconstruct the time of an event from other available information. Perhaps the most important criteria for episodic memory are the knowledge of what happened and that the event happened *to me*. In other words, I must know that I experienced a specific event at a single point in time, but I do not need to accurately locate that event in time for the memory to be episodic. Because conventional time knowledge develops dramatically over middle childhood (Friedman, 2003), it will be important to ascertain in future research the relation between children's developing time knowledge and their ability to date events accurately.

Research on autobiographical memory in middle childhood has not yet explored cultural differences, and most of the studies have not tested (or at least have not reported testing) for gender differences. When a gender difference is reported, however, it is in the direction of girls providing greater recall than boys (e.g., Fivush & Schwarzmueller, 1998). For instance, Bohn and Berntsen (2008) found strong evidence of a female advantage in the length and coherence of autobiographical narratives in a sample of 9- to 15-year-old Danish children. Habermas and de Silveira (2008) also reported limited evidence of a female advantage in the coherence of German 8-year-olds' life stories. By age 5½, girls and boys differed more dramatically in their memories for recent than distant past events (Cleveland & Reese, 2008). Adult women also reported more internal states and emotions in their memories from after age 7 years than from before age 7 (Bauer *et al.*, 2003b), suggesting a widening of the gender gap in autobiographical memory by the end of early childhood. Several researchers have proposed that differences in the way parents, especially mothers, reminisce with daughters and sons are responsible for these increasing differences between girls' and boys' memories. Mothers and fathers are more elaborative in their past event talk with their young daughters than with their sons (Reese & Fivush, 1993). Peterson and Roberts (2003) found parallels between the independent autobiographical narratives of the same event by mothers and their 8- to 13-year-old daughters on measures of length, detail, and narrative quality, but no parallels in autobiographical narratives were found between fathers and their children, between mothers and their sons, or between mothers and their younger children.

By middle childhood, how many events from early childhood are still verbally accessible? Retrospective research on this question used a procedure adapted from adult memory studies, in which 7- to 10-year-old children produced and dated memories in response to cue words (Bauer *et al.*, 2007). For instance, a researcher gave children the cue word "pencil" and asked children to recall a specific memory from the past involving a pencil. A high proportion of the children's memories came from the recent past, similar to studies with adults. However, the memory distributions for children were best fit by an exponential forgetting function instead of the power function obtained in adult studies. Early memories were not yet stable at this age; children were in still the midst of forgetting their early childhood experiences. In another retrospective study, Peterson, Grant, and Boland (2005) asked children aged 6–20 years to provide their earliest memory. The 6- to 9-year-olds' earliest memory was from 36 months on average, whereas the 10- to 20-year-olds' earliest memory was from 40 months or older on average. By age 10, children's earliest memory was stable and, in line with research with adults, occurred at an average age of approximately 3½.

In a prospective memory study, van Abbema and Bauer (2005) tracked 7- to 9-year-old children's memory for events that occurred from age 3. This study showed a linear decrease in memory with age such that 7-year-olds recalled only 60% of events from age 3 that they had previously remembered, and 9-year-olds recalled only 34% of previously remembered events from age 3 (van Abbema & Bauer, 2005). In keeping with this pattern, Cleveland and Reese (2008; see Figure 2) found that 5½-year-olds could remember approximately 75% of events originally experienced at age 3. In another prospective study, Fivush and Schwarzmueller (1998) found that 8-year-olds remembered up to 75% of previously remembered events from age 3 but recalled still higher percentages of events from later ages (88% from age 4 and 95% from age 6). Taken together, these studies indicate that childhood amnesia is progressing in earnest during middle childhood.

Summary of autobiographical memory in middle childhood. Very little autobiographical memory research has focused on this age period, so knowledge is limited. The existing evidence suggests continued growth in children's ability to provide details of past events in their autobiographical narratives and to locate past events in time and place. Thus, an increasing number of children's autobiographical narratives fit the criteria for episodic memories and indicate true recollection. The ability to chronologically order an autobiographical narrative is also achieved during this period. Like adults, children at this age can produce accurate memories and can date those memories accurately (Bauer *et al.*, 2007). Children's ability to date an event accurately, however, does not appear to depend on the volume of their accurate memory for that event (Friedman & Lyon, 2005).Thus, memory for the time and the content of an event are independent and probably involve different processes. Little is known about continued cultural differences in autobiographical narratives in this period, but the limited evidence available suggests that differences between girls' and boys' autobiographical narratives continue to widen in middle childhood. Children are rapidly forgetting their earliest experiences during middle childhood.

D. AUTOBIOGRAPHICAL MEMORY IN ADOLESCENCE

It is in adolescence that the pinnacle of autobiographical memory, the life story, is born. The life story *is* autobiography. The life story is based on one's memory for specific events, but goes beyond the single autobiographical narratives discussed so far. In the life story, an individual is able to tell a story of their whole life, incorporating what they remember with what they simply know about their lives, and integrating those memories and stories thematically. Life stories are an essential element of personality in adults (McAdams, 1996, 2006).

The youngest age at which experimenters have tried to elicit whole life stories from children is 8 years. Habermas and de Silveira (2008) used a structured interview procedure with 8- to 20-year-olds in which participants first nominated the 7 most important events from their lives. Then the interviewer prompted them to tell a story of their whole lives, including the preselected events. Even the 8-year-old children could tell a story of their whole lives when prompted in this fashion, in contrast to previous reports that children of this age were unable to respond at all or gave only a single event narrative (see Habermas & Bluck, 2000). However, the youngest children's life stories lacked critical elements. For instance, 8-year-olds rarely posited causal or temporal connections across life events and did not show insight into the meaning of life events for understanding the self. Twelve-year-olds displayed better causal and temporal links across events and showed some insight into those events, but did not demonstrate full understanding of life's turning points or the consequences of events. Sixteen-year-olds were more advanced in their understanding of life events, but the life story continued to develop in terms of temporal/causal understanding and insight into young adulthood at age 20. Thus, although 8-year-olds can tell a life story, it is not until adolescence that they freely provide information about the meaning of personally experienced events for the self-concept or for their futures, and these insights continue to develop into young adulthood (see Table I).

The life story clearly encompasses more than the ability to narrate single events, which children have mastered by middle childhood. Disparate past events must be connected in thematic ways to produce a life story as opposed to an unconnected series of event narratives. Another critical element in the life story is knowledge of the typical life course, represented in *life scripts*, which differ across cultures. Which major events, such as getting married, are expected to happen in a life, and when in that life are those events expected to occur? Bohn and Berntsen (2008) compared 9- to 15-year-old children's written narratives of single events and life stories in relation to their understanding of life scripts. To assess life scripts, children were asked to imagine a newborn child and to nominate the 10 most important events that would happen in that child's life. Children's life scripts were compared to a prototypical life script provided by adults. As in Habermas and de Silveira (2008), most (72%) of even the youngest children were able to complete the life story task by providing more than a single-event narrative, but the youngest children wrote more coherent narratives about single events than about the life story. From 11 years onwards, adolescents' life stories were more likely to start at birth, whereas most of the younger children's life stories began at some point after birth, suggesting an inability to integrate known and remembered events in middle childhood. Not until mid-adolescence were most participants able to project their lives into the future. The ability to imagine a future for oneself that follows in a logical and coherent manner from one's past is one of the hallmarks of a mature life story (McAdams, 1996). Most importantly, the coherence of life stories (as defined by the use of a classic narrative structure), but not the coherence of single-event narratives, was correlated with children's and adolescents' understanding of life scripts. A mature life story involves more than being able to connect events; life stories also entail cultural knowledge about which events should be considered significant.

In adolescence, then, major autobiographical developments occur in the life story. Personally remembered events are integrated with cultural and familial knowledge about life events into a coherent autobiography (see Reese & Fivush, 2008). Contrary to assertions that a life story is not possible until mid-adolescence (Habermas & Bluck, 2000), it appears that the rudiments of a life story are present by middle childhood (Bohn & Berntsen, 2008; Habermas & de Silveira, 2008). The life story matures dramatically in structure and insight over early and mid-adolescence, however, and continues to develop into young adulthood.

By the end of adolescence, how much is remembered of one's earliest experiences? The bulk of the research on childhood amnesia has been conducted with young adults at around age 20 (see Jack & Hayne, 2007 for a review). Participants are asked to recall and date their earliest memory, excluding memories that originated solely from photos or family stories about the event. In most of these studies, the earliest memories are elicited in written form, but sometimes participants are interviewed about early memories instead. This retrospective procedure dates back to the 19th century, when Henri and Henri (1898) interviewed more than 100 adults about their earliest memory. Another method of eliciting early memories is to ask participants to recall an event with a known date, such as the birth of a sibling. The age at which events from early childhood can be recalled is remarkably similar across these different procedures. In most Anglo middle-class samples, the average age of earliest memory is between 3 and 3½ years (e.g., Mullen, 1994). If a sibling was born before the participant was 3 years old, the participant is unlikely to recall any accurate information about the event as verified by a parent (Sheingold & Tenney, 1982). If a sibling was born after the participant was 3 years old, however, the participant is likely to recall at least some accurate information about the sibling's arrival. Some studies using the targeted event method have arrived upon an earlier age of first memory, at around 2 years (e.g., Usher & Neisser, 1993), most likely because of differences in the questioning or validation procedures (see Jack & Hayne, 2007). In some studies, women are able to recall events from earlier in childhood compared to men, although the effect size of this gender difference is small (e.g., Mullen, 1994). Across many studies, however, women report a greater amount of information than do men about their earliest memories, in line with the previously discussed episodic advantage for women (e.g., MacDonald, Uesiliana, & Hayne, 2000).

The age and volume of early memories also varies as a function of the culture of the participant. Participants from all Asian cultures studied to date report later first memories, on average between 4 and 4½ years, than do participants from Anglo cultures, especially North American culture (Conway *et al.*, 2005; Mullen, 1994; Wang, 2001a). In at least one study with Asian participants, however, the gender difference was reversed, such that Asian women reported *later* first memories than did Asian men (MacDonald *et al.*, 2000). In contrast, Māori New Zealand adults report significantly earlier first memories, on average between 2½ and 3 years, than do European-descent adults (Hayne & MacDonald, 2003; MacDonald *et al.*, 2000). One possible reason for these cultural differences in earliest memories is that European cultures focus more on the individual self, whereas in Asian cultures, the focus is on the self with others (Wang, 2008a). An individual's personal memories are not prized as much in cultures with a focus on interdependence. An individual focus is linked to more elaborative interactions between European American mothers and their children about early memories, and an interdependent focus to less elaborative interactions between Chinese mothers and their children about early memories (Wang, 2007). By late preschool, European

American children already tell more elaborative autobiographical narratives than do Asian children, who tend to focus on general past experiences rather than specific memories (Han, Leichtman, & Wang, 1998). The earlier memories of Māori adults may also be linked to their narrative environment, but the findings to date in this regard are not straightforward. Māori mothers tell more elaborate stories about significant life events with their children relative to their stories about everyday life events, but Māori mothers are actually less elaborative than European mothers when telling stories of everyday past experiences with their children (Reese, Hayne, & MacDonald, 2008). My colleagues and I are currently exploring a wider range of Māori parent–child interactions to elucidate this effect.

In a procedure designed to test childhood amnesia using the same technique from childhood to adolescence, participants are presented with a timeline of each year in their lives, accompanied by photos of themselves (Tustin & Hayne, 2008). Participants are encouraged to provide and date memories from different ages. By late adolescence (18–20 years), European-descent participants' earliest memory in this procedure is in line with ages derived from other retrospective methods (i.e., between 3 and 3½ years). The age of earliest memory, however, is considerably earlier for younger participants using this method: 5- to 9-year-olds recall events that occurred on average between 1 and 2 years, and 12- to 13-year-olds recall events from 2- to 2½ years. This research once again points to the beginning of childhood amnesia in childhood, but using this highly scaffolded procedure, forgetting appears to begin slightly later (past age 9) compared to other less scaffolded procedures (Cleveland & Reese, 2008; Peterson *et al.*, 2005; van Abbema & Bauer, 2005).

Summary of autobiographical memory in adolescence. By adolescence, the main focus of autobiographical memory research is on the life story as the fullest expression of autobiography. Life stories arise out of children's autobiographical narratives in middle childhood but continue to develop into late adolescence. Changes in the life story are not due to how much is remembered but to how past events are interpreted and integrated into a coherent narrative. By the end of adolescence, early memories have stabilized, showing the same pattern as in adulthood. As noted in the middle childhood section, a female advantage in the volume and quality of autobiographical memories is clearly evident in adolescence across individual autobiographical memories and in the coherence of the life story. A female advantage for the age and volume of earliest memory is also evident but is less robust.

Now that I have presented the major monuments along the road to autobiography, I turn to the theories proposed to explain these developmental changes, and I evaluate the evidence to support those theories.

III. Origins of Autobiographical Memory

A. CONTEMPORARY THEORIES OF AUTOBIOGRAPHICAL MEMORY DEVELOPMENT

Theories of the development of autobiographical memory abound. Some of these theories focus on a critical skill or prerequisite to autobiographical memory. For instance, *self-recognition theory* (Howe *et al.*, 2003; Howe & Courage, 1993, 1997) posits that children's ability to recognize their physical selves in a mirror in the second year of life marks the start of autobiographical memory. Before self-recognition is achieved, infants and toddlers are capable of long-term memory, but those memories are not autobiographical or self-relevant according to this theory. The rate at which children accrue self-knowledge after mirror self-recognition then determines the frequency, richness, and durability of their autobiographical memories. Povinelli (1995) concurs that self-recognition is the foundation on which autobiographical memory rests, but asserts that it is children's awareness of a past and future self at around age 4 that is the critical skill, because only then children can experience a continuous sense of self over time (see Povinelli, 2001 for a review).

Other "critical skill" theories also propose a later onset of autobiographical memory, and accordingly, more advanced prerequisites to autobiographical memory. *Autonoetic theory* (e.g., Perner & Ruffman, 1995; Perner, 2000, 2001) hypothesizes that the critical prerequisite for memories to count as episodic and autobiographical is the ability to understand the phenomenological difference between re-experiencing an event versus simply knowing about an event. To be capable of autobiographical memory, one must know that a memory can only be autobiographical if the memory resulted from a direct experience, as opposed to a memory that resulted from hearing about the event or gaining knowledge in some other indirect fashion. In the case of direct experience, the resulting memory will be accompanied by a sense of recollection or *autonoesis*. True episodic memory should thus be linked to children's abilities to introspect about knowledge sources, such as knowing that one can only report on sensory qualities of an object if one feels the object rather than simply sees the object (Perner, Kloo, & Gornik, 2007).

"Integrated" theories instead account for the development of auto-biographical memory via a complex interplay among biological, cognitive, linguistic, and social-cognitive advances, but all of these theories highlight the important role of social interaction (Bauer, 2007b; Fivush & Nelson, 2004; Nelson & Fivush, 2004; Reese, 2002a, 2002b; Welch-Ross, 1995). Children do not develop long-term memories in a vacuum. Even infants' skill at deferred imitation is shaped by their interactions with caregivers (Bauer & Burch, 2004). From around the time that children start to reference past events verbally in the second year of life, adults follow up on these references with requests for children to expand on their verbal memories (Eisenberg, 1985; Hudson, 1991; Sachs, 1983). Even in these very early conversations about the past, parents already differ dramatically in their styles of discussing autobiographical memories with their children (Farrant & Reese, 2000; Fivush & Fromhoff, 1988; see Table III for examples and Fivush, Haden, & Reese, 2006 for a review). Some parents are highly elaborative in their requests for more information, framing their requests in open-ended forms, and their requests incorporate richly descriptive cues. Other parents are much less elaborative in their reminiscing style. These parents ask their children fewer questions, and their requests are likely to be closed-ended, with only a yes or no response required, or even a repetition of a prior request. Importantly, parents' elaborative reminiscing style does not appear to be part of a generally elaborative conversational style. Parents who elaborate during reminiscing do not necessarily elaborate in their conversations during free-play (Haden & Fivush, 1996) or book-reading with their children (Laible, 2004). All of the integrated theories of autobiographical memory propose that a child whose primary caregiver adopts a highly elaborative reminiscing style will have earlier, richer, and longer-lasting autobiographical memories than those of a child whose primary caregiver uses a less elaborative reminiscing style (Fivush & Reese, 1992; Nelson, 1993). In contrast to critical-skill theories, however, integrated theories place more emphasis on the multiple influences on autobiographical memory.

Most integrated theories also resist stating an exact age at which autobiographical memory begins (e.g., Bauer, 2007b). Instead, integrated theories focus on the gradual emergence of autobiographical memory out of earlier capacities and experiences. However, integrated theories still differ on whether autobiographical memory is an early or late development.

Since the late 1990s, I have been developing an integrated theory of autobiographical memory that I will call *emergent recollection* (Reese, 1999; Reese, 2002a, 2002b; Reese & Fivush, 2008). I have proposed that

Table III

Examples of Mothers' High and Low Elaborative Reminiscing Styles with Preschool Children

---

High elaborative maternal reminiscing style

M: And what else did we do that weekend that there was the big celebrations on?
C: I don't uhh. I had a lollipop
M: Yes, you had a lollipop. And did you wear something special?
C: What was it?
M: You tell me
C: I don't know
M: Don't you remember what you wore?
C: No
M: You and I got dressed up in some old fashioned clothes, didn't we? What were the old fashioned clothes?
C: Um, because we wanted to pick up Jessie
M: Very good. We had to go and look after Jessie, didn't we?
C: Mmm
M: And was Jessie dressed up?
C: Yes
M: And what did she have on?
C: A bonnet
M: A bonnet, good girl. And did you wear a bonnet?
C: Yes
M: You did, and you looked really pretty. (pause) And you wore a dress, and a very old fashioned thing over the top of the dress. What was that thing called?
C: Umm, a bress
M: Yeah, a dress, with an apron. Remember the white apron that went over the front? It was very pretty

Low elaborative maternal reminiscing style

M: Do you remember going to the RSPCA?
C: Yep
M: Do you remember going there, with playcentre?
C: Yep
M: Do you remember what we did?
C: Yeah
M: What did we look at?
C: Uh
M: Do you remember what we saw there? What?
C: Toys
M: Did we see toys? Ohh
C: And paint
M: Oh, did we? Um, do you remember who we went with?
C: You
M: Me. Who else did we go with?
C: Leah
M: Leah, yeah we did. Who else?
C: Sssusan
M: No, we went to playcentre
C: Darlene
M: Yeah we went with Darlene. We went with lots of people. And what else did we do?

Table III

(*Continued*)

C:	And see Santa
M:	No, we didn't see Santa
C:	At Christmas we seed Santa
M:	Yeah, but we're talking about the RSPCA, do you know what's at the RSPCA? The animals. Remember the animals?
C:	Yeah
M:	What animals did we see?
C:	What are the ladies doing?
M:	Don't worry about what they're doing. Do you remember the animals?
C:	Yep
M:	What animals were there?
C:	Uh

Note: M, Mother; C, child.

self-awareness, attachment security, language, and social interaction all contribute in the first two years of life to children's verbal memory, which then stabilizes but continues to develop over the preschool years (Reese, 2002a). These factors are hypothesized to interact in complex ways to affect the existence and richness of autobiographical memories. Children with a more secure attachment to their primary caregivers will more readily benefit from their caregivers' reminiscing style because the trust in the relationship enables more effective internalization of memory skills (Reese & Farrant, 2003). Children with an earlier onset of self-recognition will benefit from a caregiver's elaborative reminiscing style at an earlier age because they are hypothesized to be better able to use a parent's elaborations to cue and enrich their memories (Reese & Newcombe, 2007). Likewise, children with advanced language capabilities will be better able to encode and store their caregivers' elaborative talk. Self-awareness, attachment security, and linguistic competence are not seen as prerequisites to autobiographical memory in the emergent recollection theory. Rather, nonverbal declarative memory is developing in a continuous fashion across the first several years of life (see Hayne, 2004). As I reviewed earlier, children's earliest verbal memories arise out of their nonverbal memories and already contain the seeds of the "what," "where," "when," and "to me" components of episodic memory. I also proposed that some of children's earliest verbal memories are accompanied by, and arise from, a mental replay of the event (cf. Perner & Dienes, 2003). Young preschoolers may not yet be aware that these mental replays are representations of the past (Fivush & Nelson, 2006), nor are they able to report on their awareness of an event as based on recollection.

I believe, however, that those criteria set the bar for episodic memory too high. An experience of recollection is very different from an awareness of that experience, much less the ability to verbalize that awareness. I propose that children show evidence of recollection in their reminiscing by age 3 years, and possibly even younger, through their inclusion of personal references, mental state words, temporal terms, and location information (e.g., Nelson, 1989; Rudek & Haden, 2005).

Certainly recollection continues to develop in later childhood and adolescence. The development of self-awareness, attachment security, language, and an elaborative reminiscing style merely increase the odds that a memory will be retained past early childhood. When a personal memory from a specific point in time is retained in the long term, it has the potential to become a memory of personal significance and thus part of one's autobiography (Reese, 1999). As such, autobiography is an emergent property of children's early memories. Even a memory that was encoded before mirror self-recognition, for instance, could later become imbued with self-relevant features and with personal meaning, in the same way that a memory can later become integrated with words that were not available at the time of encoding (Morris & Baker-Ward, 2007). Thus, in emergent recollection theory, autobiography evolves from earlier episodic memories. All episodic memories are candidates for becoming autobiographical memories.

Other integrated theories also posit a gradual emergence of autobiographical memory as a function of multiple influences. *Social cultural developmental theory* (Fivush & Nelson, 2004; Nelson & Fivush, 2004) proposes a complex progression of skills and influences leading to autobiographical memory late in early childhood, when children develop a sense of self as enduring in time. The multiple influences on autobiographical memory include language, self-awareness, and theory of mind, but also later-developing temporal concepts and narrative skills. Finally, parent–child conversations are critical for autobiographical memory in this theory, including specific social interactions in which parent and child disagree about their perspectives on a memory. These multiple influences are not simply added together to create autobiographical memory, but are synthesized into a qualitatively different perception of self as continuous in time (Fivush & Nelson, 2006). The primary focus of this theory is on the functions of autobiographical memory for self-understanding and entry into the community by the end of early childhood (cf. Ornstein *et al.*, 2006; Pillemer, 2003, for other functional theories of autobiographical memory).

Bauer (2007b) offered a fresh perspective on the development of autobiographical memory by noting that the "problem" of childhood amnesia could be accounted for simply by more rapid rates of loss compared to retention of memories before age 4, combined with more rapid rates of retention than loss of memories after age 6. Moreover, Bauer advocated a move away from specifying criteria for autobiographical memory, such as autonoesis or one-time experiences. Instead, memories can be viewed as closer to or farther away from the prototypical specific, one-point-in-time episodic variety. Memories based on repeated experiences may be less prototypical versions of autobiographical memories, but can nonetheless be recalled, at times vividly, and can shape our sense of self.

All contemporary theorists of autobiographical memory agree that neurological factors, self-awareness, cognitive change, and language are important to its development (see Conway, Singer, & Tagini, 2004 for an integrated theory of adults' autobiographical memory). In the latest versions of even the critical-skill theories, social interaction is acknowledged as a major force in the expression of autobiographical memories (Howe, 2003; Perner *et al.*, 2007). The field is thus converging on a shared understanding of many of the contributors to autobiographical memory. Theorists still disagree, however, on whether episodic or autobiographical memory is an earlier or later accomplishment during early childhood, and they also disagree on whether autonoetic awareness should be a defining feature of episodic or autobiographical memories. Some theories equate episodic with autobiographical memories but others differentiate the two. Finally, theorists continue to disagree about the course of autobiographical memory development: is it gradual and continuous, or marked by sharp qualitative change? In the following section, I review the evidence for cognitive, linguistic, social, and emotional sources of influence in children's and adolescents' developing autobiographical memory competence, evaluating contemporary theories in the process.

B. SOURCES OF AUTOBIOGRAPHICAL MEMORY DEVELOPMENT

1. Cognitive Sources

Several theories of autobiographical memory have proposed one or more cognitive changes as the prerequisite skill for autobiographical memory. The first major cognitive influence to consider is the effect of self-recognition in the second year of life on autobiographical memory (Howe *et al.*, 2003; Howe & Courage, 1993, 1997; cf. Wheeler, Stuss, & Tulving, 1997). At present, there is little evidence to suggest that the onset of self-recognition results in a qualitative shift in remembering. Children who show earlier self-recognition do initially advance faster in their nonverbal and verbal memory skills compared to children who show later self-recognition (Harley & Reese, 1999; Prudhomme, 2005), but the direct contribution of self-recognition to verbal memory drops out after age 2½ years (Reese, 2002a; Reese & Newcombe, 2007). Moreover, the critical piece of evidence needed to support this theory is that autobiographical memory is not possible until the advent of self-recognition. Again, when does a memory count as autobiographical? Must the memory be expressed verbally? Howe *et al.* (2003) proposed a measure of nonverbal autobiographical recall to circumvent the problems with verbal definitions of autobiographical memory. In this task, the child helps an experimenter hide a stuffed Tinky-Winky doll (from the popular television show *Teletubbies*) in a filing cabinet. On a separate visit to a different room in the lab, the child is asked to find Tinky-Winky. Children who go into the correct room and who search for the toy in the filing cabinet are deemed to exhibit nonverbal autobiographical recall because they are demonstrating two of Tulving's criteria for episodic memory: the "what" and "where." Howe *et al.* (2003) reported that children do not display recall in this task until they have passed the mirror test of self-recognition.

Clearly this task does measure the "what" and the "where" of children's long-term memory for a specific event. However, I believe that children's performance on this task is no more (or less) autobiographical than their performance in deferred imitation. Children show recall on this task at a later age than on a typical deferred imitation task, and after they have achieved self-recognition, only because the task is more difficult. First, children's retrieval is tested in a different context (room) from encoding, and only verbal, not physical cues, are present at the time of retrieval. Thus, children's ability to perform this task may not depend on self-awareness per se, but on their growing representational flexibility (see Hayne, 2004) and their ability to use solely verbal cues for memory retrieval (Morgan & Hayne, 2007). Tulving's (1985, 2002) remaining criteria for a test of episodic memory—the knowledge of "when" and that this event happened to *me*, accompanied by a sense of recollection—are not demonstrated in this task. It is difficult to conceive of a nonverbal, behavioral test of autobiographical memory that would satisfy these criteria.

I proposed earlier that verbal recall is a better indicator of episodic and autobiographical memory than nonverbal recall, but certainly not all verbal memory is episodic or autobiographical. Children who supply a correct verbal response to a parent's question about a past event may not be relying on episodic recall. For example, a child who responds with "Dad" to his mother's question "Who was at the rugby with us?" may be relying on general knowledge (Dad is usually present at family events) or may simply have made a lucky guess, not engaged in true recollection.

However, a child who initiates a verbal reference to a past event, uncued by a parent, is likely to be mentally re-experiencing that event. These spontaneous verbal references to the past occur from the second year of life. They are difficult to capture experimentally because the cues for any one memory are highly idiosyncratic (see Reese, 1999). Despite this difficulty, I propose that the best test of Howe *et al.*'s (2003) theory will be to track simultaneously children's self-recognition and their spontaneous verbal references to the past. If children indeed do not spontaneously refer to the past before self-recognition, then firmer support for Howe *et al.*'s theory will be obtained.

Other cognitive theorists of autobiographical memory, however, assert that the critical cognitive skill and accompanying autobiographical memories occur much later in childhood, at approximately 4 years, long after self-recognition and verbal memory initiations have commenced. Prospective evidence, however, does not support a dramatic shift in autobiographical memory at age 4. Children can easily tell an unprompted recount of a past event before this age (see Table I). The few existing studies of a link between theory of mind abilities and autobiographical memory offer scant evidence at best for qualitative change in episodic memory as a function of metacognitive advances. Perner and Ruffman (1995) did note a correlation between children's theory of mind and their free recall of a set of pictures, even after their receptive language and cued recall performance had been taken into account. However, children's age was not controlled in this study, so this link could simply be due to increases in both theory of mind and free recall with age. When Naito (2003) controlled for age as well as verbal intelligence, only children's memory for the source of their knowledge, not their free recall, was correlated with their theory of mind performance. Thus, theory of mind is most likely correlated with other metacognitive advances such as the awareness of different knowledge states, not with episodic memory per se.

One intriguing demonstration of a possible qualitative shift in autobiographical memory at this age, however, is that older children with advanced theory of mind demonstrated greater memory for a directly experienced event (putting cards in a box) as opposed to an indirectly experienced event (seeing the pictures on the cards only later from a video) (Perner *et al.*, 2007). Younger children with less developed theory of mind showed the opposite pattern, in which they recalled indirectly experienced events slightly better than directly experienced events. Perner *et al.* acknowledged that these different memory patterns in younger and older children did not necessarily suggest that theory of mind is a prerequisite to episodic memory, only that there is a link between the two. It is possible that these different memory patterns with age are due to refinements in episodic memory that come with source monitoring skills between ages 4 and 6.

Other studies have examined links between theory of mind and children's autobiographical memory for real-world events. Welch-Ross (1997) found a concurrent correlation between children's theory of mind skills and their verbal memory for naturally occurring experiences, but Reese and Cleveland (2007) found no evidence of this same link longitudinally once appropriate controls for children's language skills were put into place. Kleinknecht and Beike (2004) demonstrated correlations between children's theory of mind and their narrative ability when retelling a fictional story, but found no links between theory of mind and preschool children's autobiographical memory, as measured by their verbal memory for a field trip to a museum. Therefore, although most of the theories of autobiographical memory as a late development incorporate theory of mind as a prerequisite for true recollection, the basic link between theory of mind and episodic memory necessary to support these theories has not been established. Instead, theory of mind is associated with improvements in source memory or in language skills, but not with episodic or autobiographical memory specifically. As Perner *et al.* (2007, p. 473) pointed out, "Although source memory is an important part of episodic memory it should not be equated with it. The ability to recall the source of information does not require episodic memory, because it can be based on knowing and need not be remembered."

To summarize, self-recognition is linked with steeper growth rates in children's verbal memory over the second year of life, but does not appear to be a prerequisite for, or a lasting influence upon, children's autobiographical memory. Nor is theory of mind a prerequisite to autobiographical memories as hypothesized, but theory of mind may contribute to children's ability to remember the sources of their memories.

2. Linguistic Sources

Children's developing language skill is a salient candidate for strengthening their memories (Farrant & Reese, 2000; Nelson, 1996; Simcock & Hayne, 2002, 2003). Language development may enhance autobiographical memory in at least two ways. First, growth in vocabulary and syntax enables children to express, and perhaps even to encode, their memories in increasingly sophisticated ways. In studies with independent measures of children's language skill, children with advanced language demonstrate richer verbal *and* nonverbal memories in the early preschool period (Farrant & Reese, 2000; Harley & Reese, 1999; Reese *et al.*, 2008; Simcock & Hayne, 2003). Children's vocabulary development uniquely predicts their developing autobiographical memory in early childhood, even after accounting for other powerful factors such as nonverbal memory skill, attachment security, self-recognition, and their conversations with parents about those memories (Reese, 2002a). Given that parents' conversational style is also driven to some extent by children's language capability (Farrant & Reese, 2000), this test is a conservative measure of the strong role of children's language in their early memory development. Second, as discussed previously, the act of putting a memory into words makes it more likely that the memory will be retained, and in a richer fashion, in the long term. In an experimental study of adult-child talk on preschool children's verbal memory for a staged zoo event, children recalled their own memory provisions from the adult-led conversations in the later test better than they recalled the adults' talk (McGuigan & Salmon, 2004). Young children's recall is especially robust for those items that both mother and child talked about together during the event (Hedrick *et al.*, in press b).

The role of language in memory diminishes with age, however. By the end of the preschool years, and continuing into adolescence, children's concurrent language skills are no longer correlated with their verbal memories (Cleveland & Reese, 2008; Jack *et al.*, 2009), nor is their language skill strongly correlated with the coherence of their autobiographical narratives (Reese *et al.*, 2009). At age 5½ years, however, their memories of distant events from early childhood remain correlated with their language skill from that period (Cleveland & Reese), suggesting that early language abilities do shape early memories in an enduring way.

Therefore, although language propels children's autobiographical memory in the early years, language ceases to be a critical influence for memories formed after that time. When children enter school, they all possess the basic language for remembering events in a verbal form, so vocabulary is no longer a delimiting factor in their memories. So far, though, most studies with older children have measured language only in terms of vocabulary. It is certainly possible that language is still important for autobiographical memory at older ages, but the dimension of language that is important has changed. For instance, narrative skill may yet emerge as an important influence on autobiographical memories at older ages (Nelson, 1996). In early childhood, children's event memory was largely unrelated to their fictional narrative skills, but was related to their autobiographical narrative skills (Kleinknecht & Beike, 2004). Studies with older children have not included narrative measures that are independent of children's autobiographical memory; the narrative measure in these studies is instead embedded in the autobiographical memory measure. In future research with older children, narrative measures that do not rely on children's memory, such as their ability to create a fantasy narrative, could be included alongside personal narrative measures in order to test this hypothesis. Experimental research using a narrative elaboration technique (NET; Saywitz & Snyder, 1996) is relevant in this regard. School-aged children who were trained to use narrative forms showed better event recall than children in a control group who were not trained (Brown & Pipe, 2003). Therefore, higher-order language skills may continue to affect children's recall by helping them to organize the material to be remembered and expressed.

3. Social and Emotional Sources

Children's social and emotional development is predicted to influence their autobiographical memories in several ways. First, children's temperament is hypothesized to shape their autobiographical memories. Research in this area has been more exploratory than programmatic, exploring the links between temperament and memory without clear predictions about which aspects of temperament should be related to autobiographical memory. The findings, all of which rely on parent reports of temperament, are mixed. With younger children in imitation tasks, Bauer and Burch (2004) found that different aspects of children's temperament were linked to memory as a function of task difficulty. Toddlers with more active temperaments performed better on easier memory sequences, whereas toddlers who were more interested and persistent performed better on more challenging memory sequences.

In the preschool years once verbal memory can be measured, children who were more adaptable produced greater recall for a staged Circus Day event (Geddie, Fradin, & Beer, 2000). Children with greater effortful control used more explanations of internal states, a measure of narrative sophistication and memory processing, in their autobiographical memories with mothers (Bird, Reese, & Tripp, 2006). Laible (2004) reported that dyadic talk about negative emotions was positively related to children's negative reactivity, and negatively related to their extraversion. Lewis (1999) reported no associations between child temperament and children's autobiographical memory. Children's temperament is thus not a straightforward predictor of their autobiographical memory.

Attachment security is another dimension of children's social and emotional development that is theoretically linked to autobiographical memory development. Children with a secure attachment to their primary caregivers are expected to have richer and more evaluated autobiographical memories, presumably because their caregivers have discussed past events more openly and in a more emotional way with their children

(Bowlby, 1988; Bretherton & Munholland, 1999). The evidence to date supports this prediction. Securely attached preschoolers have richer and more emotional conversations about the past with their mothers than do insecurely attached children (Bost *et al.*, 2006; Farrar, Fasig, & Welch-Ross, 1997; Laible, 2004; Laible & Thompson, 2000; Newcombe & Reese, 2004; Reese & Farrant, 2003). The impact of attachment security appears to extend to children's independent event memory. Securely attached 4-year-olds recalled longer and more detailed independent autobiographical narratives than did insecurely attached children (McCabe, Peterson, & Connors, 2006). Securely attached children remembered positive lab events more accurately than negative lab events, whereas the reverse pattern was true for insecurely attached children (Belsky, Spritz, & Crnic, 1996). Securely and insecurely attached children did not differ, however, in their memory for nonemotional aspects of events, such as when and where the event took place (Newcombe & Reese, 2004). In a retrospective study with Italian adults, Peterson, Smorti, and Tani (2008) found that young men who reported having better early relationships with parents also reported more episodic memories of positive events from early childhood. Therefore, attachment security and a positive relationship with parents are linked to children's and young adults' autobiographical memory, especially for the emotional aspects of events.

A third important dimension of children's socioemotional development for autobiographical memory is their understanding of emotions. Children with greater emotion understanding are predicted to have richer and more durable autobiographical memories because of their enhanced ability to process and retain the emotional aspects of events (Wang, 2008b). Children's emotion knowledge is developing alongside their verbal memory from the second year of life, but only one study to date has explored the link between the two. Wang (2008b) measured emotion knowledge, internal state language, and autobiographical memory in European American, Chinese American, and Chinese preschoolers longitudinally from ages 3 to 4½, controlling for children's vocabulary skills. From ages 3 to 3½ years, the relations between emotion knowledge and autobiographical memory were bidirectional. At age 3½, however, children's emotion knowledge uniquely predicted their specific event memory at age 4½, across cultures and regardless of language skill. Children's event memory at age 3½ did not uniquely predict their later emotion knowledge. Thus, an understanding of emotions appears to help children create stronger and more specific autobiographical memories. Moreover, children's emotion knowledge mediated the link between their earlier language skill and their later event memory. Language facility helps children's emotion understanding, which in turn may help children understand and process events, thus strengthening their autobiographical memory.

Because children's emotion understanding is also linked to secure attachment (e.g., Laible, 2004), it is possible that emotion understanding mediates the relation between attachment security and autobiographical memory. Future research that includes measures of both attachment security and emotion understanding as predictors of autobiographical memory will help elucidate these effects. In Laible's (2004) study, both attachment security and emotion knowledge were assessed concurrently, but emotion knowledge was only used as an outcome variable in analyses, not as a predictor of autobiographical memory. An indirect effect of attachment security on autobiographical memory is plausible given that early attachment security drops out as a direct predictor of children's autobiographical memory by age 5½ years (Reese, 2008).

The study of the socioemotional foundations of autobiographical memory also needs to extend into the school years. By middle childhood, children can be reliably and validly assessed on the Big Five dimensions of personality: openness, conscientiousness, extraversion, agreeableness, and neuroticism (Measelle *et al.*, 2005). Adults who tell more mature life stories rate themselves as higher on the traits of openness and extraversion, and lower on the trait of neuroticism (Bauer, McAdams, & Sakaeda, 2005). If childhood temperament is indeed the basis of later personality (Roberts & DelVecchio, 2000), and given the mixed findings of a link between temperament and autobiographical memory, at what point in development does personality become linked to autobiographical memory? And would the same dimensions of personality that are important for adults' life stories also be important for children's autobiographical memories? Nor do we know the mechanism for these relations between personality and memory in either adults or children. Does personality shape the content, the richness, and the durability of one's memories? Or is it conceivable that one's memories could also shape one's personality? In other words, how do our experiences, and most importantly, our interpretations of those experiences, forge our personalities?

4. Social Interaction Sources

All of the integrated theories of autobiographical memory development propose an important role for social interaction. From before the time that children begin to reference past events, adults are asking children about those past events. And the way that adults talk to children about the past varies dramatically, with some adults asking a preponderance of open-ended questions containing new information about the event and con-firming their children's responses, and other adults asking children fewer and less informative questions about the event (Engel, 1995; Fivush & Fromhoff, 1988; McCabe & Peterson, 1991; see Table III). Thus, adults differ in the degree to which they use an *elaborative reminiscing* style with children. Although adults also differ in the frequency with which they repeat their own questions and statements about a past event, in effect badgering children to respond to a specific question, a repetitive reminiscing style (Reese & Fivush, 1993) is not consistently related to children's verbal memory, either in the same conversation or in the long-term.

In contrast, an elaborative reminiscing style is linked to increases in children's verbal memory, both in the same conversation and over time (e.g., Reese, Haden, & Fivush, 1993; see Fivush *et al.*, 2006 for a review). Children whose parents, and their mothers in particular, use an elaborative reminiscing style demonstrate richer verbal memories with their mothers from as early as age 2 (Farrant & Reese, 2000; Hudson, 1990). Their conversations have already become bidirectional at this point, with both partners offering information about the past event, although the conversations become even more collaborative when children are between 4 and 5 years old (Reese *et al.*). By as early as 2½ years, the children of mothers with a highly elaborative reminiscing style also offer richer accounts of the past to other adults, such as a researcher whom they have just met (Farrant & Reese; Hudson).

These individual differences in mothers' reminiscing style do not appear to be a function of general differences in their conversational styles, because mothers with a highly elaborative reminiscing style are not necessarily more elaborative in other kinds of conversations (see Fivush *et al.*, 2006). Mothers are consistent in their reminiscing style across different types of past events, however. A mother with a highly elaborative reminiscing style when discussing a shared past event with her child is also likely to be highly elaborative when discussing an unshared past event at her child's preschool, or an instance of past misbehavior on the part of her child (e.g., Leyva *et al.*, 2008; Reese & Brown, 2000; Reese & Newcombe, 2007). Mothers' style of reminiscing is thus a separate dimension of interaction that is not simply a function of their talkativeness.

An elaborative reminiscing style is only weakly correlated with mothers' education levels and socioeconomic status. Mothers with more education and higher socioeconomic status talk far more with their children about present and past events than do mothers with less education and lower socioeconomic status (Hart & Risley, 1995), but they are not specifically more elaborative in their reminiscing with their children (Reese & Newcombe, 2007). Even among low-income mothers of diverse ethnic and language backgrounds, their level of elaborative reminiscing about shared events uniquely predicts their children's independent reminiscing with a researcher (Leyva *et al.*, 2008).

One known correlate of mothers' reminiscing style is attachment, both their own attachment orientation and their children's attachment security. Mothers who are secure (or autonomous) in their attachment orientation toward their own early childhood experiences, as measured in the Adult Attachment Interview (Main, Goldwyn, & Hesse, 2002), are more likely to adopt a highly elaborative reminiscing style with their children about shared past experiences (Reese, 2008). Mothers with a highly elaborative and evaluative reminiscing style are also more likely to have children who are securely attached themselves (Fivush & Vasudeva, 2002; Laible, 2004; Laible & Thompson, 2000; Reese & Farrant, 2003). Moreover, mothers and their securely attached children enjoy more collaborative conversations about the past over time, mutually influencing their partners' evaluations of the past event (Newcombe & Reese, 2004; see Reese *et al.*, in press, for narrative examples). Mothers and their insecurely attached children, in contrast, do not positively influence each others' use of an elaborative and evaluative reminiscing style over time (Newcombe & Reese; Reese & Farrant). At present, children's attachment security in these studies has only been measured at the outset of each study, so it is unclear whether children's attachment security leads to more elaborative and collaborative reminiscing, or whether elaborative and collaborative reminiscing also shapes children's attachment security. In order to assess both possibilities, it is vital that new research in this area includes multiple measures of attachment security and mother–child reminiscing over the period in which children are forming internal working models of self and of others, from approximately 1½ to 3½ years (Bretherton & Munholland, 1999).

Experimental research confirms and clarifies the effect of adults' elaborative reminiscing style on children's autobiographical memory. In these studies, an adult (usually a researcher or the mother) adopts an elaborative conversational style when discussing an experimental event with the child, and then children's event memory is tested after a delay. Children in control conditions experience less elaborative talk or no event talk at all. This research shows that elaborative talk during and after an event helps children to remember core features and details from the event, primarily in their verbal recall (Boland, Haden, & Ornstein, 2003;

McGuigan & Salmon, 2004), but also in their nonverbal recall (McGuigan & Salmon, 2004, 2006). The effects of discussion can be quite specific such that children evidence greater memory only for those items discussed, and not for items that were not discussed (Conroy & Salmon, 2006). Only at older ages (5 and above) do children also benefit in their recall from verbal and nonverbal preparation before the event (La Rooy, Pipe, & Murray, 2007; McGuigan & Salmon, 2004, 2005; Priestley, Roberts, & Pipe, 1999; Sutherland *et al.*, 2003). The benefits of elaborative talk during and after the event appear to be additive for young children's memory, such that elaborative talk a few days after an event amplifies the effects of elaborative talk during the event (Hedrick, Haden, & Ornstein, in press a; cf. Ornstein *et al.*, 2006 for a review).

Longitudinal research verifies the unique importance of mothers' elaborative reminiscing style for children's later autobiographical memory, even after controlling for important factors such as children's attachment security, language, self-recognition, and nonverbal memory (Harley & Reese, 1999; Reese, 2002a). This longitudinal work is bolstered by a growing body of experimental work in which researchers instruct mothers in elaborative reminiscing techniques with their young children, and then measure short- and long-term influences on children's verbal memory. In an initial small-scale study, children of mothers instructed to ask more open-ended questions about past events and to confirm their children's responses gave longer and more detailed autobiographical narratives two years after the start of the intervention at age 3½ (Peterson, Jesso & McCabe, 1999). A large-scale study of over 100 mother-child dyads extended these findings in several ways. Reese and Newcombe (2007) instructed mothers of toddlers to become more elaborative in their reminiscing, and then assessed children's verbal memory at 2½ and 3½ years. Children of instructed mothers provided more memory information in mother-child conversations at age 2½ compared to children of mothers in the control group who did not receive specific instruction in reminiscing. By age 3½, the effect of maternal elaboration had extended to children's independent reminiscing with a researcher, but only for children who began the study with advanced self-recognition (Figure 3). Early recognizers whose mothers received instruction gave more detailed and more accurate information about past events than did children of mothers in the control group, even after covarying children's initial language development. There were no main effects of self-awareness for children's autobiographical memory in this study, but there were main effects of maternal reminiscing on children's memory with their mothers at both ages. Therefore, maternal reminiscing style is a strong and independent influence on children's autobiographical memory. At young ages, however,

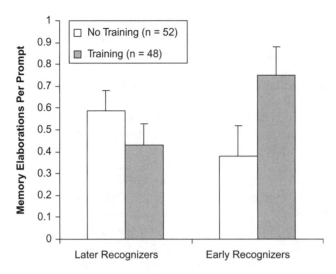

Fig. 3. Children's memory units per researcher prompt at age 3½ as a function of self-recognition at age 1½ and maternal elaboration training from 1½ to 2½ years (from Reese & Newcombe, 2007, Figure 3).

children's ability to benefit from an elaborative reminiscing style in their independent memory depends upon their level of self-awareness (cf. Wang, 2006; Welch-Ross, 2001). Children with a firmer cognitive sense of self more readily internalize mothers' reminiscing styles. This work now needs to be extended to older ages to test the continuing influences of maternal reminiscing style and self-awareness on childhood amnesia and adolescents' life stories.

A separate dimension from elaboration of adults' reminiscing style is the degree to which adults support children's perspectives on a memory. This dimension, termed *autonomy support* (from Deci & Ryan, 1987; Grolnick *et al.*, 2002), is coded independently by considering the degree to which each maternal conversational turn supports or redirects the child's version of the memory. Autonomy support is uncorrelated with mothers' level of elaboration and uniquely predicts children's verbal memory with mothers in the early preschool years (Cleveland & Reese, 2005) and children's levels of engagement when reminiscing with others (Cleveland, Reese, & Grolnick, 2007; Leyva *et al.*, 2008). Because children's engagement in reminiscing is strongly correlated with their provisions of verbal memory, especially at young ages (Farrant & Reese, 2000; Leyva *et al.*, 2008), adults' autonomy support is an additional factor to consider in children's autobiographical memory. When maternal elaboration and autonomy support are compared directly, however, maternal elaboration is a stronger influence than autonomy support on the volume and accuracy of children's verbal memory (Cleveland & Reese; Cleveland *et al.*).

Another important extension of the social interaction literature is the study of cultural differences in mother–child reminiscing and children's autobiographical memory. In a longitudinal study of Chinese, Chinese American immigrants, and European American mother–child dyads, Wang (2006) replicated earlier findings that Chinese mothers are less elaborative with their children than are European American mothers (Wang, 2001b), and that Chinese children produce sparser autobiographical memories from a young age compared to European American children (Han *et al.*, 1998). At age 3, children's agentic self-concept, defined as their private self-descriptions (*I'm happy*) minus their public and collective self-descriptions (*I'm a girl*), uniquely predicted their independent verbal memory with a researcher. In contrast, maternal reminiscing style predicted both children's shared and independent verbal memory. Moreover, children's agentic self-concept and mothers' reminiscing style mediated the effects of culture on children's memory. Thus, cultural differences in children's (and perhaps adults') autobiographical memories are transmitted through social interaction but also through children's self-concept from a young age.

Does parental reminiscing continue to exert an impact on children's autobiographical memory beyond the preschool years? Only a few studies have examined parent-child reminiscing beyond preschool, and no study has yet tracked changes in parents' reminiscing as their children move from early childhood into adolescence. Several studies have examined family reminiscing with older children and adolescents (Fivush, Bohanek, & Duke, 2008; Weeks & Pasupathi, in press). In one study, for instance, preadolescents conversed with their families about positive and negative events (Bohanek *et al.*, 2006). Families' reminiscing styles varied along a dimension of collaboration, with some families engaging in highly coordinated memory conversations with equal and integrated input from all family members. Other families engaged in less coordinated conversations in which individuals took separate turns or actively imposed their perspectives on others. Families with a coordinated perspective had preadolescents, especially girls, with higher self-esteem. The aim of these studies was to explore the role of family reminiscing for children's well-being, so children's autobiographical memory was not assessed separately. Still, it would be interesting to know if parents who are elaborative when reminiscing with their preschoolers grow to become coordinated when reminiscing with their preadolescents. Similar to the research contrasting during- and postevent talk, are there additive effects for children's autobiographical memory when parents are consistently elaborative and then coordinated in their reminiscing across children's development?

In a cross-sectional study that compared mother-child reminiscing with preschool and school-aged children (ages 3–4 versus 7–8 years), mothers were more elaborative when talking about past events with school-aged children than with preschoolers (Reese *et al.*, 2008). Older children in turn made more verbal memory contributions to these conversations than did younger children. This finding concurs with longitudinal research over the preschool years showing that mothers become ever more elaborative in their reminiscing as children grow older and contribute more to the conversations (Reese *et al.*, 1993). Given that parents grow more elaborative in their reminiscing as children age, and children become better able to build upon parental reminiscing, it is possible that reminiscing conversations in middle childhood have an even greater effect on autobiographical memory than did parent-child reminiscing during early childhood.

5. Evaluating Theories of the Origins of Autobiographical Memory

In the only study to date to follow children's autobiographical memory from preschool to adolescence, Jack *et al.* (2009) demonstrated that adolescents reported earlier first memories if their mothers had used an elaborative reminiscing style with them in early childhood (Figure 4). Taken together with the research on social interaction effects during early childhood on children's autobiographical memory, it is clear that children whose parents adopt an elaborative reminiscing style have more durable memories from early childhood. This pattern is consistent with the research on childhood amnesia, such that adults in cultures with less elaborative reminiscing styles demonstrate later first memories. These results are also in line with all of the integrated theories of autobiographical memory in assigning a prominent role to mother-child interactions in autobiographical memory development.

Social interaction is of course not the only source of influence on autobiographical memories in and from early childhood, as integrated theories propose. As illustrated by the empty upper-right half of Figure 4, none of the adolescents with highly elaborative mothers had late first memories, but there were some adolescents with less elaborative mothers who had early first memories (as seen in the lower-left half of the figure).

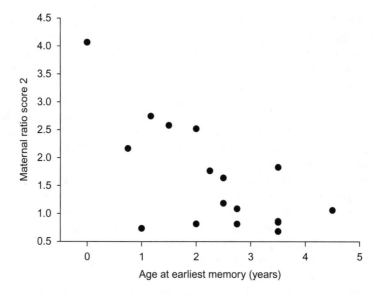

Fig. 4. Age of adolescents' earliest memory as a function of maternal elaborative reminiscing (open-ended elaborative questions divided by total repetitions) during early childhood (from Jack et al., 2009, Figure 1).

Therefore, having an elaborative parent seems to ensure that one will have early memories, but an elaborative reminiscing environment is not the only route to early memories. Autobiographical memory is multiply determined. Children's language development and their self-awareness exert an influence on autobiographical memory, and secure attachment is important for the child's ability to benefit from a mother's elaborative reminiscing style.

Based on the evidence reviewed here, and in line with emergent recollection theory, I propose that children demonstrate some elements of true recollection before the age at which they acquire the metacognitive skills hypothesized to be necessary for autobiographical memory. An advanced understanding of mind may fine-tune their autobiographical memories, but does not appear to enable recollection. Children are capable of remembering the "what," "where," "when," and "to me" aspects of events long before age 4. Less cognitive aspects of an understanding of mind, such as children's emotion understanding, also appear to enrich and extend children's early memories, probably because children with greater emotion understanding can better appreciate the personal significance of an event.

IV. Consequences of Autobiographical Memory

Individual differences in autobiographical memory are evident in early childhood and these differences extend into adolescence. Do these individual differences in autobiographical memory matter for other aspects of development? So far, the research has focused primarily on the benefits of maternal reminiscing for other aspects of children's development besides autobiographical memory, such as children's strategic memory, literacy, theory of mind, emotion understanding, narrative, self-concept, prosocial behavior, and psychological well-being (see Fivush *et al.*, 2006; Wareham & Salmon, 2006 for reviews). Given that maternal reminiscing style strongly influences children's autobiographical memory, however, it is possible that children's autobiographical memory mediates some of these effects on other aspects of development.

Most existing studies have not directly tested for mediation of maternal reminiscing effects on children's development via their autobiographical memory. However, these studies can be assessed for the initial criterion for mediation: was children's autobiographical memory a significant predictor of the proposed outcome? Note that I could not assess studies that did not include a separate measure of children's memory (e.g., Laible, 2004; Laible & Song, 2006; Ontai & Thompson, 2008). When I evaluated existing research for the possibility that advances in autobiographical memory spill over to other aspects of development, I discovered two distinct patterns. For most of the proposed cognitive and social-cognitive outcomes of autobiographical memory—vocabulary, literacy, theory of mind, and emotion understanding to be specific—the initial criterion for mediation is not met. Children's autobiographical memory is either uncorrelated with the target outcome, or is only correlated as an outcome variable itself in longitudinal correlations (Peterson *et al.*, 1999; Reese, 1995; Reese & Cleveland, 2007; Wang, 2008b), especially once language controls are put into place. For instance, in an experimental study, mothers who were instructed in elaborative reminiscing had children with better understanding of the causes of emotions after 6 months compared to a control group of mothers and children, but the same children did not yet show evidence of advanced memory development (Wareham *et al.*, in press). The best explanation so far is that maternal reminiscing as a rich source of conversation directly affects these cognitive and social-cognitive skills, not indirectly via children's autobiographical memory. Of course, it is possible that other factors besides children's autobiographical memory mediate these effects of maternal reminiscing style on children's cognitive and social-cognitive skills. For instance, children's symbolic understanding may mediate the link between maternal reminiscing and children's literacy.

For most of the proposed narrative and socioemotional outcomes of autobiographical memory, however, the initial criterion for mediation via children's autobiographical memory *is* met. For instance, in the area of narrative development, children's growing participation in memory conversations across preschool predicted their story comprehension and production of fictional narratives (Reese, 1995). Children's autobiographical memory also correlates with their attachment security (e.g., Belsky *et al.*, 1996; McCabe *et al.*, 2006) and with the organization of their self-concept in early childhood (Bird & Reese, 2006). Most compelling, preadolescents with a greater knowledge of family history experience greater psychological well-being (Duke, Lazarus, & Fivush, 2008; Fivush *et al.*, 2008), and adolescents' life stories correlate with their self-esteem (McLean & Breen, 2009; McLean, Breen, & Fournier, in press; Reese *et al.*, in press). Thus, although these tests of mediation via autobiographical memory need to be conducted formally, it is possible that possessing richer autobiographical memories leads to stronger socioemotional skills, and specifically to a stronger self-concept and to psychological well-being. This link is consistent with research revealing greater well-being among adults who can tell more mature and coherent life stories (Baerger & McAdams, 1999; Bauer *et al.*, 2005).

The mechanism for these effects also needs to be elucidated. Putting experiences into words, especially past emotional experiences, appears to enhance well-being in adults. Pennebaker (1997) and colleagues have amply demonstrated the benefits of writing and talking about past emotional experiences, especially when causes and insights are emphasized in the process. Working through emotional experiences after the emotions have subsided may be especially helpful because resolution and integration are easier when not in the heat of the moment (Fivush, 2001). An exciting avenue for future research will be to explore how richer autobiographical memories in childhood lead to happier, more articulate, and more self-assured adolescents.

V. From Neurology to Narrative: A Synthesis of Autobiographical Memory Development from Infancy to Adolescence

My goal in this chapter was to synthesize contemporary theories and research on autobiographical memory from infancy to adolescence. In Reese (2002b), I advocated that autobiographical memory researchers adopt a dynamic systems perspective by undertaking six tasks (Thelen & Smith, 1998): (1) define the variable of interest; (2) map the trajectory of children's memories at different ages and under different conditions; (3) conduct intensive longitudinal studies of children's memory from 1 to 5 years; (4) identify transition points of rapid change; (5) discover the main sources of influence on children's developing memories; and (6) test these hypotheses experimentally. I am happy to report that collectively the field has made progress on all of these fronts.

In response to Tasks 1 and 2, we continue to elucidate the nature of children's and adolescents' memories, from their deferred imitation to their life stories. One question that immediately pops to mind is "Are we even looking at the same phenomenon over this age span?" Based on the continuity in findings that emerges across these radically different methods, I argue that yes, we are looking at the same phenomenon. Children increasingly demonstrate their recall of "what," "where," and "when" with age across these methods, and their recall gradually shows greater evidence of recollection and integration. However, the choice of method is confounded with age, such that lab-based and experimental procedures dominate the infancy literature, and in middle childhood and adolescence most studies are based on interviews about naturally occurring events. We can not devise a verbal test of autobiographical memory for infants under one year, but we can continue to search for a nonverbal test of autobiographical memory for young children. We should also expand upon the brain-imaging research beyond infancy (see Riggins *et al.*, 2009).

We have made tremendous progress with respect to the third task of mapping these memories across time. Many longitudinal datasets of autobiographical memory development from early to middle childhood now exist (e.g., Cleveland & Reese, 2005, 2008; Fivush & Schwarzmueller, 1998; Hedrick *et al.*, in press b; van Abbema & Bauer, 2005; Wang, 2006) and no doubt several more are waiting in the wings. Conclusions from these datasets differ depending upon whether we view children's memories prospectively or retrospectively, however. Viewed prospectively, children's memory still appears to be relatively continuous. Their verbal memories become increasingly detailed and recollective across the preschool years. Qualitative shifts only appear in hindsight, when the data are viewed retrospectively. For instance, in the Cleveland and Reese (2008) dataset, children's memories underwent a dramatic drop-off between ages 2 and 2½, but only from the perspective of the 5½-year-olds' recall. At the time that the memories were being formed, development appeared to be continuous and gradual (Reese, 2002a). Thus, we are closer to identifying transition points in children's memories (Task 4), but we may only be able to see these transition points in retrospect, when memories have been consolidated as firmly autobiographical. At present, there is no strong evidence for a qualitative shift in children's memories between ages 3 and 5 years as proposed in several theories, but perhaps we will begin to see these transition points from the perspective of middle childhood or early adolescence, once further forgetting has taken place. In line with dynamic systems approaches (e.g., van Geert & Steenbeek, 2005), I advocate the use of intensive longitudinal case studies to identify these transition points in children's memories. These case studies will be difficult because they will need to take place over longer time spans than in infancy to observe change, but if enough case studies are collected, we can merge them to model the process of development.

I believe that we have made the greatest advances in response to the last two recommended tasks. Through correlational and experimental long-itudinal studies, we are now much surer of the role of various endogenous and exogenous factors in children's autobiographical memory. We also are starting to understand how these various sources interact. In particular, adults' reminiscing style is a strong influence on children's autobiographi-cal memory, but it interacts with other factors such as children's early self-awareness (Reese & Newcombe, 2007) and adults' style of discussing events as they unfold (Hedrick *et al.*, in press a).

Given the healthy development of the field, what is left to discover about autobiographical memory from infancy to adolescence? The first order of business is to continue to follow children from these longitudinal studies as they move through adolescence. Do the same exogenous sources of influence, such as maternal reminiscing style, continue to act on autobiographical memory development in the same way? Do fathers start to play a larger role in shaping their children's autobiographical memories (Reese, Haden, & Fivush, 1996; but cf. Peterson & Roberts, 2003)? One potential new endogenous influence is children's developing understand-ing of conventional time during middle childhood. The ability to mentally manipulate longer time scales (e.g., months and years) may interact with children's event memory skills to help them integrate past events and create mental timelines of their lives. Another possible research avenue is to explore how older children's advanced perspective-taking interacts with new forms of parent-child and peer reminiscing to enable children to consider a past event from multiple perspectives (Reese & Fivush, 2008), including how they might react to the same situation differently in the future. Perspective-taking may help adolescents consider alternate versions of the life story, both when selecting events most meaningful to the self, and in projecting different future selves.

Finally, it will be imperative to discover how adolescents find and create meaning in their lives. What are the influences on their understanding of the causes and consequences of life events and the relevance of events for self? What are the critical social and cognitive skills for creating coherence in a life? Habermas and de Silveira (2008) have illustrated that coherence is not simply a function of sheer intelligence. Instead, the ability to filter out less relevant events may be important for selecting events to include in the life story. Besides reminiscing with peers and parents, what are the other contributors to this ability in adolescence? We need to explore adolescents' meaning-making in a range of media—literature, movies, role-playing games, and social networking sites—that allows the adolescent to enter the mind of a character and to adopt alternative identities.

By the end of childhood, autobiographical memory is largely stable. It is at this point that the real work of memory begins as preadolescents and adolescents start to use memory for the service of the self. What does one do with the memories of early childhood that remain? How are these early memories integrated with new memories that are constantly being accumulated? And how does this integration translate into benefits for adolescents' well-being? Here I offer my tentative hypotheses based on the limited data available at present, with the goal of extending the emergent recollection theory into adolescence.

When children first begin to use autobiographical memory for self-understanding, and there is some indication that girls do this slightly earlier than boys, the insights gained may actually decrease, at least temporarily, their well-being (see McLean *et al.*, in press; Reese *et al.*, in press). Self-reflection can be, and perhaps should be, discomforting. By mid-adolescence, the ability to find the positive aspects of a negative experience is linked to positive self-esteem, especially for boys (McLean & Breen, 2009). Of course, many roadblocks along the way can prevent these positive spin-offs of autobiographical memory. Adolescents who focus excessively and unproductively on the past, as in the case of rumination, can become depressed (e.g., Nolen-Hoeksema *et al.*, 2007). I predict, however, that adolescents who experienced rich, elaborative, and emotional conversations about the past in early and middle childhood will be able to use memories in the service of self more effectively than those adolescents who experienced fewer and less detailed conversations about their experiences (cf. McLean & Breen, 2009). These adolescents will have a richer store of specific self-relevant memories to draw upon in creating and interpreting their life stories.

Cultural differences in the relationship between autobiographical memory and well-being should also emerge in adolescence. In cultures in which memories are prized and discussed frequently, such as in Māori culture (Reese *et al.*, 2008), the connection between memory and well-being may occur earlier in adolescence than in cultures in which individual memories are not discussed as elaboratively, such as in many Asian cultures. The implications of such findings for interventions with adolescents are numerous, but first we will need to discover at what point in development autobiography becomes intertwined with well-being for young men and women in different cultures. Then the real work for researchers will be to translate our knowledge of autobiographical memory development into a form that practitioners who work with children and adolescents can use.

REFERENCES

Alvarado, M. C., & Bachevalier, J. (2000). Revisiting the maturation of medial temporal lobe memory functions in primates. *Learning and Memory, 7*, 244–256.

Baerger, D. R., & McAdams, D. P. (1999). Life story coherence and its relation to psychological well-being. *Narrative Inquiry, 9*, 69–96.

Barr, R., & Hayne, H. (2000). Age-related changes in imitation: Implications for memory development. In C. Rovee-Collier, L. P. Lipsitt, & H. Hayne (Eds.), *Progress in infancy research* (Vol. 1, pp. 21–67). Hillsdale, NJ: Erlbaum.

Barr, R., Dowden, A., & Hayne, H. (1996). Developmental changes in deferred imitation by 6- to 24-month-old infants. *Infant Behavior and Development, 19*, 159–170.

Barr, R., Vieira, A., & Rovee-Collier, C. (2001). Mediated imitation at 6 months of age: Remembering by association. *Journal of Experimental Child Psychology, 79*, 229–252.

Barr, R., Rovee-Collier, C. A., & Campanella, J. (2005). Retrieval protracts deferred imitation by 6-month-olds. *Infancy, 7*, 263–283.

Bauer, P. J. (2007a). Recall in infancy: A neurodevelopmental account. *Current Directions in Psychological Science, 16*, 142–146.

Bauer, P. J. (2007b). *Remembering the times of our lives: Memory in infancy and beyond.* Mahwah, NJ: Lawrence Erlbaum Associates.

Bauer, P. J. (2008). Toward a neuro-developmental account of the development of declarative memory. *Developmental Psychobiology, 50*, 19–31.

Bauer, P. J., & Burch, M. M. (2004). Developments in early memory: Multiple mediators of foundational processes. In J. M. Lucariello, J. A. Hudson, R. Fivush, & P. J. Bauer (Eds.), *The development of the mediated mind* (pp. 101–125). Mahwah, NJ: Lawrence Erlbaum.

Bauer, P. J., & Wewerka, S. S. (1995). One- to two-year olds' recall of events: The more expressed, the more impressed. *Journal of Experimental Child Psychology, 80*, 174–200.

Bauer, P. J., Wenner, J. A., Dropik, P. L., & Wewerka, S. S. (2000). Parameters of remembering and forgetting in the transition from infancy to early childhood. *Monographs of the Society for Research in Child Development, 65*, 1–204.

Bauer, P. J., Wiebe, S. A., Waters, J. M., & Bangston, S. K. (2001). Reexposure breeds recall: Effects of experience on 9-month-olds' ordered recall. *Journal of Experimental Child Psychology, 80*, 174–200.

Bauer, P. J., Wiebe, S. A., Carver, L. J., Waters, J. M., & Nelson, C. A. (2003a). Developmental in long-term explicit memory late in the first year of life: Behavioral and electrophysiological indices. *Psychological Science, 14*, 629–635.

Bauer, P. J., Stennes, L. M., & Haight, J. C. (2003b). Representation of the inner self in autobiography: Women's and men's use of internal states language in personal narratives. *Memory, 11*, 27–42.

Bauer, P. J., van Abbema, D. L., Wiebe, S. A., Cary, M. S., Phill, C., & Burch, M. M. (2004). Props, not pictures, are worth a thousand words: Verbal accessibility of early memories under different conditions of contextual support. *Applied Cognitive Psychology, 18*, 373–392.

Bauer, J. J., McAdams, D. P., & Sakaeda, A. R. (2005). Interpreting the good life: Growth memories in the lives of mature, happy people. *Journal of Personality and Social Psychology, 88*, 203–217.

Bauer, P. J., Wiebe, S. A., Carver, L. J., Lukowski, A. F., Haight, J. C., Water, J. M., & Nelson, C. A. (2006). Electrophysiological indexes of encoding and behavioural indexes of recall: Examining relations and developmental change late in the first year of life. *Developmental Neuropsychology, 29*, 293–320.

Bauer, P. J., Burch, M. M., Scholin, S. E., & Güler, O. E. (2007). Using cue words to investigate the distribution of autobiographical memories in childhood. *Psychological Science, 18*, 910–916.

Belsky, J., Spritz, B., & Crnic, K. (1996). Infant attachment security and affective-cognitive information processing at age 3. *Psychological Science, 7*, 111–114.

Bird, A., & Reese, E. (2006). Emotional reminiscing and the development of an autobiographical self. *Developmental Psychology, 42*, 613–626.

Bird, A., Reese, E., & Tripp, G. (2006). Parent–child talk about past emotional events: Associations with child temperament and goodness-of-fit. *Journal of Cognition and Development, 7*, 189–210.

Bohanek, J. G., Marin, K. A., Fivush, R., & Duke, M. P. (2006). Family narrative interaction and children's sense of self. *Family Process, 45*, 39–54.

Bohn, A., & Berntsen, D. (2008). Life story development in childhood: The development of life story abilities and the acquisition of cultural life scripts in late middle childhood to adolescence. *Developmental Psychology, 44*, 1135–1147.

Boland, A. M., Haden, C. A., & Ornstein, P. A. (2003). Boosting children's memory by training mothers in the use of an elaborative conversational style as an event unfolds. *Journal of Cognition and Development, 4*, 39–65.

Bost, K. K., Shin, N., McBride, B. A., Brown, G. L., Vaughn, B. E., Coppola, G., Verissimio, M., Monteiro, L., & Korth, B. (2006). Maternal secure base scripts, children's attachment security, and mother-child narrative styles. *Attachment & Human Development, 8*, 241–260.

Bowlby, J. (1988). *A secure base: Clinical applications of attachment theory.* London: Routledge Press.

Bretherton, I., & Munholland, K. A. (1999). Internal working models in attachment relationships: A construct revisited. In J. Cassidy & P. R. Shaver (Eds.), *Handbook of attachment: Theory, research, and clinical applications* (pp. 89–111). New York: The Guilford Press.

Brown, D., & Pipe, M.-E. (2003). Variations on a technique: Enhancing children's recall using narrative elaboration training. *Applied Cognitive Psychology, 17*, 377–399.

Bruck, M., & Ceci, S. J. (1999). The suggestibility of children's memory. *Annual Review of Psychology, 50*, 419–439.

Carver, L. J., & Bauer, P. J. (1999). When the event is more than the sum of its parts: Long-term recall of event sequences by 9-month-old infants. *Memory, 7*, 147–174.

Carver, L. J., & Bauer, P. J. (2001). The dawning of a past: The emergence of long-term explicit memory in infancy. *Journal of Experimental Psychology: General, 130*, 726–745.

Champion, T., Seymour, H., & Camarata, S. (1995). Narrative discourse of African American children. *Journal of Narrative and Life History*, *5*, 333–352.

Cheatham, C. L., & Bauer, P. J. (2005). Construction of a more coherent story: Prior verball recall predicts later verbal accessibility of early memories. *Memory*, *13*, 516–532.

Cleveland, E. S., & Reese, E. (2005). Maternal structure and autonomy support in conversations about the past: Contributions to children's autobiographical memory. *Developmental Psychology*, *41*, 376–388.

Cleveland, E. S., & Reese, E. (2008). Children remember early childhood: Long-term recall across the offset of childhood amnesia. *Applied Cognitive Psychology*, *22*, 127–142.

Cleveland, E. S., Reese, E., & Grolnick, W. (2007). Children's engagement and competence in personal recollection: Effects of parents' reminiscing goals. *Journal of Experimental Child Psychology*, *96*, 131–149.

Collie, R., & Hayne, H. (1999). Deferred imitation by 6-month-old infants: More evidence for declarative memory. *Developmental Psychobiology*, *35*, 83–90.

Conroy, R., & Salmon, K. (2006). Talking about parts of a past experience: The impact of discussion style and event structure on memory for discussed and nondiscussed information. *Journal of Experimental Child Psychology*, *95*, 278–297.

Conway, M. A., Singer, J. A., & Tagini, A. (2004). The self and autobiographical memory: Correspondence and coherence. *Social Cognition*, *22*, 491–529.

Conway, M. A., Wang, Q., Hanyu, K., & Haque, S. A. (2005). Cross-cultural investigation of autobiographical memory: On the universality and cultural variation of the reminiscence bump. *Journal of Cross-Cultural Psychology*, *36*, 739–749.

Courage, M. L., Edison, S. C., & Howe, M. L. (2004). Variability in the early development of visual self-recognition. *Infant Behavior & Development*, *27*, 509–532.

Deci, E. L., & Ryan, R. M. (1987). The support of autonomy and the control of behavior. *Journal of Personality and Social Psychology*, *6*, 1024–1037.

Dudycha, G. J., & Dudycha, M. M. (1933). Adolescents' memories of preschool experiences. *Journal of Genetic Psychology: General*, *42*, 468–480.

Duke, M. P., Lazarus, A., & Fivush, R. (2008). Knowledge of family history as a clinically useful index of psychological well-being and prognosis: A brief report. *Psychotherapy Theory, Research, Practice, Training*, *45*, 268–272.

Eisenberg, A. R. (1985). Learning to describe past experiences in conversation. *Discourse Processes*, *8*, 177–204.

Engel, S. (1995). *The stories children tell: Making sense of the narratives of childhood*. New York: W. H. Freeman.

Farrant, K., & Reese, E. (2000). Maternal style and children's participation in reminiscing: Stepping stones in children's autobiographical memory development. *Journal of Cognition and Development*, *1*, 193–225.

Farrar, J. M., Fasig, L. G., & Welch-Ross, M. K. (1997). Attachment and emotion in autobiographical memory development. *Journal of Experimental Child Psychology*, *67*, 389–408.

Fenson, L., Dale, P. S., Reznick, J. S., Thal, D., Bates, E., Hartung, J. P., Pethick, S., & Reilly, J. S. (1993). *MacArthur communicative development inventories*. San Diego: Singular Publishing Group.

Fivush, R. (2001). Owning experience: The development of subjective perspective in autobiographical memory. In C. Moore & K. Lemmon (Eds.), *The self in time: Developmental perspectives* (pp. 35–52). Mahwah, NJ: Erlbaum.

Fivush, R., & Fromhoff, F. (1988). Style and structure in mother–child conversations about the past. *Discourse Processes*, *11*, 337–355.

Fivush, R., & Hamond, N. (1990). Autobiographical memory across the preschool years: Toward reconceptualizing childhood amnesia. In R. Fivush & J. A. Hudson (Eds.), *Knowing and remembering in young children* (pp. 223–248). New York: Cambridge University Press.

Fivush, R., & Nelson, K. (2004). Culture and language in the emergence of autobiographical memory. *Psychological Science, 15*, 573–577.

Fivush, R., & Nelson, K. (2006). Parent–child reminiscing locates the self in the past. *British Journal of Developmental Psychology, 24*, 235–251.

Fivush, R., & Reese, E. (1992). The social construction of autobiographical memory. In M. A. Conway, D. Rubin, H. Spinnler, & W. Wagenaar (Eds.), *Theoretical perspectives on autobiographical memory* (pp. 115–132). The Netherlands: Kulwer Academic Publishers.

Fivush, R., & Schwarzmueller, A. (1998). Children remember childhood: Implications for childhood amnesia. *Applied Cognitive Psychology, 12*, 455–473.

Fivush, R., & Vasudeva, A. (2002). Remembering to relate: Socioemotional correlates of mother–child reminiscing. *Journal of Cognition and Development, 3*, 73–90.

Fivush, R., Kuebli, J., & Clubb, P. A. (1992). The structure of events and event representations: A developmental analysis. *Child Development, 63*, 188–201.

Fivush, A., Haden, C., & Adam, S. (1995). Structure and coherence of preschoolers' personal narratives over time: Implications for childhood amnesia. *Journal of Experimental Child Psychology, 60*, 32–56.

Fivush, R., Haden, C. A., & Reese, E. (1996). Remembering, recounting and reminiscing: The development of autobiographical memory in social context. In D. Rubin (Ed.), *Remembering our past: An overview of autobiographical memory* (pp. 377–397). Cambridge, MA: Cambridge University Press.

Fivush, R., Sales, J. M., Goldberg, A., Bahrick, L., & Parker, J. (2004). Weathering the storm: Children's long-term recall of Hurricane Andrew. *Memory, 12*, 104–118.

Fivush, R., Haden, C. A., & Reese, E. (2006). Elaborating on elaborations: The role of maternal reminiscing style in cognitive and socioemotional development. *Child Development, 77*, 1568–1588.

Fivush, R., Bohanek, J., & Duke, M. (2008). The intergenerational self: Subjective perspective and family history. In F. Sani (Ed.), *Individual and collective self-continuity* (pp. 131–144). New York: Psychology Press.

Friedman, W. J. (2003). The development of a differentiated sense of the past and the future. In R. V. Kail (Ed.), *Advances in child development and behavior* (Vol. 31, pp. 229–269). San Diego, CA: Academic Press.

Friedman, W. J. (2004). Time in autobiographical memory. *Social Cognition, 22*, 591–605.

Friedman, W. J., & Lyon, T. D. (2005). Development of temporal-reconstructive abilities. *Child Development, 76*, 1202–1216.

Geddie, L., Fradin, S., & Beer, J. (2000). Child characteristics which impact accuracy of recall and suggestibility in preschoolers: Is age the best predictor? *Child Abuse and Neglect, 24*, 223–235.

Goldman-Rakic, P. S. (1987). Circuitry of primate prefrontal cortex and regulation of behaviour by representational memory. In F. Plum (Ed.), *Handbook of physiology, the nervous system, higher functions of the brain* (Vol. 5, pp. 373–417). Bethesda, MD: American Physiological Society.

Grolnick, W. S., Gurland, S. T., DeCourcey, W., & Jacob, K. (2002). Antecedents and consequences of mothers' autonomy support: An experimental investigation. *Developmental Psychology, 38*, 143–155.

Habermas, T., & Bluck, S. (2000). Getting a life: The emergence of the life story in adolescence. *Psychological Bulletin, 126*, 748–769.

Habermas, T., & de Silveira, C. (2008). The development of global coherence in life narratives across adolescent: Temporal, causal, and thematic aspects. *Developmental Psychology, 44,* 707–721.

Haden, C. A., & Fivush, R. (1996). Contextual variation in maternal conversational styles. *Merrill-Palmer Quarterly, 42,* 200–227.

Han, J. J., Leichtman, M. D., & Wang, Q. (1998). Autobiographical memory in Korean, Chinese, and American children. *Developmental Psychology, 34,* 701–713.

Harley, K., & Reese, E. (1999). Origins of autobiographical memory. *Developmental Psychology, 35,* 1338–1348.

Hart, B., & Risley, T. R. (1995). *Meaningful differences in the everyday experience of young American children.* Baltimore, MD: Paul H. Brookes Publishing Co.

Hayne, H. (2004). Infant memory development: Implications for childhood amnesia. *Developmental Review, 24,* 33–73.

Hayne, H., & MacDonald, S. (2003). The socialization of autobiographical memory in children and adults: The roles of culture and gender. In R. Fivush & C. A. Haden (Eds.), *Autobiographical memory and the construction of a narrative self: Developmental and cultural perspectives* (pp. 99–120). Mahwah, NJ: Lawrence Erlbaum Associates.

Hayne, H., Boniface, J., & Barr, R. (2000). The development of declarative memory in human infants: Age-related changes in deferred imitation. *Behavioral Neuroscience, 114,* 77–83.

Hedrick, A. M., Haden, C. A., & Ornstein, P. A. (in press a). Elaborative talk during and after an event: Conversational style influences children's memory reports. *Journal of Cognition and Development.*

Hedrick, A. M., San Souci, P., Haden, C. A., & Ornstein, P. A. (in press b). Mother-child joint conversational exchanges during events: Linkages to children's memory reports over time. *Journal of Cognition and Development.*

Henri, V., & Henri, C. (1898). Earliest recollections. *Popular Science Monthly, 53,* 108–115.

Herbert, J., Gross, J., & Hayne, H. (2006). Age-related changes in deferred imitation between 6 and 9 months of age. *Infant Behavior and Development, 29,* 136–139.

Howe, M. L. (2000). *The fate of early memories: Developmental science and the retention of childhood experiences.* Washington, DC: American Psychological Association.

Howe, M. (2003). Memories from the cradle. *Current Directions in Psychological Science, 12,* 62–65.

Howe, M. L., & Courage, M. L. (1993). On resolving the enigma of infantile amnesia. *Psychological Bulletin, 113,* 305–326.

Howe, M. L., & Courage, M. L. (1997). The emergence and early development of autobiographical memory. *Psychological Review, 104,* 499–523.

Howe, M., Courage, M. L., & Edison, S. C. (2003). When autobiographical memory begins. *Developmental Review, 23,* 471–494.

Hudson, J. A. (1990). The emergence of autobiographical memory in mother–child conversation. In R. Fivush & J. A. Hudson (Eds.), *Knowing and remembering in young children* (pp. 166–196). Cambridge, UK: Cambridge University Press.

Hudson, J. A. (1991). Learning to reminisce: A case study. *Journal of Narrative and Life History, 1,* 295–324.

Jack, F., & Hayne, H. (2007). Eliciting adults' earliest memories: Does it matter how we ask the question? *Memory, 15,* 647–663.

Jack, F., MacDonald, S., Reese, E., & Hayne, H. (2009). Maternal reminiscing style during early childhood predicts the age of adolescents' earliest memories. *Child Development, 80,* 496–505.

James, W. (1890/1950). *Principles of psychology.* Chicago: Encylopedia Britannica.

Keller, H., Kärtner, J., Borke, J., Yovsi, R., & Kleis, A. (2005). Parenting styles and the development of the categorical self: A longitudinal study on mirror self-recognition in Cameroonian Nso and German families. *International Journal of Behavioral Development, 29*, 496–504.

Klein, P. J., & Meltzoff, A. N. (1999). Long-term memory, forgetting, and deferred imitation in 12-month-old infants. *Developmental Science, 2*, 102–113.

Kleinknecht, E., & Beike, D. R. (2004). How knowing and doing inform an autobiography: Relations among preschoolers' theory of mind, narrative, and event memory skills. *Applied Cognitive Psychology, 18*, 745–764.

Laible, D. (2004). Mother–child discourse in two contexts: Links with child temperament, attachment security, and socioemotional competence. *Developmental Psychology, 40*, 979–992.

Laible, D., & Song, J. (2006). Constructing emotional and relational understanding: The role of affect and mother–child discourse. *Merrill-Palmer Quarterly, 52*, 44–69.

Laible, D., & Thompson, R. (2000). Mother–child discourse, attachment security, shared positive affect, and early conscience development. *Child Development, 71*, 1424–1440.

La Rooy, D., Pipe, M.-E., & Murray, J. E. (2007). Enhancing children's event recall after long delays. *Applied Cognitive Psychology, 21*, 1–17.

Lewis, K. (1999). Maternal style in reminiscing: Relations to child individual differences. *Cognitive Development, 14*, 381–399.

Lewis, M., & Brooks-Gunn, J. (1979). *Social cognition and the acquisition of the self.* New York: Plenum Press.

Leyva, D., Reese, E., Grolnick, W., & Price, C. (2008). Elaboration and autonomy support in low-income mothers' reminiscing: Links to children's autobiographical narratives. *Journal of Cognition and Development, 9*, 363–389.

Liston, C., & Kagan, J. (2002). Memory enhancement in early childhood. *Nature, 419*, 896.

MacDonald, S., Uesiliana, K., & Hayne, H. (2000). Cross-cultural and gender differences in childhood amnesia. *Memory, 8*, 365–376.

Main, M., Goldwyn, R., & Hesse, E. (2002). *Adult attachment scoring and classification systems*, Version 7.0. Unpublished manuscript, University of California at Berkeley.

Mandler, J., & Johnson, N. (1977). Remembrance of things parsed: Story structure and recall. *Cognitive Psychology, 9*, 111–151.

McAdams, D. P. (1996). Personality, modernity, and the storied self: A contemporary framework for studying persons. *Psychological Inquiry, 7*, 295–321.

McAdams, D. P. (2006). The role of narrative in personality psychology today. *Narrative Inquiry, 16*, 11–18.

McCabe, A., & Bliss, L. S. (2003). *Patterns of narrative discourse: A multicultural, life span approach.* Boston: Pearson Education Inc.

McCabe, A., & Peterson, C. (1991). Getting the story: A longitudinal study of parental styles in eliciting narratives and developing narrative skill. In A. McCabe & C. Peterson (Eds.), *Developing narrative structure* (pp. 217–253). Hillsdale, NJ: Lawrence Erlbaum Associates.

McCabe, A., Peterson, C., & Connors, D. M. (2006). Attachment security and narrative elaboration. *International Journal of Behavioral Development, 30*, 398–409.

McDonough, L., Mandler, J. M., McKee, R. D., & Squire, L. R. (1995). The deferred imitation task as a nonverbal measure of declarative memory. *Proceedings of the National Academic of Sciences, 92*, 7580–7584.

McGuigan, F., & Salmon, K. (2004). The time to talk: The influence of the timing of adult-child talk on children's event memory. *Child Development, 75*, 669–686.

McGuigan, F., & Salmon, K. (2005). Pre-event discussion and recall of a novel event: How are children best prepared? *Journal of Experimental Child Psychology, 91*, 342–366.

McGuigan, F., & Salmon, K. (2006). The influence of talking on showing and telling: Adult–child talk and children's verbal and nonverbal event recall. *Applied Cognitive Psychology*, *20*, 365–381.

McLean, K. C., & Breen, A. V. (2009). Processes and content of narrative identity development in adolescence: Gender and well-being. *Developmental Psychology*, *45*, 702–710.

McLean, K. C., Breen, A. V., & Fournier, M. A. (in press). Constructing the self in early, middle, and late adolescent boys: Narrative identity, individuation, and well-being. *Journal of Research on Adolescence*.

Measelle, J. R., John, O. P., Ablow, J. C., Cowan, P. A., & Cowan, C. P. (2005). Can children provide coherent, stable, and valid self-reports on the Big Five Dimensions: A longitudinal study from ages 5 to 7. *Journal of Personality and Social Psychology*, *89*, 90–106.

Meltzoff, A. N. (1995). What infant memory tells us about infantile amnesia: Long-term recall and deferred imitation. *Journal of Experimental Child Psychology*, *59*, 497–515.

Minami, M. (1996). Japanese preschool children's and adults' narrative discourse competence and narrative structure. *Journal of Narrative and Life History*, *6*, 349–373.

Morgan, K., & Hayne, H. (2007). Nonspecific verbal cues alleviate forgetting by young children. *Developmental Science*, *10*, 727–733.

Morris, G., & Baker-Ward, L. (2007). Fragile but real: Children's capacity to use newly acquired words to convey preverbal memories. *Child Development*, *78*, 448–458.

Mullen, M. K. (1994). Earliest recollections of childhood: A demographic analysis. *Cognition*, *52*, 55–79.

Naito, M. (2003). The relationship between theory of mind and episodic memory: Evidence for the development of autonoetic consciousness. *Journal of Experimental Child Psychology*, *85*, 312–336.

Nelson, K. (1989). Monologue as representation of real-life experience. In K. Nelson (Ed.), *Narratives from the crib* (pp. 27–71). Cambridge, MA: Harvard University Press.

Nelson, K. (1993). The psychological and social origins of autobiographical memory. *Psychological Science*, *4*, 1–8.

Nelson, K. (1996). *Language in cognitive development: The emergence of the mediated mind.* Cambridge, UK: Cambridge University Press.

Nelson, K., & Fivush, R. (2004). The emergence of autobiographical memory: A social cultural developmental theory. *Psychological Review*, *111*, 486–511.

Nelson, K., & Ross, G. (1980). The generalities and specifics of long-term memory in infants and young children. *New Directions for Child Development*, *10*, 87–101.

Newcombe, R., & Reese, E. (2004). Evaluations and orientations in mother–child narratives as a function of attachment. *International Journal of Behavioral Development*, *28*, 230–245.

Nolen-Hoeksema, S., Stice, E., Wade, E., & Bohon, C. (2007). Reciprocal relations between rumination and bulimic, substance abuse, and depressive symptoms in female adolescents. *Journal of Abnormal Psychology*, *116*, 198–207.

Ontai, L. L., & Thompson, R. A. (2008). Attachment, parent–child discourse and theory-of-mind development. *Social Development*, *17*, 47–60.

Ornstein, P. A., Haden, C. A., & Elischberger, H. B. (2006). Children's memory development: Remembering the past and preparing for the future. In E. Bialystok & F. I. M. Craik (Eds.), *Lifespan cognition: Mechanisms of change* (pp. 143–161). New York: Oxford University Press.

Pennebaker, J. W. (1997). Writing about emotional experiences as a therapeutic process. *Psychological Science*, *8*, 162–166.

Perner, J. (2000). Memory and theory of mind. In E. Tulving & F. I. M. Craik (Eds.), *The Oxford handbook of memory* (pp. 297–312). New York: Oxford University Press.

Perner, J. (2001). Episodic memory: Essential distinctions and developmental implications. In C. Moore & K. Lemmon (Eds.), *The self in time: Developmental perspectives* (pp. 181–202). Mahwah, NJ: Lawrence Erlbaum Associates.

Perner, J., & Dienes, Z. (2003). Developmental aspects of consciousness: How much theory of mind do you need to be consciously aware? *Consciousness and Cognition, 12*, 63–82.

Perner, J., & Ruffman, T. (1995). Episodic memory or autonoetic consciousness: Developmental evidence and a theory of autobiographical memory development. *Journal of Experimental Child Psychology, 59*, 516–548.

Perner, J., Kloo, D., & Gornik, E. (2007). Episodic memory development: Theory of mind is part of re-experiencing experienced events. *Infant and Child Development, 16*, 471–490.

Pesco, D., & Crago, M. (1996). "We went home, told the whole story to our friends": Narratives by children in an Algonquin community. *Journal of Narrative and Life History, 6*, 293–321.

Peterson, C., & McCabe, A. (1983). *Developmental psycholinguistics: Three ways of looking at a child's narrative*. New York: Plenum.

Peterson, C., & Rideout, R. (1998). Memory for medical emergencies experienced by 1- and 2-year-olds. *Developmental Psychology, 34*, 1059–1072.

Peterson, C., & Roberts, C. (2003). Like mother, like daughter: Similarities in narrative style. *Developmental Psychology, 39*, 551–562.

Peterson, C., Jesso, B., & McCabe, A. (1999). Encouraging narratives in preschoolers: An intervention study. *Journal of Child Language, 26*, 46–67.

Peterson, C., Grant, V. V., & Boland, L. D. (2005). Childhood amnesia in children and adolescents: Their earliest memories. *Memory, 13*, 622–637.

Peterson, C., Smorti, A., & Tani, F. (2008). Parental influences on earliest memories. *Memory, 16*, 569–578.

Pillemer, D. B. (2003). Directive functions of autobiographical memory: The guiding power of the specific episode. *Memory, 11*, 193–202.

Pillemer, D. B., Wink, P., DiDonato, T. E., & Sanborn, R. L. (2003). Gender differences in autobiographical memory styles of older adults. *Memory, 11*, 525–532.

Piolino, P., Hisland, M., Ruffeveille, I., Matuszewski, V., Jambaqué, I., & Eustache, F. (2007). Do school-age children remember or know the personal past? *Consciousness and Cognition, 16*, 84–101.

Povinelli, D. J. (1995). The unduplicated self. In P. Rochat (Ed.), *Advances in psychology, The self in infancy: Theory and research* (Vol. 112, pp. 161–192). Amsterdam: North-Holland/Elsevier.

Povinelli, D. J. (2001). The self: Elevated in consciousness and extended in time. In C. Moore & K. Lemmon (Eds.), *The self in time: Developmental perspectives* (pp. 75–96). Mahwah, NJ: Lawrence Erlbaum Associates.

Priel, B., & de Schonen, S. (1986). Self-recognition: A study of a population without mirrors. *Journal of Experimental Child Psychology, 41*, 237–250.

Priestley, G., Roberts, S., & Pipe, M.-E. (1999). Returning to the scene: Reminders and context reinstatement enhance children's recall. *Developmental Psychology, 35*, 1006–1019.

Prudhomme, N. (2005). Early declarative memory and self-concept. *Infant Behavior and Development, 28*, 132–144.

Reese, E. (1995). Predicting children's literacy from mother–child conversations. *Cognitive Development, 10*, 381–405.

Reese, E. (1999). What children say when they talk about the past. *Narrative Inquiry, 9*, 1–27.

Reese, E. (2002a). A model of the origins of autobiographical memory. In H. Hayne & J. Fagan (Eds.), *Progress in infancy research* (Vol. 2, pp. 215–260). Mahwah, NJ: Lawrence Erlbaum.

Reese, E. (2002b). Social factors in the development of autobiographical memory: The state of the art. *Social Development, 11,* 124–142.

Reese, E. (2008). Maternal coherence in the adult attachment interview is linked to maternal reminiscing and to children's self concept. *Attachment and Human Development, 10,* 451–464.

Reese, E., & Brown, N. (2000). Reminiscing and recounting in the preschool years. *Applied Cognitive Psychology, 14,* 1–17.

Reese, E., & Cleveland, E. (2007). Mother–child reminiscing and children's understanding of mind. *Merrill-Palmer Quarterly, 52,* 17–43.

Reese, E., & Farrant, K. (2003). Social origins of reminiscing. In R. Fivush & C. Haden (Eds.), *Autobiographical memory and the construction of the narrative self: Developmental and cultural perspectives* (pp. 29–49). Mahwah, NJ: Lawrence Erlbaum.

Reese, E., & Fivush, R. (1993). Parental styles of talking about the past. *Developmental Psychology, 29,* 596–606.

Reese, E., & Fivush, R. (2008). Collective memory across the lifespan. *Memory, 16,* 201–212.

Reese, E., & Newcombe, R. (2007). Training mothers in elaborative reminiscing enhances children's autobiographical memory and narrative. *Child Development, 78,* 1153–1170.

Reese, E., Haden, C. A., & Fivush, R. (1993). Mother–child conversations about the past: Relationships of style and memory over time. *Cognitive Development, 8,* 403–430.

Reese, E., Haden, C. A., & Fivush, R. (1996). Mothers, fathers, daughters and sons: Gender differences in autobiographical reminiscing. *Research on Language and Social Interaction, 29,* 27–56.

Reese, E., Hayne, H., & MacDonald, S. (2008). Looking back to the future: Māori and Pakeha mother–child birth stories. *Child Development, 79,* 114–125.

Reese, E., Haden, C. A., Baker-Ward, L., Bauer, P. J., Fivush, R., & Ornstein, P. (2009). *Coherence of personal narratives across the lifespan: A multidimensional model.* Manuscript under review.

Reese, E., Chen, Y., Jack, F., & Hayne, H. (in press). Emerging identities: Narrative and self in early adolescence. In K. McLean & M. Pasupathi (Eds.), *Narrative development in adolescence.* New York: Springer.

Richmond, J., & Nelson, C. A. (2007). Accounting for change in declarative memory: A cognitive neuroscience perspective. *Developmental Review, 27,* 349–373.

Riggins, T., Miller, N. C., Bauer, P. J., Georgieff, M. K., & Nelson, C. A. (2009). Electrophysiological indices of memory for temporal order in early childhood: Implications for the development of recollection. *Developmental Science, 12,* 209–219.

Roberts, B. W., & DelVecchio, W. F. (2000). The rank-order consistency of personality traits from childhood to old age: A quantitative review of longitudinal studies. *Psychological Bulletin, 126,* 3–25.

Rudek, D. J., & Haden, C. A. (2005). Mothers' and preschoolers' mental state language during reminiscing over time. *Merrill-Palmer Quarterly, 51,* 523–549.

Sachs, J. (1983). Topic selection in parent–child discourse. *Discourse Processes, 2,* 145–153.

Saywitz, K. J., & Snyder, L. (1996). Narrative elaboration: Test of a new procedure for interviewing children. *Journal of Consulting and Clinical Psychology, 64,* 1347–1357.

Sheffield, E. G., & Hudson, J. A. (2006). You must remember this: Effects of video and photograph reminders on 18-month-olds' event memory. *Journal of Cognition and Development, 7,* 73–93.

Sheingold, K., & Tenney, Y. J. (1982). Memory for a salient childhood event. In U. Neisser (Ed.), *Memory observed* (pp. 202–212). San Francisco: Freeman.

Simcock, G., & Hayne, H. (2002). Breaking the barrier? Children fail to translate their preverbal memories into language. *Psychological Science, 13,* 225–231.

Simcock, G., & Hayne, H. (2003). Age-related changes in verbal and nonverbal memory during early childhood. *Developmental Psychology*, *39*, 805–814.

Squire, L. R. (1992). Declarative and nondeclarative memory: Multiple brain systems supporting learning and memory. *Journal of Cognitive Neuroscience*, *4*, 232–243.

Sutherland, R., Pipe, M.-E., Schick, K., Murray, J., & Gobbo, C. (2003). Knowing in advance: The impact of prior event information on memory and event knowledge. *Journal of Experimental Child Psychology*, *84*, 244–263.

Thelen, E., & Smith, L. B. (1998). Dynamic systems theories. In R. M. Lerner (Ed.), *Handbook of child psychology: Theoretical models of human development* (5th ed., Vol. 1, pp. 563–634). New York: Wiley.

Thorne, A. (2000). Personal memory telling and personality development. *Personality and Social Psychology Review*, *4*, 45–56.

Tulving, E. (1985). Memory and consciousness. *Canadian Psychology*, *26*, 1–12.

Tulving, E. (2002). Episodic memory: From mind to brain. *Annual Review of Psychology*, *53*, 1–25.

Tustin, K., & Hayne, H. (2008). *Defining the boundary: Age-related changes in childhood amnesia*. Manuscript under review.

Usher, J. A., & Neisser, U. (1993). Childhood amnesia and the beginnings of memory for four early life events. *Journal of Experimental Psychology: General*, *122*, 155–165.

van Abbema, D., & Bauer, P. J. (2005). Autobiographical memory in middle childhood: Recollections of the recent and distant past. *Memory*, *13*, 829–845.

van Geert, P., & Steenbeek, H. (2005). Explaining after by before: Basic aspects of a dynamic systems approach to the study of development. *Developmental Review*, *25*, 408–442.

Wang, Q. (2001a). Culture effects on adults' earliest childhood recollection and self-description: Implications for the relation between memory and the self. *Journal of Personality and Social Psychology*, *81*, 220–233.

Wang, Q. (2001b). "Did you have fun?" American and Chinese mother–child conversations about shared emotional experiences. *Cognitive Development*, *16*, 693–715.

Wang, Q. (2004). The emergence of cultural self-constructs: Autobiographical memory and self-description in European American and Chinese children. *Developmental Psychology*, *40*, 3–15.

Wang, Q. (2006). Relations of maternal style and child self-concept to autobiographical memories in Chinese, Chinese immigrant, and European American 3-year-olds. *Child Development*, *77*, 1794–1809.

Wang, Q. (2007). "Remember when you got the big, big bulldozer?" Mother–child reminiscing over time and across cultures. *Social Cognition*, *25*, 455–471.

Wang, Q. (2008a). Being American, being Asian: The bicultural self and autobiographical memory in Asian Americans. *Cognition*, *107*, 743–751.

Wang, Q. (2008b). Emotion knowledge and autobiographical memory across the preschool years: A cross-cultural longitudinal investigation. *Cognition*, *108*, 117–135.

Wareham, P., & Salmon, K. (2006). Mother–child reminiscing about everyday experiences: Implications for psychological interventions in the preschool years. *Clinical Psychology Review*, *26*, 535–554.

Wareham, P., Salmon, K., Dadds, M. R., & Allen, J. (in press). Training mothers in emotion-rich, elaborative reminiscing: Influences on autobiographical memory and emotion knowledge. *Journal of Cognition and Development*.

Weeks, T., & Pasupathi, M. (in press). Autonomy, identity, and joint autobiographical remembering in adolescence. In K. McLean & M. Pasupathi (Eds.), *Narrative development in adolescence*. New York: Springer.

Welch-Ross, M. (1995). An integrative model of the development of autobiographical memory. *Developmental Review, 15*, 338–365.

Welch-Ross, M. K. (1997). Mother–child participation in conversation about the past: Relationships to preschoolers' theory of mind. *Developmental Psychology, 33*, 618–629.

Welch-Ross, M. K. (2001). Personalizing the temporally extended self: Evaluative self-awareness and the development of autobiographical memory. In C. Moore & K. Lemmon (Eds.), *The self in time: Developmental perspectives* (pp. 97–120). Mahwah, NJ: Lawrence Erlbaum Associates.

Wheeler, M. A., Stuss, D. T., & Tulving, E. (1997). Toward a theory of episodic memory: The frontal lobes and autonoetic consciousness. *Psychological Bulletin, 121*, 331–354.

THE DEVELOPMENT OF TEMPERAMENT FROM A BEHAVIORAL GENETICS PERSPECTIVE

Kimberly J. Saudino

PSYCHOLOGY DEPARTMENT, BOSTON UNIVERSITY, BOSTON,
MA, 02215, USA

I. Genes, Environments, and Development

Development refers to changes over time. The study of child development, then, is interested in what characteristics change or remain stable as children develop and the processes that bring about developmental change and continuity. The goal of developmental behavioral genetics research is to determine the extent to which both genes and environments contribute to behavioral development. Genetic factors often are viewed as constants in the developmental process. This likely is a result of the belief that genetic factors are immutable, contributing only to behavioral stability. However, this static view of genetic influences on behavior is not accurate. Genes are dynamic in nature, changing in the quantity and quality of their effects as the organism changes developmentally. Moreover, different genes can be involved at different stages of

201

Advances in Child Development and Behavior
Patricia Bauer : Editor

development. Thus, genetic factors can be sources of change as well as continuity in behavioral development. This chapter examines the types of questions that can be asked in developmental behavioral genetics and the methods used to answer these questions. By way of example, the focus is on findings in from the temperament literature, but the concepts presented can be extended to any phenotype of interest.

II. Exploring Genetic and Environmental Influences on Temperament

Behavioral genetic research is well-suited to the study of temperament. Although there are many different theories of child temperament each differing in the specific types of behaviors that are viewed as falling under the rubric of temperament (e.g., positive emotionality, negative emotionality, shyness, activity level, attention/persistence, inhibitory control), most agree that temperament refers to stable, early appearing individual differences in behavioral tendencies that have *a biological or constitutional basis* (Goldsmith *et al.*, 1987). Soon after birth, children show a great deal of variation in those behavioral dimensions considered to be temperamental. For example, some children cry easily and intensely, whereas others are more easy going; some are highly active and always on the go, whereas others are more sedentary; some attend and persist in tasks for long periods of time, whereas others' attention wanders quickly. It is these individual differences and the variations in between that are of interest to behavioral geneticists. That is, we are interested in understanding why children differ in their temperaments. Temperament theories suggest that such individual differences have a biological or constitutional foundation. This can be investigated using behavioral genetic methods which explore the extent to which genetic and environmental factors contribute to individual differences in behavior. In addition, longitudinal behavioral genetic designs allow us to explore the genetic and environmental factors that influence continuity and change in temperament across age.

A. BEHAVIOR GENETIC METHODS

The question of the relative importance of genes (nature) and environments (nurture) on behavior has had a long history dating back to ancient times when philosophers debated whether ideas were innate or acquired through ones senses. Although debated for several hundred years, this question was not empirically evaluated until the late 19th century when Galton (1822–1911) studied "heredity genius" (i.e., mental ability) by examining approximately 1000 men identified as "eminent" and found that these men belonged to only 300 families (Galton, 1869).[1] Moreover, as compared to more distant relatives, relatives who were more closely related to "eminent" men were themselves more likely to be eminent (i.e., the likelihood of relatives of eminent men being identified as eminent was associated with the degree of genetic relatedness). This was the first family study of a behavioral trait in humans. Although Galton's conclusion that mental ability was solely due to genetic inheritance is not justified on the basis of a family study (see below regarding the limitation of family studies), this study and Galton's work that followed are important for demonstrating that individual differences in mental ability and other behaviors may have a genetic basis. Galton also proposed using twins and adoptees to examine the role of genetic influences on behavioral variation. As indicated below, the twin and adoption designs are the workhorses of modern behavioral genetics. Galton's early designs were not quite the same as those currently used (e.g., his twin study did not compare identical and fraternal twins). Nonetheless, the notion of comparing the behavioral similarities of individuals of varying genetic relatedness remains the basis of behavioral genetic methodology, and Galton can be considered the father of behavioral genetics.

To estimate the relative influence of genes and environments on behavioral variability, modern behavioral genetic methods involve decomposing the observed (i.e., phenotypic) variance of a trait into genetic and environmental variance components. *Heritability*, the genetic effect size, is the proportion of phenotypic variance that can be attributed to genetic factors. The remaining variance is attributed to environmental factors which comprise all nonheritable influences including prenatal factors. Environmental variance can be further decomposed into shared and nonshared environmental influences. These two types of environmental influences have very different effects on the resemblances of family members. *Shared environmental variance* is familial resemblance that is not explained by genetic variance. This comprises environmental influences that are shared by family members such as family demographics, family members, one's rearing neighborhood, shared friends, even the number of televisions or books in the household. If shared environments are important to individual differences in temperament, they should enhance the similarity of family members. That is, they should make family members more similar in behavior irrespective of genetic similarity.

---

[1]Much of this historical perspective comes from Plomin, DeFries, and McClearn (1990b).

Nonshared environmental variance is a residual variance that includes environmental influences that are unique to each individual. These unique environmental influences operate to make members of the same family *different* from one another. Possible sources of nonshared environmental variance include differential parental treatment; extrafamilial relationships with friends, peers, and teachers; and nonsystematic factors such as accidents or illness (Plomin, Chipuer, & Neiderhiser, 1994). In addition, measurement error is also a source of nonshared environmental variance.

To estimate genetic, shared and nonshared environmental contributions to individual differences in temperament or other behaviors of interest, behavioral genetics research examines pairs of individuals who vary systematically in their genetic and/or environmental similarity. The logic underlying all behavioral genetic designs is quite simple: If genetic influences are important to a trait or behavior, then behavioral similarity should covary with genetic relatedness (i.e., individuals who are more genetically similar should be more behaviorally similar). In other words, traits that are genetically influenced should "run in families." Relatives should be more similar for the behavior than randomly paired individuals and the more closely related the family members, the more similar they should be for the behavior (e.g., 1st degree relatives >2nd degree relatives >3rd degree relatives > unrelated individuals). However, there is a problem with simply studying family members (i.e., family studies): relatives share environments as well as genes. In fact, the more genetically related relatives are, the more similar their environments (Plomin, 1990). Therefore, family members may resemble each other for environmental as well as genetic reasons, and simple family studies cannot separate the two.

1. Twin Design

The two designs most frequently used to disentangle genetic and environmental sources of variance in temperament are the twin design and the adoptive/nonadoptive sibling design. The twin method involves comparing genetically identical (monozygotic or MZ) twins with fraternal (dizygotic or DZ) twins who share approximately 50% of their segregating genes. Segregating genes refer to genes that *differ* in the population. Over 99% of the human genome is similar between all individuals (Venter, 2007), but these genetic effects are of little interest to behavioral geneticists because they cannot explain variation in the population—only genes that differ among individuals can contribute to individual differences. If a trait is genetically influenced, the two-fold greater genetic similarity of MZ twins is expected to make them more behaviorally similar than DZ twins. Intraclass correlations typically serve as indices of cotwin similarity (Galton can also be credited with developing the concept of correlation). An MZ correlation that is significantly greater than the DZ correlation suggests genetic influence. DZ twin resemblance that exceeds that predicted by the genetic hypothesis (i.e., a DZ correlation that exceeds one-half the MZ correlation) indicates familial resemblance that is not explained by genetic factors and suggests the presence of shared environmental influences. Because MZ twins share all their genes, differences within pairs of identical twins can only be due to environmental influences that are unique to each individual. Thus MZ correlations that are less than unity indicate nonshared environmental influences (i.e., environments that result in differences between relatives).

The standard twin model is depicted as a path diagram in Figure 1. This model is sometimes referred to as the "ACE" model. The rectangles represent the phenotypic variances of each twin. The circles represent latent genetic and environmental factors. The curved double-headed arrows indicate correlations between the variables they connect, whereas the single-headed arrows represent partial regressions of the measured variable on the latent variable. The "A" factors refer to additive genetic influences—the sum of the average effect of all genes that influence a trait. On the basis of the degree of genetic relatedness, the A factors correlate, as indicated by the r_g paths, 1.0 and .5 for MZ and DZ twins, respectively. The "C" factors refer to the influence of shared rearing environments on

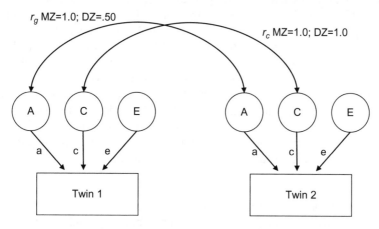

Fig. 1. *Univariate genetic model. Twin 1 and Twin 2 are measured variables for the two twins (i.e., the phenotype of each twin). A, C, and E are latent variables representing additive genetic variance, shared environmental variance, and nonshared environmental variance, respectively.* r_g *and* r_c *are the genetic and shared environmental correlations between twins. The single-headed arrows a, c, and e represent paths, partial regressions of the measured variable on the latent variable.*

twin resemblance. Because twins in the standard twin design are reared in the same family, the correlation for shared environment (i.e., r_c) is 1.0 for both MZ and DZ twins. Finally, the "E" factors reflect nonshared environmental variance and measurement error. Nonshared environmental influences are unique to each member of a twin pair and, therefore, are depicted in the path diagram as residual arrows for each twin representing the remaining variance not explained by genetics or shared environment. The path coefficients, a, c, and e, are partial regressions that indicate the relative influence of the latent variables on the phenotype. When path coefficients have been standardized, the percent variance explained by a latent variable is the square of the path coefficient. Fitting this model to data from MZ and DZ twins allows the estimation of the proportions of variance in the population that are due to genetic and shared and nonshared environmental influences.

This model may at first appear somewhat complex, but it simply expresses the same expectations as those used in the more basic correlational analyses. For example, using the temperament dimension shyness as our phenotype of interest, an individual's tendency to behave with wariness when meeting strangers may be due to a combination of three factors: genes (A), environments that are common or shared among family members (C), and environments that are uniquely experienced by the individual (E). The model depicts sources of covariance among twin siblings. That is, twin siblings may resemble each other (i.e., correlate) in terms of shyness because they share genes and/or they share environments. However, if genes contribute to variability in shyness, MZ twins should be more similar in shyness than DZ twins because they share 100% of their genes, whereas DZ twins share on average 50% of their segregating genes. Nonshared environments cannot contribute to familial resemblance in shyness for either MZ or DZ twins because they are specific to each individual and by definition, result in differences between individuals. Because MZ twins are genetically identical and share the same common family environments, the only reason why they might differ in shyness is due to nonshared environmental influences.

2. Adoptive/Nonadoptive Sibling Design

The adoptive/nonadoptive sibling design shares a similar logic to the twin design, but compares the similarity of groups of adoptive and nonadoptive sibling pairs. Genetic influences are implied when nonadoptive siblings who share approximately 50% of their segregating genes are more similar than adoptive siblings who are not genetically related. Shared environmental influences are suggested when genetically unrelated adoptive siblings resemble each other. The standard ACE model can also be fit to data from adoptive and nonadoptive siblings to estimate heritability and shared and nonshared environmental variances. In this case, the A factors would be uncorrelated (i.e., $r_g = 0$) for genetically unrelated adoptive siblings and would correlate .5 for nonadoptive siblings. As with the twin design, the correlation for shared environment (i.e., r_c) is 1.0 for both adoptive and nonadoptive siblings because both sibling types have shared rearing environments.

Continuing with the shyness example from above, this model again explains sources of covariance (i.e., familial resemblance for shyness), but this time for adoptive and nonadoptive sibling pairs. Because adoptive siblings are genetically unrelated, the correlation between adoptive siblings can only arise due to shared environments. That is, adoptive siblings can resemble each other for shyness only if shared environmental influences contribute to variability in this temperament dimension. In contrast, like all first-degree relatives reared in the same family, nonadoptive siblings may resemble each other for shyness because of shared genes and/or shared environments. Therefore, genetic influences on shyness would be implied if nonadoptive siblings were more similar than adoptive siblings.

3. Important Considerations

It should be noted that these simple models require a number of important assumptions. For example, the models assume that genetic variance is additive in nature (i.e., there are no genetic dominance or epistasis), mating is random with respect to temperament, there is no selective placement specific to temperament for the adoptive siblings, the effects of genotype–environment interaction are negligible, and that there are no sex differences at the level of etiology. Previous research suggests that, at least for temperament and personality, these assumptions are generally tenable (Saudino *et al.*, 1995). Nonetheless, with more complex models, large samples, and in, some instances, additional data (e.g., data from parents can inform on questions of assortative mating and selective placement; data from opposite sex twins allows tests of sex-limited genetic/ environmental influences), it is possible to explicitly test these assumptions. For our purposes, however, these simple models are sufficient for a basic understanding of the behavioral genetic literature to be discussed in this chapter.

It is also important to consider that like all statistics, estimates of heritability, shared and nonshared environmental variances have a certain degree of error. Consequently, estimates of genetic and environmental variances may vary across studies. Large samples and more reliable measures of the phenotype (i.e., behavior under study) result in more accurate estimates. As is the case for most research in psychology, the reader should not view variance estimates from behavioral genetic studies as exact point estimates and, where available, should consider the confidence intervals surrounding the estimates when evaluating research findings.

Finally, although twin and adoption analyses are useful for estimating the relative influences of genes and environments on individual differences in temperament, the genetic and environmental effects in these analyses are anonymous. That is, these quantitative genetic designs indicate the magnitude of genetic influence, but do not identify specific genes responsible for heritability. Similarly, although these designs can tell us about the impact of shared and nonshared environments on temperament, they do not provide information about the specific environments that influence the behaviors under study.

B. WHAT EXPLAINS INDIVIDUAL DIFFERENCES IN TEMPERAMENT?

Twin studies provide strong evidence of genetic influences on temperament. In general, twin research consistently finds that MZ cotwins are more similar than DZ cotwins across a wide variety of temperament dimensions including emotionality, activity, shyness, sociability, attention/persistence, approach, adaptability, distress, positive affect and negative affect (Braungart *et al.*, 1992; Cyphers *et al.*, 1990; Goldsmith, Buss, & Lemery, 1997; Robinson *et al.*, 1992; Saudino & Cherny, 2001a). Findings from adoption studies are more mixed. When assessed through parent ratings, adoption studies yield little evidence of genetic influences on temperament (Gagne, Saudino, & Cherny, 2003; Plomin *et al.*, 1991; Schmitz, 1994), but genetic effects on temperament are apparent when teacher, tester, or observer ratings are employed (Braungart *et al.*, 1992; Gagne *et al.*, 2003; Schmitz *et al.*, 1996). The fact that genetic influences on temperament are found in adoption studies using more objective measures of temperament suggests that the failure to detect genetic influences in adoption studies using parent ratings is likely due to the presence of parent rater biases which exaggerate differences between siblings and lead to underestimates of genetic influence in adoption studies (see Saudino *et al.*, 1995; Saudino *et al.*, 2004). Summarizing across designs and methods, the overall conclusion is there is little doubt that temperament is genetically influenced. Although estimates of heritability vary across samples, they generally fall within the range of .20 to .60, suggesting that genetic differences among individuals account for approximately 20–60% of the variability of temperament within a population. That is, the reason why people differ from one another in their temperaments is in part because they differ genetically. With few exceptions (e.g., soothability and rhythmicity, which show little genetic influence), there is no consistent pattern of differential heritability across dimensions. In other words, across most research, there is little evidence to suggest that some temperament dimensions are more heritable than others.

Genetic factors are important to temperament but the environment is also very important. Heritabilities in the range of .20 to .60 mean that the remaining 80–40% of the variance in temperament is attributed to environmental factors. However, behavioral genetics research suggests that the types of environments traditionally assumed to influence child behavior may not operate the way we think they do. Most developmental research exploring environmental influences on temperament has considered between-family effects such as parenting style (e.g., authoritative, permissive) and family functioning (e.g., Eriksson & Pehrsson, 2003; Leve, Scaramella, & Fagot, 2001). In behavioral genetics terms, these types of environments would fall under the rubric of shared environments since they are assumed to operate on a family-wide basis. A particularly interesting finding that frequently emerges from twin and adoption studies is that shared family environment accounts for only a small portion of variance in most temperament dimensions (e.g., Braungart *et al.*, 1992; Cyphers *et al.*, 1990; Gagne *et al.*, 2003; Robinson *et al.*, 1992; Saudino & Cherny, 2001a, 2001b). A good example comes from the Colorado Adoption Project which that found correlations for tester-rated temperament in infancy were approximately .00 for genetically unrelated adoptive siblings—which provides a direct test of shared family environment—and .20 for genetically related nonadoptive siblings (Braungart *et al.*, 1992). Thus, being raised in the same family did not make adoptive siblings resemble each other in their temperaments. Only siblings who shared genes were similar in temperament.

There are some exceptions to the general finding of no shared environmental influences on temperament. For example, positive affect and related behaviors (e.g., smiling, interest in others) display moderate shared environmental influences during infancy and early childhood (Cohen, Dibble, & Grawe, 1977; Goldsmith *et al.*, 1997; Goldsmith & Campos, 1986; Goldsmith & Gottesman, 1981; Goldsmith *et al.*, 1999; Lytton, 1980) perhaps reflecting the influence of maternal personality and attachment security on this temperament dimension (Goldsmith *et al.*, 1999). Overall, however, it seems that growing up in the same family does not make family members resemble each other in their temperaments. Family members are similar in temperaments primarily because of shared genes, not shared environments.

The finding that the environment does not contribute to familial resemblance in temperament does not mean that the environment is unimportant. The environmental factors that influence temperament are those that are unique to family members (i.e., nonshared environmental influences) and make family members different. These effects are substantial and provide an important focus for researchers interested in environmental effects on temperament. Behavioral genetics research suggests that instead of examining environmental factors that differ *across* families, it will be more profitable to focus on environmental factors that differ *within* families (e.g., differential parenting). Researchers need to consider why individuals within the same family differ so much with regard to temperament. This will involve studying more than one individual per family and exploring the association of experiential differences within a family with differences in temperament. For example, one study used the MZ difference method to examine possible sources of nonshared environmental influences on temperament in middle childhood (Deater-Deckard, Petrill, & Thompson, 2007). MZ within-pair differences on temperament dimensions were correlated with within-pair experiential differences (i.e., birth weight and differential parenting). Because differences between MZ co-twins can only be due to nonshared environmental influences, this method provides a test of "pure" environmental influences that are not contaminated with genetic effects. Results indicated that within pairs, the twin who was rated lower in the temperament dimensions of surgency and negative affect, and higher in the dimension of effortful control was heavier at birth, received less maternal negativity and more maternal positivity. These results suggest that differences in birth weight[2] and parenting may be important sources of nonshared environmental influences accounting for temperamental differences between MZ twins. A caveat is that it is difficult to know the direction of effects given that parenting and temperament were assessed contemporaneously. Differences in parenting could result in differences in temperament, but it is also possible that differences in temperament could result in differential parental treatment. This research is a good start at exploring nonshared environmental influences on temperament, however, longitudinal studies exploring the association of experiential differences within a family with differences in temperament are sorely needed to identify specific

---

[2]The reader may be surprised that birth weight is considered to be an environmental variable, but environmental influences in behavioral genetics is broadly defined as all nonheritable influences, including biological events.

nonshared environments (i.e., experiences) that impact the development of temperament. A limiting factor for research of this type is the general lack of environmental measures that are specific to the individual. Thus, the development of such measures will play an important role in advancing our understanding of temperament.

1. How You Measure Temperament is Important

There are many different methods for assessing temperament. The most frequently employed method is the parent rating questionnaire which asks parents to rate their children's typical behaviors on a series of questions designed to tap various temperament dimensions. Questions may be global (e.g., "Child has lots of energy") or specific in nature (e.g., "When playing inside the house, how often did your child climb over furniture?"). Observational measures such as tester ratings or observed behavioral coding (e.g., the Laboratory Temperament Assessment Battery [Lab-TAB]; Goldsmith *et al.*, 1994) are sometimes used to provide a measure of temperament, typically within the laboratory situation. Although behavioral observations involve a limited sample of the child's behavior, they may be more objective than parent ratings and observing children in the same standard situation facilitates comparisons among children. In addition to parent and observer ratings, some dimensions of temperament are amenable to methods of assessment that do not require human inferences about child behavior, for example, computer-based measures of attention and mechanical measures of activity level. It is generally assumed that all these different methods of assessment are tapping the same underlying constructs. Behavioral genetics research can provide a strong test of this assumption by exploring the extent to which different methods of assessing temperament have a common etiology (i.e., are influenced by the same genetic and environmental factors).

As indicated earlier, behavioral genetic analyses of temperament in infancy and childhood provide convincing evidence that most temperament dimensions are at least moderately genetically influenced. This is true when temperament is assessed through parents, trained observers, or mechanical/computerized measures (e.g., Goldsmith *et al.*, 1999; Polderman *et al.*, 2007; Saudino & Eaton, 1991, 1995; Saudino, Plomin, & DeFries, 1996). However, the fact that temperament is consistently heritable across different methods of assessment does not necessarily mean that the different methods of assessing temperament tap the same genetic and environmental effects. Phenotypic correlations between parent ratings and observational or mechanical measures of temperament are typically modest (e.g., Saudino *et al.*, 2004; Seifer *et al.*, 1994), indicating that, to some extent, different methods are influenced by different factors. Thus, it is possible that the genetic and environmental factors that influence one method of assessing temperament may differ from those that influence another. This can be examined through multivariate behavioral genetic analyses that explore genetic and environmental contributions to the *covariance* between two measures (or methods in this case) rather than the variance of each measure considered separately (Plomin *et al.*, 2001). That is, to what extent do genetic effects on a parent-rating measure of temperament (e.g., shyness) overlap with observer ratings of the same dimension?

The few behavioral genetic studies that have explored the question of genetic overlap across temperament methods have found evidence of genetic variance unique to specific methods of assessment. For example, a multitrait-multimethod approach to infant twin data comprising three temperament dimensions (activity, emotional tone, sociability) assessed three different ways (tester rating, playroom observation, parent rating) found substantial method-specific genetic variance (Philips & Matheny, 1997). Similarly, a twin study examining the etiological overlap between activity assessed with actigraphs (mechanical motion recorders) and parent and teachers' ratings of hyperactivity in middle childhood found that although there was genetic variance common to all three measures, there was also genetic variance specific to the actigraph and parent ratings (Wood *et al.*, 2008). Genetic correlations between methods ranged from .21 between actigraphs and teacher ratings to .48 between parent and teacher ratings, indicating that less than 50% of the genetic effects overlap across methods. Thus, although the different methods all assess activity, they are to some extent influenced by different genetic factors.

A problem with these two studies, however, is that methods are confounded with situations. That is, the different methods of assessing temperament were used in different situations (e.g., parent report in the home, observer report or actigraphs in the laboratory, teacher report in the school). Under these circumstances, it is difficult to determine whether the unique genetic variance is specific to the method or to the situation in which temperament was assessed. A more rigorous test of method-specific genetic effects comes from a twin study of activity level that employed multiple measures of activity level within the *same* situation, thereby controlling for situational influences (Saudino, in press). In the Boston University Twin Project (BUTP), the activity level of 2-year-old twins was assessed in the home and the laboratory. In both situations, mechanical motion recorders (actigraphs) provided an objective measure of the physical forces that are associated with human activity. Parent ratings of temperament provided a second measure of activity level in the home and observer ratings of activity level were obtained in the laboratory.

The phenotypic correlation between the two measures of activity in the home was modest ($r = .25$), whereas the correlation between the two laboratory measures of activity was substantial ($r = .67$). Multivariate genetic analyses exploring genetic and environment sources of covariance found that there was no covariance between environmental effects influencing parent-rated and actigraph activity level in the home. The environments that influenced differences among individuals on parents' ratings of activity were not the same as those that influenced individual differences in actigraph measures. Genetic factors explained all of the phenotypic correlation, but the genetic correlation between parent-rated and actigraph-assessed activity level was only moderate. Approximately 38% of the genetic effects overlapped across the two methods. Thus, there is a considerable amount of genetic variance that is unique to each measure (i.e., 62%). In other words, although genetic factors mediated the phenotypic association between the two variables, there is substantial genetic variance on parent-rated activity that is independent of genetic variance on actigraph activity, and vice versa. Although the genetic overlap between the two methods was only moderate, it is these overlapping genetic effects that account for the correlation between the two methods. Because both measures assessed activity in the same situation, the independent genetic and environmental variances reflect method-specific, not situation-specific, effects. Thus, to some extent, the parent ratings and actigraph measures of activity level differ at the level of genetic and environmental etiology. Interestingly, although parent ratings had little genetic overlap with actigraph-assessed activity level in the home, this was not the case for observer ratings of activity level in the laboratory. A genetic correlation of .95 between the two laboratory measures of activity level suggests that the two measures are essentially influenced by the same genetic effects. There was also modest overlap in nonshared environmental influences on both laboratory measures.

These findings highlight the need to consider how temperament is measured when conducting research. The fact that different measures of the same temperament domain, activity level in this case, can have different etiologies means that researchers should not assume that all measures of temperament are interchangeable. Findings with one method may not generalize to another, not because of contextual factors, but because different methods engage different processes.

2. Where You Measure Temperament is Important

Although developmentalists frequently acknowledge the importance of contextual factors on temperament (e.g., Mangelsdorf, Schoppe, & Buur,

2000), situational effects on temperament rarely have been considered from a behavioral genetic perspective. Because temperament is expected to display cross-situational consistency (Goldsmith *et al.*, 1987), questions of genetic and environmental contributions to situational change have largely been ignored by temperament researchers. However, different situations place different demands on the individual and elicit different behaviors. We tend to think that behavioral change across situations is due to environmental factors, but this need not be the case. It is possible that genetic influences contribute to behavioral change as the individual goes from situation to situation. That is, individual differences in temperamental responding to specific situations might be influenced by genetic effects (Philips & Matheny, 1997).

Multivariate genetic analyses can be used to explore the extent to which genetic effects on a measure of temperament in one situation are shared with genetic effects on another measure of the same dimension in a different situation. *Cross-situational* genetic effects are genetic influences that overlap across different situations and contribute to the stability of temperament across situations. *Contextual* genetic influences are genetic effects that are unique to a specific situation and contribute to situational changes in temperament. Because, as indicated in the previous section, different methods of assessing temperament may tap different genetic influences, when investigating the possibility of contextual/situational-specific genetic influences on temperament, it is important to use the same method across situations. For some dimensions of temperament (e.g., emotionality), this may be difficult because different informants are often needed for different situations (e.g., home and school). To date, only a handful of behavioral genetic studies of observed shyness and mechanically assessed activity level have examined situational influences while controlling for method effects.

In the MacArthur Longitudinal Twin Study (Emde & Hewitt, 2001; Plomin *et al.*, 1990a) observed measures of shyness were obtained based on children's initial reactions to examiners in the home and laboratory at 14 and 20 months of age. Each child's behavior was videotaped and scored for the occurrence of discrete behaviors such as approach to the examiner, approach to a proffered toy, proximity to mother, clinging to mother, self-soothing, vocalization, and crying. The phenotypic correlations between observer-assessed shyness in the laboratory and home during infancy were modest, but there was substantial overlap between the genetic influences involved in both situations (Cherny *et al.*, 1994; Cherny *et al.*, 2001). This finding of cross-situational genetic effects for shyness in the laboratory and the home means that genetic factors contribute to the stability of shyness across the two situations. As might be expected, differences between shyness in the laboratory and in the home were due primarily to environmental factors, but there were some small contextual, or situationally specific, genetic influences on shyness in the home. Although shyness in the laboratory and the home are largely influenced by the same genetic factors and situational change is largely due to environmental factors, there are some modest genetic influences on shyness that are specific to the home environment.

Two twin studies have used actigraphs to assess activity level in various situations. The results suggest that genetic factors contribute to both continuity and change across situations—provided that the situations are substantially different from each other. For example, school-aged twins wore motion recorders in a laboratory cognitive testing situation and during a 25-minute break in testing (Wood *et al.*, 2007). Activity level was significantly heritable in both situations and the genetic correlation between the two situations was estimated as 1.0, indicating complete overlap between the genetic influences operating on the two situations (i.e., there were no situation-specific genetic influences). The genetic effects that influenced motor activity in the test situation also influenced activity in the break situation. Given that there was complete genetic overlap across situations, one must conclude that genetic factors contribute to stability, not change. Although there was also moderate environmental overlap across situations, there were substantial environmental influences that were situation specific (i.e., unique to each situation). Thus, within the laboratory, genes contribute to cross-situational consistency and differences between the two situations were due solely to environmental influences. It is possible, however, that the two laboratory situations were not were sufficiently different to reasonably expect that they would have different genetic etiologies.

When actigraphs were used with more diverse situations, evidence for situation-specific genetic variance emerged. In the BUTP the activity level of toddler twins was assessed in the home, laboratory test and laboratory play situations (Saudino & Zapfe, 2008). Phenotypic correlations revealed substantial consistency in activity level across the laboratory test and play situations ($r = .53$) but activity in the two laboratory situations were more modestly associated with activity at home (Test $r = .34$; Play $r = .33$). Multivariate genetic analyses indicated that the covariation between activity level in the home, test, and play situations was best described by a common latent factor accounting for approximately 40% of the variance in activity level. Thus, to some extent, the same activity phenotype was assessed in all situations. Individual differences in this underlying activity phenotype were due only to genetic influences indicating that what is common across all situations is genetic. For this young sample, neither shared nor nonshared environmental influences contributed significantly to cross-situational consistency in activity. The reason why activity was similar across situations is because to some extent, the same genetic effects are operating across situations. As found by Wood *et al.* (2007), the genetic correlation between activity in two laboratory situations was 1.0 (i.e., there was complete overlap between the genetic influences on activity in the test and play situations). This was not the case for activity level beyond the laboratory. Genetic correlations across home and laboratory situations indicated that approximately 68% of the genetic factors that influence activity in the home also influenced activity in the laboratory test and play situations. Although there was considerable genetic overlap between activity level in the home and the laboratory, there were also genetic influences unique to the home situation. In other words, as was previously found for shyness, there were genetic influences specific to activity in the home situation. In fact, approximately 50% of the genetic variance on activity in the home was situation-specific (i.e., half of the genetic effects that influence activity in the home are independent of the genetic effects that influence the common activity phenotype that was consistent across situations), indicating context-specific genetic effects for activity level. Thus, when situations are sufficiently different (i.e., home versus laboratory), genetic factors contribute to both cross-situational consistency *and* situational change.

An interpretation of the situation-specific effects found for both shyness and activity level is that different contexts provide different views of temperament and thus engage different genetic influences on processes relevant to each context. The fact that, to some extent, different genetic influences operate on across different situations means that researchers will need to carefully consider the situation in which temperament is assessed. The situation matters! This is true not only for behavioral geneticists, but for anyone interested in temperament. Links between temperament and behavioral outcomes may differ depending on the situation in which temperament is assessed. Moreover, we need to remember that behavioral differences between situations can have a genetic basis (i.e., contextual differences are not necessarily environmental). These findings have important implications not just for developmentalists but also for molecular genetics researchers seeking to find specific genes associated with temperament. Researchers are just beginning to identify genes associated with childhood behavioral dimensions and disorders and replication of results across studies is a critical component to this line of study. Quantitative behavioral genetics findings of situationally-specific genetic effects suggest that, in some instances, failures to replicate molecular genetic findings may be due to situational differences between studies.

III. Genetic and Environmental Contributions to the Development of Temperament

Although issues of heritability and environmental variances, method-specific genetic effects, and cross-situational and situation-specific genetic effects on temperament are important to developmental researchers, the findings discussed thus far are not really developmental in nature. That is, the focus has not been on age-related change. For the developmentalist, the major marker of genetic and environmental change is age (Plomin, DeFries, & Fulker, 1988). Consequently, age is a variable that must be considered when examining the etiology of temperament from a developmental perspective. There are two basic questions that can be explored in developmental behavioral genetics. The first inquires about differential heritability or changes in heritability across ages (i.e., does the relative influence of genetic factors increase or decrease as the child develops?). This issue is important because the investigation of differential heritability over age may serve to elucidate time-points wherein transitions occur in development. The second question explores the role of genetic influences on age-to-age change or continuity of individual differences during development (i.e., to what extent is behavioral change or continuity in temperament due to genetic influences?). This question addresses the process by which developmental change takes place.

A. DIFFERENTIAL HERITABILITY ACROSS AGE

The dynamic nature of gene action throughout the lifespan raises the question of differential heritability of temperament as a function of age. The fact that a temperament dimension is genetically influenced at one age does not guarantee that the same dimension will be genetically influenced at another. The degree of genetic influence or, indeed, whether a temperament trait is heritable may vary across age. Genes switch on and off throughout development, and there may be changes in the quantity and quality of genetic effects across age. Similarly, the environments that we experience differ across age and the role of the environment on individual differences in temperament may change as environments change. Consequently, there may be developmental changes in the relative influence of genes and environments on temperament. As a result, one should not assume that behavioral genetics findings about the etiology of temperament at one age apply to another.

The question of differential heritability across age asks whether the relative contribution of genetic and environmental influences on behavior (e.g., temperament) changes with development. As indicated earlier, heritability is the proportion of phenotypic variance that is due to genetic differences between individuals and the remaining variance is due to environmental (shared and nonshared) effects. Since it is a proportion, this means that if heritability changes across age, there must also be some change in environmental variance. If, for example, heritability were to increase with development, there must also be some decrease in the magnitude of environmental influences on the behavior in question. In terms of the twin design, an increase in heritability as a function of age would be the consequence of an increased difference between MZ and DZ co-twin resemblances. This would transpire if MZ co-twin similarity increased to a greater extent than DZ co-twin similarity, or conversely, if the DZ co-twin similarity decreased to a greater extent than that of MZ co-twins (Plomin *et al.*, 1988).

Does the heritability of temperament differ across age? On a strictly intuitive level, most people might predict that the importance of the environment might increase with age. That is, as children develop, they are exposed to more diverse environments which may influence temperament, and therefore, the importance of genetic factors on temperament might wane. Empirical research does not support this notion. Many studies find no evidence of differential heritability across age (e.g., Cyphers *et al.*, 1990; Gagne *et al.*, 2003; McCartney, Harris, & Bernieri, 1990; Plomin *et al.*, 1993; Saudino, 2008; Saudino & Cherny, 2001b). Moreover, when developmental differences in genetic influences on temperament are suggested, it tends to be in the direction of *increased* genetic variance (e.g., Braungart *et al.*, 1992; Buss, Plomin, & Willerman, 1973; Ganiban *et al.*, 2008; Stevenson & Fielding, 1985). A striking example comes from the Louisville Twin Study which found that observer-rated temperament displayed no evidence of genetic influences during the neonatal period (Riese, 1990) but was moderately heritable in later infancy and early childhood (Matheny, 1983, 1989).

A number of explanations for a trend toward increasing genetic influences on temperament can be entertained. First, genetic influences on temperament in early infancy might be masked because of perinatal environmental influence (Torgersen, 1985). For example, although there is considerable evidence for genetic influences on temperament in infancy and early childhood, as indicated above, a study of temperament in neonates found no evidence of genetic influences (Riese, 1990). When assessed within just a few days of their birth, MZ twins were not more similar than DZ twins on observed behaviors such as activity, irritability, and responsiveness to stimuli. However, within-pair differences in birth weight and Apgar scores were significantly associated with differences in observed temperament suggesting that prenatal and birth conditions may play a role in the similarity within twin pairs assessed at very young ages. Second, Plomin and DeFries' (1985) "amplification model" might apply. According to this developmental model, genetic effects that create small individual differences in infancy become magnified with age. For example, Plomin (1986a) suggests that small differences in neuroanatomy or neurophysiology in early development may cascade into larger behavioral differences as children age. The third explanation has to do with niche-picking. Scarr and McCartney (1983) suggest a shift from passive to reactive and active genotype-environment correlations as an explanatory mechanism for why DZ twins become increasingly different with development. The similarity of DZ twins' early environments, which are passively correlated with their genotypes, give way as they actively select environments correlated with their different genotypes. Because MZ twins select highly correlated environments a shift from passive to active genotype-environment correlations would not decrease their similarity. Under this process, with development DZ twins become less similar relative to MZ twins and estimates of heritability, therefore, increase.

These three hypotheses explaining age-related increases in heritability are intriguing. However, because the pattern of increasing heritability across age is not found in all studies, a more plausible explanation might lie within the measures used to assess temperament. Temperament measures may have differential reliability or validity across age. Most research examining the etiology of temperament employs parent or observer ratings. Unreliability of the ratings would reduce the likelihood of finding significant genetic effects. For temperament and personality, the measurement properties of the assessment techniques, especially during infancy, are often weak and are apt to systematically affect the probability of finding genetic influences (Goldsmith, 1983). It has been suggested that during early infancy there may not be enough behavior to obtain a good assessment of temperament (Buss & Plomin, 1984). Additionally, it may be harder for judges to differentiate behavior in infants. If the reliability of the rating measure improves from infancy to early childhood, then the probability of finding a genetic influence would improve concomitantly. Although for temperament rating measures the study of differential reliability across age has, for the most part, been neglected, it has been acknowledged that measures may have lower reliability at younger ages (Baydar, 1995; Goldsmith, 1983; Mathiesen & Tambs, 1999; Torgersen, 1985).

Similarly, differential measurement validity across age could produce a pattern of variable heritability. Rater bias might increase with age. Parent ratings of temperament are prone to contrast effects—rater biases that magnify existing behavioral differences between co-twins and thereby inflate heritability estimates (Saudino, Cherny, & Plomin, 2000; Saudino *et al.*, 2004). It is interesting to note that many of the studies suggesting increasing genetic influences on parents' ratings of temperament also showed a trend toward increasing contrast effects (e.g., Buss *et al.*, 1973; Stevenson & Fielding, 1985; Torgersen, 1981). Additionally, apparent differences in heritability for temperament might reflect differences in item content or in the factor structure of the measure at different ages. Indeed, when differential heritability is evident in studies employing observer ratings, concurrent changes in factor structure are often present (e.g., Goldsmith & Gottesman, 1981; Matheny, 1983; Wilson & Matheny, 1986).

The use of mechanical measures to assess the temperament dimension of activity level addresses the possibility that differential heritability may be artifacts of age-related differences in the psychometric properties and/ or in the content of the instruments used to assess temperament. That is, problems of possible age differences in reliability, factor structure, or rater biases do not emerge when activity level is assessed with motion recorders. As a result, with such measures, age differences in heritability would not be confounded with methodological issues. Although differential herit-ability across age is evident in several ratings-based studies of activity level (e.g., Buss *et al.*, 1973; Goldsmith & Gottesman, 1981; Matheny, 1983; Stevenson & Fielding, 1985; Torgersen, 1981; Wilson & Matheny, 1986), this has not been the case when motion recorders have been used to assess activity across infancy and toddlerhood (Saudino, 2008; Saudino & Eaton, 1995). For example, longitudinal analyses of actigraph-assessed activity level in the laboratory found that genetic influences accounted for approximately 50% of the variance at both 2 and 3 years of age (Saudino, 2008). Perhaps more striking is a cross-sectional analysis of actometer-assessed activity level that found heritabilities of approximately .40 for a sample of 7-month-old infants and a sample of young adolescents mean age 14 years (Saudino, 2000). Of course, as indicated earlier, methods of assessment are not interchangeable, so it is possible that earlier findings of differential heritability for some measures (i.e., measures other than motion recorders) are real. The problem is that one cannot tell until the methodological issues are resolved.

B. GENETIC CONTRIBUTIONS TO DEVELOPMENTAL CONTINUITY AND CHANGE

Although the evidence for differential heritability across age is mixed, what is clear is that beyond the neonatal period, there is consistent evidence of genetic influences on temperament throughout the lifespan.

Studies of temperament in infancy, early childhood, middle childhood, adolescence, and adulthood yield the similar conclusion that individual differences in temperament are in part due to genetic differences among individuals. The fact that temperament is heritable at different ages does not mean, however, that the same genetic influences operate at each age. That is, the genes that influence temperament in infancy may differ from those that influence temperament in later developmental periods. This is true even when estimates of heritability are equivalent across age. For example, in the MacArthur Longitudinal Twin Study, the heritability of behavioral inhibition was approximately .40 at 14, 20, and 24 months of age (Saudino & Cherny, 2001b). However, although genetic factors explain similar proportions of variance in behavioral inhibition at each age, this does not mean that the same genes are operating at each age (see below). Similarly, age differences in the magnitude of heritability estimates does not mean that the genes that operate on temperament differ from one age to the next—only that there is a difference in the extent to which genetic factors contribute to behavioral variability. So, simply examining heritability estimates across age does not answer the interesting developmental questions. That is, do the same genes influence temperament at different ages? Do new genetic effects emerge across development? In other words, what is the role of genetic factors in continuity and change in temperament?

1. Methods to Assess Genetic and Environmental Contributions to Continuity and Change

From a developmental perspective, the measurement of within-person change is more interesting than cross-sectional age differences because the measurement of change is more informative about underlying processes (Wohlwill, 1973). For the same reason, genetic influences on continuity and change are more interesting than the presence or absence of genetic influences at various ages. The question of differential heritability is essentially cross-sectional and does not address mechanisms of change. However, by using behavioral genetic methods within a longitudinal design, we are able to determine the extent to which developmental change and continuity are due to genetic and environmental factors.

In an early attempt to explore genetic influences on developmental change in temperament, the Louisville Twin Study examined twin concordances for age-to-age change profiles across infancy and early childhood (Matheny, 1989; Wilson & Matheny, 1986). MZ twins demonstrated greater resemblances than DZ twins on age-to-age change profiles for laboratory measures of activity, task orientation, affect-extraversion, emotional tone, and surgency, suggesting that across infancy and early childhood the developmental patterns for these temperament traits are, in part, regulated by genetic influences. A problem with the analysis of change profiles is that they do not reveal the extent to which the genetic effects that influence temperament are consistent from one age to another (Plomin & Nesselroade, 1990). This can be addressed by assessing genetic contributions to phenotypic continuity and change across age. The finding of genetic influences on continuity implies that there is some overlap between the genetic factors that affect a trait across age (Plomin, 1986b). Longitudinal analyses of genetic contributions to phenotypic continuity permit the estimation of the extent to which genetic effects on a trait at one age overlap with genetic effects at another age (i.e., genetic correlation) and, furthermore, whether new genetic influences on the trait emerge across time. Such analyses can therefore provide important information about developmental processes.

In twin and adoptive/nonadoptive designs, the role of genetic influences on developmental continuity and change is assessed through cross-sibling cross-age covariances. Using the twin design as an example, the twin's score at Time 1 is correlated with the other twin's score at Time 2. If phenotypic stability is mediated by genetic factors, then the cross-twin cross-age correlations for MZ twins should be greater than the DZ twin cross-correlation. The logic behind this is quite simple. An MZ intraclass correlation that exceeds the DZ intraclass for a single occasion suggests genetic influences at that moment. A simple two-occasion (cross-age) correlation is a typical measure of phenotypic stability. Thus, an MZ cross-twin cross-age correlation that exceeds the DZ cross-twin cross-age correlation suggests a genetic contribution to age-to-age phenotypic stability.

Although correlational analyses can give an impression of genetic and environmental sources of variance and covariance across age, model-fitting analyses are required to provide accurate estimates of these effects. There are various longitudinal behavioral genetic models, however, the Cholesky decomposition model is widely used in the developmental literature and is the model used in the temperament research reviewed below. The model illustrated as a path diagram in Figure 2 depicts possible genetic and environmental contributions to continuity and change across three ages. A_3, C_3, and E_3, represent genetic, shared environmental, and nonshared environmental effects, respectively, that are common across all three ages; A_2, C_2, and E_2 are the respective effects that are common to ages 2 and 3 independent of what is common to all ages; and A_1, C_1, and E_1 represent the genetic and environmental effects that are unique to age 3. Genetic continuity refers to genetic effects that persist across time. In the model this is suggested when two or more path coefficients within a common A

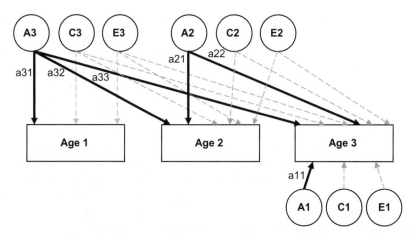

Fig. 2. *Longitudinal path model of genetic and environmental sources of change and continuity. The three rectangles represent the phenotypic variances at ages 1, 2, and 3. The latent variables A3, C3, and E3 are the common genetic factor, the common shared environmental factor, and the nonshared environmental factor, respectively, that are shared at all ages. A2, C2, and E2 are the common factors that are shared across ages 2 and 3 independent of what is shared at all three ages. A1, C1, and E1 represent the genetic, shared environmental, and nonshared environmental influences that are unique to the phenotype at age 3 independent of effects at ages 1 and 2. A_{11} to A_{33} are genetic path coefficients.*

factor are significant. For example, genetic continuity across all ages is implied when all the paths in the A_3 factor are significant. However, if only the a_{31} and a_{32} paths were significant, it would suggest genetic continuity across ages 1 and 2, but not across ages 1 and 3. Under this model genetic contributions to change are conceptualized as new genetic effects at one age that are independent of genetic effects at an earlier age. For example, paths a_{21} and a_{11} represent new genetic effects that emerge at ages 2 and 3, respectively.

2. Sources of Continuity and Change in Temperament

The Cholesky model was used to examine genetic and environmental sources of continuity and change in observer ratings of activity, affect/ extraversion, task orientation, shyness, and behavioral inhibition assessed at 14, 20, 24, and 36 months of age in the MacArthur Longitudinal Twin Study (Saudino & Cherny, 2001b; Saudino *et al.*, 1996). The assessment situation was similar across age, thus ruling out situations as a possible explanation of change. The average age-to-age phenotypic stability correlation was .24 (range .00–.39), indicating that for these temperament dimensions change predominates over continuity across infancy and toddlerhood. Nonetheless, for most dimensions, genetic influences appear to mediate whatever continuity exists. Although modest, the age-to-age stability correlations for activity, affect/extraversion, and behavioral inhibition were almost entirely due to genetic factors. That is, what persists across age is genetic in nature. Shyness was an exception in that both genetic and shared environmental influences contributed to developmental continuity.

If genetic factors explain continuity, what explains developmental change? The answer to some extent varies across temperament dimensions, but for all dimensions new nonshared environmental influences emerged at each age. Thus, individual differences in the development of early temperament are in part due to differences within the family environment, such as differential treatment, experiences, or accidents. For shyness, both shared and nonshared environmental influences contributed to developmental change. It is somewhat puzzling that substantially different shared environments influenced shyness across age, and it is possible that this effect is the result of observing both twins together (Cherny *et al.*, 1994). That is, the novel person would serve as a common experience (i.e., shared environment) that influenced both co-twins behavior. Because the novel person differed across age, this could explain the new shared environmental influences at each age.

With the exception of shyness, genetic factors also appear to contribute to developmental change. New genetic effects emerged at 20, 24, and 36 months of age for behavioral inhibition; at 20 months for affect/extraversion; and at 36 months for both activity and task orientation. Thus, for these temperament dimensions genetic factors influence both continuity and change in temperament across age. The new genetic effects on affect/extraversion at 20 months of age are intriguing because this is the age when children's socio-cognitive competencies (e.g., self-awareness and other-awareness) dramatically increase (Asendorpf & Baudonnière, 1993; Asendorpf, Warkentin, & Baudonnière, 1996). Thus, the novel genetic effects for affect/extraversion observed within the laboratory situation at 20 months might be a result of these new processes coming online. It should be noted, however, that although significant, genetic change for affect/extraversion is modest—the genetic correlations indexing the degree of genetic overlap across age were high, and it would appear that nonshared environmental influences account for most developmental change in this dimension.

The issue of genetic change is thornier for behavioral inhibition, activity, and task orientation. For these dimensions, genetic change coincided with subtle changes in the measures used to assess temperament. That is, although the measures used at each age are presumed to reflect the same temperamental dimension, there were differences in item content and/or factor structure. As indicated earlier, different methods of assessing temperament can tap different genetic effects. This raises the possibility that changes in the construct across age may result in the emergence of new genetic effects from one measurement period to the next simply because different behaviors are being assessed. Consequently, it is difficult to distinguish between changes due to development and changes due to measurement.

Again, how you measure temperament is important. In order to disentangle changes due to development from changes due to measurement, it is critical that the measure be invariant across age. This can be a concern for the study of temperament because many parent- and observer-rating measures have age-appropriate versions, which although conceptually linked, differ in content (e.g., the Infant Behavior Questionnaire (Rothbart, 1981) and Child Behavior Questionnaire (Rothbart *et al.*, 2001)). Two longitudinal studies in which measures did not differ across age suggest that genetic change in temperament might be real. In the Nonshared Adolescent Development Project parents rated the temperaments of their children twice approximately 2.5 years apart (Ganiban *et al.*, 2008). Although parent ratings are prone to contrast effects that can affect estimates of genetic influence, these rater biases were controlled for in the longitudinal models. As was found for toddlers, stability in temperament across early to mid-adolescence was largely due to genetic effects and change was due to both genetic and nonshared environmental influences. For mothers' and fathers' ratings of their adolescent children's temperaments, most of the genetic variance in Time 2 ratings was independent of the genetic effects on Time 1 ratings (i.e., approximately 55% and 75% of the genetic variance for mothers' and fathers' ratings, respectively, at time 2 was unique to the second time period). Similar genetic innovations have also been observed for adolescent twins self-ratings of personality (Gillespie *et al.*, 2004), but studies of adult personality find little evidence of genetic change across age (McGue, Bacon, & Lykken, 1993; Viken *et al.*, 1994).

Although it has been suggested that puberty may explain the new genetic effects on adolescent temperament (Ganiban *et al.*, 2008), work with objectively-assessed activity level finds that genetic change on temperament occurs in toddlerhood as well. In the BUTP age-to-age stability for actigraph activity between 2 and 3 years of age was .32, .40, and .43 in the play, test, and home situations, respectively. For the measure of activity level in the home, the genetic effects that influenced activity at age 2 years were entirely overlapping with those at age 3 years (Saudino, 2008).

Genetic factors contributed to continuity not change. Developmental change for activity in the home was due to environmental factors (both shared and nonshared). This was not the case for activity within the two laboratory situations. The phenotypic stability for both laboratory play and test measures of activity was entirely due to genetic factors, indicating that, once again, genes, not environments, contribute to continuity across age. However, developmental change in activity level in the laboratory was due to both nonshared environmental and genetic influences. For activity in both the laboratory situations, significant new genetic effects emerged at age 3. That is, when activity was longitudinally assessed within the laboratory, genes contributed to both continuity and change. Approximately 65% of the genetic variance on activity in the play situation and 48% of the genetic variance in the test situation was unique to age 3. These findings mirror those from the MacArthur Longitudinal Twin Study which also found novel genetic variance on observed activity within the laboratory at age 3, however, the use of actigraphs to assess activity level across age rules out measure differences as a source of change and allows for more interesting hypotheses regarding the new genetic variance. It is possible that the new genetic effects in the laboratory situations may reflect children's increased self-control/self-regulation or adaptability to novel social situations. It is interesting that these novel genetic effects at age 3 years are not apparent in the home situation, once again reminding us that we need to consider situations when exploring genetic effects on behavior.

More longitudinal research with careful consideration of assessment methods (i.e., measure invariance across age) is needed to fully understand the etiology of developmental change in temperament. Nonetheless, the research to date demonstrates an interesting developmental pattern. From a phenotypic perspective, personality in adulthood is quite stable. Behavioral genetics research suggests that this stability is due to genetic factors. In contrast to findings with adults, in children and adolescents, temperament and personality are much less stable and although genes contribute to stability during these earlier periods, there is also evidence of novel genetic effects emerging with age. Developmental change in temperament and personality is, in part, a biological process. Across all studies, the environmental influences that were most associated with developmental change were of the nonshared variety. The question of which specific nonshared environmental influences on developmental change has generally gone unexplored, but there are a number of interesting possibilities. For example, individual differences in changes in temperament may be due to differences within the family environment, such as differential treatment, different peer groups, experiences, or accidents. Identifying specific nonfamilial environmental factors that influence developmental change remains an important goal for future temperament research.

IV. Conclusions

As would be predicted from temperament theory that assumes a biological basis to individual differences in children's behavioral tendencies, twin and adoption studies provide substantial evidence to suggest that temperament is genetically influenced. This is true for most dimensions of temperament and across most developmental periods (i.e., infancy, early childhood, middle childhood, adolescence, and adulthood). However, the story is not that simple. Research employing multivariate behavioral genetic methods reveal that genetic influences largely explain the behavioral consistency of temperament across methods of assessment, situations, and age. This probably comes as no surprise and fits with the commonly held static view of genetic effects. Genetic contributions to behavioral consistency are only part of the story. In accordance with a more dynamic view of genetic effects, genes also contribute to behavioral differences or change in temperament across methods, situations, and age. The finding that there are unique genetic influences on temperament across measures, situations, and age has important implications for developmental researchers interested in temperament. Specifically, findings based on a single assessment of temperament may not generalize to other assessments. When evaluating developmental change, it is essential to consider and control for methodological and contextual sources of "change" across age. This is true for both phenotypic research as well as behavioral genetic research. Such measurement-related issues often go unexamined because many consider them to be uninteresting. However, until these issues are resolved, we will not get a full understanding of behavioral development.

Acknowlegement

This work was supported in part by grant MH062375 from the National Institute of Mental Health.

REFERENCES

Asendorpf, J. B., & Baudonnière, P.-M. (1993). Self-awareness and other-awareness: Mirror self-recognition and synchronic imitation among unfamiliar peers. *Developmental Psychology, 29*(1), 88–95.

Asendorpf, J. B., Warkentin, V., & Baudonnière, P.-M. (1996). Self-awareness and other-awareness. II: Mirror self-recognition, social contingency awareness, and synchronic imitation. *Developmental Psychology, 32*(2), 313–321.

Baydar, N. (1995). Reliability and validity of temperament scales of the NLSY child assessments. *Journal of Applied Developmental Psychology, 16*(3), 339–370.

Braungart, J. M., Plomin, R., DeFries, J. C., & Fulker, D. (1992). Genetic influences on tester-rated infant temperament as assessed by Bayley's Infant Behavior Record: Nonadoptive and adoptive siblings and twins. *Developmental Psychology, 28*, 40–47.

Buss, A. H., & Plomin, R. (1984). *Temperament: Early developing personality traits.* Hillsdale, NJ: Erlbaum.

Buss, A. H., Plomin, R., & Willerman, L. (1973). The inheritance of temperaments. *Journal of Personality, 41*, 513–524.

Cherny, S. S., Fulker, D. W., Corley, R. P., Plomin, R., & DeFries, J. C. (1994). Continuity and change in infant shyness from 14 to 20 months. *Behavior Genetics, 24*, 365–379.

Cherny, S. S., Saudino, K. J., Fulker, D. W., Plomin, R., Corley, R. P., & DeFries, J. C. (2001). The development of observed shyness from 14 to 20 months: Shyness in context. In R. N. Emde & J. K. Hewitt (Eds.), *Infancy to early childhood: Genetic and environmental influences on developmental change* (pp. 269–282). New York: Oxford University Press.

Cohen, D. J., Dibble, E., & Grawe, J. M. (1977). Fathers' and mothers' perceptions of children's personality. *Archives of General Psychiatry, 34*, 480–487.

Cyphers, L. H., Phillips, K., Fulker, D. W., & Mrazek, D. A. (1990). Twin temperament during the transition from infancy to early childhood. *Journal of the American Academy of Child and Adolescent Psychiatry, 29*, 392–397.

Deater-Deckard, K., Petrill, S. A., & Thompson, L. A. (2007). *Nonshared environmental influences on temperament in middle childhood.* Paper presented at the Society for Research in Child Development.

Emde, R. N. & Hewitt, J. K. (Eds). (2001). *The transition from infancy to early childhood: Genetic and environmental influences in the MacArthur Longitudinal Twin Study.* New York: Oxford University Press.

Eriksson, O. S., & Pehrsson, G. (2003). Relationships between the family's way of functioning and children's temperament as rated by parents of pre-term children. *Journal of Child Health Care, 7*, 89–100.

Gagne, J. R., Saudino, K. J., & Cherny, S. S. (2003). Genetic influences on temperament in early adolescence: A multimethod perspective. In S. Petrill, R. Plomin, J. C. DeFries, & J. K. Hewitt (Eds.), *The transition to early adolescence: Nature and nurture* pp. 166–184.

Galton, F. (1869). *Hereditary genius: An inquiry into its laws and consequences.* London: Macmillan.

Ganiban, J. M., Saudino, K. J., Ulbricht, J., Neiderhiser, J. M., & Reiss, D. (2008). Continuity and change in temperament during adolescence. *Journal of Personality and Social Psychology, 95*, 222–236.

Gillespie, N. A., Evans, D. E., Wright, M. M., & Martin, N. G. (2004). Genetic simplex modeling of Eysenck's dimensions of personality in a sample of young Australian twins. *Twin Research, 7*(6), 637–648.

Goldsmith, H. H. (1983). Genetic influences on personality from infancy to adulthood. *Child Development, 54*, 331–355.

Goldsmith, H. H., & Campos, J. J. (1986). Fundamental issues in the study of early temperament: The Denver twin temperament study. In M. E. Lamb, A. L. Brown, & B. Rogoff (Eds.), *Advances in developmental psychology* (Vol. 4, pp. 231–283).

Goldsmith, H. H., & Gottesman, I. I. (1981). Origins of variation in behavioral style: A longitudinal study of temperament in young twins. *Child Development, 52*, 91–103.

Goldsmith, H. H., Buss, A., Plomin, R., Rothbart, M. K., Thomas, A., Chess, S., *et al.* (1987). Roundtable: What is temperament? Four approaches. *Child Development, 58,* 505–529.

Goldsmith, H. H., Reilly, H. H., Lemery, K. S., Longley, S., & Prescott, A. (1994). Manual for the Preschool Laboratory Temperament Assessment Battery.

Goldsmith, H. H., Buss, K. A., & Lemery, K. S. (1997). Toddler and childhood temperament: Expended content, stronger genetic evidence, new evidence for the importance of environment. *Developmental Psychology, 33,* 891–905.

Goldsmith, H. H., Lemery, K. S., Buss, K. A., & Campos, J. J. (1999). Genetic analyses of focal aspects of infant temperament. *Developmental Psychology, 35,* 972–985.

Leve, L. D., Scaramella, L. V., & Fagot, B. I. (2001). Infant temperament, pleasure in parenting, and marital happiness in adoptive families. *Infant Mental Health Journal, 22,* 545–558.

Lytton, H. (1980). *Parent-child interaction: The socialization processes observed in twin and singleton families.* New York: Plenum.

Mangelsdorf, S. C., Schoppe, S. J., & Buur, H. (2000). The meaning of parental reports: A contextual approach to the study of temperament and behavior problems in childhood. In V. J. Molfese & D. L. Molfese (Eds.), *Temperament and personality development across the lifespan* (pp. 1–32). Mahwah, NJ: Earlbaum.

Matheny, A. P. (1983). A longitudinal twin study of stability of components from Bayley's infant behavior record. *Child Development, 54,* 356–360.

Matheny, A. P. (1989). Children's behavioral inhibition over age and across situations: Genetic similarity for a trait during change. *Journal of Personality, 57,* 215–235.

Mathiesen, K. S., & Tambs, K. (1999). The EAS temperament questionnaire—factor structure, age trends, reliability, and stability in a Norwegian sample. *Journal of Child Psychology and Psychiatry, 40*(3), 431–439.

McCartney, K., Harris, M. J., & Bernieri, F. (1990). Growing up and growing apart: A developmental meta-analysis of twin studies. *Psychological Bulletin, 107,* 226–237.

McGue, M., Bacon, S., & Lykken, D. T. (1993). Personality stability and change in early adulthood: A behavioural genetic analysis. *Developmental Psychology, 29,* 96–109.

Philips, K., & Matheny, A. P. (1997). Evidence for genetic influence on both cross-situation and situation-specific components of behavior. *Journal of Personality and Social Psychology, 73,* 129–138.

Plomin, R. (1986a). *Development, genetics, and psychology.* Hillsdale, New Jersey: Lawerence Erlbaum.

Plomin, R. (1986b). Multivariate analysis and developmental behavioral genetics: Developmental change as well as continuity. *Behavior Genetics, 16,* 25–43.

Plomin, R. (1990). *Nature and nurture: An introduction to human behavioral genetics.* Belmont, CA: Brooks Cole.

Plomin, R., & DeFries, J. C. (1985). *Origins of individual differences in infancy: The Colorado adoption project.* Toronto: Academic Press.

Plomin, R., & Nesselroade, J. R. (1990). Behavioural genetics and personality changes. *Journal of Personality, 58,* 191–220.

Plomin, R., DeFries, J. C., & Fulker, D. W. (1988). *Nature and nurture during infancy and early childhood.* New York: Harvard University Press.

Plomin, R., Campos, J. J., Corley, R., Emde, R. N., Fulker, D. W., Kagan, J., *et al.* (1990a). Individual differences during the second year of life: The MacArthur Longitudinal Twin Study. In *Individual differences in infancy: Reliability, stability, and predictability* pp. 431–455).

Plomin, R., DeFries, J. C., & McClearn, G. E. (1990b). *Behavioral genetics. A primer* (2nd ed.). New York: W. H. Freeman.

Plomin, R., Coon, H., Carey, G., DeFries, J. C., & Fulker, D. (1991). Parent-off spring and sibling adoption analyses of parental ratings of temperament in infancy and early childhood. *Journal of Personality, 59*, 705–732.

Plomin, R., Emde, R. N., Braungart, J. M., Campos, J., Corley, R., & Fulker, D. W. (1993). Genetic change and continuity from 14 to 20 months: The MacArthur longitudinal twin study. *Child Development, 64*, 1354–1376.

Plomin, R., Chipuer, H. M., & Neiderhiser, J. M. (1994). Behavioral genetic evidence for the importance of nonshared environment. In E. M. Hetherington, D. Reiss, & R. Plomin (Eds.), *Separate social worlds of siblings: Importance of nonshared environment on development*. Hillsdale, NJ: Lawrence Erlbaum Associates.

Plomin, R., DeFries, J. C., McClearn, G. E., & McGuffin, P. (2001). *Behavioral genetics* (4th Ed.). New York: Worth Publishing.

Polderman, T. J. C., Posthuma, D., De Sonneville, L. M. J., Stins, J. F., Verhulst, F. C., & Boomsma, D. I. (2007). Genetic analyses of the stability of executive functioning during childhood. *Biological Psychology, 76*(1), 11–20.

Riese, M. L. (1990). Neonatal temperament in monozygotic and dizygotic twin pairs. *Child Development, 61*, 1230–1237.

Robinson, J. L., Kagan, J., Reznick, J. S., & Corley, R. (1992). The heritability of inhibited and unihibited behavior: A twin study. *Developmental Psychology, 28*, 1030–1037.

Rothbart, M. K. (1981). Measurement of temperament in infancy. *Child Development, 52*, 569–578.

Rothbart, M. K., Ahadi, S. A., Hershey, K., & Fisher, P. (2001). Investigations of temperament at three to seven years: The children's behavior questionnair. *Child Development, 72*, 1394–1408.

Saudino, K. J. (2000). *How you measure it counts. Genetic influences on activity level*. Paper presented at the Development 2000: A Conference on Developmental Psychology.

Saudino, K. J. (2008). *Sources of continuity and change in activity level in early childhood: Different situations, different results (partly)*. Paper presented at the Annual Meetings of the Behavior Genetics Association.

Saudino, K. J., & Cherny, S. S. (2001a). Parent ratings of temperament in twins. In R. N. Emde & J. K. Hewitt (Eds.), *The transition from infancy to early childhood: Genetic and environmental influences in the MacArthur longitudinal twin study* (pp. 73–88). New York: Oxford University Press.

Saudino, K. J., & Cherny, S. S. (2001b). Sources of continuity and change in observed temperament. In R. N. Emde & J. K. Hewitt (Eds.), *The transition from infancy to early childhood: Genetic and environmental influences in the MacArthur longitudinal twin study* (pp. 89–110). New York: Oxford University Press.

Saudino, K. J., & Eaton, W. O. (1991). Infant temperament and genetics: An objective twin study of motor activity level. *Child Development, 62*, 1167–1174.

Saudino, K. J., & Eaton, W. O. (1995). Continuity and change in objectively assessed temperament: A longitudinal twin study of activity level. *British Journal of Developmental Psychology, 13*, 81–95.

Saudino, K. J., & Zapfe, J. A. (2008). Genetic influences on activity level in early childhood: Do situations matter? *Child Development, 79*, 930–943.

Saudino, K. J., McGuire, S., Reiss, D., Hetherington, E. M., & Plomin, R. (1995). Parent ratings of EAS temperaments in twins, full siblings, half siblings, and step siblings. *Journal of Personality and Social Psychology, 68*, 723–733.

Saudino, K. J., Plomin, R., & DeFries, J. C. (1996). Tester-related temperament at 14, 20, and 24 months: Environmental change and genetic continuity. *British Journal of Developmental Psychology, 14*, 129–144.

Saudino, K. J., Cherny, S. S., & Plomin, R. (2000). Parent ratings of temperament in twins: Explaining the "too low" DZ correlations. *Twin Research, 3,* 224–233.

Saudino, K. J., Wertz, A. E., Gagne, J. R., & Chawla, S. (2004). Night and day: Are siblings as different in temperament as parents say they are? *Journal of Personality and Social Psychology, 87,* 698–706.

Saudino, K. J. (in press). Do different measures tap the same genetic influences? A multi-method study of activity level in young twins. *Developmental Science.*

Scarr, S., & McCartney, K. (1983). How people make their own environments: A theory of genotype-environment effects. *Child Development, 54,* 424–435.

Schmitz, S. (1994). Personality and temperament. In J. C. DeFries, R. Plomin, & D. W. Fulker (Eds.), *Nature and nurture during middle childhood* (pp. 120–140). Malden, MA: Blackwell Publishing.

Schmitz, S., Saudino, K. J., Plomin, R., & Fulkner, D. W. (1996). Genetic and environmental influences on temperament in middle childhood: Analyses of teacher and tester ratings. *Child Development, 67,* 409–422.

Seifer, R., Sameroff, A. J., Barrett, L. C., & Krafchuck, E. (1994). Infant temperament measured by multiple observations and mother reports. *Child Development, 65,* 1487–1490.

Stevenson, J., & Fielding, J. (1985). Ratings of temperament in families of young twins. *British Journal of Developmental Psychology, 3,* 143–152.

Torgersen, A. M. (1981). Genetic factors in temperamental individuality. A longitudinal study of same-sexed twins from 2 months to 6 years of age. *Journal of the American Academy of Child Psychiatry, 20,* 702–711.

Torgersen, A. M. (1985). Temperamental differences in infants and 6-year-old children: A follow-up study of twins. In The biological basis of personality and behavior: Theories, measurement techniques, and development (Vol. 1, pp. 227–239). Washington, DC: Hemisphere.

Venter, J. C. (2007, September 4). First diploid human genome sequence shows we're surprisingly different. *Science Daily.*

Viken, R. J., Rose, R. J., Kaprio, J., & Koskenvuo, M. (1994). A developmental genetic analysis of adult personality: Extraversion and neuroticism from 18 to 59 years of age. *Journal of Personality and Social Psychology, 66*(4), 722–730.

Wilson, R. S., & Matheny, A. P., Jr. (1986). Behavior genetics research in infant temperament: The Louisville Twin Study. In R. Plomin & J. Dunn (Eds.), *The study of temperament: Changes, continuities and challenges* (pp. 81–97). Hillsdale, NJ: Erlbaum.

Wohlwill, J. F. (1973). *The study of behavioral development.* Oxford, UK: Academic Press.

Wood, A. C., Saudino, K. J., Rogers, H., Asherson, P., & Kuntsi, J. (2007). Genetic influences on mechanically-assessed activity level in children. *Journal of Child Psychology and Psychiatry, 48,* 695–702.

Wood, A. C., Rijsdijk, F., Saudino, K. J., Asherson, P., & Kuntsi, J. (2008). High heritability for a composite index of children's activity level measures. *Behavior Genetics, 38*(3), 266–276.

DEVELOPMENTAL CHANGES IN COGNITIVE CONTROL THROUGH ADOLESCENCE

Beatriz Luna

LABORATORY OF NEUROCOGNITIVE DEVELOPMENT, WESTERN PSYCHIATRIC
INSTITUTE AND CLINIC, UNIVERSITY OF PITTSBURGH MEDICAL CENTER,
PITTSBURGH, PA 15213, USA

I. INTRODUCTION

II. WHAT IS MATURING IN THE BRAIN DURING ADOLESCENCE?
    A. SYNAPTIC PRUNING: INCREASING REGIONAL PROCESSING
       EFFICIENCY
    B. MYELINATION: SPEEDED NEURONAL TRANSMISSION

III. WHAT EXECUTIVE PROCESSES IMPROVE DURING
    ADOLESCENCE?
    A. WHAT IMPROVES IN THE ABILITY TO VOLUNTARILY INHIBIT
       A RESPONSE?
    B. WHAT IMPROVES IN THE ABILITY TO USE WORKING
       MEMORY?
    C. WHAT DRIVES DEVELOPMENTAL INCREASES IN SPEED OF
       PROCESSING?

IV. WHAT HAVE DEVELOPMENTAL NEUROIMAGING STUDIES
    REVEALED ABOUT MATURATION OF THE COGNITIVE SYSTEM?
    A. WHAT CHANGES IN BRAIN FUNCTION ACCOUNT FOR
       DEVELOPMENTAL CHANGES IN INHIBITORY CONTROL?
    B. WHAT CHANGES IN BRAIN FUNCTION ACCOUNT FOR
       DEVELOPMENTAL CHANGES IN WORKING MEMORY?

V. LIMITATIONS IN DEVELOPMENTAL STUDIES OF BRAIN
    FUNCTION

VI. THE TRANSITION TO WIDELY DISTRIBUTED CIRCUITRY

VII. HOW DOES IMMATURITY IN EXECUTIVE PROCESSING INFORM
    US ABOUT REAL LIFE DECISION MAKING?

REFERENCES

I. Introduction

The main purpose of this review is a better understanding of the developmental transition in behavior from adolescence to adulthood. To

Advances in Child Development and Behavior
Patricia Bauer : Editor

distinguish our focus from earlier (infancy) and later (aging) phases of development, we will refer to processes of "maturation," to emphasize the nature of this phase as a time when improvements are reaching a plateau and stable levels of adult behavior are achieved. During this phase of development many processes are changing that affect decision making including social, emotional, and cognitive aspects of behavior. In this review, I focus on the processes underlying the maturation of voluntary control of behavior (also referred to as cognitive control and executive function) because of its basic role in decision making.

Development refers to the mechanisms of change that ultimately lead to maturity in adulthood. Although much is known about the significant advances that occur in infancy and childhood, relatively less is known of the mechanisms that support the later parts of development in adolescence as mature-level behavior is approached. This chapter focuses on this particular phase of development as we transition from immature mechanism to mature adult-level behavior. Early development involves the *acquisition* of abilities that significantly change behavior, but as maturity is reached the changes are more subtle and involve the *sophistication* of abilities. This process begins in adolescence and can be conceptualized as occurring at the bend in the curve of development just before when the curve flattens representing adult stability (Figure 1). An important question during this phase of development is: what are the mechanisms that support this transition into mature levels of cognitive control of behavior? This is a phase of development when much of behavior appears adult-like, yet there is still pervasive evidence for limits in the efficacy of cognitive control. For example, adolescents are vulnerable to psychopathology, such as schizophrenia and mood disorders (Angold, Costello, & Worthman, 1998; Kessler *et al.*, 1994). In addition, sensation and novelty seeking peak in adolescence (Chambers, Taylor, & Petenza, 2003; Spear, 2000) and are associated with extreme sports, drug use, and unprotected sex. These behaviors appear to be characterized by poor judgment and decision making with limited appreciation for long-term consequences and are often impulsive in nature.

A significant landmark of this phase of development is the maturation to adult levels of the flexible and controlled manner of voluntarily guiding goal-directed behavior. In contrast to exogenously driven behavior (i.e., reflexive, automatic, and guided by outside stimuli) that is present early in development, endogenously driven behavior (i.e., voluntary, planned, and driven by internal goals) matures later. Central to endogenous behaviors are executive processes such as voluntary response inhibition and working memory that allow planned responses. When planning a response,

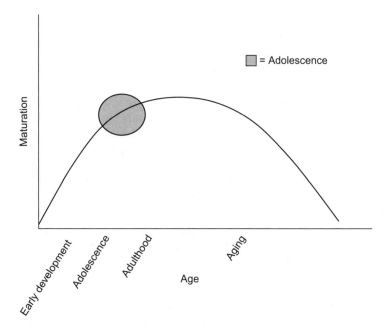

Fig. 1. *Depiction of developmental change across the age span. Adolescence is highlighted as a unique stage past childhood when adult-level stability is coming on-line.*

alternatives often must be considered and goal inappropriate responses that may be more reflexive need to be suppressed. This process is referred to as response inhibition and is central to cognitive control (Fuster, 1997). Working memory refers to the 'sketch pad' that allows us to retain relevant information on-line to make a planned goal-directed response and it is also central to cognitive control (Fuster, 1997). These processes, as described later in this chapter, are present in infancy but continue to improve throughout adolescence into adulthood and may underlie the emergence of adult-like behavior. We discuss what is known to be unique regarding the cognitive control of behavior during adolescence.

The emergence of cognitive control is driven by continuous interaction of environmental and biological factors. Biological mechanisms determine a timeline when environmental factors can have a lasting effect, and the environment establishes the course of biological mechanisms. For example, in the process of synaptic pruning (discussed later), the environment determines which synapses will be kept and which will not be needed but biological mechanisms determine the times in development when different parts of the brain will be most affected. In terms of cognitive control, brain development constrains the processes that can be performed at different ages. Characterizing the state of brain mechanisms during adolescence can help determine the nature of the cognitive tools that are available or not during this period. The interaction of brain and behavior thus becomes crucial in understanding maturation. These interactions have been studied with functional magnetic resonance imaging (fMRI); later we discuss what neuroimaging has revealed regarding onset of adult-like behavior in adolescence.

Adolescence commonly is considered to encompass 12–17 years of age, with the precise timing varying with gender and puberty (Spear, 2000). Puberty occurs when secretion of hormones in the pituitary gland stimulate ovarian development in females and spermatogenesis in males (Ojeda, Ma, & Rage, 1995). The timing is determined by age as well as metabolic and neuronal factors. Gonad hormone levels have direct effects on molecular mechanisms throughout the brain (McEwen, 2001) including influencing cortical development. Mood and social processes are affected by hormonal changes (Alsaker, 1996) which influence sex steroid receptors in the hippocampus and are associated with the regulation of the neurotransmitter dopamine (DA) especially in the part of the midbrain, namely the nucleus accumbens (NAcc), known to be critical in reward processing (Chambers *et al.*, 2003). There is no clear association between puberty and cognitive processes. Some studies have found a link between spatial abilities and pubertal timing (Petersen, 1976; Waber, Mann, Merola, & Moylan, 1985), but others have not (Orr, Brack, & Ingersoll, 1988; Strauss & Kinsbourne, 1981). Puberty may influence the degree to which one can exert cognitive control in situations of high arousal but in itself may not be directly linked to the development of cognitive control. Still, it is a pivotal aspect of this stage of development that must not be over-looked.

In this chapter, I analyze available evidence regarding the behavioral and brain processes present during adolescence. I discuss immaturities in the brain and how these may limit voluntary control. I also discuss the evidence indicating continuing development of cognitive control through adolescence, assessing the nature of what is still immature during this period. A critical review of the results of neuroimaging studies provides a forum to integrate the mechanisms of how brain and behavior interact during this time. A developmental theory emphasizing the role of the integration of widely distributed circuitry underlying the transition from adolescence to adulthood is contrasted against the traditional view that cognitive development is primarily driven by the unique protracted maturation of prefrontal cortex. Finally, I delineate a theory of maturation that is specific to this time of development and can be used to make predictions of behavioral performance.

II. What is Maturing in the Brain during Adolescence?

Identifying the progression of structural brain maturation in adolescence can further understanding of the brain functional systems that are available to support complex behavior such as cognitive control. The gross morphology of the brain is apparent early in life. The delineation of cortical folding in the brain is in place by birth (Armstrong *et al.*, 1995). The brain rapidly changes from a smooth surface to a convoluted one postnatally with well-defined sulci and gyri that are organized in predetermined fashion and that have different functional roles and cytoarchitecture. This early gyrification indicates the potential early in life for brain structure to support distinct regional specialization. The gyrification index, the ratio of exposed versus entire cortical contour, reaches adult levels in the second decade of life (Armstrong *et al.*, 1995). The brain achieves 95% of adult levels of size and weight by 7–11 years of age and adult weight by adolescence (Caviness *et al.*, 1996; Giedd *et al.*, 1996). These later changes in brain morphology are believed to be the result of processes such as synaptic pruning and myelination (Huttenlocher, 1990; Yakovlev & Lecours, 1967). I discuss each in turn.

A. SYNAPTIC PRUNING: INCREASING REGIONAL PROCESSING EFFICIENCY

Humans are born with an over-abundance of neuronal synaptic connections. After the first two years of life, throughout infancy, and into adolescence, synaptic connections that are used remain and those that are not used are eliminated or *pruned* through activity-dependent stabilization (Rauschecker & Marler, 1987). This process is largely understood to be a mechanism of plasticity that allows the brain to mold to a best fit with the individual's environment. The loss of unused connections enhances the computational capacity and speed of information processing of regional circuitry.

The early morphological studies characterizing these changes indicated that different parts of the brain pruned on different schedules. The initial study measured synapses in primary visual cortex in the occipital lobe and compared this to the rate of elimination in the middle frontal gyrus, a critical prefrontal region implicated in executive reasoning (Huttenlocher, 1990). Visual cortex reached maturity by 7 years of age whereas middle frontal gyrus did not reach adult levels until 17 years of age. A later study found that auditory cortex matured by 12 years of age (Huttenlocher & Dabholkar, 1997). These results are frequently cited to indicate that unlike non-human primate cortex, which develops concurrently across the brain (Rakic *et al.*, 1986), the human brain develops in a hierarchical fashion with sensory areas developing before executive regions. These results have major implications for developmental theory by suggesting that the maturation of cognitive control is guided to a great degree by the late maturation of prefrontal cortex (Casey, Giedd, & Thomas, 2000; Diamond, 2002).

Although the morphological findings are not in dispute, they focused on small regions that do not represent the entire brain. Neuroimaging studies allow assessment of changes across the whole brain. Positron emission tomography (PET) measures brain metabolism, which reflects levels of brain activity. In the resting state, glucose metabolism is believed to reflect synaptic activity and age-related changes in resting state glucose metabolism are believed to indirectly reflect synaptic pruning. Specifically, PET results indicate that resting state glucose metabolism achieve mature levels in many brain regions (e.g., parietal and temporal regions), during adolescence, not simply in frontal regions (Chugani, 1998). In addition, MRI has been used to measure gray matter thickness, which is believed to be determined, in large part, by synaptic pruning. Reductions in gray matter have been found throughout the cortex in association areas, notably in frontal and temporal regions (Gogtay *et al.*, 2004; Toga, Thompson, & Sowell, 2006) as well as basal ganglia (Sowell *et al.*, 1999). Association areas are unique in connecting different regions and supporting complex integration of function. Association areas within each of the cortical lobes demonstrate continued thinning into adolescence with temporal language-related regions developing last (Gogtay *et al.*, 2004) (Figure 2). These findings are important because they imply that the late maturation of cognitive control may not be guided by prefrontal specialization alone but by the ability to integrate information in association cortex throughout different regions of the brain.

B. MYELINATION: SPEEDED NEURONAL TRANSMISSION

Myelination is the process of insulating nerve tracts with glial cells. It significantly increases the speed of neuronal transmission (Drobyshevsky *et al.*, 2005). The increase in the speed of neuronal transmission allows for distant regions to integrate function, enhancing the efficiency of information processing and importantly supporting the integration of widely distributed circuitry needed for complex behavior (Goldman-Rakic *et al.*, 1993).

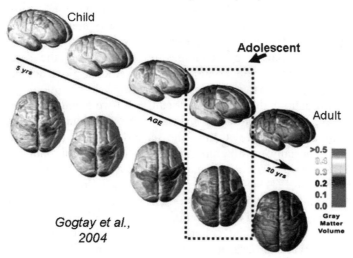

Fig. 2. *View of cortical surface of the brain generated from longitudinal MRI scans. Darkening shade represents degree of gray matter thinning. We have added a box surrounding the brains that represent adolescence (Figure transformed to black and white and reprinted from Gogtay* et al., *2004, 101(21), 8174–8179, with permission from PNAS).*

Myelination increases through adolescence (Wozniak & Lim, 2006). A classic histological study by Yakovlev and Lecours (1967) is widely cited to refer to the maturation of myelination throughout adolescence and, similarly to Huttenlocher and Dabholkar (1997), has been used as evidence for a posterior to anterior maturation of the brain. Motor and sensory areas were found to myelinate early in the first decade of life whereas associative areas in frontal, parietal, and temporal regions were found to continue to myelinate into the second decade of life. This finding has been used to indicate that frontal regions myelinate last. However, the findings indicate that frontal, parietal, and temporal areas all show similar protracted myelination. These results have been confirmed and expanded to provide evidence for protracted development of hippocampal structures as well (Benes, 1989). Similar to synaptic pruning, an implication of hierarchical maturation of the brain is that development is guided by the emergence of prefrontally guided executive function. However, evidence for protracted myelination throughout cortex supports the view that development may be guided by the establishment of mature connectivity that supports the integration of function of widely distributed circuitries throughout the brain known to support executive function (Goldman-Rakic, 1988). Given that the changes in white matter are a gradual enhancement of established connections, these results also support the notion that the nature of the protracted progressions through adolescence is a refinement of executive control processes that are in place early in development.

Although neuroimaging techniques do not provide the same high level of spatial resolution as morphological studies, they do allow the whole brain to be assessed *in vivo* providing information regarding changes throughout the extended circuitry. T1-weighted magnetic resonance images, which allow the measurement of white matter volume, indicate its continued growth into the second decade of life throughout the brain, especially frontotemporal regions that underlie language processes (Paus *et al.*, 1999; Pfefferbaum *et al.*, 1994). In addition, Diffusion Tensor Imaging (DTI) has been used as an indirect measure of developmental changes in myelination (Klingberg *et al.*, 1999; Mukherjee & McKinstry, 2006). DTI is a non-invasive magnetic resonance imaging method that measures the coherence of water diffusion in the brain parenchyma. Water diffuses in an anisotropic manner. That is, it does not have a preferred direction of movement. However, within the boundaries of white matter tracts, water diffuses in a predominantly preferred direction allowing the definition of white matter. Greater coherence of water diffusion reflects better integrity of white matter of which myelination has been found to be a major contributor (Moseley *et al.*, 1990; Song *et al.*, 2003).

Fractional anisotropy is often used as a measure of the index of directionally dependent diffusion reflecting white matter integrity. Fractional anisotropy values increase throughout childhood and adolescence, then stabilize in the second or third decade of life, paralleling known increases in myelination (Ben Bashat *et al.*, 2005; Li & Noseworthy, 2002). Studies have found age-related increases in fractional anisotropy across cortex in the major groups of tracts that provide functional integration supporting fine motor control, language processing, and executive control, such as the internal capsule (connects cortical and subcortical regions), corticospinal tract (connects cortex and spinal chord), arcuate fasciculus (connects temporal, parietal, and frontal regions), and corpus callosum (connects left and right hemispheres) (Ashtari *et al.*, 2007; Schmithorst *et al.*, 2002). Fractional anisotropy values have been found to be correlated with cognitive performance. Across different cortical regions, values of fractional anisotropy are associated with diverse measures of cognitive performance, including working memory, reaction time, reading, and IQ. For example, increases in fractional anisotropy in fronto-parietal regions have been found to correlate with cognitive performance especially in visuo-spatial tasks (Liston *et al.*, 2006; Nagy, Westerberg, & Klingberg, 2004).

This pattern of enhanced connectivity across cortical regions is supported by findings from studies of electroencephalography (EEG), which measures the brain's electrical activity. The correlations of resting state brain electrical activity across different brain regions provides a measure of the number and strength of brain connections (Otnes & Enochson, 1972). EEG studies indicate enhanced connectivity with development across neocortical regions throughout adolescence, primarily between frontal and other cortical areas (Thatcher, Walker, & Giudice, 1987). These results underscore the importance of functional integration throughout the brain as a significant aspect of later stages of development as adulthood is reached.

Taken together, synaptic pruning and myelination indicate that adolescence is marked by refinements across the brain that support integration of information and thereby foster higher-order cognitive processes (Goldman-Rakic, 1988). Although the establishment of widely distributed processing is nearing adult levels in adolescence, continued increases in myelination through this period indicate persistent limitations in connectivity. The circuitry available in adolescence thus would allow for approximations to adult control of behavior but with remaining immaturities limiting both efficient higher computations afforded by synaptic pruning and the establishment of widely distributed circuitry. These enhancements in regional circuitry and connectivity support a more effective manner in which executive cortical systems can affect basic subcortical response systems that support mature executive control of behavior.

III. What Executive Processes Improve during Adolescence?

In parallel with maturation of brain mechanisms, *behavior* is becoming more controlled and voluntary during adolescence. Executive function is used to define the processes that allow for cognitive or voluntary control of behavior including response planning and preparation, response inhibition, and working memory that support cognitive flexibility, abstract thought, and rule-guided behavior. Executive function is apparent early in development but continues to improve through adolescence. Evidence for early executive function comes from 7- to 12-month-olds who are able to perform the A not B task, which requires the use of working memory and inhibitory control (Diamond & Goldman-Rakic, 1989). Continued improvements through childhood in executive function are reflected in performance on neuropsychological tests that measure processes associated with prefrontal cortex (Davies & Rose, 1999; Levin *et al.*, 1991). These results indicate that prefrontally supported executive functions are present early in development but have a protracted development through childhood as these processes become better defined. Importantly, it highlights that the phase of development from childhood through adolescence is characterized by refinement of existing processes and not the emergence of new ones.

Thus, understanding development has to go beyond the integration of prefrontal circuitry. To understand the more complex underpinning of the brain and development association it is imperative that we investigate the basic components of executive function. Voluntary planned behavior requires the ability to retain online the goal of the response (using working memory), to plan and prepare the response, and the ability to filter out task irrelevant responses (response inhibition). These processes take place in the context of an information processing stream in which stimuli and task demands are initially perceived then processed and then an appropriate response is generated. In this section, I discuss what aspects of executive function improve during childhood and adolescence.

A. WHAT IMPROVES IN THE ABILITY TO VOLUNTARILY INHIBIT A RESPONSE?

As mentioned earlier, response inhibition, or the ability to suppress task-irrelevant responses for task-appropriate responses, is central to voluntary control of behavior (Davidson *et al.*, 2006; Fuster, 1989; Miller & Cohen, 2001). Most response inhibition tasks include competing responses including some that may be extremely prepotent, such as reflexive responses to external stimuli (e.g., antisaccade task, see further) or learned automatic responses (e.g., go-no-go task, see further), yet are task inappropriate. The ability to voluntarily inhibit responses provides flexibility to choose actions and for behavior to be guided by a task goal. Voluntary response inhibition is available early in infancy as demonstrated by studies using different paradigms wherein infants must suppress attention to a distractor stimulus to produce the most task appropriate response (Amso & Johnson, 2005; Bell & Fox, 1992; Diamond & Goldman-Rakic, 1989). Moreover, there is evidence that these early processes are supported by frontal systems (Bell & Fox, 1992). Studies of inhibitory performance through childhood indicate that what improves is the *rate* of correct inhibitory responses, not the ability to generate a correct inhibitory response (Bedard *et al.*, 2002; Luna *et al.*, 2004; Ridderinkhof, Band, & Logan, 1999; Van den Wildenberg & van der Molen, 2004; Williams *et al.*, 1999; Wise, Sutton, & Gibbons, 1975). These results suggest that the neural components that support the basic ability to inhibit a response as an isolated event are available early in development.

Studies have measured response inhibition by using tasks that require cessation of a reflexive response or suppression of interference from established responses that are incompatible with the goal of the task. Many such tasks have been used to measure developmental improvements in response inhibition. I expand on those that have been used most frequently, such as the go-no-go, flanker, stop signal, antisaccade, and Stroop tasks. In the go-no-go task subjects are presented with two types of stimuli, one that requires that participants press a response key, and one that requires that they refrain from responding. The "go" response is established by presenting a higher rate of response stimuli therefore requiring response inhibition for the infrequent "stop" stimuli. The typical flanker task presents a central arrowhead that is surrounded by arrowheads that are either in the same direction (compatible) or in the opposite direction (incompatible). Response inhibition is required to suppress distraction in incompatible trials which is reflected by a higher error rate and longer reaction times. In the stop-signal task, subjects are presented with a go signal which indicates that a response must be made (e.g., button press), however, some trials show a "stop" signal at different times after the "go" signal has been presented. This task requires inhibition of an already initiated response. Participants performing the antisaccade task are instructed to avoid looking at a visual stimulus that appears at an unpredictable location and time and instead look to an unpredictable location. Response inhibition is required to inhibit the reflexive response to look toward a light. Finally, the Stroop task is a prototypical neuropsychological task of response inhibition in which subjects must verbally say the color of the font of a color word that is sometimes in incompatible ink (e.g., "red" in green font). Participants must inhibit the tendency to say the word and instead say the font color. These tasks have been viewed as assessing different aspects of inhibitory control with the go-no-go, antisaccade, and stop signal task viewed as requiring active inhibition of motor commands and the Stroop and flanker tasks as tapping into focused attention (Kok, 1999).

On these tasks, younger children typically inhibit inappropriate responses on an above-chance number of trials. However the number of correct inhibitory responses throughout a task increases significantly with maturity. Therefore, one of the processes that improve throughout childhood and adolescence is the ability to inhibit *consistently* throughout a block of several trials. The process that supports the *flexible and consistent use* of the ability to inhibit responses is what becomes better established in adulthood. Inhibitory control requires top-down modulation of response-related processes guided by a goal, while suppressing reactive responses. Immaturities in synaptic pruning and especially myelination could hamper the top-down modulation of behavior, that is, the ability for executive cortical regions to have an effect on subcortical sensory and motor regions by limitations in speed and efficiency in which information is processed. This is especially true of long connections and distributed circuitries that integrate function of frontal areas with parietal regions and subcortical regions that are known to underlie executive functions (Goldman-Rakic, 1988).

The trajectory of late development of inhibitory control is shown in our studies of 245 8- to 30-year-old healthy individuals who performed an antisaccade task (Luna *et al.*, 2004). In this task, participants were asked to refrain from looking at a visual cue that appeared in an unpredictable location in the periphery and instead to look in the opposite location. Even the youngest children were able to perform some correct antisaccades, indicating that the ability to inhibit a single response is available early in development. However, performance improved dramatically with age and reached adult levels of performance by 14–15 years of age (Figure 3). These results have been consistent across a range of studies (e.g., Fukushima, Hatta, & Fukushima, 2000; Klein & Foerster, 2001).

One aspect of behavior that may significantly contribute to consistent performance is the process of establishing a *response state*. In addition to the actual voluntary suppression of a reactive response, other sensory and cognitive demands must be orchestrated for inhibition to occur consistently. The attention literature has referred to this process as the establishment of a task-related state that allows for the executive organization and control of the processes guiding cognitive events (Logan & Gordon, 2001). The ability to retain a response state has been found to have a unique brain circuitry that is distinct from the circuitry supporting other aspects of cognitive processes (Dosenbach *et al.*, 2006). Because developmental improvements are evident in the number of correct inhibitory responses and not the ability to make a single inhibitory response, there may be developmental limitations in the ability to establish an inhibitory response state. Therefore the implications are that what characterizes development through adolescence is not the emergence of a new cognitive ability but the ability to efficiently

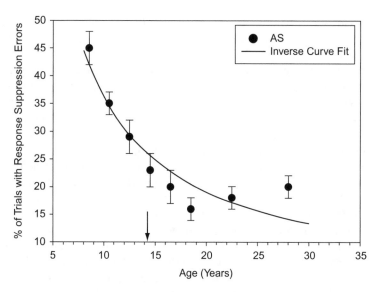

Fig. 3. Solid circles depict the M±1 standard error of the M (SEM) for the percent of trials with a response suppression failure in the antisaccade (AS) task. Thick lines depict the inverse curve fit on the response suppression failures by age in years. The arrow depicts the age at which change point analyses indicate adult level of performance was reached (reprinted from child development, 75(5), 1357–1372, with permission from the society for research in child development).

use this tool in a flexible and consistent fashion by effectively establishing a response state. Furthermore, the implications would also suggest that the circuitry that supports response state, which is unique to this process (Dosenbach *et al.*, 2006), would also be immature. As discussed later, neuroimaging findings indicate that the circuitry supporting response state shows a protracted development through adolescence (Fair *et al.*, 2007).

B. WHAT IMPROVES IN THE ABILITY TO USE WORKING MEMORY?

To enact a voluntary response, there has to be a representation of the goal that is kept on-line. This process is referred to as working memory (Baddeley, 1986). Working memory, such as response inhibition, is central to executive function (Fuster, 1997; Miller & Cohen, 2001) and given its interaction with response inhibition is often considered to be part of the same process (Miller & Cohen, 2001). In other words, response inhibition and working memory may always operate in tandem. Yet studies have found evidence for independent developmental trajectories for working memory and response inhibition (Asato, Sweeney, & Luna, 2006; Luciana *et al.*, 2005; Miyake *et al.*, 2000).

Working memory, similar to inhibitory control, also shows a prolonged development through adolescence (Demetriou *et al.*, 2002; Luna *et al.*, 2004). Working memory tasks typically present a stimulus or instructions that have to be remembered over a delay period, which sometimes can have an interfering stimulus or manipulation requirement. For example, in the oculomotor-delayed response task, subjects must remember the location of a briefly presented stimulus. After the to-be-remembered stimulus is presented there is a delay period during which the information (e.g., location, and sequence of letters) is maintained in working memory. In some working memory tasks, participants are asked to engage in a distraction during the delay period (e.g., counting numbers) which makes the task more difficult. After the delay period subjects have to make a response that is guided by the information that was kept on-line in working memory. The accuracy of that response with respect to the information initially presented is used to characterize the integrity of working memory. There is a consistent finding that although children can guide their behavior by instruction held in working memory, their responses are less accurate than those of adults. For example, children can identify the overall location of a previously presented cue (Luciana *et al.*, 2005; van Leijenhorst, Crone, & van der Molen, 2007) but are inferior to adults at the *precision* of this response (Luna *et al.*, 2004; Zald & Iacono, 1998). Measuring the precision of a working memory response allows detection of subtle differences in working memory performance that emerge in late childhood and adolescence. That is, processes that allow for the maintenance of general information regarding a working memory representation are available early in development. Later into adolescence general working memory processes are fine-tuned, which supports more detailed representations to be maintained on-line.

Typical tasks, such as those using verbal stimuli to probe working memory mechanisms, are not well-suited for characterizing of the level of fine tuning of working memory mechanism that occurs in adolescence. Language processes themselves continue to develop into adulthood, limiting the ability to assess age-related changes particular to working memory. Spatial working memory tasks, therefore, are better suited for developmental studies given that basic visual processes are available early in development and they allow for subtle changes in accuracy to be assessed. We have used the memory-guided saccade task, also known as the oculomotor-delayed response task, to characterize developmental improvements in working memory. Single-cell studies using this task have shown that the neural circuitry underlying working memory is recruited during this task, supporting its applicability to study the brain basis of working memory (Funahashi, Inoue, & Kubota, 1997; Hikosaka & Wurtz, 1983). Participants fixate a central target while a cue is briefly presented at an unpredictable location in the periphery and participants must remember the location during a delay period with no distraction or manipulation involved. The response to the memory-guided saccade task usually involves two or more saccadic eye movements. The first is a large saccade that approximates the target location and is driven both by processes supporting voluntary responses (directing the eyes to move with no visual guidance) and the working memory representation of the location of the previous target. Afterwards there are smaller corrective eye movements, which are more predominantly driven by the working memory representation and performance monitoring processes. We found that the accuracy of the initial saccade became adult-like by approximately 15 years of age (Figure 4). However, the last corrective saccade that provided precision continued to show improvements into the early twenties (Luna *et al.*, 2004).

These results suggest that although the ability to initiate a voluntary response guided by working memory reaches maturity in adolescence, corrective responses that afford precision continue to improve after adolescence. These results were present across different delay periods, suggesting that maintenance processes alone do not account for developmental differences but that also encoding may have developmental improvements. That is, the spatial resolution of the ability to encode a representation in working memory may be more refined in the adult system. Thus, although working memory is evident in infancy (Diamond & Goldman-Rakic, 1989), the ability to use working memory precisely and flexibly develops through adolescence. This is a recurring theme in cognitive maturation: Basic abilities are available early in life, while sophisticated use of cognitive abilities improves into adulthood. These results parallel those from response inhibition and from the timeline of brain maturation showing organization and specialization of central processes that are present early in life.

The protracted development of response inhibition and working memory underlie the late appearance into adolescence of adult-level performance in neuropsychological tasks (for reviews see: Diamond, 2002; Welsh, 2002). Neuropsychological tasks involve an array of processes including working memory and response inhibition that underlie planning

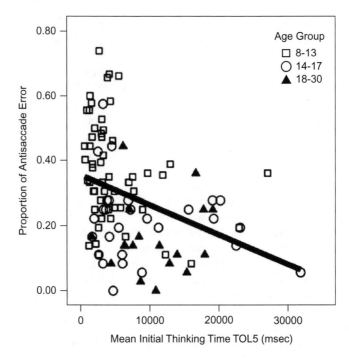

Fig. 4. Mean±1 standard error of the accuracy to initiate a memory-guided saccade (solid circles) and the accuracy of the final gaze location (open circles) in the ODR task for each age group. Thick lines indicate the inverse curve fit for these data across the age range studied. Arrows depict the age at which change point analyses indicate adult levels of performance were reached (reprinted from neuropsychologia, 44(12), 2259–2269, with permission from Elsevier).

and rule-guided behavior. The Wisconsin Card Sort, a widely used neuropsychological test, requires that participants match cards based on their own perception of the dimension at play (e.g., "red" figures) and are given feedback if they are correct. Then unexpectedly the dimension on which to match the cards changes (e.g., shape) and responses based on the old criterion are incorrect. Different performance components are scored to assess set shifting. Working memory is required to keep on-line the previous successful rule while inhibition is needed to suppress the tendency to perseverate responses that are no longer valid. In the Tower of London, participants need to arrange stimuli in as few steps as possible to match a presented arrangement. For example, subjects are presented with three columns on which 5 disks of distinct colors are arranged. Their task is to arrange the disks to match the presented arrangement. Working memory is needed to keep on-line the arrangement of cues as well as the possible steps to match the target arrangement.

Response inhibition is needed to suppress responding to the apparently easiest yet task inappropriate steps. Stroop and Contingency Naming Tasks require keeping the task instruction in working memory while suppressing the more established response. Performance on the Wisconsin Card Sort can appear mature by childhood (Chelune & Baer, 1986; Somsen, 2007) however performance on the Tower of London task continues to improve into adolescence (Asato *et al.*, 2006). Our results indicate that underlying developmental improvements in the Tower of London task are improvements in inhibitory control and working memory. Therefore, underlying improvements in neuropsychological tasks are improvements in central cognitive abilities.

There are mechanisms separate from central working memory processes that also can limit performance, including processing interference and failure to use strategies. Owing to immaturities in inhibition, children experience greater interference from distractors than adults, undermining the ability to show mature working memory performance in tasks that present competing stimuli in the delay period (Bjorklund & Harnishfeger, 1990; Dempster, 1981). Similarly, strategies such as verbal rehearsal or making associations between to-be remembered items during working memory maintenance also can enhance performance by using systems in addition to working memory, such as long-term memory, to assist in task performance. Results show that in working memory tasks in which it is possible to use strategies, such as verbal rehearsal of the to-be-remembered stimuli, adults take advantage of this more so than adolescents (Cowan, Saults, & Morey, 2006; van Leijenhorst *et al.*, 2007). These results highlight that developmental differences in working memory tasks may be related to strategy use rather than or in addition to age-related changes in working memory per se.

Taken together the literature indicates the presence of working memory abilities early in development that support executive function. What continues to improve into adolescence is the ability to perform complex tasks, be more precise, and control distraction, resulting in more efficient and adaptable working memory. Abstract thought and decision making benefit from an efficient and adaptable working memory system and immaturities in this system can therefore limit decision making.

C. WHAT DRIVES DEVELOPMENTAL INCREASES IN SPEED OF PROCESSING?

The speed with which stimuli and instructions are processed to produce a response indicates efficiency of information processing and is considered

Beatriz Luna

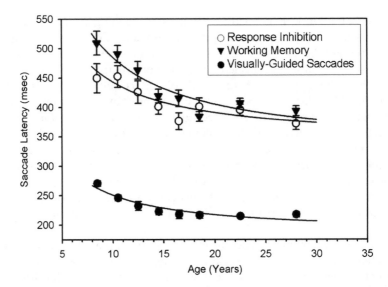

Fig. 5. M ± 1 standard error of the M (SEM) of the latency to initiate a saccade in each task for each age group. Solid circles depict the latency to initiate a saccade to a visual stimulus during the visually guided saccade (VGS) task. Open circles depict the latency to initiate an eye movement to the opposite location of a visual target in the antisaccade (AS) task. Solid triangles depict the latency to initiate an eye movement to a remembered location in the oculomotor-delayed response (ODR) task. Thick lines indicate the inverse curve fit on the M latency to initiate an eye movement response in millisececond by age in years. Arrows depict the ages at which change point analyses indicate adult levels of performance were reached (reprinted from child development, 75(5), 1357–1372, with permission from the society for research in child development).

a mental capacity (Kail & Salthouse, 1994). Processing speed is believed to reflect the integrity of the brain processes underlying functional integration such as myelination and synaptic pruning (described earlier), which support improvements in cognitive processes such as response inhibition and working memory (Kail, 1993; Luna *et al.*, 2004). Across reflexive and cognitive tasks, processing speed has been found to increase exponentially throughout childhood and adolescence (Hale, 1990; Kail, 1993). Developmental decreases in reaction time have been found using simple reaction time tasks where the speed to look at a visual target is assessed (Fischer, Biscaldi, & Gezeck, 1997; Fukushima *et al.*, 2000) as well as those that have cognitive demands such as inhibitory control (Luna *et al.*, 2004; Munoz *et al.*, 1998) (Figure 5). Developmental improvements in speed of processing have also been found in manual reaction time (Elliott, 1970) and visual matching tasks (Fry & Hale, 1996). Regardless of the actual latency to initiate responses, which are extended in tasks with cognitive demands, there is a similar developmental profile with maturity being reached in adolescence. The fact that improvements in reaction time to an automatic response are similar to those with a cognitive load suggests that the development of speed of processing is independent from cognitive processing and in fact may assist the development of executive processes.

IV. What have Developmental Neuroimaging Studies Revealed about Maturation of the Cognitive System?

The co-occurrence in adolescence of changes in brain processes such as synaptic pruning and myelination that support cognition and speed of processing as well as changes in cognition and behavior suggest an important link between brain and behavior through development. However, investigating the association between changes in brain structure and behavior does not provide information regarding the maturity of dynamic brain function. That is, although pruning and myelination throughout cortical and subcortical regions are still occurring through adolescence, we do not know how this affects the functioning brain systems and which aspects of the system are associated with behavioral improvements.

One way to investigate functional circuits during cognitive function across development is with neuroimaging methods. fMRI is a non-invasive technique that provides an indirect measure of neuronal activity by measuring regional changes in blood oxygen levels that result from increased metabolism in areas of neuronal activity. Since the late 1990s, fMRI has been used to study cognitive development and the results have had a great impact in how we understand the brain behavior relations during development.

A. WHAT CHANGES IN BRAIN FUNCTION ACCOUNT FOR DEVELOPMENTAL CHANGES IN INHIBITORY CONTROL?

Response inhibition is supported by a widely distributed circuitry of which prefrontal areas are undoubtedly central. Different regions of prefrontal cortex have been implicated in unique aspects of inhibitory control such as inferior frontal gyrus supporting interference resolution during response *execution* versus dorsolateral prefrontal cortex and anterior cingulate cortex supporting response *selection* (Nee, Wager, & Jonides, 2007). Prefrontal cortex is highly interconnected within itself and with other cortical and subcortical regions of the brain, permitting quick executive control by suppressing internal and external inputs and disrupting any ongoing behavior. Its contributions to inhibition are in the preparatory activity in anticipation of an inhibitory response (Nyffeler *et al.*, 2007) and in organizing the temporal processes of the task (Fuster, 1997).

The literature on the development of executive function has focused primarily on the contributions of age-related changes in regional processes of prefrontal cortex. However, given evidence that the beginning of complex executive behavior is present early in life and that age-related improvement in inhibition take the form of an increase in the rate of successful executive inhibitions, structural changes in prefrontal cortex alone cannot account for the bulk of developmental changes. Early in development prefrontal cortex has the capacity to perform complex computations supporting executive function as evidenced by the ability to perform executive responses. Improvements through childhood in the ability to flexibly use executive function, which is supported by a widely distributed circuitry (Dosenbach *et al.*, 2006), suggest that a significant contributor to the development of executive function is the integration of brain function, which in turn is supported by continued myelination known to occur during this period. Continued myelination in turn enhances the ability of prefrontal cortex to effectively influence on the rest of the brain (Chugani, Phelps, & Mazziotta, 1987; Olesen *et al.*, 2003; Thatcher, 1991). Furthermore, other cortical association areas also undergo protracted refinements that may allow them to perform complex computations that can collaborate with prefrontal cortex in providing inhibitory control.

For example, inhibition of reflexive visually guided eye movements in the antisaccade task is supported by a circuitry including cortical and subcortical regions wherein preparatory activity is crucial to successful inhibitory control. In this task, participants are instructed to avoid looking at a peripheral visual target, which appears at an unpredictable time and location, and to look instead toward the mirror location. Single-cell studies in non-human primates have found that preparatory activity in eye movement regions predicts successful inhibitory responses (Everling & Munoz, 2000). During the preparation to make an inhibitory eye movement, activity in subcortical (superior colliculus) and cortical systems (frontal eye fields and intraparietal sulcus) that generate eye movements is dampened while activity in the regions supporting fixation (the suppression of eye movements) is increased. Dorsolateral prefrontal cortex and medial prefrontal cortex also show preparatory activity. Unlike superior colliculus, frontal eye field, and intraparietal sulcus, which also show activity during saccade response, prefrontal cortex is only recruited in the preparatory phase, indicating that it is involved in response planning only

(Brown, Vilis, & Everling, 2007). The instruction to inhibit a response is processed in prefrontal cortex, which then influences oculomotor cortical and subcortical regions, with the goal being to influence the superior colliculus in a timely fashion to stop the reflexive saccadic response. These results indicate that inhibiting an impending saccade relies on the concerted activity of prefrontal, premotor, and subcortical regions. The ability to make correct antisaccades in childhood indicates that this circuitry is available during this period. However, as described previously, the *proportion* of correct inhibitory responses increases with age, indicating that this circuitry is engaged in a more reliable and more consistent fashion with age.

Most developmental fMRI studies of response inhibition focus exclusively on results in specific regions of prefrontal cortex as opposed to larger neural systems. Across studies there have been findings indicating that aspects of the inferior frontal gyrus (Brodmann's areas 45 and 46 or BA 45/46) and premotor regions (BA46) increase activation with age (Bunge *et al.*, 2002; Rubia *et al.*, 2000). These regions have been found across inhibitory tasks such as the go-no-go (Rubia *et al.*, 2006; Tamm, Menon, & Reiss, 2002), flankers (Bunge *et al.*, 2002), stop tasks (Rubia *et al.*, 2007), Stroop (Adleman *et al.*, 2002; Marsh *et al.*, 2006), and antisaccade tasks (Luna *et al.*, 2001), with equivalent performance or with behavior that changes with age. Most studies have interpreted this finding as reflecting the late structural changes in prefrontal cortex that may allow this region to better participate in inhibitory control and therefore show more activity. However these same studies as well as others also have found evidence for age-related *decreases* in other prefrontal regions including inferior and medial frontal gyri. A go-no-go study with 8- to 20-year-olds showed both increased activation in the medial frontal gyrus as well as *decreases* in the inferior frontal gyrus (Tamm *et al.*, 2002). Age-related increases in the participation of the medial frontal gyrus was interpreted as reflecting actual improvements in the brain for supporting inhibitory processes, whereas age-related decreases in inferior frontal gyrus participation were thought to reflect developmental differences in the effort required to exert inhibitory control. The interpretation of developmental increases and decreases in brain function is an area of the literature that needs clarification and I discuss this in detail later.

Some of the developmental results can be interpreted in the context of the functions that certain prefrontal regions are known to support. For example, increased recruitment of inferior frontal gyrus, which often includes BA 45 (Broca's area) and premotor regions (BA 6), may indicate both increases in the capability of inhibiting a response as well as the use of strategies for enhancing a basic inhibitory function. The recruitment of BA 45, which is an area central to speech production, could represent a verbal strategy that is being implemented by adults but not by younger participants. Increases in activation in premotor regions, which as described previously are known to support preparatory activity in inhibitory control, may indicate enhanced ability to plan for stopping a response. Our work using the antisaccade task has indicated that the frontal eye fields (BA 6) show enhanced activity when adults perform better than younger participants (Luna *et al.*, 2001).

The ability to detect errors and monitor performance is crucial to inhibitory control and has been fond to be supported by a well-delineated neural circuitry of which the anterior cingulate cortex is central (Braver *et al.*, 2001; Carter *et al.*, 1998). Initial studies found that the integration of the anterior cingulate cortex as well as prefrontal systems improves with development, perhaps enhancing the ability to influence overall performance influenced by error commission. Rubia *et al.* (2007) found that when equating performance across childhood to adulthood in an inhibitory task by adapting the task by skill level, adults still demonstrated increased recruitment of anterior cingulate and prefrontal cortex, suggesting a more mature anterior cingulate cortex structure that can participate in performance monitoring. The anterior cingulate cortex has connections with prefrontal cortex as well as striatal and brain stem regions (Devinsky, Morrell, & Vogt, 1995) making it particularly suitable to detect errors and influence behavior. An adult study examining the evolution of anterior cingulate cortex participation in error commission during the antisaccade task indicated different stages of error processing (Polli *et al.*, 2005). To make a correct inhibitory response it is necessary to suppress activity in "default-mode" regions, which supports the state of brain systems when they are not engaged in an active task, that persists during rest and undermines focused goal directed responses and recruit a rostral part of the anterior cingulate cortex (Simpson, *et al.*, 2001). After an error has been committed, regions that integrate the failure of the response to benefit future performance are recruited, including a dorsal aspect of the anterior cingulate cortex. Results indicate that inhibitory errors are characterized by failure to deactivate the rostral anterior cingulate cortex, which was evident immediately after an error and by the later recruitment of dorsal anterior cingulate cortex to influence performance. It is important to determine whether performance monitoring shows protracted development and hence accounts for developmental improvements in performance. Our own developmental fMRI study demonstrated increased activity in anterior cingulate during errors of inhibition that was specific to different stages of error processing. The

7.5 sec   10.5 sec

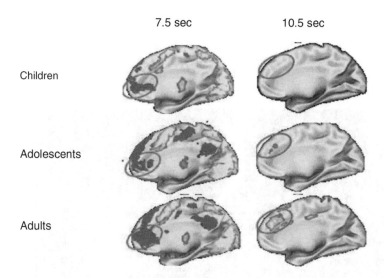

Children

Adolescents

Adults

Fig. 6. From Velanova et al., 2008. Activity in medFG/rACC and dACC across time for correct and error AS trials in each age group on the partially inflated medial cortical surface of the right hemisphere for correctly performed antisaccade trials (reprinted from cerebral cortex, 18(11), 2505–2522, with permission from Oxford University press).

ventral anterior cingulate cortex had equivalent activation in initial stages of error processing across age groups. However, during the second stage of error processing only adults recruited the dorsal anterior cingulate cortex reflecting immaturities even in adolescence (Velanova, Wheeler, & Luna, 2008) (Figure 6). These results imply that whereas the detection of errors may be available early in development, later stages that may influence subsequent behavior may have a protracted development.

When taking into consideration circuitries that include frontal regions, fMRI studies have found evidence indicating that age-related integration of fronto-striato-thalamic and fronto-cerebellar neural pathways support enhanced inhibitory control and correlate with better performance in a range of inhibitory tasks (Rubia *et al.*, 2006; Rubia *et al.*, 2007). Our own work provides evidence for a more circuit based maturation (Luna *et al.*, 2001). Using the antisaccade task we found that activity in dorsolateral prefrontal cortex showed increased activation from childhood to adolescence whereas its participation decreased from adolescence to adulthood. Instead, adults recruited a much more distributed circuitry including premotor and parietal eye fields as well cerebellum (Figure 7). Age-related increases in the participation of parietal and cerebellar regions also have been found in other developmental studies of inhibition (Bunge *et al.*, 2002;

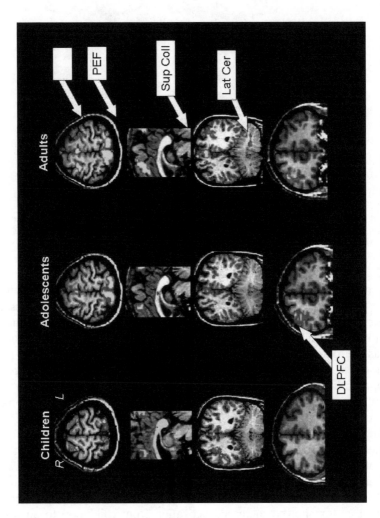

Fig. 7. From Luna et al., 2001. Mean group activity during a block antisaccade task for children, adolescents, and adults overlaid on top of the structure of a representative subject (reprinted from neuroimage, 13(5), 786–793, with permission from Elsevier).

Rubia *et al.*, 2006) as well as recruitment of frontostriatal and frontocerebellar pathways (Andersen *et al.*, 1990; Rubia *et al.*, 2007). These results indicate that developmental improvements are supported by the integration of a distributed brain system and not by the enhanced participation of prefrontal cortex alone.

As discussed previously, the ability to establish a response set may be a crucial element in maturation of inhibitory control and may have an independent developmental trajectory. A distinct circuitry including dorsal anterior cingulate cortex, medial prefrontal cortex, and bilateral anterior insula has been found to be recruited across different tasks (e.g., verb generation, matching, and motor timing) when maintaining a task-set compared to periods of rest (Dosenbach *et al.*, 2006). Our initial results reveal important developmental improvements in the ability to retain an inhibitory response state that are separate from those that support the ability to make a single correct inhibitory response. The circuitry supporting the ability to make a single correct response is present by childhood but shows decreased participation with age. The decreases in activity may reflect the reduced effort for older participants to perform a correct inhibitory response relative to younger children. Developmental changes in the ability to retain an inhibitory *state,* however, indicate *increases* in activity in prefrontal and posterior regions suggesting that the circuitry is more successfully recruited with age. These results support the proposal that inhibitory processes are available by childhood whereas the ability to flexibly and consistently execute control continues to improve through adolescence and may be primary in age related improvements in executive function.

B. WHAT CHANGES IN BRAIN FUNCTION ACCOUNT FOR DEVELOPMENTAL CHANGES IN WORKING MEMORY?

As is the case for response inhibition, there is a widely distributed circuitry known to underlie working memory in the adult, including premotor, parietal, temporal, and subcortical regions (Passingham & Sakai, 2004; Sweeney *et al.*, 1995). However, the focus of most research, including developmental fMRI studies, has largely been on the contributions of prefrontal systems. Prefrontal regions undoubtedly play a role in central aspects of working memory but many studies indicate that other regions, mainly in parietal areas, also play an important role. Prefrontal areas apparently support executive aspects of working memory such as the manipulation of information, whereas parietal regions appear to support the actual storage (ability to maintain information on line) of information in working memory (D'Esposito *et al.*, 1999; Postle *et al.*, 2006). Our studies on the mature system have also indicated that maintenance is supported by parietal regions (Geier, Garver, & Luna, 2007).

fMRI studies consistently indicate that prefrontal systems are engaged in working memory processes as early as 8 years of age but the magnitude of engagement varies with age. Studies that use the n-back task, where responses depend on keeping on-line the arrangement of previous cues, show equivalent prefrontal recruitment in children and adults (Nelson *et al.*, 2000; Thomas *et al.*, 1999). However, most studies that use working memory tasks that examine task manipulation and the accuracy of responses show age-related increases in the recruitment of prefrontal cortex (Ciesielski *et al.*, 2006). These increases have been found to be due to immaturities in the ability to manipulate information in working memory (Crone *et al.*, 2006; Olesen *et al.*, 2007), to gen'-erate an accurate response (Klingberg, Forssberg, & Westerberg, 2002; Scherf, Sweeney, & Luna, 2006), and to suppress distractors (Olesen *et al.*, 2007).

We performed the memory-guided task in children, adolescents, and adults in an fMRI study to investigate circuit-level changes with development (Scherf *et al.*, 2006). In the memory-guided saccade task subjects must remember the location of a peripheral target that is presented briefly in an unexpected location in the periphery. After a varying delay period (typically 1 to 10 sec), during which the location of the target is sustained in working memory, subjects must move their eyes in the absence of a visual target to the location they remembered the target to have been. The accuracy of the memory-guided eye movement is used to assess the fidelity of the working memory response. Dorsolateral prefrontal cortex was found to be recruited across age groups. However, similar to our results with response inhibition, the magnitude of right dorsolateral prefrontal cortex participation followed an inverted "U" shape, peaking in adolescence. These results may be due to the fact that children do not perform at adolescent or adult levels, which may be due to immaturities in executive processes supported by prefrontal systems. In contrast, adolescents perform similar to older participants and use prefrontal executive systems, but it may be more difficult for them to perform at adult levels, which results in increased recruitment of prefrontal cortex.

The implications for adolescent behavior are similar to those of inhibitory control: Although adolescents may demonstrate executive function that is similar to that of adults, their functional circuitry resembles that of adults performing a more difficult task. Additionally, as shown in Figure 8, activity across brain regions becomes more evenly distributed

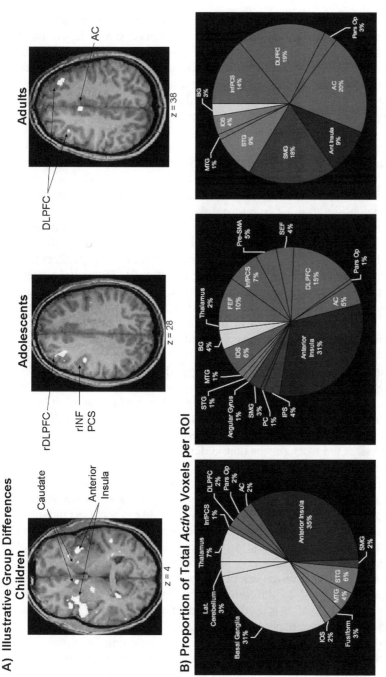

Fig. 8. From Scherf et al., 2006. Imaging results from both magnitude and extent of activation analyses. (A) Axial brain slices depicting regions of significant brain activity in each age group. Children showed stronger activation bilaterally in the caudate nucleus, the thalamus, and anterior insula. Adolescents showed the strongest right DLPFC activation, and adults showed concentrated activation in left prefrontal and posterior parietal regions. (B) Pie charts depict the distribution of brain activation across all brain regions recruited. Children showed disproportionate amount of activity in basal ganglia and adolescents in right dorsolateral prefrontal cortex. In contrast, adults showed more equally distributed recruitment of regions (reprinted from journal of cognitive neuroscience, 18, 1045–1058, with permission from MIT press).

with age, suggesting that as we reach adulthood there is more distributed function across the brain which may decrease the need to recruit prefrontal systems. The hypothesis that integration across the brain is central to cognitive development (Edin *et al.*, 2007; Olesen *et al.*, 2003) is supported by DTI studies (described earlier) showing that age related improvements in working memory are related to increased functional connectivity within cortical regions and in corticosubcortical pathways.

V. Limitations in Developmental Studies of Brain Function

A number of factors underlying differences across studies need to be taken into consideration when interpreting the results reported here. The most controversial in the literature has been the issue of how to interpret age-related differences in brain function when performance also differs by age. On the one hand, differences in performance could simply reflect that unique strategies are adopted and may not capture developmental change in the brain processes themselves. On the other hand, equating performance also limits what can be characterized to purely differences in effort. Higher cognitive loads or increased complexity of tasks require overall more "effort" in adults. Age-related changes in effort may be due to the use of unique strategies but may also reflect decreases in the recruitment of basic brain processes engaged in adulthood. Moreover, equating performance can misrepresent developmental differences such as in comparing children who are outliers in that they perform at adult levels with adults who are also outliers in performing at low levels. Finally, only considering tasks in which performance is similar across ages limits the ability to assess the mechanisms that underlie the inability of children and adolescents to perform at adult levels.

There is no clear solution to this problem except for integrating different interpretations in the results. When groups differ in performance, there is the possibility of defining what the circuitry looks like when it is immature. In this manner, the regions that fail to be recruited and the alternative circuitry that has been used can provide insight into the immaturities of specific brain systems. However, as stated earlier, the developmental differences may be due to the use of unique strategies that recruit specific brain systems and not to differences in the integrity of brain systems themselves. When learning is used as a model for development, age related differences in the use of strategies and their related brain circuitry is supported. Studies with adults in which simple learning tasks are used indicate that the circuitry that is initially recruited when a task is novel is qualitatively different from the circuitry that is recruited once the behavior has been learned. This may reflect a shift in the strategies that are used and would not indicate immaturities in the ability to use the learned systems (Ungerleider, Doyon, & Karni, 2002).

When performance is equivalent, the developmental differences become somewhat obscured because now the task has become simpler and the differences can only be attributed to differences in the degree to which executive regions need to be recruited. A typical finding when performance is equated is that younger children rely more on executive regions needed to perform the task, which is similar to results in adults when cognitive load is increased. However, similar performance could also be achieved by the use of different strategies.

Even so, the question remains regarding why children do not use adult strategies. Strategy use may be the result of learned responses with similar demands and be independent from brain maturation. However, immaturities in brain regions and connectivity could also undermine the ability to recruit strategies that are supported by complex circuitry. Parametric studies where different levels of cognitive complexity can be assessed would assist in the ability to see if similar strategies can be used for easier tasks. Lack of age-related differences at simple versus complex levels of cognition would indicate that basic brain systems are available but need further specialization or that processes specific to cognitive complexity are not being accessed. Parametric manipulations also allow for identifying at what level of cognitive complexity there is a failure to instate the proper circuitry. Similarly, longitudinal designs could be used to assess the availability of different circuitries at the individual level, as well as changes in brain structure using DTI or measures of gray matter thinning. Another approach is to use tasks that have minimal opportunity for strategy formation. Oculomotor tasks that tap into cognitive systems are not as amenable to strategies given that the responses are quick and to unpredictable locations. The go-no-go task and stop tasks are similar in this respect as there is little preparation to stop an automatic response and verbal cues are not used. These tasks which appear simple compared to typical neuropsychological tasks that involve many cognitive processes, can inform us regarding the status of basic aspects of individual systems. There are processes that are common and therefore basic to executive function that these simpler tasks can help us model. For example, inhibitory control always requires top-down modulation from frontal executive systems to processes related to motor responses. Characterizing the status of inhibitory control using these tasks that focus on specific aspects of executive function can inform us regarding their availability at different stages of development. Evidence of limitations in performance or in the recruitment of brain systems supporting these "basic" systems would indicate that central processes are still immature undermining the ability to perform more complicated tasks.

There also are methodological issues that affect how we interpret developmental neuroimaging results. fMRI studies can be performed using a "blocked" design, where brain activity represents the collective activity of a block of similar trials, or an "event-related" design where brain activity is assessed at the single trial level. In block designs, periods (typically lasting 10–40 s) of experimental trials with cognitive demands (e.g., Stroop) are compared to periods of a baseline task with minimal cognitive demands (e.g., fixation). The brain regions that show significant increases in activity in the experimental versus baseline blocks are deemed to support processes underlying the cognitive demands of the experimental period. Because of the engagement of continuous performance of a specific behavior, the block design offers optimal signal to identify the brain regions participating in a task. In this design, however, error and correct trials are grouped and processes supporting the ability to retain a task state are also included therefore measuring more than the processes of interest. Event-related designs provide an alternative by allowing the characterization of brain function that underlies a single trial. This approach generates lower signal than the block design and necessitates more trials. The benefit of event related designs is that it allows for only correct trials to be assessed therefore comparing similar performance since the same behavior is being generated. Additionally, if sufficient incorrect trials are performed, the brain circuitry underlying error commission also can be investigated. An ideal approach would be to use a mixed block event related fMRI design that permits the assessment of correct and incorrect trials as well as the block-level processes that can reflect the status of response state, which as indicated earlier, may be key in understanding the basis of developmental improvements in cognitive control.

Another factor that can affect the definition of changing circuitry is the level of analyses. The gross morphology of the brain is stable from childhood on, but the continued thinning of gray matter into adolescence could result in some age-related anatomical differences. Voxel-wise analyses, where comparisons are made on the 1–5 mm area that the data was acquired, could be affected by subtle anatomical differences. Fitting the variable anatomy of a group of subjects to a common brain atlas is crucial in ensuring that the same regions are being compared. However, the match may not always be to 1–5 mm resolution and the identical voxels may not always correspond across subjects. Region of interest (ROI) based analyses can overcome this limitation as a large region of voxels are selected to perform analyses (e.g., Brodmann's Area 6 in the precentral sulcus, which defines the Frontal Eye Field) and these can be more consistently matched across individuals and groups of individuals. How regions of interest are defined is also a contributing factor. Hypothesis-driven selection of regions is highly regarded in the field because it is theory driven and protects from spurious findings. However, mapping developmental changes in brain function is still at the early stage of discovery where exploratory analyses are essential. Limiting studies to only investigating the regions that have already been implicated in the literature, such as prefrontal cortex, assumes that this is where developmental change will occur and limits the ability to test other possibilities.

There are well-delineated approaches that can be used that allow exploratory analyses to avoid the pitfalls of fishing expeditions. One approach is to select regions of interest based on the circuitry generated from analyses of adults. The question then becomes the extent to which younger groups use the same regions, when they do, whether they are used in the same magnitude and manner. Inspection of the temporal development of the fMRI signal changes within a region becomes crucial. When groups differ in activation, many qualitatively different processes might be involved and each has distinct implications for development. The most common interpretation of age-related differences in activation is that both groups recruited a region but one group activated it to a larger magnitude. If the older group showed higher activity than the younger group, this would be interpreted as indicating that although children recruit this region for the task, region-wise immaturities do not allow the level of processing needed to support performance at adult levels. That is, that due to for example, immature myelination, this region is not being integrated into the circuitry to the required level. If the younger group demonstrates higher activity this would be interpreted as indicating that due to lack of specialization (diffuse to focal theory, Durston *et al.*, 2006), or larger exerted effort, the younger group had to drive the region to a higher degree. For example, lack of synaptic pruning may result in a larger extent of grey matter being recruited to activate the region. Alternatively, the task may be perceived as more difficult by younger subjects and may need a higher degree of involvement to be effective such as in executive regions of prefrontal cortex.

However, there are many other possibilities including that different groups are using the region in qualitatively different manners. For example, one group may actively engage the region while the other actively suppresses it, or one group simply does not engage that region at all. Both groups may recruit a similar region but may be using it to support different aspects of behavior such as response preparation or response execution, or for maintaining information on line. These results would indicate a more complex change in development where regions are online early but their role is still being defined.

Another approach that can be taken to examine developmental differences is to see how activity changes in comparison to adult activation. This can be of value in identifying which brain regions younger subjects are not accessing. However, this approach undermines the ability to characterize the alternate circuitry that may be being used by the younger group. That is, it is quite possible that younger subjects recruit completely different regions than the older group. For example, children may be recruiting regions in parietal cortex to compensate for immaturities in prefrontal systems but these would not be captured if older subjects did not also recruit this region. Identifying alternative circuitries would allow us to determine the circuitry that younger subjects are using to perform a task. Consequently, another approach defines regions based on a main effect of task across subject groups therefore identifying the regions that were relevant to the task at hand regardless of developmental differences. Compensatory regions only recruited by younger subjects or supplementary regions recruited by older subjects would also be evident. In this manner, the possibility that older subjects are using supplementary regions in posterior areas while showing reduced activity in prefrontal regions could suggest a mechanism by which the mature system can better distribute function. Another limitation present in many studies is the erroneous reporting of age differences in regions that were not recruited during the main task but that appear significant during age comparisons. Regions that are not statistically defined to participate in a task are part of background activity that contributes to artifact. These results should not be interpreted.

The task used for baseline comparison also is crucial. It is important that the baseline comparison task used in a study does not itself have developmental differences. Differences in the comparison task would undermine the ability to assess developmental changes in the experimental task. For example, a Stroop study found a set of regions that showed age-related differences in *deactivation* that were hard to interpret. As the authors acknowledged, this may have been due to developmental differences in how the baseline condition (congruent name and color) was processed (Marsh *et al.*, 2006). The baseline condition used in this task was to say the name of the color word that was printed in an ink color that corresponded to the letter ("red" in red ink). This baseline task was used to assess activity in the experimental task where participants had to say the name of the color word that was printed in a font color that did not correspond to the color word ("red" in green ink). There may have been differences in language processes in children that undermined the ability to assess the experimental condition.

Finally, the ages chosen to represent different developmental stages can influence outcomes. Some studies group children and adolescents into a homogenous group (Rubia *et al.*, 2000, 2006) limiting the ability to observe differences between childhood and adolescence and developmental differences in general. Given the variability in individual development, there are no steadfast ages that define a particular period. Adolescence defined through pubertal staging can vary tremendously starting as young as 10 and continuing to late teens. Several factors can help determine appropriate ages. Pubertal assessments can help *post hoc* to investigate possible stage related differences. Narrowing the age range can increase the probability of including participants within a stage (e.g., 13–17 years for adolescence as opposed to 10–19 years). Optimally, a task should be used for which behavioral performance has been established across different ages and this information can be used to guide the appropriate age ranges to test.

An alternative is to consider age as a continuous variable and analyze the data with regression-based approaches. This approach can be very useful in capturing linear trends. Although many developmental changes in behavior from childhood to adulthood are linear, studies have found that age-related changes in cognitive control and speed of processing are best represented by a log function or curvilinear approaches that can integrate the period of adolescence when adult plateau levels are reached (Kail, 2007; Luna *et al.*, 2004). However, the large samples required for typical regression analyses can make this approach less feasible for imaging work, where relatively small samples are the norm.

VI. The Transition to Widely Distributed Circuitry

Adolescence differs qualitatively from childhood in that adolescents can appear to have mature cognitive control. Our developmental studies on both response inhibition and working memory show that adolescents typically behave at adult-like levels (Luna *et al.*, 2004; Scherf *et al.*, 2006). Adolescents recruit many of the same circuits that adults use, yet there are important differences that are telling of the adolescent period. Adolescents appear to use dorsolateral prefrontal cortex to a higher magnitude than adults while not recruiting the other regions to the same degree. In the response inhibition task, adolescents showed more activity in the dorsolateral prefrontal cortex than adults and less in frontal and parietal eye fields known to be involved in response preparation. In a working memory task, adolescents also recruited dorsolateral prefrontal cortex to a higher degree than adults but did not show the distribution of function and temporal involvement evident in the adult system. These results suggest that although the adolescent can demonstrate adult-level cognitive control, the circuitry being recruited to perform at this level may not be optimal for the flexible and consistent performance evident in adults. Limitations in the ability to have consistent performance may make adolescents vulnerable to making errors.

Prefrontal cortex is recruited early in development and undergoes refinement both in focalization of function—reflective of improved efficiency—and in increased participation, indicating optimal organization of function. In other words, by childhood prefrontal processing is available and developmental change thereafter consists of establishing reliable circuitry. Cognitive control is supported by a widely distributed circuitry that is highly functionally integrated (Goldman-Rakic, 1988). The strengthening of functional connectivity across cortex and subcortical regions with development supports access to this widely-distributed circuitry that supports cognitive control. Regional changes undoubtedly also contribute to developmental change. Decreases in gray matter in association areas through development (Gogtay *et al.*, 2004), reflective of regressive events including synaptic pruning, indicate that there are important changes occurring at the regional level. That is, that localized neuronal computations become more efficient which may support more rapid and complex computations underlying complex behavior such as cognitive control. The combination of both enhanced regional computational processing and long distance functional integration, supported by myelination, across the brain would support both the ability to enact a goal directed plan and to effectively implement it throughout the brain.

The substantial behavioral changes observed from childhood to adolescence (Luna *et al.*, 2004) are accompanied by consistent changes in prefrontal participation. Performance changes are significant yet subtle from adolescence to adulthood and prefrontal recruitment may actually decrease during this period. We propose that the years from childhood to adolescence represents a significant shift to prefrontally mediated behavior (Fassbender *et al.*, 2004; Fuster, 1997). However, from adolescence to adulthood there is a qualitatively different shift in which adults distribute function across cortex more evenly, which allows cognition to be more efficiently supported and relieves prefrontal cortex from being primary in determining executive function. This could imply that there is less reliance on executive processes or that executive processes are achieved by circuitry other than prefrontal systems. For example, there is evidence that parietal regions support the mnemonic aspects of working memory while prefrontal cortex is preferentially involved in the manipulation of information (Postle, Berger, & D'Esposito, 1999). The adult system may reflect a better distribution of function among regions that support executive function (e.g., parietal and prefrontal recruitment) while adolescents may depend primarily on prefrontal systems.

Taken together, developmental fMRI studies indicate that the prefrontal cortex is involved in cognitive control early in childhood and that its relative participation becomes magnified and restricted with age. However, the ability to demonstrate flexible and reliable cognitive control characterizes the transition to adult-level performance, and this process necessitates a widely distributed circuitry (Goldman-Rakic, 1988). Most studies have focused primarily on the role of prefrontal cortex and have not considered the impact of a circuit-based mechanism. Evidence that functional integration across neocortex is present throughout adolescence (Chugani, 1998; Thatcher *et al.*, 1987) indicates that, in conjunction with developmental improvements in the intrinsic computational capacity of prefrontal cortex, there is increased integration of prefrontal cortex with other brain regions during adolescence. Several studies have indicated that additional areas become active in adulthood, including parietal, striatal, and cerebellar regions (Luna *et al.*, 2001; Tamm *et al.*, 2002), which through connections with prefrontal cortex, may establish an efficient circuitry supporting mature cognitive control.

Recent work delineating developmental changes in brain circuitries underlying cognitive control support the proposal that development is supported by the integration of widely distributed circuitries. Characterizing the association of the temporal evolution of signal changes across brain regions recruited for a cognitive task can inform us regarding the strength of the relationship between regions which is believed to reflect functional connectivity. Functional connectivity in fronto-parietal and fronto-striatal-thalamic pathways during performance of inhibitory and working memory tasks have been found to strengthen from adolescence to adulthood (Edin *et al.*, 2007; Stevens, Kiehl, Pearlson, & Calhoun, 2007).

Functional connectivity also can be assessed by cross correlating spontaneous neural activity during rest (not performing a cognitive task) using rs-fcMRI (resting state functional connectivity MRI). Resting state fMRI in contrast to fMRI can assess capability of basic connectivity of large brain circuits that can be used for cognitive processing. Fair *et al.* (2007) assessed the strength of connection of two circuitries known to support cognitive control. The frontoparietal network supports cognitive abilities such as inhibitory control and working memory (Dosenbach *et al.*, 2006). The cingulo-opercular network, which includes the anterior cingulate cortex, insula, anterior prefrontal cortex, and thalamus, underlies the ability to retain a response state. As described earlier, *response state* refers to the ability to orchestrate cognitive demands to apply cognitive abilities in a consistent and flexible manner. Results indicated that these circuitries continue to reorganize through adolescence by becoming distinct and segregated from one another and by integrating long distance connections. Specifically, regions in medial prefrontal cortex initially part of the frontoparietal network that supports cognitive abilities such as inhibition and working memory, become part of the cingulo-opercular network supporting response state. These results imply that the nature of development is the process of specializing and segregating circuitries that support task ability and response state. Therefore, both the ability to perform a response guided by cognitive control as well as the ability to retain a response state improves with development as the circuits that support these distinct processes become independent.

The mechanisms by which these circuits develop are not known. Synaptic pruning and myelination interacting with experience may support the development of these circuits. As synaptic pruning supports more efficient computations at the regional level, brain regions can more effectively coordinate activity with other regions. Myelination would support the ability for regions to interact in a timely fashion but spontaneous synchronous activity such as through Hebbian process independent of myelination may also underlie development (Fair *et al.*, 2007). Experience would provide the guidance for which regions become entrained to work in a collaborative fashion.

Immaturities in brain function across development especially in adolescence, when mature performance is available, reflect a system in transition that therefore may be particularly vulnerable to limitations in cognitive control and may contribute to the emergence of psychopathology and risk-taking behavior. We propose that similar to adults who are more prone to error when performing a difficult task, the adolescent may be overall more vulnerable to error due to the yet immature circuitry recruited. This implies that the nature of "maturation" as the transition from immature to adult-level cognitive control is a switch to a more organized and efficiently recruited distributed circuitry. This transition from adolescence to adult brain integration however may be a period of vulnerability to impaired development that could contribute to the emergence of psychopathology that occurs at this time. Characterizing a normative system allows the investigation of the abnormal development usually associated with failures of cognitive control, specifically, disorders such as ADHD, Tourette's, and autism (Luna *et al.*, 2002; Luna & Sweeney, 1999). Major psychopathology is characterized by impaired executive function and its appearance in adolescence (Luna & Sweeney, 2001). Comparing a normative template of developmental changes in brain systems with groups of individuals with psychopathology could contribute to identifying the basis of impaired brain mechanisms. Additionally, characterizing periods of immaturities and the nature of the changes in brain systems in typical populations could potentially provide insight into risk-taking behavior, which is recognized as a failure in decision making that is supported by cognitive control and peaks in adolescence (Chambers *et al.*, 2003; Spear, 2000). Risk-taking behavior can lead to substance abuse which typically begins in adolescence (Call *et al.*, 2002; Resnick *et al.*, 1997). Understanding individual variability in the development of brain systems could inform us of individuals that may be vulnerable to substance abuse.

VII. How does Immaturity in Executive Processing Inform us about Real Life Decision Making?

Adolescence is the peak of sensation seeking and risk-taking behavior across species (Hodes & Shors, 2005; Stansfield & Kirstein, 2006). Sensation seeking is believed to be important for obtaining experience in independent decision making needed for survival as an adult. Risk-taking behavior occurs when sensation-seeking involves decision making that results in a risk to survival. Drug use, unprotected sex, and extreme sports are examples of risk-taking behavior. During adolescence, sensation seeking becomes increasingly appetizing as anxiety is not associated with risk-taking to the same degree as in adulthood (Hodes & Shors, 2005). The ability to control desired sensation seeking behavior for safe lower risk behaviors requires the ability to inhibit responses and to make goal directed plans in working memory. The decision making processes involved in risk-taking behavior are many, including motivation and reward processing in addition to inhibitory processing. The inhibitory processes involved in risk-taking behavior are also multi-dimensional involving an array of domains (visual, somatosensory, auditory) and cognitive processes (language, reasoning).

In order to understand the brain basis of such a complex process it is useful to begin by investigating basic aspects of this model. It would be of significance to understand the status of basic aspects that allow proper decision making. Probing the integrity of basic executive processes can provide insight into the capability of successful decision-making. If these are not yet at adult levels, then they already indicate a limitation in the general process of decision making. Investigating basic processes of cognition allows for direct comparisons to be made between brain and behavior. Risk-taking behavior *per se* is not a unitary concept that can be readily and directly examined. Breaking down its main components such as response inhibition and working memory allows us to begin to understand the brain behavior relationships that underlie adolescent behavior. Using tasks that tap into basic aspects of cognitive control allows us to directly examine the neural basis of individual components of complex decision making such as is involved in risk-taking behavior. The inferences that can be made are limited but highly relevant. What can be said is that immaturities in the neural circuitry of basic executive function contribute to limitations in decision making.

Studies indicating immaturities in the ability to make simple inhibitory motor responses suggests that adolescents still have limitations in implementing basic cognitive control. Children however, also have limitations in inhibitory control but they do not demonstrate the degree of risk-taking behavior evident in adolescence. The added peak in sensation seeking in adolescence coupled with immature cognitive control however could add to processes that lead to risk taking behavior. Given additional variables that make decision making more difficult, an immature executive system becomes an important factor in risk-taking behavior. Therefore, athough these basic studies can not explain or justify risk-taking behavior, they enlighten us regarding the limitations that are specific to the adolescent system. Importantly, it provides a model as to the neural basis of poor decision making. I propose that adolescents have the ability to make executive decisions. However they demonstrate limitations in the ability to effectively exert top-down modulation and possibly to establish a response state that can affect clear decision making. Additionally, immature reward processing can further influence cognitive control. Studies that provide a view of the integrity of brain functional systems of basic cognitive components can provide a template for understanding the limitations that are unique to adolescent decision making.

REFERENCES

Adleman, N. E., Menon, V., Blasey, C. M., White, C. D., Warsofsky, I. S., Glover, G. H., & Reiss, A. L. (2002). A developmental fMRI study of the Stroop Color-Word task. *NeuroImage*, *16*(1), 61–75.

Alsaker, F. D. (1996). Annotation: The impact of puberty. *Journal of Child Psychology and Psychiatry*, *37*(3), 249–258.

Amso, D., & Johnson, S. P. (2005). Selection and inhibition in infancy: Evidence from the spatial negative priming paradigm. *Cognition, 95*(2), B27–B36.

Andersen, R. A., Asanuma, C., Essick, G., & Siegel, R. M. (1990). Corticocortical connections of anatomically and physiologically defined subdivisions within the inferior parietal lobule. *The Journal of Comparative Neurology, 296*, 65–113.

Angold, A., Costello, E. J., & Worthman, C. M. (1998). Puberty and depression: The roles of age, pubertal status and pubertal timing. *Psychological Medicine, 28*(1), 51–61.

Armstrong, E., Schleicher, A., Omran, H., Curtis, M., & Zilles, K. (1995). The ontogeny of human gyrification. *Cerebral Cortex, 5*(1), 56–63.

Asato, M. R., Sweeney, J. A., & Luna, B. (2006). Cognitive processes in the development of TOL performance. *Neuropsychologia, 44*(12), 2259–2269.

Ashtari, M., Cervellione, K. L., Hasan, K. M., Wu, J., McIlree, C., Kester, H., Ardekani, B. A., Roofeh, D., Szeszko, P. R., & Kumra, S. (2007). White matter development during late adolescence in healthy males: A cross-sectional diffusion tensor imaging study. *NeuroImage, 35*(2), 501–510.

Baddeley, A. (1986). *Working memory*. New York: Oxford University Press.

Bedard, A. C., Nichols, S., Barbosa, J. A., Schachar, R., Logan, G. D., & Tannock, R. (2002). The development of selective inhibitory control across the life span. *Developmental Neuropsychology, 21*(1), 93–111.

Bell, M. A., & Fox, N. A. (1992). The relations between frontal brain electrical activity and cognitive development during infancy. *Child Development, 63*(5), 1142–1163.

Ben Bashat, D., Ben Sira, L., Graif, M., Pianka, P., Hendler, T., Cohen, Y., & Assaf, Y. (2005). Normal white matter development from infancy to adulthood: Comparing diffusion tensor and high b value diffusion weighted MR images. *Journal of Magnetic Resonance Imaging, 21*(5), 503–511.

Benes, F. M. (1989). Myelination of cortical-hippocampal relays during late adolescence. *Schizophrenia Bulletin, 15*(4), 585–593.

Bjorklund, D. F., & Harnishfeger, K. K. (1990). The resources construct in cognitive development: Diverse sources of evidence and a theory of inefficient inhibition. *Developmental Review, 10*(1), 48–71.

Braver, T. S., Barch, D. M., Gray, J. R., Molfese, D. L., & Snyder, A. (2001). Anterior cingulate cortex and response conflict: Effects of frequency, inhibition and errors. *Cerebral Cortex, 11*, 825–836.

Brown, M. R., Vilis, T., & Everling, S. (2007). Frontoparietal activation with preparation for antisaccades. *Journal of Neurophysiology, 98*(3), 1751–1762.

Bunge, S. A., Dudukovic, N. M., Thomason, M. E., Vaidya, C. J., & Gabrieli, J. D. (2002). Immature frontal lobe contributions to cognitive control in children: Evidence from fMRI. *Neuron, 33*(2), 301–311.

Call, K. T., Reidel, A. A., Hein, K., McLoyd, V., Petersen, A., & Kipke, M. (2002). Adolescent health and well-being in the twenty-first century: A global perspective. *Journal of Research on Adolescence, 12*(1), 69–98.

Carter, C. S., Braver, T. S., Barch, D. M., Botvinick, M. M., Noll, D., & Cohen, J. D. (1998). Anterior cingulate cortex, error detection, and the online monitoring of performance. *Science, 280*, 747–749.

Casey, B. J., Giedd, J. N., & Thomas, K. M. (2000). Structural and functional brain development and its relation to cognitive development. *Biological Psychology, 54*(1–3), 241–257.

Caviness, V. S., Kennedy, D. N., Bates, J. F., & Makris, N. (1996). The developing human brain: A morphometric profile. In R. W. Thatcher, G. Reid Lyon, J. Rumsey, & N. A. Krasnegor (Eds.), *Developmental neuroimaging: Mapping the development of brain and behavior* (pp. 3–14). New York: Academic Press.

Chambers, R. A., Taylor, J. R., & Petenza, M. N. (2003). Developmental neurocircuitry of motivation in adolescence: A critical period of addiction vulnerability. *American Journal of Psychiatry, 160*(6), 1041–1052.

Chelune, G. J., & Baer, R. A. (1986). Developmental norms for the Wisconsin Card Sorting test. *Journal of Clinical and Experimental Neuropsychology, 8*(3), 219–228.

Chugani, H. T. (1998). A critical period of brain development: Studies of cerebral glucose utilization with PET. *Preventive Medicine, 27*(2), 184–188.

Chugani, H. T., Phelps, M. E., & Mazziotta, J. C. (1987). Positron emission tomography study of human brain functional development. *Annals of Neurology, 22*(4), 487–497.

Ciesielski, K. T., Lesnik, P. G., Savoy, R. L., Grant, E. P., & Ahlfors, S. P. (2006). Developmental neural networks in children performing a categorical N-back task. *NeuroImage, 33*(3), 980–990.

Cowan, N., Saults, J. S., & Morey, C. C. (2006). Development of working memory for verbal-spatial associations. *Journal of Memory and Language, 55*(2), 274–289.

Crone, E. A., Wendelken, C., Donohue, S., van Leijenhorst, L., & Bunge, S. A. (2006). Neurocognitive development of the ability to manipulate information in working memory. *Proceedings of the National Academy of Sciences of the United States of America, 103*(24), 9315–9320.

Davidson, M. C., Amso, D., Anderson, L. C., & Diamond, A. (2006). Development of cognitive control and executive functions from 4 to 13 years: Evidence from manipulations of memory, inhibition, and task switching. *Neuropsychologia, 44*(11), 2037–2078.

Davies, P. L., & Rose, J. D. (1999). Assessment of cognitive development in adolescents by means of neuropsychological tasks. *Developmental Neuropsychology, 15*(2), 227–248.

Demetriou, A., Christou, C., Spanoudis, G., & Platsidou, M. (2002). The development of mental processing: efficiency, working memory, and thinking. *Monographs of the Society for Research in Child Development, 67*(1), 1–155 discussion 156.

Dempster, F. N. (1981). Memory span: Sources of individual and developmental differences. *Psychological Bulletin, 89*(1), 63–100.

D'Esposito, M., Postle, B. R., Ballard, D., & Lease, J. (1999). Maintenance versus manipulation of information held in working memory: An event-related fMRI study. *Brain and Cognition, 41*(1), 66–86.

Devinsky, O., Morrell, M. J., & Vogt, B. A. (1995). Contributions of anterior cingulate cortex to behavior. *Brain, 118*, 279–306.

Diamond, A. (2002). Normal development of prefrontal cortex from birth to young adulthood: Cognitive functions, anatomy, and biochemistry. In D. T. Stuss & R. T. Knight (Eds.), *Principles of frontal lobe function* (pp. 466–503). New York: Oxford University Press.

Diamond, A., & Goldman-Rakic, P. S. (1989). Comparison of human infants and rhesus monkeys on Piaget's AB task: Evidence for dependence on dorsolateral prefrontal cortex. *Experimental Brain Research, 74*(1), 24–40.

Dosenbach, N. U., Visscher, K. M., Palmer, E. D., Miezin, F. M., Wenger, K. K., Kang, H. C., Burgund, E. D., Grimes, A. L., Schlaggar, B. L., & Petersen, S. E. (2006). A core system for the implementation of task sets. *Neuron, 50*(5), 799–812.

Drobyshevsky, A., Song, S. K., Gamkrelidze, G., Wyrwicz, A. M., Meng, F., Derrick, M., Meng, F., Li, L., Ji, X., Trommer, B., Beardsley, D. J., Lou, N. L., Back, S. A., & Tan, S. (2005). Developmental changes in diffusion anisotropy coincide with immature oligodendrocyte progression and maturation of compound action potential. *Journal of Neuroscience, 25*(25), 5988–5997.

Durston, S., Davidson, M. C., Tottenham, N., Galvan, A., Spicer, J., Fossella, J. A., et al. (2006). A shift from diffuse to focal cortical activity with development. *Developmental Science, 9*(1), 1–8.

Edin, F., Macoveanu, J., Olesen, P. J., Tegner, J., & Klingberg, T. (2007). Stronger synaptic connectivity as a mechanism behind development of working memory-related brain activity during childhood. *Journal of Cognitive Neuroscience, 19*(5), 750–760.

Elliott, R. (1970). Simple reaction time: Effects associated with age, preparatory interval, incentive-shift and mode of presentation. *Journal of Experimental Child Psychology, 9*, 86–107.

Everling, S., & Munoz, D. P. (2000). Neuronal correlates for preparatory set associated with pro-saccades and anti-saccades in the primate frontal eye field. *Journal of Neuroscience, 20*(1), 387–400.

Fair, D. A., Dosenbach, N. U., Church, J. A., Cohen, A. L., Brahmbhatt, S., Miezin, F. M., Barch, D. M., Raichle, M. E., Petersen, S. E., & Schlaggar, B. L. (2007). Development of distinct control networks through segregation and integration. *Proceedings of the National Academy of Sciences of the United States of America, 104*(33), 13507–13512.

Fassbender, C., Murphy, K., Foxe, J. J., Wylie, G. R., Javitt, D. C., Robertson, I. H., & Garavan, H. (2004). A topography of executive functions and their interactions revealed by functional magnetic resonance imaging. *Brain Research. Cognitive brain research, 20*(2), 132–143.

Fischer, B., Biscaldi, M., & Gezeck, S. (1997). On the development of voluntary and reflexive components in human saccade generation. *Brain Research, 754*(1–2), 285–297.

Fry, A. F., & Hale, S. (1996). Processing speed, working memory, and fluid intelligence: Evidence for a developmental cascade. *Psychological Science, 7*(4), 237–241.

Fukushima, J., Hatta, T., & Fukushima, K. (2000). Development of voluntary control of saccadic eye movements. I. Age-related changes in normal children. *Brain and Development, 22*(3), 173–180.

Funahashi, S., Inoue, M., & Kubota, K. (1997). Delay-period activity in the primate prefrontal cortex encoding multiple spatial positions and their order of presentation. *Behavioural Brain Research, 84*(1–2), 203–223.

Fuster, J. M. (1989). *The prefrontal cortex* (2 ed.). New York: Raven Press.

Fuster, J. M. (1997). *The prefrontal cortex* (3 ed.). New York: Raven Press.

Geier, C. F., Garver, K. E., & Luna, B. (2007). Circuitry underlying temporally extended spatial working memory. *Neuoimage, 35*(2), 904–915.

Giedd, J. N., Snell, J. W., Lange, N., Rajapakse, J. C., Casey, B. J., Kozuch, P. L., et al. (1996). Quantitative magnetic resonance imaging of human brain development: Ages 4–18. *Cerebral Cortex, 6*(4), 551–560.

Gogtay, N., Giedd, J. N., Lusk, L., Hayashi, K. M., Greenstein, D., Vaituzis, A. C., Nugent, T. F., 3rd, Herman, D. H., Clasen, L. S., Toga, A. W., Rapoport, J. L., & Thompson, P. M. (2004). Dynamic mapping of human cortical development during childhood through early adulthood. *Proceedings of the National Academy of Sciences of the United States of America, 101*(21), 8174–8179.

Goldman-Rakic, P. S. (1988). Topography of cognition: Parallel distributed networks in primate association cortex. *Annual Review of Neuroscience, 11*, 137–156.

Goldman-Rakic, P. S., Chafee, M., & Friedman, H. (1993). Allocation of function in distributed circuits. In T. Ono, L. R. Squire, M. E. Raichle, D. I. Perrett, & M. Fukuda (Eds.), *Brain mechanisms of perception and memory: From neuron to behavior* (pp. 445–456). New York: Oxford University Press.

Hale, S. (1990). A global developmental trend in cognitive processing speed. *Child Development, 61*(3), 653–663.

Hikosaka, O., & Wurtz, R. H. (1983). Visual and oculomotor functions of monkey substantia nigra pars reticulata. III. Memory-contingent visual and saccade responses. *Journal of Neurophysiology, 49*, 1268–1284.

Hodes, G. E., & Shors, T. J. (2005). Distinctive stress effects on learning during puberty. *Hormones and Behavior*, *48*(2), 163–171.

Huttenlocher, P. R. (1990). Morphometric study of human cerebral cortex development. *Neuropsychologia*, *28*(6), 517–527.

Huttenlocher, P. R., & Dabholkar, A. S. (1997). Regional differences in synaptogenesis in human cerebral cortex. *Journal of Comparative Neurology*, *387*(2), 167–178.

Kail, R. (1993). Processing time decreases globally at an exponential rate during childhood and adolescence. *Journal of Experimental Child Psychology*, *56*(2), 254–265.

Kail, R. (2007). Longitudinal evidence that increases in processing speed and working memory enhance children's reasoning. *Psychological Science*, *18*(4), 312–313.

Kail, R., & Salthouse, T. A. (1994). Processing speed as a mental capacity. *Acta Psychologica*, *86*(2–3), 199–225.

Kessler, R. C., McGonagle, K. A., Zhao, S., Nelson, C. B., Hughes, M., Eshleman, S., Wittchen, H. U., & Kendler, K. S. (1994). Lifetime and 12-month prevalence of DSM-III-R psychiatric disorders in the United States. Results from the National Comorbidity Survey. *Archives of General Psychiatry*, *51*(1), 8–19.

Klein, C., & Foerster, F. (2001). Development of prosaccade and antisaccade task performance in participants aged 6 to 26 years. *Psychophysiology*, *38*(2), 179–189.

Klingberg, T., Vaidya, C. J., Gabrieli, J. D. E., Moseley, M. E., & Hedehus, M. (1999). Myelination and organization of the frontal white matter in children: A diffusion tensor MRI study. *Neuroreport*, *10*(13), 2817–2821.

Klingberg, T., Forssberg, H., & Westerberg, H. (2002). Increased brain activity in frontal and parietal cortex underlies the development of visuospatial working memory capacity during childhood. *Journal of Cognitive Neuroscience*, *14*(1), 1–10.

Kok, A. (1999). Varieties of inhibition: Manifestations in cognition, event-related potentials and aging. *Acta Psychologica*, *101*(2–3), 129–158.

Levin, H. S., Culhane, K. A., Hartmann, J., Evankovich, K., & Mattson, A. J. (1991). Developmental changes in performance on tests of purported frontal lobe functioning. *Developmental Neuropsychology*, *7*, 377–395.

Li, T. Q., & Noseworthy, M. D. (2002). Mapping the development of white matter tracts with diffusion tensor imaging. *Developmental Science*, *5*(3), 293–300.

Liston, C., Watts, R., Tottenham, N., Davidson, M. C., Niogi, S., Ulug, A. M., & Casey, B. J. (2006). Frontostriatal microstructure modulates efficient recruitment of cognitive control. *Cerebral Cortex*, *16*(4), 553–560.

Logan, G. D., & Gordon, S. E. (2001). Executive control of visual attention in dual-task situations. *Psychological Review*, *108*(2), 393–434.

Luciana, M., Conklin, H. M., Hooper, C. J., & Yarger, R. S. (2005). The development of nonverbal working memory and executive control processes in adolescents. *Child Development*, *76*(3), 697–712.

Luna, B., & Sweeney, J. A. (1999). Cognitive functional magnetic resonance imaging at very-high-field: Eye movement control. *Topics in Magnetic Resonance Imaging*, *10*(1), 3–15.

Luna, B., & Sweeney, J. A. (2001). Studies of brain and cognitive maturation through childhood and adolescence: A strategy for testing neurodevelopmental hypotheses. *Schizophrenia Bulletin*, *27*(3), 443–455.

Luna, B., Thulborn, K. R., Munoz, D. P., Merriam, E. P., Garver, K. E., Minshew, N. J., Keshavan, M. S., Genovese, C. R., Eddy, W. F., & Sweeney, J. A. (2001). Maturation of widely distributed brain function subserves cognitive development. *NeuroImage*, *13*(5), 786–793.

Luna, B., Minshew, N. J., Garver, K. E., Lazar, N. A., Thulborn, K. R., Eddy, W. F., & Sweeney, J. A. (2002). Neocortical system abnormalities in autism: An fMRI study of spatial working memory. *Neurology, 59*(6), 834–840.

Luna, B., Garver, K. E., Urban, T. A., Lazar, N. A., & Sweeney, J. A. (2004). Maturation of cognitive processes from late childhood to adulthood. *Child Development, 75*(5), 1357–1372.

Marsh, R., Zhu, H., Schultz, R. T., Quackenbush, G., Royal, J., Skudlarski, P., & Peterson, B. S. (2006). A developmental fMRI study of self-regulatory control. *Human Brain Mapping, 27*(11), 848–863.

McEwen, B. S. (2001). Invited review: Estrogens effects on the brain: Multiple sties and molecular mechanisms. *Journal of Applied Psychology, 91*, 2785–2801.

Miller, E. K., & Cohen, J. D. (2001). An integrative theory of prefrontal cortex function. *Annual Reviews in Neuroscience, 24*, 167–202.

Miyake, A., Friedman, N. P., Emerson, M. J., Witzki, A. H., Howerter, A., & Wager, T. D. (2000). The unity and diversity of executive functions and their contributions to complex "Frontal Lobe" tasks: A latent variable analysis. *Cognitive Psychology, 41*(1), 49–100.

Moseley, M. E., Cohen, Y., Kucharczyk, J., Mintorovitch, J., Asgari, H. S., Wendland, M. F., Tsuruda, J., & Norman, D. (1990). Diffusion-weighted MR imaging of anisotropic water diffusion in cat central nervous system. *Radiology, 176*, 439–445.

Mukherjee, P., & McKinstry, R. C. (2006). Diffusion tensor imaging and tractography of human brain development. *Neuroimaging Clinics of North America, 16*(1), 19–43.

Munoz, D. P., Broughton, J. R., Goldring, J. E., & Armstrong, I. T. (1998). Age-related performance of human subjects on saccadic eye movement tasks. *Experimental Brain Research, 121*(4), 391–400.

Nagy, Z., Westerberg, H., & Klingberg, T. (2004). Maturation of white matter is associated with the development of cognitive functions during childhood. *Journal of Cognitive Neuroscience, 16*(7), 1227–1233.

Nee, D. E., Wager, T. D., & Jonides, J. (2007). Interference resolution: Insights from a meta-analysis of neuroimaging tasks. *Cognitive, Affective & Behavioral Neuroscience, 7*(1), 1–17.

Nelson, C. A., Monk, C. S., Lin, J., Carver, L. J., Thomas, K. M., & Truwitt, C. L. (2000). Functional neuroanatomy of spatial working memory in children. *Developmental Psychology, 36*(1), 109–116.

Nyffeler, T., Muri, R., Bucher-Ottiger, Y., Pierrot-Deseilligny, C., Gaymard, B., & Rivaud-Pechoux, S. (2007). Inhibitory control of the human dorsolateral prefrontal cortex during the anti-saccade paradigm-a transcranial magnetic stimulation study. *European Journal of Neuroscience, 26*(5), 1381–1385.

Ojeda, S. R., Ma, Y. M., & Rage, F. (1995). A role for TGF in the neuroendocrine control of female puberty. In T. M. Plant & P. A. Lee (Eds.), *The neurobiology of puberty* (pp. 103–117). Bristol: Journal of Endocrinology Limited.

Olesen, P. J., Nagy, Z., Westerberg, H., & Klingberg, T. (2003). Combined analysis of DTI and fMRI data reveals a joint maturation of white and grey matter in a fronto-parietal network. *Cognitive Brain Research, 18*(1), 48–57.

Olesen, P. J., Macoveanu, J., Tegner, J., & Klingberg, T. (2007). Brain activity related to working memory and distraction in children and adults. *Cerebral Cortex, 17*(5), 1047–1054.

Orr, D. P., Brack, C. J., & Ingersoll, G. (1988). Pubertal maturation and cognitive maturity in adolescents. *Journal of Adolescent Health Care, 9*, 273–279.

Otnes, R. K., & Enochson, L. D. (1972). *Digital time series analysis* (1 ed.). New York: Wiley.

Passingham, D., & Sakai, K. (2004). The prefrontal cortex and working memory: Physiology and brain imaging. *Current Opinion in Neurobiology, 14*(2), 163–168.

Paus, T., Zijdenbos, A., Worsley, K., Collins, D. L., Blumenthal, J., Giedd, J. N., Rapoport, J. L., & Evans, A. C. (1999). Structural maturation of neural pathways in children and adolescents: In vivo study. *Science, 283*(5409), 1908–1911.

Petersen, A. C. (1976). Physical androgyny and cognitive functioning in adolescence. *Developmental Psychology, 12*(6), 524–533.

Pfefferbaum, A., Mathalon, D. H., Sullivan, E. V., Rawles, J. M., Zipursky, R. B., & Lim, K. O. (1994). A quantitative magnetic resonance imaging study of changes in brain morphology from infancy to late adulthood. *Archives of Neurology, 51*(9), 874–887.

Polli, F. E., Barton, J. J., Cain, M. S., Thakkar, K. N., Rauch, S. L., & Manoach, D. S. (2005). Rostral and dorsal anterior cingulate cortex make dissociable contributions during antisaccade error commission. *Proceedings of the National Academy of Sciences of the United States of America, 102*(43), 15700–15705.

Postle, B. R., Berger, J. S., & D'Esposito, M. (1999). Functional neuroanatomical double dissociation of mnemonic and executive control processes contributing to working memory performance. *Proceedings of the National Academy of Sciences of the United States of America, 96*(22), 12959–12964.

Postle, B. R., Ferrarelli, F., Hamidi, M., Feredoes, E., Massimini, M., Peterson, M., Alexander, A., & Tononi, G. (2006). Repetitive transcranial magnetic stimulation dissociates working memory manipulation from retention functions in the prefrontal, but not posterior parietal, cortex. *Journal of Cognitive Neuroscience, 18*(10), 1712–1722.

Rakic, P., Bourgeois, J. P., Eckenhoff, M. F., Zecevic, N., & Goldman-Rakic, P. S. (1986). Concurrent overproduction of synapses in diverse regions of the primate cerebral cortex. *Science, 232*(4747), 232–235.

Rauschecker, J. P., & Marler, P. (1987). What signals are responsible for synaptic changes in visual cortical plasticity? In J. P. Rauschecker & P. Marler (Eds.), *Imprinting and cortical plasticity* (pp. 193–200). New York: Wiley.

Resnick, M. D., Bearman, P. S., Blum, R. W., Bauman, K. E., Harris, K. M., Jones, J., *et al.* (1997). Protecting adolescents from harm. Findings from the national longitudinal study on adolescent health. *JAMA, 278*(10), 823–832.

Ridderinkhof, K. R., Band, G. P. H., & Logan, G. D. (1999). A study of adaptive behavior: Effects of age and irrelevant information on the ability to inhibit one's actions. *Acta Psychologica, 101*, 315–337.

Rubia, K., Overmeyer, S., Taylor, E., Brammer, M., Williams, S. C., Simmons, A., *et al.* (2000). Functional frontalisation with age: Mapping neurodevelopmental trajectories with fMRI. *Neuroscience and Biobehavioral Reviews, 24*(1), 13–19.

Rubia, K., Smith, A. B., Woolley, J., Nosarti, C., Heyman, I., Taylor, E., & Brammer, M. (2006). Progressive increase of frontostriatal brain activation from childhood to adulthood during event-related tasks of cognitive control. *Human Brain Mapping, 27*(12), 973–993.

Rubia, K., Smith, A. B., Taylor, E., & Brammer, M. (2007). Linear age-correlated functional development of right inferior fronto-striato-cerebellar networks during response inhibition and anterior cingulate during error-related processes. *Human Brain Mapping, 28*(11), 1163–1177.

Scherf, K. S., Sweeney, J. A., & Luna, B. (2006). Brain basis of developmental change in visuospatial working memory. *Journal of Cognitive Neuroscience, 18*, 1045–1058.

Schmithorst, V. J., Wilke, M., Dardzinski, B. J., & Holland, S. K. (2002). Correlation of white matter diffusivity and anisotropy with age during childhood and adolescence: A cross-sectional diffusion-tensor MR imaging study. *Radiology, 222*(1), 212–218.

Simpson, J. R., Jr., Snyder, A. Z., Gusnard, D. A., & Raichle, M. E. (2001). Emotion-induced changes in human medial prefrontal cortex: I. During cognitive task performance. *Proceedings of the National Academy of Sciences of the United States of America*, *98*(2), 683–687.

Somsen, R. J. (2007). The development of attention regulation in the Wisconsin Card Sorting Task. *Developmental Science*, *10*(5), 664–680.

Song, S. K., Sun, S. W., Ju, W. K., Lin, S. J., Cross, A. H., & Neufeld, A. H. (2003). Diffusion tensor imaging detects and differentiates axon and myelin degeneration in mouse optic nerve after retinal ischemia. *NeuroImage*, *20*(3), 1714–1722.

Sowell, E. R., Thompson, P. M., Holmes, C. J., Jernigan, T. L., & Toga, A. W. (1999). *In vivo* evidence for post-adolescent brain maturation in frontal and striatal regions. *Nature Neuroscience*, *2*(10), 859–861.

Spear, L. P. (2000). The adolescent brain and age-related behavioral manifestations. *Neuroscience and Biobehavioral Reviews*, *24*, 417–463.

Stansfield, K. H., & Kirstein, C. L. (2006). Effects of novelty on behavior in the adolescent and adult rat. *Developmental Psychobiology*, *48*(1), 10–15.

Stevens, M. C., Kiehl, K. A., Pearlson, G. D., & Calhoun, V. D. (2007). Functional neural networks underlying response inhibition in adolescents and adults. *Behavioural Brain Research*, *181*(1), 12–22.

Strauss, E., & Kinsbourne, M. (1981). Does age of menarche affect the ultimate level of verbal and spatial skills? *Cortex*, *17*, 323–326.

Sweeney, J. A., Mintun, M. A., Kwee, S., Wiseman, M. B., Brown, D. L., Rosenberg, D. R., & Carl, J. R. (1995). PET studies of voluntary saccadic eye movements and spatial working memory. *Schizophrenia Research*, *15*, 100.

Tamm, L., Menon, V., & Reiss, A. L. (2002). Maturation of brain function associated with response inhibition. *Journal of the American Academy of Child and Adolescent Psychiatry*, *41*(10), 1231–1238.

Thatcher, R. W. (1991). Maturation of the human frontal lobes: Physiological evidence for staging. *Developmental Neuropsychology*, *7*(3), 397–419.

Thatcher, R. W., Walker, R. A., & Giudice, S. (1987). Human cerebral hemispheres develop at different rates and ages. *Science*, *236*(4805), 1110–1113.

Thomas, K. M., King, S. W., Franzen, P. L., Welsh, T. F., Berkowitz, A. L., Noll, D. C., *et al.* (1999). A developmental functional MRI study of spatial working memory. *NeuroImage*, *10*(3 Pt 1), 327–338.

Toga, A. W., Thompson, P. M., & Sowell, E. R. (2006). Mapping brain maturation. *Trends in Neurosciences*, *29*(3), 148–159.

Ungerleider, L. G., Doyon, J., & Karni, A. (2002). Imaging brain plasticity during motor skill learning. *Neurobiology of learning and memory*, *78*(3), 553–564.

Van den Wildenberg, W. P. M., & van der Molen, M. W. (2004). Developmental trends in simple and selective inhibition of compatible and incompatible responses. *Journal of Experimental Child Psychology*, *87*(3), 201–220.

van Leijenhorst, L., Crone, E. A., & van der Molen, M. W. (2007). Developmental trends for object and spatial working memory: A psychophysiological analysis. *Child Development*, *78*(3), 987–1000.

Velanova, K., Wheeler, M. E., & Luna, B. (2008). Maturational changes in anterior cingulate and frontoparietal recruitment support the development of error processing and inhibitory control. *Cerebral Cortex*, *18*(11), 2505–2522.

Waber, D. P., Mann, M. B., Merola, J., & Moylan, P. M. (1985). Physical maturation rate and cognitive performance in early adolescence: A longitudinal examiniation. *Developmental Psychology*, *21*(4), 666–681.

Welsh, M. C. (2002). Developmental and clinical variations in executive functions. In D. L. Molfese & V. J. Molfese (Eds.), *Developmental variations in learning: Applications to social, executive function, language, and reading skills* (pp. 139–185). Mahwah: Lawrence Erlbaum.

Williams, B. R., Ponesse, J. S., Schachar, R. J., Logan, G. D., & Tannock, R. (1999). Development of inhibitory control across the life span. *Developmental Psychology, 35*(1), 205–213.

Wise, L. A., Sutton, J. A., & Gibbons, P. D. (1975). Decrement in Stroop interfence time with age. *Perceptual and Motor Skills, 41,* 149–150.

Wozniak, J. R., & Lim, K. O. (2006). Advances in white matter imaging: A review of in vivo magnetic resonance methodologies and their applicability to the study of development and aging. *Neuroscience & Biobehavioral Reviews, 30*(6), 762–774.

Yakovlev, P. I., & Lecours, A. R. (1967). The myelogenetic cycles of regional maturation of the brain. In A. Minkowski (Ed.), *Regional development of the brain in early life* (pp. 3–70). Oxford: Blackwell Scientific.

Zald, D. H., & Iacono, W. G. (1998). The development of spatial working memory abilities. *Developmental Neuropsychology, 14*(4), 563–578.

Author Index

A

Accredolo, L., 36
Adam, S., 147
Adamson, L., 4, 18, 32–3, 35
Adleman, Leonard Max, 253
Adolphs, R., 43
Akhtar, N., 86
Alibali, M. W., 69
Als, H., 18
Alsaker, F. D., 236
Alvarado, M. C., 149
Alvarez, J. M., 108
Amso, D., 242
Andersen, R. A., 257
Anderson, D., 8
Anderson, J. R., 65
Angold, A., 234
Argyle, M., 60
Armstrong, E., 237
Arterberry, M. E., 9
Asato, M. R., 246, 249
Aschersleben, G., 89
Asendorpf, J. B., 224
Ashtari, M., 240
Aslin, R. N., 58
Astington, J. W., 56, 58, 69, 78, 83
Atran, S., 116

B

Bachevalier, J., 149
Bacon, S., 225
Baddeley, A., 245
Baer, R. A., 249
Baerger, D. R., 186
Baillargeon, R., 73, 78–80, 84, 92–3
Baird, J. A., 5, 85
Bakeman, R., 4, 32–3, 35
Baker-Ward, L., 147, 152, 169
Baldwin, D. A., 63, 79, 85, 88
Baldwin, J., 40
Bales, D. W., 131
Band, G. P. H., 243

Bandura, A., 117
Banerjee, M., 73
Banks, M. S., 7
Barillas, Y., 34–5, 40
Barna, J., 9, 11
Baron-Cohen, S., 32, 34–5, 59, 69, 93
Barr, R., 8–9, 146–50, 153
Barrera, M. E., 8
Barresi, J., 3, 5–6
Bartsch, K., 36, 69, 73, 78, 87
Bates, E., 34, 36–7
Bateson, M. C., 39
Baudonnière, P.-M., 224
Bauer, J. J., 177, 186
Bauer, P., 8–9, 147–50, 152–3, 155, 158–60, 164, 166, 169–70, 175, 187
Baydar, N., 219
Bedard, A. C., 243
Beeghly, M., 35
Beeghly-Smith, M., 92
Beer, J., 175
Behne, T., 44–5, 84
Beike, D. R., 173–4
Bell, M. A., 242
Bellagamba, F., 86
Belsky, J., 176, 186
Ben Bashat, D., 240
Benes, F. M., 239
Bennett, R. T., 57
Berger, J. S., 266
Berndt, T. J., 108
Bernieri, F., 218
Berntsen, D., 147, 159, 162
Bird, A., 175, 186
Biscaldi, M., 250
Bjorklund, D. F., 249
Blackwell, L., 117
Blakemore, S.-J., 43
Bliss, L. S., 155
Bloom, P., 90
Bluck, S., 147, 161–2
Bohanek, J., 182
Bohn, A., 147, 159, 162
Boland, A. M., 179
Boland, L. D., 160

Subject Index

A

ability
  acquisition of, 234
  sophistication of, 234
  traits and, 109–10, 112–13, 115–16, 121,
    132–4
  see also skill development
academic ability, traits and, 109–10, 121, 132
accidental action imitation, 86–8, 90
ACE model, 205, 207, 222–3
acquisition of abilities, 234
actigraphs, 212–13, 215, 220, 226
actions:
  desires and, 69
  infants, 5–6, 77
  intention-in-action, 85–7
  see also goal-directed actions
Active Intermodal Mapping theory, 12,
    13–17
activity level studies, 212–13, 215–16, 220,
    224–6, 263–4
additive genetic influences, 205, 207
adolescence:
  age range definitions, 236, 264
  autobiographical memory, 146, 158,
    161–4, 182–4, 186–8
  cognitive control maturation, 233–75
  heritability of temperament, 220–1, 225
  working memory, 234–5, 241, 245–50,
    257–9, 265, 267, 269
  see also older children
adoptive/nonadoptive sibling studies, 203,
    206–9, 222–3
Adult Attachment Interviews, 179
adulthood, transition to, 233–4, 236, 262–3,
    265–8
  see also age-related change
affect:
  attunement, 14, 16–17, 27–30, 32–3, 36–7
  behavioral genetics, 224
  vocal expressions, 74–5
Affect Sharing Model, 12, 13–14, 16
affective dyadic communication, 16
African-American children, 154–5

age ranges *see* adolescence; infants; middle
    childhood; older children; preschool
    children; toddlers; young children
age-related change:
  brain function studies, 259–5
  differential heritability, 217–25
  fractional anisotropy, 240
  memory development, 150, 160, 246, 249,
    258–9
  response inhibition, 252–4
  trait reasoning, 106–14, 123–4, 127–8, 135,
    137–8
  working memory, 246, 249, 258–9
agentic self-concept, 182
aggression, 121–2
amnesia (childhood), 157, 160, 162–4,
    169–70, 183
amplification model, temperament, 219
anisotropy, fractional, 240
anterior cingulate cortex, 251, 254–5, 257
antisaccade task, 243, 244, 250, 252–6
  see also saccade task
antisocial behavior:
  theory of mind development, 58
  trait reasoning, 109–12, 116–17, 125–6
appearances vs traits, 118–20
Asian cultures, 155, 163–4, 190
  see also Chinese children
assessment methods, behavioral genetics,
    221–3
  see also measurement methods
assimilation, recognitory, 6
association areas, cortex, 238–9
attachment security, 175–7, 179
attention, 56–7, 65–68
  coordinated, 32–5, 40, 44–5
  definition, 65
  emotions and, 76
  joint attention hypothesis, 34–5,
    37, 39
  maintaining, 14
  precursor hypothesis, 89
  redirecting, 33–5
  sharing, 13, 28–9, 33–5,
    38, 68

Contents of Previous Volumes

303